I0616747

PEOPLES OF THE WORLD
North Americans

PEOPLES OF THE WORLD
North Americans

Joyce Moss • George Wilson

The Culture, Geographical Setting, and Historical Background of 37 North American Peoples

FIRST EDITION

 Gale Research Inc. • *DETROIT* • *NEW YORK* • *LONDON*

Joyce Moss
George Wilson
Illustrator: Lynn Van Dam

Gale Research Inc. staff

Production Manager: Mary Beth Trimper
External Production Assistant: Shanna Philpott

Art Director: Arthur Chartow
Graphic Designer: Bernadette M. Gornie
Keyliner: C. J. Jonik

Production Supervisor: Laura Bryant
Internal Production Associate: Louise Gagné
Internal Production Assistant: Yolanda Y. Latham

Printed in the United States of America

Published in the United States by Gale Research Inc.
Published simultaneously in the United Kingdom
by Gale Research International Limited
(An affiliated company of Gale Research Inc.)

In memory of all the individuals—the Native Americans, Latin Americans, Africans, Asians, and Europeans— who perished in forging the fabric that is North America.

Table of Contents

Preface

Layer upon layer of native and ethnic groups have peopled North America. It has been said that as technology spreads and these groups join the mainstream, they are losing their individuality. *Peoples of the World: North Americans* was written to expose the individuality that remains in the continent's society. Once the "melting pot" notion taught that cultures blended together to produce American citizens. This notion has since given way to the "salad bowl" concept, which holds that the various cultures maintain their own identities while contributing to the North American whole. Abiding by the later philosophy, this work profiles separate cultures and presents their contributions to the whole. In the process, the interaction between groups is revealed.

A great social experiment has been taking place in North America. The array of cultural groups within its borders makes it a microcosm of the world, and the social experiment is the ability of these groups to co-exist. This they have done, sometimes less than peacefully. Friction has arisen between groups competing in the American job market, for example, but cooperation prevailed in the fighting of two World Wars.

Roughly 500 years have passed since the Indian and Inuit peoples who first occupied the continent were joined by immigrant groups. The country has flourished in this time, due to both the natives and immigrants. A secondary purpose of this work is to reveal the achievements that have given this continent a culture as remarkable in its own right as the heritage in the old countries of Asia, Europe, or Africa.

It is a heritage that began with the native groups, which is why wide coverage is given to them in this work. Preceding immigrants from Europe was a great mix of natives, ranging from Arctic peoples occupying snowhouses (the Netsilik) to desert Indians inhabiting hogans (Navajo) to forest Indians congregating in longhouses (Seneca). They were joined by Mexicans, who settled territory that would become part of North America, and by Italian, Jewish, Arab, Polish, Chinese, African, Irish, and other immigrants. Together these groups made the continent what it has become today.

It is the conviction of the authors that to truly understand events, one must come to know the individuals behind them, and this requires learning about their ethnic upbringing and their people's experiences on the continent. Therefore, the entries that follow focus on the human dimension in historical and current events. Each cultural group takes on a personality of its own because of the habits, values, and ties to events that characterize its people. Becoming familiar with these cultural personalities is a key to understanding both the events and individuals.

Peoples of the World: North Americans is envisioned as a reference for school libraries. A visual resource, providing information in an easy-to-use dictionary format, this work will also be beneficial to public libraries, especially those that serve a student population. Designed with young readers in mind—those at the junior high level and up—it collects information currently available only in many resources and updates this information to the present.

Acknowledgements

For review of the selection of cultural groups and entries on them, the authors are grateful to William Roy, Associate Professor of Sociology, University of California at Los Angeles. The authors had invaluable aid in updating information from individuals who belong to the respective cultures. Grateful acknowledgement is particularly extended to these individuals:

African Americans—Henry Palmer, Ed.D.
Chinese Americans—Nancy Chung
Dakota (Sioux)—Ray Baird
Filipino Americans—Soledad Reginaldo
Irish Americans—Brigette Flynn
Japanese Americans—Shizue Takagaki
Jewish Americans—Rabbi Stanley Chyet
Mexican Americans—José Longoria
Mormons—Steven Farnsworth
Polish Americans—Eugene Brycki
Russian Americans—Faina Plyan
Seminole—Dan Factor
Tlingit—Elizabeth Woods

The editors appreciate assistance in compiling research from Denise Berger, Nancy Fister, Jennifer Lord, Joanna Pearlstein, Ann Dichter, Eric Vollmer, and Colin Wells. Special thank yous are extended to Colin Wells for his fine contributions on the Asian and other American cultures and to Linda Metzger of Gale Research for her insightful editing of the manuscript.

Copyright Acknowledgements

Acknowledgement for the use of copyrighted material on the following pages is hereby made in accordance with publishers' directives.

Page 24—From *The Blacks in America 1492–1976* by Irving J. Sloan. Reprinted by permission of Oceana Publications © 1977.

Page 73—From *To Paris: Poems by Samuel Hazo* by Samuel Hazo. Reprinted by permission of New Directions © 1981.

Photograph Acknowledgements

Introduction

Thousands of years ago (exactly how many thousands is the subject of scientific investigation), bands of wanderers crossed the Bering Strait from Asia to North America. As migration grew, settlers moved along the Pacific northwest coast, among the islands of northern Canada to Greenland, and south through the United States Great Plains. The settlements developed into grand civilizations by 1215 A.D., the year the Magna Carta granted rights to serfs in England. Over time North America's ancient societies rose and fell, disintegrating before Christopher Columbus appeared on the continent. Replacing them were smaller, loosely joined bands of peoples, collectively called the North American Indians. There were also small bands collectively called the Inuit (Eskimo), but they were far fewer and less widespread, inhabiting Arctic regions. In contrast, Indians spanned the continent. Perhaps two to three million of them lived in North America when the first Europeans arrived in the 1500s.

Interaction Between Native and Immigrant Groups

The migration of Europeans became a flood sweeping over the land— French, British, Spanish, and Dutch settlers each in their own separate areas. By the 1700s, these new settlers outnumbered the Indians by at least four to one, often pushing them onto the least desirable land, driven by a hunger for gold and land. Indians rebelled, and there was bloodshed. In Mexico, there was rebellion, too, but the situation differed. Its Indians mixed with larger society, albeit often by force as slave type laborers. In contrast, Indians to the north isolated themselves from the new society. Areas of the United States and Canada have thus seen slow assimilation of native groups into the mainstream.

The Indians began on separate territories, basing their lifestyles on environments affected first by trade with outsiders and then by the intrusion of those outsiders. Native groups struggled to adapt, sometimes fighting for their land, sometimes moving and adjusting to a new environment. They owned property on a collective basis, but this was foreign to the European settlers, who broke up territory held in common and doled out allotments piecemeal to Indians. Over a century has passed since America's immigrants took it upon themselves to make the Indian over in their own image. Officials have finally accepted the existence of separate Indian nations, though their individual governments are subject to national government in the United States and Canada.

Assimilation and Pluralism

There were similarities in the experiences of the immigrant peoples. Language was the first stumbling block, but each group experienced others: resistance to Catholicism for the Irish, low wages for the Mexicans, neighborhood restrictions for the Japanese, land ownership prohibitions against Jews, and slavery for African Americans. Newcomers from the same culture banded together in North America.

Almost everywhere the pattern of assimilation into larger society has been the same. Immigrants flock to areas populated by earlier newcomers from the same culture, creating minisocieties within the larger American culture. They learn the language and mores of the new nation in a secure context, moving gradually into the mainstream. Reservations provide this type of context for the Indians.

Though native and immigrant groups came to participate in larger society, they would also respond to it in ways that allowed them to preserve their own identities. Poles formed a network of Polish American organizations. In their separate churches, Africans created variations in worship, and the Amish retreated from surrounding society altogether. Meanwhile, the groups introduced customs of their own into the larger American culture, and some were adopted by it. Examples are sushi (Japanese), blues music (African), the Spanish language (Mexican), and moccasins (American Indian).

Coverage of Immigrant and Native Cultures

A great many native and non-native groups reside in North America. The U.S. Census Bureau recognizes over 500 Indian peoples alone. Obviously all the native and non-native groups that live on the continent cannot be detailed in a work of this scope. Therefore, the authors made a representative selection based on a few main criteria:

- Coverage of different geographic locations
- Size of population
- Earliest and most recent cultures
- Variety of lifestyles

The native groups represent various regions of North America, and the immigrant groups originated in different regions of the world: Europe,

Africa, Asia, and Latin America.* Included in the collection are profiles of large groups and smaller groups that are emerging today (Arab Americans, for example) or have maintained a highly distinct lifestyle over the years (such as the Amish). Overall, the selection draws on both old and new ingredients from the continent's "salad bowl" of culture.

*While Mexico is part of North America, its heritage is Latin American; therefore, its cultures appear in *Peoples of the World: Latin Americans.*

Format and Arrangement of Entries

Peoples of the World: North Americans is arranged into two sections: Old Cultures and Cultures of Today. Old Cultures provides brief overviews of the continent's ancient peoples. Organized alphabetically by people name, Cultures of Today includes both the native and immigrant groups. The entry for each of the groups is arranged as follows:

A dictionary-style definition introduces the entry, pronouncing the people's name, describing the group in brief, and furnishing the key facts of population, location, and language. (Populations are estimates based on the available United States census figures and on the latest statistics available for the group.)

Following this introduction are detailed descriptions under three main headings: Geographical Setting, Historical Background, and Culture Today. (In the case of the old societies, this heading is simply Culture.)

For quick access to information, subheadings appear under main headings. The Culture Today section for example, may include the following categories:

Food, Clothing and Shelter
Religion
Education
Business
Family Life
The Arts

Due to the unique experience of the groups, the subheadings vary somewhat across the entries.

Each entry in Cultures of Today concludes with a section headed For More Information, which is a selective guide for readers wanting to conduct further research on the featured group. This section lists reading materials and appropriate organizations to contact.

Other Helpful Features

To assist readers in understanding details, each entry includes a map that highlights the current geographical distribution of the featured group. Line drawings and photographs also illustrate the entries. Because primary source material enlivens historical facts for the reader, the writings include excerpts from poems, speeches, journals, etc., when such material is available and appropriate. All quoted material is identified parenthetically within the text of the entries; for complete bibliographic identification, the reader should consult the bibliography included in the book's back matter.

Although every effort is made to explain foreign or difficult terms within the text, a glossary has been compiled as a further aid to the reader. A comprehensive subject index provides another point of access to the information contained in the entries.

Comments and Suggestions

Your comments on this work, as well as your suggestions for future *Peoples of the World* volumes or future editions of *North Americans*, are welcome. Please write: Editors, *Peoples of the World*, Gale Research Inc., 835 Penobscot Bldg., Detroit, Michigan 48226-4094; or call toll-free 1-800-347-4253.

The Old Cultures

ANASAZI
(ana´ sazee)

Former residents of the Southwest believed to be the ancestors of the Hopi.

Population: Unknown.
Location: The canyons of present-day Arizona, New Mexico, and Colorado.
Language: Unknown.

Geographical Setting

The Southwest region, in which the four states of Utah, Colorado, New Mexico, and Arizona come together, is a high sandstone plateau cut by deep canyons that are the results of the wanderings of the Colorado River, the Little Colorado River, and the San Juan River. The lower levels of this region are covered with sage and juniper; the upper levels contain piñon pine. The region has harsh winters and hot summer temperatures. There is little rainfall. Small streams wander through some canyons. Here the flat canyon bed can support a small, subsistence farming society.

Historical Background

About two thousand years ago, settlers began to move into the canyon lands from the north. At first these people were probably nomadic hunters, roaming the many canyon floors of the southwest. These were the first of the ancient people known now as the Anasazi. Farther south, along the Mogollon Rim (an abrupt cliff rising across east central Arizona), another group, the Mogollons, was developing its own culture, while still farther south and west the Hohokam society was growing along the Gila River. Between 100 and 500 A.D., the Mogollons learned to make pots and decorate them, to fashion stone tools, and to build houses of the most abundant material in their mountain region, rock. At about the same time, the

Hohokam were learning to farm, growing corn and developing irrigation systems. The Hohokam were also traders with the peoples of Mexico and with their northern neighbors.

The land of the Anasazi and their neighbors.

Meanwhile, the Anasazi were becoming builders and farmers. Their first permanent houses were pit houses in the canyon floors. Later they constructed shelters of stone on the canyon floors. About 500 A.D., they began to build more enduring, free-standing stone structures, and still later they began to build large apartment-like complexes in the depressions in the canyon walls.

Decline. For more than a thousand years, the Anasazi flourished in this desert region. But in the 13th century, they began to abandon their cliff homes. The decline of the Anasazi coincided with a great drought that struck the four-corners region between 1276 and 1299. Some students of the Anasazi feel that the effect of this drought on the food and water supply of the land caused the disbanding of the old culture. Others think that pressure from newcomers to the area resulted in the disintegration of the Anasazi society. Whatever the reason, the Anasazi or ancient people began to be replaced by today's occupants of the region, the Hopi first and the Navajo.

Culture

The early Anasazi. Before 500 A.D., the Anasazi had not developed the ability to form clay into useful shapes. They were, instead, basket makers, making large and small baskets with such proficiency that some of their containers were strong enough and sufficiently tightly-woven to carry water. Yucca fibers were stripped and used for basket making. From their pit houses, the first Anasazi hunted and grew corn for food. Using stakes to poke holes in the soil, they planted several grains of corn in each hole and covered the grains with as much as 12 inches of soil.

About 500 A.D., a new weapon, a spear thrower called an *atlatl,* improved the ability to hunt the small game on the plateau. At the same time, communities began to include a larger pit house, the *kiva,* for religious ceremony and serious business meetings. And the sixth century saw the development of pottery making. Pots replaced baskets for many chores. Large pots for water and grain storage were made using a molding method in which clay was rolled into long ropes, then coiled into the form of the pot.

Betatakin in Arizona is the remains of an Anasazi village.

Cliff dwellings. About 700 A.D., the Anasazi began to abandon their canyon floor pit houses and to build houses of stone in depressions in the walls of the cliffs. First in Chaco Canyon in New Mexico, then in the Mesa Verde area of Colorado, and finally in Kayenta in Arizona, huge canyons running for many miles and with many side canyons, the Anasazi built apartmentlike structures four, five, or more stories high. One cliff building, now called Pueblo Bonito, contained more than 800 rooms and provided housing for thousands of inhabitants. There were living quarters, storage rooms for grain, and meeting places, the kivas, all built high above the canyon floor in a cave in the perpendicular canyon wall. Steps were carved in the wall to allow the residents to reach their farm land and their source of water. In other places ladders of timbers across which steps were lashed with string made from hides led to the canyon floor or from one apartment level to another. The rooms were mostly without windows. Entrance was through a hole in the roof or through low doorways built into the stone walls.

Food. At the same time, the Anasazi developed new skills for survival in the canyonlands. About 700 A.D., the bow and arrow became the main hunting tool, replacing the spear and *atlatl*. Cotton was added to the farm products of corn and squash. The cotton was twisted into thread and woven into blankets and other articles of clothing. The cliff dwellers also learned to make stronger axes by grooving the heads to hold a handle more firmly. They learned to make large nets from cotton and yucca fibers and to use these nets for trapping the most abundant source of meat and fur, rabbits.

Arts. Some Anasazi became artists, making jewelry from stone, shell, and metal. They also crafted pottery, which they decorated with geometrical designs using paints made from plants and rocks. Such designs also ornamented woven pieces such as carrying straps and sacks.

Appearance. The Anasazi were short, stocky people. Often they had lighter colored hair than most of today's residents of the area. Men kept their hair long while women often bobbed theirs. They wore simple skirts and loin cloths made at first from animal skins and later from woven fibers of yucca and cotton. A typical costume might have been a sort of apron woven from yucca fiber. Sandals were also made from yucca fiber. For warmth, the first Anasazi turned to fur blankets and mantles, mostly of rabbit fur, then later to woven blankets of cotton.

Disappearance. The Anasazi left no written records that would tell of their history or religious beliefs. However, anthropologists believe that some time in the 13th century, the Anasazi began to abandon their cliff houses and give way to new groups of people who would live in the canyons or on the mesas: the Pueblo, Hopi, Zuni, and Navajo people of today.

For More Information

See these reading materials:

Cummings, Byron. *The First Inhabitants of Arizona and the Southwest.* Tucson, Arizona: Cummings Publication Council, 1953.

Koppen, Philip. *The Smithsonian Book of North American Indians.* Washington, DC: Smithsonian Books, 1986.

Pike, Donald G. *Anasazi: Ancient People of the Rock.* Palo Alto, California: American West Publishing Company, 1974.

MOUND BUILDERS

Early inhabitants of central North America.

Population: Unknown.
Location: North America from the Rocky Mountains to the Atlantic Ocean and from the Great Lakes to the Gulf of Mexico.
Language: Probably various languages related to those of the Plains Indians.

Geographical Setting

Signs of the Mound Builders have been found in many places but are most frequent in the Mississippi and Ohio valleys.

As the early inhabitants of North America moved southward from Alaska, they found a wide range of climates and natural resources with which to contend. Following the rivers and edges of the mountain ranges, these migrants found great forest areas in what is now Canada and the northern United States, and south of that a great plains area carved by the Missouri, Mississippi, and Ohio Rivers. Here the rivers had piled up sediment for centuries, providing good soil for forest and grassland and a plentiful supply of wild life. The most abundant natural resources were soil, wood, bone, and fur. The migrants settled in small groups along the waterways from the cold climate north of the Great Lakes to the more temperate climate of the lower Mississippi Valley.

Historical Background

Perhaps as long ago as 8,000 years ago, bands of people began to settle along the rivers of central North America. Here they built independent villages, some housing as many as 2,000-3,000 people. Wood, stone, and earth were the building materials with which the various groups built large structures that stand today as mounds in Ohio, Virginia, Tennessee, and other places as far west as the Rockies and as far east as the Atlantic Ocean. Living in a time before humans had discovered the uses of metals, some Mound Builders constructed fortified cities guarded by fences of soil, inside of which they mounded other structures for worship, celebration, and burial. So varied are the mound structures that the Stone Age Mound Builders are now considered to be of many different stocks and to be the ancestors of the American Indians that inhabited the land at the time Europeans arrived in the Americas.

Probably less a separate people than an activity of the ancestors of today's American Indians, the mound building idea spread throughout the land that became the central United States over a long period of time; as early as 3,000 B.C. until 1,500 A.D. In that time, they were separated into groups and developed a variety of languages, the precursors of the Indian languages encountered by the first Europeans. Left behind are emblems of their work, large constructions of earth that required moving tons of soil. The Mound Builders did not have a written language, so what is known about their cultures has been gathered through careful excavation of their mounded towns and worship sites. Thomas Jefferson was among the first to explore an ancient mound and record what was found. His excavation of a mound in Virginia revealed that that mound had been a burial ground. The mounds of the Mound Builders served many purposes, some of which remain a mystery today. For example: why did the early mound builders in Ohio build a giant earthen serpent with jaws 75 feet wide and body extending for a quarter of a mile? Or why, in the area of Wisconsin, did they build earthen effigies of buffalo, moose, fox, wolf, panther, and lynx? Many questions remain unanswered, but as other mounds have been explored, more is becoming known about these ancient people.

The mounds vary. Some, such as the one excavated by Thomas Jefferson, contained layer upon layer of skeletons carefully arranged with stone slabs separating them. Some small mounds contain the remnants of earthen altars. Others appear to be mounds of earth on which homes were built. Pots, jewelry, and tools buried with the people of the mounds tell us something of their way of life. They suggest a culture that developed several thousand years B.C. and continued until it took the many shapes of the Indian cultures that were in the Americas at the time Europeans arrived.

Culture

Early food and shelter. The first Mound Builders were hunters, surviving on game and wild plants. As early as 3,000 B.C., hunters and gatherers had built a worship center at a place called Poverty Point in Louisiana and had established a city there. On a point of land overlooking a bayou, these workers carried earth by the basket load to build rows of broad steps in the shape of a horseshoe. Inside the horseshoe steps, which seem to have been building sites for homes, a great square was elevated. Just outside the living area, workers built a 70-foot-high mound and several smaller mounds for celebrations and burials. Eventually, perhaps as many as 3,000 people lived at Poverty Point in the center of a culture that reached out for 300 miles along the Mississippi River. These people made hunting tools and fish hooks from bone and shell. They fired clay into balls that could be heated and then dropped into pots of stew or soup for cooking. The people of Poverty Point traded up and down the Mississippi. At the time that Poverty Point flourished (until about 500 B.C.), agricultural skills had not developed. The entire city survived by hunting and fishing. The evidence gathered from Poverty Point and other sites in Tennessee, Virginia and West Virginia presents a picture of a well-developed society before the disappearance of the mound building society about 1,000 years ago.

Agriculture. Later, the Mound Builders took up agriculture and learned to cultivate corn. They may have lived in fortified villages around their places of worship. Mounds at the Pinson Center in Tennessee show that a great earthen wall was built around an area in which people built houses, a large mound for worshiping, and other smaller ones that were burial sites. Some investigators attribute the mounds to the hard work of the women of the community. Carrying baskets of earth from other places, they piled up great hills of earth and flattened the tops into an outdoor arena for worship and play. Some of the mounds contain more than a million baskets of earth.

Arts. Over their long history, the people of Pinson became efficient weavers, basket makers, potters, and toolmakers. They made necklaces and other jewelry of stone, bone, and shell. In one location, a cache of tools has been found, revealing fine knives, chisels, and hammers made from carefully crafted hard rock such as chert. Mound Builders in some places also learned to hammer art objects and tools from copper. The material gathered at the Pinson Indian Mound Complex has led one investigator, Mildred Y. Payne, to suggest a typical village life.

Later shelter and clothing. According to Payne's account, the people of Pinson lived in single-room homes made of wood frames covered with branches scattered around a central mound that was used as a ceremonial ground. The men in the village made tools from bone and stone and hunted for game. The women were left to do the hard work of maintaining the mound and building other mounds for worship and burial. Women were also expected to bear children and rear large families, prepare food, tend crops, and make clothing. Men and women wore clothing for the seasons. In the warm summer, women wore a strip of hide from which was woven an apron of bark or grass. Men wore loincloths. In winter, fur wraps afforded protection against the cold and dampness.

At least some of the communities of Mound Builders appear to have been monarchies. Aristocratic families had mounds built on which they constructed homes above and apart from the other community people. These rulers lived more comfortably and ate more food than their neighbors. Often they appear to have been the religious leaders of the community.

Food was abundant most of the time. There was time for game playing. Similar to present-day La Crosse, one game of the Mound Builders was played on a specially constructed field raised on a mound. The playing field was also the site of dancing at night to the rhythm of drums and rattles. On the days of big games, men players painted their bodies and attached feathers for decorations on knees and elbows

Many mound-building communities traded with near and distant neighbors. Some traded pearl-like shell for such items as salt. In other communities, workers made stone beads and tools for trade. The mound building societies may have traded with people as far away as Northern Canadians and the people of Central America.

About 500 B.C., the civilization around Poverty Point began to disintegrate. A thousand years later, the same decay reached Pinson.

Eventually, individual groups of Indians adopted the toolmaking and hunting habits of their ancestors and became the Indian groups known by the early settlers from Europe.

For More Information

See these reading materials:

Shetrone, Henry Clyde. *The Mound Builders.* Port Washington, New York: Kennikat Press, 1967.

Silverberg, Robert. *Mound Builders of Ancient America.* New York: New York Graphic Society, 1968.

THULE
(too´ lee)

Ancestors of the Inuit living in the far north.

Population: Unknown. There were probably fewer than 1,000,000 Native American in all of Alaska, Canada, and Greenland at the time of Columbus.
Location: Arctic and Subarctic north from Alaska to Greenland.
Languages: Various dialects, which anthropologists relate in two distinct language groups.

Geographical Setting

Thule people spread across the far North America into Greenland.

The far north of Canada and Alaska is jagged and rough. Toward the center of the North American continent, the coastline is broken into thousands of islands of varying sizes. These islands trail off north and east as if being pulled by a larger island, Greenland, away from the main continent. Here the climate is cold, most of the time near or below freezing. Most of the land is covered for much of the year with ice and snow. But the ruggedness of the coastline has provided some spots with low shrubs and even lower plant life of the tundra. Here walrus, seal, and whale come to spawn and spend some of each year. Inland, the country becomes forest land and grazing land for large animals such as the caribou. In this arctic and subarctic region, a people adapted to life in the cold and with tools for hunting large game were among the first settlers to North America.

Historical Background

Thousands of years ago, migrants from Asia crossed the Bering Strait and hunted along the coast of Alaska. The earliest direct evidence of a culture in the North is a settlement on Anangula Island, part of the Aleutian chain. Here a community of several hundred people survived for 500 years from 6,750 B.C. to 6,250 B.C. Waves of small groups of people fanned out along the Alaskan coastline. These became known as the Norton people, distinguished by pit houses, stone lamps, a simple boat made of the skin of sea mammals called a *kayak*, and the invention of the toggle spearhead for hunting walrus and seals. The Norton people were makers of small stone tools fashioned from the hard volcanic rocks, chert and obsidian. Eventually a new wave moved farther east from Alaska across northern Canada toward Baffin Island. These people developed a crescent-shaped knife, the *ulu*, and became efficient makers of tools ground and polished from slate. The Dorset also developed the use of copper and iron, although they could only fashion tools from these metals by hammering. The Dorset had no knowledge of smelting. To the pit houses of earlier North people, they added houses built of hides supported by whale ribs.

About 800 A.D., the Dorset people began to be replaced by another group from Alaska, the Thule. Master whale hunters and developers of the *umiak,* a more seaworthy boat, the Thule culture spread across Canada and across the ocean to Greenland. The Thule people came to occupy more territory than any other culture, spreading 6,000 miles from west to east. In fact, the word *thule* means "far off places," and Thule has become the name of the farthest community of these Northern people in Greenland.

Culture

Life in the arctic depended largely upon two abilities: the ability to endure the bitter cold and the ability to hunt the large marine mammals of the North. Animals such as seals, walrus, and then whales dominated the way of life of the Thule. These animals provided nearly all of the food for the Thule.

Food, clothing, and shelter. Women sewed the animal hides into clothing, using strips of sinew for thread and bone for needles. Tough hide was formed into thimbles to help with the sewing. The clothes for men and women were much the same. Both men and women wore parkas, a slip-on coat made of seal skin or caribou hide. Fur trousers, fur stockings, and fur boots completed the clothing. Another skin suit of parka and trousers made from lighter hide was worn underneath in winter and became the outer wear in summer. Even the decoration for the clothing came from the large animals. Thule women decorated their parkas with fringes of hide of different colors. To this costume the Thule added snow goggles, slitted goggles of wood or ivory, to protect against the bright sun and its reflection from the white surface of the earth. In addition, women among the Thule frequently decorated their faces with tattoos. Women often braided their hair, while the men usually cut theirs so that they had long hair in back with bangs over the forehead.

Women stayed inside the pit house most of the time and did the sewing and cooking. Men helped with the building of the houses and hunted for food. In their time at home, men sat atop the pit houses in fair weather and carved tools, geometric designs, and animal sculptures from wood, bone, ivory, or horn.

At first, Thule homes were rectangular pit houses. A bit of earth was cleared and a shallow excavation was dug out using bone tools. This pit was covered with logs, then with soil, making a thick protection from the elements. Packed snow was also used as a covering for the pit house. As the Thule moved eastward and found more whale-spawning country, some houses were made with coverings of skin stretched over frames made from the ribs of whales.

Hunting the large mammals of the North was necessary for food, clothing, and shelter. The Thule invented the umiak, a skin boat larger and more sturdy than the kayak, and were the first to be able to hunt whales by boat. The animal upon which the Thule depended became dominant in their religious beliefs. In their religion, led by shamans, the Thule believed that carvings of animals contained the spirit of the animals and would protect the people in times of conflict.

Arts. The large mammals became subjects of art. Even before the Thule culture arrived, Norton people had learned to carve animal figures from bone and ivory. The early carvings, done by the men as they sat atop their pit houses and talked, were very detailed. Building on this tradition of bone and ivory carving and of decorating tools with the carvings, the Thule developed an art that was more simple, while still representing the whales, seals, walrus, caribou, bears, dogs, and birds that they respected and worshiped. Carvings of animals on the handles of spears and knives were said to evoke the animals represented and to bring good fortune to the hunter.

Other forms of art were appreciated by the Thule. They developed musical instruments such as a tambourine-shaped drum, mostly to keep rhythm for the singing that accompanied their religious ceremonies and the slow, rhythmic dances they enjoyed. Among the Thule, religious leaders were shamans who invoked the help of the animals and were thought to be able to predict the location of animals to be hunted.

Government. The development of the umiak helped the Thule become seamen. With the umiak, they could sail in search of large sea mammals rather than waiting for them to come near the shore. The Thule knife came to be a large crescent-shaped one well suited for skinning and carving their large prey. They developed better harpoons than their predecessors, the Dorset, and floats for helping to detain and tire out the large game they hunted. Whale became the most important prey for the Thule. The whaleboat captain became head of the community and took responsibility for caring for the community's needs. The whale boat captain was the real government of the Thule community.

Continuity. The Thule borrowed from the Norton and Dorset cultures. They adopted the early interest in sculpting the animals of the North, but their carvings were more economical of detail than those of their predecessors. The Dorset had begun to form tools by polishing slate as early as 2,500 B.C., and the Thule continued this practice. By the time of the arrival of the first Europeans, the Thule had spread as far as the coast of Greenland and were among the first Native Americans to meet the newcomers. Gradually, the Thule culture gave way to that of the Inuit of today. So the story of the North people is one of continuous waves of people learning from the past and adding new methods to deal with the severe cold and limited vegetation of the far north.

For More Information

See these reading materials:

Kopper, Philip. *The Smithsonian Book of North American* Indiaans. Washington, DC: Smithsonian Books, 1986.

Spencer, Robert F., Jesse D. Jennings, et al. *The Native Americans.* New York: Harper and Row, 1965.

Cultures of Today

AFRICAN AMERICANS
(af´ reh kin eh mer´ uh kins)

Black Americans whose ancestors were born in Africa.

Population: 28,151,000 (1985).
Location: United States, mainly the South.
Language: English, Black English, Gullah.

Geographical Setting

Major population areas of African Americans.

It is hardly surprising that some 53 percent of the black population in the United States resides in the South. Over 90 percent of them descend from Africans brought to the region as slaves to raise tobacco, rice, sugar, and cotton. After the Civil War, blacks remained mainly in the South until the early 1900s. The demand for factory workers in World War I drew many to the Northeast and more to the Midwest. Early real estate agreements not to sell homes to blacks outside a given area encouraged the growth of black ghettos, or slum neighborhoods, in these regions.

Blacks have moved to every region of the country. In the 1970s there was a reverse migration. Northern blacks migrated back to the South, where a movement from farms to cities had already occurred. Today Alabama and Mississippi have three of the nation's most densely populated black counties. These appear in the Black Belt, an area named for rich black soil under rolling grassland. The Black Belt is important to slave history, for it was largely here that cotton had its heyday.

Historical Background

Slave trade. In the beginning, slavery was accepted nationwide. Patriots such as George Washington and Thomas Jefferson owned slaves. At the root of the practice was the concept of *chattel slavery*, a system that regarded and treated people as property. Officially, early America defined slaves as less than human. In the Constitution, a black qualified as three-fifths of a person when setting up Congressional districts. It is hardly surprising, then, that the *slavers* (slave ships) treated blacks as cargo.

Records of the first slave ships bound for America date back to 1645. Taken from Africa below the Sahara Desert, most black slaves were captured in wars or kidnapped by slave raiders. They spoke different languages particular to various groups, such as the Ewe, Wolof, Hausa, Ashanti, Kongo, and Ibo. The captured formed a human chain. Linked by a rope, many of them marched hundreds of miles to the "slave" coast of West Africa to be chosen and branded.

Crowded aboard slave ships, men lay or sat shackled together. Often the males lay *spoon fashion*, breast to back, to fit the greatest number on deck. Otherwise they might sit in rows, with men crowded onto one another's laps, legs overlapping legs. They were released twice a day for meals and exercise. Women and children had more freedom.

Many passengers died from disease or starvation. Others drowned themselves, and there were over 155 mutinies. Of the mutinies, the most famous is the *Amistad* incident. Cinque, an African prince, won a revolt on the *Amistad*, but two crew members made a trick landing in Connecticut, then turned the matter over to authorities. Charged with piracy and murder, Cinque was defended in the Supreme Court by John Quincy Adams. Adams won, and Cinque returned to Africa, then became a slave trader himself. In 1841, 135 blacks sailing from Virginia to Louisiana on the *Creole* attacked the crew, then took the ship to the British colony Nassau, where they escaped slavery.

Such victories were rare, however. More often Africans sent to the New World became slaves, merchandise in a land with a foreign language and strange customs. The last slave ship, the *Clothilde*, docked in Alabama in 1859. Having arrived, the slaves, like those who preceded them, were hurled into a land whose customs and language were foreign. It mattered not whether they had been princes or farmers back in Africa. Over the years, though, their customs would influence the surrounding society in the South, and it would influence them. An African American culture developed.

Plantation life. African *survivals*, customs from Africa, appeared in music, folklore, religion, food, and farm life. As in Africa, slaves in America built thatched roofs for their cabins. They ate peanuts, sesame seeds, yams, and rice. Their numbers grew, slaves bearing black or mulatto (of black and white parentage) children. Most respected among slaves were the older blacks from Africa. The invention of the cotton gin in 1793 escalated the need for slave labor, so additional slaves were imported from Africa. Thereafter, plantation life developed around the cotton crop.

Slaves who were field hands rose before dawn, prepared breakfast, fed the animals, and rushed to the fields. There they hoed, built fences, cut trees, cleared land, and planted sugar, tobacco, or cotton until sunset. Then they tended the livestock and cooked a meal before a horn sounded bedtime. In cotton-picking season, men would gin cotton until nine at night. The house slaves gardened, cooked, sewed, churned milk, and tended horses, all under the watchful eyes of whites. Though their chores might have been easier than a field hand's, they were least respected by other slaves.

Home in the slave quarters consisted of a roughly built, one-room log cabin with a dirt floor. Cracks were plentiful, bringing in wind and rain. Crowded, each cabin housed at least two families. Slaves used their own homemade furniture and utensils. Packing boxes became tables; straw-covered boards or mattresses of corn shucks became beds. Some slaves slept on the ground. With the abundance of cotton, clothing was inexpensive and simple. Food consisted mostly of bacon or pork and Indian corn provided by the master.

While some masters were exceptionally cruel or kind, most were neither one or the other. The typical slave owner hired doctors for his sick slaves and punished those who lied, stole, or fought. Punishment might be as harsh as 50 to 75 lashes of the whip. Among the cruelest methods employed by masters were tarring and feathering, branding, and maiming. A planter in Mississippi is known to have applied 1,000 lashes to a slave, which serves as an example of extremely brutal treatment. In contrast, Dr. James Green Carson of Mississippi bought his slaves labor-saving machines and punished his own children for being impolite to his slaves.

How did the black slaves react to their situations? Many of them quietly rebelled against their master's demands. Outwardly the slaves seemed compliant, but this was a sham, a mask worn for their own protection. The celebrated black poet Paul Laurence Dunbar explains this proud form of privacy (Dunbar as cited in Sloan 1977, p. 132).

Why should the world be over-wise,
In counting all our tears and sighs?
Nay, let them only see us, while
We wear the mask.

Most slaves picked cotton, albeit grudgingly. They had no choice, but they set their own pace. In Mississippi, an average field hand picked 140 pounds of cotton a day. Yet during an 1830 cotton-picking race 14 slaves each gathered over 320 pounds. Often field hands put in a minimum of effort to get by, which bespoke wisdom in figuring out that minimum. A slave song provides further evidence of such wisdom (Douglass 1985, pp. 252–3).

We raise de wheat,
Dey gib us de corn;
We bake de bread,
Dey giv us de cruss;
We sif de meal,

Dey gib us de huss;
We peal de meat,
Dey gib us de skin
And dat's de way
Dey takes us in.

Slaves had little opportunity to be educated, so few learned to read. Those who did earned great respect in the slave quarters. Aside from the readers, others who won high status were slaves who worked away from the plantation—draymen who drove carts, steamboat men, and drovers who herded cows and horses. Also respected were slaves who provided slave clothing and housing—the carpenters, the shoemakers, the seamstresses. A sense of community existed in the quarters, a sharing of skills and goods.

The foundation of the community was the slave family. There was a pattern to courtship, or wooing. Suitors would speak in riddles to discover if a woman was available (Hampton Folklore Society as cited in Blassingame 1979, p. 158).

My dear miss, de worl' is a howlin' wilderness full of devourin'
animals, and you has got to walk through hit. Has you made
up yer min' to walk through hit by yerself, or wid som bol' wahyer?

For the slave, love and marriage came with special fears—having to watch a spouse mistreated or sold down the river. Most men wanted to marry a woman from another plantation so they would not have to suffer seeing their wife beaten, insulted, or overworked without being able to raise a hand in her defense. A slave owner, though, preferred his male slaves to marry his female slaves so their children would be his.

The majority of black families survived the perils of slavery. Though an owner could split up the family by selling a wife or child, two thirds of all slave families escaped this fate. The black husband and father faced obstacles, though. Instead of him, the slave owner provided food and clothing for the family, made decisions about their work, even decided arguments. The ways a male slave could gain status in his family's eyes were limited to hunting and fishing to break the monotonous diet. Or he might build furniture and partitions for privacy in the slave cabin. In their early years, slave children lived carefree lives, keeping their young masters company, picking berries, raiding watermelon patches, playing with them on an equal basis. By age ten, this changed as slave boys, for example, went off to pick cotton. Their parents had taught them charity, honesty, and survival tactics by then. Keep quiet around whites, the children learned, and be obedient to avoid pain or death. Still, many children would fight the overseer who whipped their mother.

Rebels. Adult slaves fought back in two ways—by escaping and by armed rebellion. The runaways built hidden communities in swamps or mountains of the South. Some joined Indians. By 1836, 1,200 maroons, or runaways, lived in Florida's Seminole Indian towns (see SEMINOLES). Other slaves stole away individually. Facing great odds, they fled overseers in hot pursuit with bloodhounds and guns in hand. If a runaway was caught, he might be sold down South or whipped and handcuffed, a cowbell placed around his neck to alert the overseer of his whereabouts.

Among the rebels were Gabriel Prosser, Denmark Vesey, and Nat Turner. In 1800, Gabriel Prosser, a Virginia slave, was betrayed in a plot to lead thousands in an attack on Richmond. Prosser was hanged. In 1822, Denmark Vesey recruited 9,000 slaves to launch a revolt in South Carolina. He too was betrayed, then hung with 36 others. Less than ten years later, Nat Turner launched his devastating rebellion. Born a slave on the plantation of Benjamin Turner, at age 31 he aimed to wreak vengeance on planters. He was a short, coal-black man who led 60 rebels through an 1831 night in military style, leaving ravaged plantations and massacred white families behind. In all, his army murdered 54 Virginia whites. A mass of alarmed,

armed whites chased Nat for two months before catching him. Afterwards, he was executed along with over 40 more blacks.

Underground Railroad. In the North, free blacks worked for the Underground Railroad and to sway public opinion against slavery. The abolitionist, or antislavery, movement was well underway by 1831. David Walker, a free black, wrote the violent 76-page pamphlet *Walker's Appeal*. Addressed to the blacks, its aim was to unify free blacks and slaves. Walker advocated violence. Killing whites was self-defense, he argued, because whites wanted blacks for slaves and would murder them. As for the whites who wanted to send free blacks back to Africa, he warned them that "America is as much our country, as it is yours." Walker dropped dead in a doorway after 1,000 dollars was offered for his body. Blacks were convinced he was poisoned. Thereafter, a steady stream of blacks wrote against slavery in newspapers like Frederick Douglass's *North Star*.

The "Underground Railroad" was not a train track but a network of secret routes for slaves escaping to freedom in the North and Canada. It operated at night. Across forests, fields, and rivers, the fugitives traveled not only on trains but also on boats, wagons, and most often on foot. Abolitionists, the blacks and whites against slavery, were "conductors," whose houses and churches became "stations" along the way. Having fled slavery himself in 1838, the free black Frederick Douglass became a conductor on the Railroad, hiding as many as 11 runaways under his roof at a time. Harriet Tubman escaped slavery in 1849 with two brothers. Chased by wild dogs, they hid in caves and graveyards before reaching Philadelphia. From there, Harriet too became a conductor, traveling South and North until she reportedly led some 300 runaways over the secret routes to freedom. Her activities were public knowledge, and at one point there was a 40,000 dollar price on her head. She survived to witness the Civil War.

Emancipation. Frederick Douglass advised President Abraham Lincoln on the condition of American blacks during the Civil War. It is estimated that some 180,000 black soldiers fought for the North, of which 40,000 died. Black fighters displayed courage in battle. Sailor Joachim Pease, for example, won a Congressional Medal of Honor for his coolness in a duel between navy ships.

Though President Abraham Lincoln signed the Emancipation Proclamation in 1863, the war dragged on until 1865. The Emancipation Proclamation declared only those slaves in the rebel states free; it was the 13th Amendment (1865) that abolished slavery throughout the nation. Four million slaves resided in the United States at the outbreak of the War. Now all surviving blacks were free. The name *slave* was replaced by *freedman.*

States set up "black codes" that spelled out the freedmen's rights. They could own property or bring a case to trial, but it was illegal for them to serve on a jury or to marry whites. Some states even forbade blacks from owning land, keeping them as close to slavery as possible. There had been talk of dividing up plantations—giving each freedman "40 acres and a mule"—but plantations remained with their old owners. Instead new state laws cancelled out freedoms in the South.

There were the literacy test, poll tax, white primary, and grandfather clause. The literacy test demanded blacks pass a reading and writing exam before voting. The poll tax required money for voting. The white primary barred blacks from voting in a primary election. To protect whites, the grandfather clause said such measures did not apply to anyone whose grandfather had voted before the Civil War.

Court cases did not help matters. After trying to ride in a white railroad car, Homer Plessy, a New Orleans black man, was arrested for defying a state law separating the races. In 1896, the Supreme Court ruled against Plessy. The case *Plessy vs. Ferguson* held that separate but equal cars, schools, and so on were legal.

Meanwhile, white groups—the Knights of the White Camelia and the infamous Ku Klux Klan—terrorized blacks. They threatened to destroy black property and kill or whip people. Lynching blacks for voting and other "crimes" grew common, killing 2,500 defenseless victims from 1889 to 1918. Records reveal causes and consequences of the lynchings (NAACP as cited in Cassity 1984, p.60).

Oklahoma, 1914
Marie Scott of Wagoner County, a seventeen-year-old Negro girl, was lynched by a mob of white men because her brother killed one of two white men who had assaulted her. She was alone in the house when the men entered, but her screams brought her brother to the rescue. In the fight that ensued one of the white men was killed. The next day the mob came to lynch her brother, but as he had escaped, lynched the girl instead. No one has ever been indicted for this crime.

Blacks fought back. As early as 1868, 200 Louisiana blacks, armed with clubs, fended off Klansmen threatening to kill black voters. That same year, groups of Tennessee blacks and Klansmen shot at each other. A Klansman, no blacks, died. In 1895, black journalist Ida B. Wells published *The Red*

Record, a statistical breakdown of lynching in the United States. Thereafter, she continued using the press to expose crimes against blacks.

Segregation. Earlier a black woman, Sojourner Truth, had tested an 1865 law against segregated horsecars in the nation's capital, Washington, DC. She boarded a horsecar, then sat next to whites. The driver ordered her to move to the front platform behind the horses or to get off the horsecar. Not only did she stay seated, but she also had the driver arrested. Two years later in New Orleans, blacks boarded cars for whites, and temporarily there was more equality. The city stopped the Jim Crow practice. (*Jim Crow* was the term for lawful segregation, taken from a song-dance "Jump Jim Crow.") Then there was a backlash. New Jim Crow laws appeared in the South in the early 1900s.

Blacks were divided about how they should respond. Booker T. Washington believed they should train for work with their hands. Once they succeeded in farming and business, whites would respect them and they would gain rights. The black leader W.E.B. Du Bois argued for full equality immediately. In 1909–1910, he helped organize the National Association for the Advancement of Colored People. The NAACP then took legal steps to end lynching and segregation in the South. It brought case after case before the Supreme Court from 1927–1950, getting it to outlaw white-only primary elections. A black lawyer, Thurgood Marshall, won over 30 cases, later becoming a justice of the Supreme Court himself. His most far-reaching victory was the 1954 case, *Brown v. the Board of Education*, which outlawed segregated schools. The Court concluded that "separate facilities are unequal." In the same decade, the NAACP toppled state laws against blacks in voting, schools, housing, and busing.

A nonviolent movement began in order to test court decisions. Like Sojourner Truth 90 years earlier, Rosa Parks refused to move from her seat on an Alabama bus in 1955. A bus boycott followed. From 1955 to 1956, blacks found other ways to get to work until bus rules changed. There were sit-ins at "white-only" restaurants, and Freedom Riders whose purpose was to ride public buses through the South and be served at stops along the way. One of the movement's leaders was a black minister, Martin Luther King, Jr.

Many blacks participated in the freedom movement, but more cheered from the sidelines. Though their tactics were nonviolent, the freedom workers suffered violence. Herbert Lee, a black farmer helping blacks register to vote in Mississippi, died from a gunshot in the head in 1961. There was a host of church bombings and burnings in Southern states. Four black girls—Addie Mae Collins, Denise McNair, Carole Robertson, and Cynthia Wesley—died in an Alabama bombing. In 1964, the bodies of black

James Chaney and his white coworkers Michael Schwerner and Andrew Goodman were discovered in a Mississippi dam. That same year Martin Luther King, Jr., won the Nobel Peace Prize for his nonviolent efforts. Peace was years away, though. King received up to 13 threats on his life a day. After the 1965 killing of black leader Malcolm X, King himself was assassinated in a 1968 protest for Tennessee garbage collectors. The decade saw race riots in the North, Midwest, and West, with more killings and with looting and burning that cost millions of dollars in property damage.

Dr. Martin Luther King, Jr. and others protest in Montgomery, Alabama in 1965.

Progress. During the 20th century, the condition of blacks improved greatly in government, education, and income. The Civil Rights Act of 1964 obligated hotels and restaurants to serve blacks. The Voting Rights Act of 1965 guaranteed protection to blacks who registered to vote. Socially, the gap between whites and blacks grew narrower. Buses of the early 1970s transported black children to white schools to balance education racially. In 1984, Jesse Jackson became the first black candidate for United States President. Four years later, in 1988, over 6,800 black officials held elected positions in the country. The number was great in contrast to blacks elected in the past, but not yet representative. Blacks formed 11.7 percent of the U.S. population, but only 1.5 percent of all elected officials. Conditions had dramatically improved by the late 1980s, but the gap was far from closed, and progress in general had slowed.

Culture Today

Government. Perhaps the greatest gains for blacks have taken place in politics. Voting was the first area of achievement. Given members of the same social class, blacks now equal or exceed whites in exercising the vote. This has influenced American relations to Africa. Generally, American blacks favor material aid to African nations and oppose apartheid (segregation) in South Africa. In the late 1980s, many American companies left South Africa, a move driven partly by pressure from American blacks.

The participation of Black Americans in government more directly affects the course of their own lives. On the most basic level, it has produced jobs in government, which employs the majority of black professionals today. Blacks have held posts in national, state, and city governments. Across levels, Andrew Young (American diplomat), Congresswoman Barbara Jordan (Texas), and Mayor Thomas Bradley (Los Angeles) serve as three of the many examples.

Business. Farm ownership was the first ambition in business. Becoming farm tenants after the Civil War, blacks lived in one-room cabins, still working from sunrise to sunset in the cotton fields. They experienced some success. Over 220,000 blacks owned farms in the South by 1920, but many more were tenants and laborers. There was a general movement to cities during the next several decades; most black males held industry or service jobs by 1962.

Joining the city labor market, blacks competed with white workers in business. They earned less than whites, so men like A. Philip Randolph formed labor unions such as the Brotherhood of Sleeping Car Porters to win higher wages and more work. Later unions not only admitted blacks but elected them to high office. Marc Stepp, for example, served as Vice President of the United Auto Workers in the 1970s. As time passed, more blacks became lawyers, doctors, and business owners. The number of professionals in the Black American population climbed to 8 percent in 1984; farmers dropped to 4.9 percent.

Income has risen for black families. As a result, about one-fifth of them had moved into the middle class by 1986. The progress has been offset by the rising number of poor blacks, though. One-third of all blacks now live below the poverty line, and this is likely to continue due to conditions in America. In recent years, unemployment has risen for all groups in the country, and the average income has fallen. This bodes ill for blacks, since past figures show they have suffered unemployment at twice the national rate and are paid less than whites. In 1985, the average income of blacks in

America was 60 percent that of whites. This imbalance mostly affects black males. Black female workers have experienced great gains in the job market. Today they earn as much as their white female counterparts.

From slavery to sharecropping to success as educators, scientists, and business owners.

Family life. To a greater degree than other groups, blacks are affected by general family trends in America. As in the general population, divorces and single-parent families have increased among blacks. The two-parent family survived slavery. Now it is losing ground. In 1986, 49 percent of black families with children were headed by a woman. The majority of children today live in households that include their mother, but not their father. Meanwhile, two-parent families remain common in middle-class homes.

It has already been established that the earning power of late 20th-century black women is considerable. In lower-class families, this often results in the mother making most of the decisions. Role models for girls are self-sufficient women who do not depend on a male for income. Living in households without fathers, many boys of the lower class have no male role models for family life.

In housing, families continue to experience segregation. Racially divided neighborhoods are typical in the major cities. In the 1970s, many blacks moved from the inner city to the suburbs. They settled adjacent to the central city, in effect, creating little ghettos within the suburbs. So neighborhoods remain unmixed, especially in the Northeast and North Central states. In 1980, the National Research Council estimated segregation in housing at 80, using 100 to stand for total separation between the races.

Food. Down-home or soul cooking for blacks refers to recipes they contributed to Southern-style meals. Cooking for their owners, house slaves added African spices to stews and rice dishes in the South. The cooks turned corn into hoe cakes, dumplings, and *spoon bread*, a soft, puddinglike dish. Made with bacon fat, the breakfast *hominy grits* is parched corn hulled, dried, and ground to meal. Slaves taught their owners to prepare dishes such as collard greens, black-eyed peas, sassafras tea, watermelon pickles, and okra and tomatoes. Many Southern recipes were theirs.

Education. Self-help is a strong current in the stream of African American development. Just as blacks began their own labor unions, they established schools. Mary Chase founded a school for blacks in Virginia after the Civil War, as did Mary D. Price in New Orleans and Miss L. Humphrey in Tennessee. Booker T. Washington founded Tuskegee Institute to train blacks in farming and industry. In 1906 the Institute started the Movable School. Loaded with teachers, supplies, and poultry, a wagon carried instruction to struggling black farms. Blacks established more schools— Hampton Institute, Howard University, Fisk University, and Bethune-Cookman College. By 1984, there were over 100 black colleges and universities.

Meanwhile, there was more desegregation in public schools. Most of the progress occurred from 1966 to 1973. Since then, desegregation in schools has slowed or stopped. This promises to slow progress for black students. Surveys chart more academic progress for black students who attend integrated schools. They often experience resegregation in the mixed school, because tracking programs isolate them. Yet they score higher on tests and are more likely to graduate from high school and college than blacks in segregated schools.

Black English. In Africa, the various peoples speak from 850 to 1,000 different languages. Early slave traders and their different-tongued prisoners needed a way to communicate. So a form of pidgin English developed. Its intention was to simplify sentence structure and vocabulary for rapid communication. Most probably an outgrowth of this pidgin English, Black English today is *not* inaccurate English.

Along the Georgia-South Carolina Sea Coast lives a small group known as the Gullah blacks. They continued to speak over 4,000 African words well into the 20th century. Living apart from whites, they have invented expressions of their own. Among them are *day clean* for "dawn" and *sweet mouth* for "flatter."

Other blacks, who lived among whites, influenced and were influenced by the surrounding speech habits. Popular words credited to Southern blacks include *okra, banjo,* and *cooter* (turtle). Elsewhere, blacks have coined terms such as *rapping, jiving, sounding,* and *gripping* for "talking."

Religion. The most renown black orators (Reverend Martin Luther King, Jr., for example) began as preachers. Religion was an early arena in which blacks were allowed to excel. At first, slaves believed in spirits and a voodoo religion that centered on a snake god. Later, the majority of blacks adopted Christianity.

The Christian notion of an afterlife appealed to the slaves, who believed that in death they would rejoin ancestors in Africa. In contrast to white Christians, slaves developed their own styles of worship. One example is "free singing." A worshiper would spontaneously lead the congregation in song, improvising a verse or moving it from one tune into another. Today the formal choir replaces free singing. A continuing tradition is call and response, a form of dialogue between a black preacher and congregation.

The early churches instructed the slaves in new behaviors (for example, Christian weddings and English words). Also churches gave slaves an avenue to status and power. Serving on a church board or as minister allowed them to control at least one aspect of their lives and brought feelings of self-worth. Famous for their speaking skills, black preachers were called upon to address white congregations,too. Protestant sects (Baptists and then Methodists) attracted the greatest following at first, and these remain strong today. Still determining their own styles of worship, most contemporary black Christians continue to frequent separate black churches. A 1987 survey indicates that 74 percent of the group considers religion extremely important. Only 60 percent attend church regularly, about as many as in other American groups today.

Religious minorities appear within the black community, too. America's black Muslim movement began in 1913 in Newark, New Jersey, then foundered until the appearance of Georgia-born Elijah Muhammad. Defining

God as a black deity, Elijah first won followers from America's ghettos. His spokesperson, Malcolm X, later recruited sports stars such as heavyweight champion Cassius Clay (Muhammed Ali). Before dying in 1975, Elijah passed leadership to his son Wallace Deen Muhammad. Wallace has favored an orthodox observance of the religion, a trend apparent among other American Muslims, too (see ARAB AMERICANS). Meanwhile, Minister Louis Farrakhan has led his own movement in the black Muslim community. African-American Jews form another minority. They mostly belong to one of three all-black sects: the Black Jews, the Black Israelites, or the Black Hebrews.

Music. Of all fields, American music is probably most indebted to black influence. Blacks not only created their own styles of music but also influenced nearly all other forms of American music.

Just as religion gave the slaves some control in life, spirituals, their religious folk songs, gave them hope. The slaves sang songs that lifted their spirits with lyrics such as "Breddren, don' get weary, breddren don' get weary, breddren don' get weary. Fo' de work is mos' done" (Blassingame 1979, p.140). A favorite, "Run, Nigger, Run" was about outsmarting white patrols in search of slaves who left the plantation without a pass. Other, less cheerful slave songs concerned hardship, love, and the thirst for freedom. Slaves would accompany the singing by *patting juba*, striking the hands on the knees, striking the hands together, then striking the right shoulder with one hand and the left with the other. Beginning in 1871, the Fisk Jubilee Singers performed spirituals, keeping alive the memory of slavery. Tobacco workers on strike in the 1940s and freedom fighters in the 1960s sang the spiritual "We Shall Overcome."

Along with spirituals, blacks developed blues, jazz, gospel, soul, and rap music. Blues music expressed sorrow, disappointment, and pain. The earliest tunes concerned Southern living—the boll weevil, cotton fields, floods, droughts, and the chain gangs. W. C. Handy published the first blues tune in 1912, then singers like Bessie Smith popularized the sound. In jazz, Scott Joplin became known as King of Ragtime, publishing "Original Rags" in 1899. Jelly Roll Morton followed 16 years later with Jelly Roll Blues (1915), regarded as the first published jazz arrangement. Then came Joseph "King" Oliver and Louis "Satchmo" Armstrong. While Joplin played piano, Armstrong favored the coronet or trumpet. They all used improvisation, instrumental vocalization, call and response. The son of a minister, Thomas Dorsey preferred gospel music to blues and jazz, then made it popular, composing over 400 gospel songs. Gospel music has been described as a blend of old religious songs, spirituals, and the blues. Sung by artists such as Aretha Franklin and Otis Redding, soul music allows for group participation and sophisticated solo passages. In "rap" music, performers talk or chat in rhyming couplets accompanied by rhythm tracks. Taking turns, the speakers discuss subjects ranging from dancing to the plight of inner city life. Rap music builds on the heritage of African chanting and on spoken lyrics sometimes used by blues and soul singers. At its barest, rap has no melody but a strong, driving beat.

Folklore and literature. In folklore, blacks created Brer Rabbit tales, John Tales, and Aunt Dicey tales to name a few. It is no accident that a weak rabbit outsmarted stronger bears, wolves, and foxes in Brer Rabbit stories. More obvious tales such as "John and His Boss-Man's Watermelon Patch" show a black laborer outsmarting a plantation owner who did not permit his laborers to raise food for themselves. In an Aunt Dicey tale, a willful, snuff-duffing former slave refuses to chop cotton for her old master once she is free; instead she insists on having a farm of her own.

Black writers treated social and family life in novels. Recognized as the first black American novel, *Clotel, the President's Daughter* by William Wells Brown appeared in 1853. A host of books by black authors followed. James Weldon Johnson wrote *The Autobiography of an Ex-Coloured Man* (1912). Arna Bontemps wrote *Black Thunder* (1936), based on the slave revolt led by Gabriel Prosser. Dealing with black life in Chicago, Richard Wright created *Native Son* (1940). Set in Harlem, New York, *Invisible Man* (1953) by Ralph Ellison took another look at black life in the North. Margaret Walker wrote *Jubilee* (1966), a family novel about life in Georgia. In *The Autobiography of Miss Jane Pittman* (1971), Ernest Gaines covered a century of life among Louisiana blacks. John Oliver Killens wrote *Great Gittin' Up Morning* (1972), based on Denmark Vesey's slave conspiracy in South Carolina.

America recognized the excellence of its African American writers. In 1987, Toni Morrison's novel *Beloved* won a Pulitzer Prize. For children, prize-winning authors include William Armstrong (*Sounder*), Mildred Taylor (*Roll of Thunder, Hear My Cry*), and Virginia Hamilton. Hamilton recalls black history for the young in *Anthony Burns: The Defeat and Triumph of a Fugitive Slave* (1989). Most celebrated among African American poets, Langston Hughes wrote verse for both children and adults.

In theater, first there were minstrel shows featuring whites in blackface who performed black humor, dance, and music. The early black actor Ira Aldridge won acclaim for his roles in Shakespearean plays. By the 1970s, noteworthy black plays had appeared—Lorraine Hansberry's *Raisin in the Sun* about family life, James Baldwin's *Blues for Mr. Charlie* about lynching and Douglas Turner Ward's *Day of Absence* about a town of whites that depends on blacks who suddenly disappear. Dramatist August Wilson won Pulitzer prizes in 1987 and in 1989. Called *Fences*, his first prize-winner dealt with the inner struggle for black identity since the Civil War.

Holidays. On January 1, 1863, President Abraham Lincoln issued the Emancipation Proclamation freeing the slaves. Blacks continue to celebrate Emancipation Day every January 1 with parades and a new reading of the Emancipation Proclamation. Like Lincoln, Martin Luther King, Jr. took action that swayed the nation. He founded a national civil rights organization (Southern Christian Leadership Conference), delivered stirring lectures across the country, wrote in support of nonviolent tactics, and led freedom rides and marches to win civil rights. The Baptist minister won the support of millions of Americans for civil rights. His "I Have a Dream" speech, delivered to an audience of 200,000 at the Lincoln Memorial, has been likened to Lincoln's Gettysburg address for its effect. To commemorate his impact on history, Americans now celebrate Martin Luther King, Jr.'s birthday on January 15.

Heroes. The list of blacks who achieved excellence spans all walks of American life. Long open to the group, sports became one of the first avenues to fame. Black boxer Peter Jackson fought Irishman James Corbett in 1891 in a 61-round draw. Thereafter sports gave rise to numerous champions—Jesse Owens in track, Joe Louis in boxing, Althea Gibson in tennis, Bill Russell in basketball, Charlie Gifford in golf, and home run champion Hank Aaron in baseball. The number of black players on professional teams also rose. In 1985, basketball had 80 percent black players, football had 52 percent, and baseball had 22 percent. Few blacks were coaches or referees, however. The group was underrepresented in positions of authority.

Blacks had helped themselves in business and education by creating their own labor unions and schools. To recognize outstanding achievement, they created their own awards for excellence. The Springarn Medal, begun by Joel E. Springarn in 1914, recognizes exceptional achievers in a variety of fields. Winners have included musicians (Roland Hayes), writers (Charles Chestnutt), teachers (Mary McLeod Bethune), doctors (Charles Drew), civil rights workers (Roy Wilkins), labor leaders (A. Philip Randolph), diplomats (Ralph Bunche), painters (Jacob Lawrence), and dancers (Alvin Ailey).

The Springarn committee showed foresight in its choices. Given to singer Marian Anderson in 1939, the Medal reached her 16 years before she performed for a mixed audience at Metropolitan Opera house. Black actor

Paul Robeson won a Springarn Medal in 1945; 19 years later, a mixed audience presented the Academy Award for Best Actor to black actor Sidney Poitier. Other awards to black artists followed. In 1975, Stevie Wonder won four Grammy Awards for excellence in American music. Trumpter Wynton Marsali won a Grammy award as top jazz solist (1983–85).

Times had changed. Too many blacks to name were recognized for their contributions to entertainment, science, the military and other fields. In the late 20th century, the average black adult, like the typical white adult, works, votes, and helps America progress. By this time the African American scientist George Washington Carver had long since conducted his agricultural research, and Dr. Percy L. Julian had isolated soya protein. In 1983, Guion Bluford became the first black astronaut sent into space on the space shuttle STS 8. Such scientists and explorers now receive widespread applause due to a century of black effort and the loss of countless lives.

Most integrated in the United States today is the army. Blacks have proven themselves time and again in military action. In 1966, Vietnam private Milton Olive III won the Congressional Medal of Honor. Grabbing a grenade, he threw his body on top of it, absorbing the blast to save others. He acted in the tradition of the great mass of unnamed black American heroes who died for their country. Released in 1989, the film *Glory* tells their story. A black regiment leads an attack for the North in the Civil War. The black soldiers die, followed by their white countrymen, who die too.

For More Information

See these reading materials:

Blockson, Charles L. *The Underground Railroad.* New York: Prentice Hall, 1987.

Spalding, Henry D., comp. and ed. *Encyclopedia of Black Folklore and Humor.* Middle Village, New York: Jonathan David Publishers, 1972.

Contact these organizations:

Afro-American Cultural Foundation, c/o Westchester Community College, 75 Grasslands Road, Valhalla, New York 19595.

Association for the Study of Afro-American Life and History, 1407 14th Street, N.W. Washington, DC 20005.

38

ALEUTS
(al´ee oots´)

An Arctic people whose ancestors were the first to inhabit the Aleutian Islands; one of the three (Aleut, Indians, and Inuit) native groups in Alaska.

Population: 8,090 (1980).
Location: Aleutian Islands, Alaska.
Language: Aleut, English, Russian.

Geographical Setting

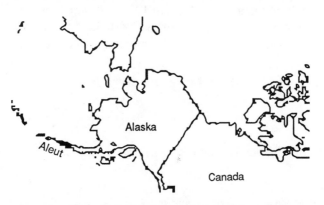

The Aleutian Islands, home of the Aleuts.

The origin of the Aleuts has been a subject of some controversy, but it is generally agreed that they came first from Asia. Some 10,000 years ago, when sea level sat far lower than it does today, a land bridge joined Asia to North America. Presently underwater, this bridge links Siberia to Alaska. It is thought that the ancestors of the Aleuts, a people named the Anangula, inhabited this land bridge.

Today's Aleuts inhabit the Alaskan Peninsula and an archipelago, or chain of islands, between the Bering Sea and the Pacific Ocean. The Aleutian

Islands stretch from the Alaskan Peninsula in a 1,000-mile arc across the Pacific Ocean to Attu, the most westerly isle. Altogether the 100 or so islands in the archipelago cover about 6,390 square miles. They are part of a volcanic underwater mountain range, the remnants of volcanic cones, some of which are still active. The island terrain is therefore rocky and mountainous. Weather-wise, cold Siberian winds flowing into warm Pacific air masses create a climate of near-constant rain, wind, and fog. Gray skies, fierce storms, and riptides are common. Grass and flowers grow plentifully, but the islands are treeless. Isolated in this ocean habitat, Aleuts live by the coastline and sustain themselves with bounty from the sea.

Historical Background

Origin. The first traces of Aleut civilization appeared at the eastern end of the archipelago. On Umnak Island evidence of life dates back about 10,000 years. It seems, however, that ancestors of today's Aleuts spread into the archipelago later in history. Mongoloid peoples appear to have migrated there from Alaska's mainland in two waves: the first wave migrated over 4,000 years ago; the second within the last 1,000 years.

Researchers argue that the Inuit (also called Eskimos) and Aleuts began as one people, separating into two groups, perhaps 3,000 years ago. While the Inuit moved inland, the Aleuts settled on the Aleutian Islands. There they divided into at least three culturally distinct groups: the Eastern Aleut, the Central Aleut, and the Attuan Aleut. Most apparent were their differences in language. According to linguists, only Attuan speech has survived to the present.

Food, clothing, and shelter. The various Aleut groups shared a basic style of life. They were all hunters and gatherers who lived in villages, practicing strict cooperation at home but conducting raids on other islands for wives and slaves. They subsisted on food and clothing from the animals they hunted, and they built semisubterranean homes, shelters sunken partly under the ground. Here, for example, are observations of groups in one region of the archipelago during the 1760s (Black 1984, p. 54-55).

> The folk on these islands...use for food animal and sea otter
> meat, also sea lions and drift whales, as well as sea fish:
> halibut and cod. Mostly, they eat it raw, but also they cook
> [their food] sometimes.... They wear bird [skin] clothing. The
> men wear inserted in their lip labrets...made of white stone.
> Their faces are tattooed, punctured by means of bone needles....

Specific habits in food, clothing, and shelter developed differently on the various islands. In some cases the Aleuts lived in a communal dwelling. Inhabitants of the westernmost island, Attu, built single-family structures.

Aleut men hunted whales, otters, and sea lions for food, or fished for halibut, salmon, and cod. They added clams, ducks, eggs, seaweed, roots, and berries to this basic diet. For hunting, men used whale ribs and whale skin to build kayaklike boats called *bidarkas*. The craft was totally enclosed except for one or two round openings on top for a hunter's body. Drawn up around his waist, gutskin prevented water from entering. The craft could travel against a current, as fast as seven miles an hour. As weapons hunters threw harpoons, lances, or barbed darts from boards. They grew accomplished at snaring sea mammals, using nets as one method of sea otter hunting. Hunters also wounded and caught whales during their search for commodities like food and oil. (The whale oil was burned in stone lamps to produce light.) Aside from the bidarka, the Aleuts built large a open boat called a *baidara*, which held up to 40 passengers.

An Aleut man and his bidarka.

The Aleuts inhabited island villages nestled between bays or sandpits. A typical village housed 50 to 150 people. For building their shelters the villagers used driftwood, whalebone, sod, and animal skins. Sometimes they constructed the *yurt*, a tent-like structure common among peoples of Asia. With the coming of summer, yurt dwellers moved into caves. Other Aleuts lived in *barbaras*—a large, oblong structures sunk three to four feet into the ground. They matted sod over a timber frames to build the barbaras. As many as 40 related families living in a single barbara were separated by stall-like dividers. The Aleuts wove dune grass into flexible mats that served as chairs, beds, and curtains. Roof openings allowed smoke to escape and residents to enter the barbara. Descending from above, they climbed down a notched log. A large village might have as many as seven barbaras.

Typical Aleut clothing.

Perhaps the most common item in clothing was the parka. Fashioned from sea otter or bird skins, furs, or intestines, the Aleut parka reached to the ankles. Unlike Inuit parkas, it generally had no hood. An exception was the *kamleika*, a hooded waterproof parka made from sea mammal intestines for hunters. Both men and women also wore a dresslike garment that hung to the calves. Using bird bones as needles and fish gut as thread, women sewed the clothing. Despite the rocky terrain, many islanders went barefoot. The Aleuts adorned themselves with accessories—ivory, beads, and rings through their nose, lips, or ears. They tattoed the hands and face, pricking the skin with needles, then rubbing it with black clay. Hunters wore artful wooden hats with elongated visors. Famous for these hats, hunters decorated them with fine ivory carvings and multicolor painting. The favored colors, derived from the local minerals and plants, were red, white, and black.

Society and politics. The small island settlements were actually family units led by a *toion*, or chief, and elders. Like other natives (see TLINGIT), the Aleuts divided their society into various classes. Their social ladder moved down from honorables to middle-class commoners to slaves. Honorables were the wealthiest Aleuts, those who hunted most expertly and won the largest share of booty in village raids.

Ongoing feuds and surprise attacks against other Aleut villages were common. Within a village, however, peace became the priority. In their rigorous environs, the village inhabitants placed high value on cooperation and generosity. They discouraged gossip or theft and used a mediator to avoid conflict when bartering among themselves. As punishment for small crimes, they rebuked the offender with silence or mocking. Enemies fought song duels, expressing hostility to their foe through lyrics. Slaves sometimes received harsher punishments than others. If they stole, judgement might call for amputating their fingers.

Russian contact. Despite their remote location, the Aleuts had extensive contact with outsiders after 1741, the year explorer Vitus Bering, sailing from Russia, first sighted the islands. Thereafter, merchant seamen voyaged to the region in quest of furs and skins for profit. They first established relations with the Aleuts that seemed to benefit both groups. The Russians brought over unknown weapons and the beer *kvass*. Drinking became a new pastime. In exchange for Russian products, Aleut hunters provided Russians with sea otters and seal skins, which were then sold to the Chinese. Time passed, and the Russians found it more profitable to employ Aleuts directly and forcibly than to peaceably exchange goods with them. Russian merchants began to treat the Aleuts brutally, pressing them into service. Merchants would kidnap wives and children, then force fathers to hunt skins as ransom to buy back their families. The Aleuts endured rape, plunder, even mass murder before finally rebelling. A conflict in 1747 with the crew of the Russians ship *Sv. Evodkim* brought death to 17 Aleut warriors. Aleut women and children were kidnapped and also killed during this conflict. In 1763, the Aleuts destroyed four Russian ships and their crew. The Russians retaliated by razing villages on two islands in this war. In the end, Russian weapons proved too powerful to withstand.

The Russians continued to hunt sea otters for profit, depleting this natural resource. They caught an average of 3,000 sea otters per year during this period. The records for one vessel show that in 1785 it collected 50 items worth 20,600 dollars. In 1787 a Russian named Gerasim Pribilof discovered herds of fur seals. Aleuts were transplanted to the islands later named for Pribilof to hunt the seals so their skins could be sold.

Not only the sea mammal population but also the Aleut population dwindled. It numbered over 15,000 when the Russians first contacted the Aleuts. By 1825, less than half that number survived. Sea otter hunts, warfare, starvation, and exposure to foreign diseases like smallpox cost thousands of Aleut lives. When merchants conscripted an Aleut to hunt on distant islands, they left his family bereft of its male provider. The Aleut family's struggle for daily survival grew grimmer.

Meanwhile, missionaries exposed the Aleuts to new ways of life in religion and marriage. Russian Orthodox priests greatly influenced Aleut life. Conversion to the Russian Orthodox Church was a priority, but the priests also changed customary behaviors. High on their list was the family. Instead of polygamy, or marriage to more than one partner, the priests taught monogamy, or marriage to only one partner. In place of the *barbara* (see above) they advocated single-family dwellings. Father Ioann Popov-Veniaminov, the most renown priest, arrived in 1824. He remained in the Aleutian Islands for ten years. Encouraging traditional Aleut interest in art, music, and basketry, Veniaminov placed high value on their traditions. He worked with an Aleut chief, Ivan Pankov, to develop an alphabet for natives in the eastern Aleutian Islands.

Life changed on the western islands, too. Before the Russians, dogs were their only domestic animal. Now cattle, pigs, chicken, and goats were imported to the region. Small changes appeared in housing: the doors were raised to ground level, for example. In 1828, another priest, Iakov Netsvetov, arrived on Atka. That same year the island began building a hospital, and a school opened. Netsvetov turned it into a parish school that attracted students from other islands. Revising Veniaminov's alphabet to suit the dialect on Atka, Netsvekov gave Aleuts there their own written language. In 1830 a church was constructed on the island. By 1840, there were churches on two of the Aleutian Islands, chapels on ten. Aleut carvings, once devoted to small figures and masks, had turned to Orthodox religious objects and church decorations.

The Russians brought Christianity, their language, the liquor kvass, monogamy, hospitals, and schools to the Aleutian Islands. Due to their reaction to Aleutian houses and dress, minor changes were made in traditional customs. The outsiders trained some Aleuts as skilled craftsmen—blacksmiths, carpenters, and bricklayers—to meet Russian needs. Also they introduced barter exchange, setting the stage for the cash economy later established under U.S. rule.

United States takeover. In 1867, the United States bought Alaska from Russia for 7,200,000 dollars in gold. Included in the purchase were the Aleutian Islands. Classified by Russia as an "uncivilized tribe," the Aleuts now fell subject to United States law, which regarded them as another native population. Their number by then had dwindled to roughly 2,000, a fraction of the 15,000 Aleuts first contacted by outsiders.

The Alaska Commercial Company and the North American Commercial Company gained control of the islands, setting up trading posts and increasing the Aleuts' need for wage labor. Again customs changed. Russians had ridiculed the Aleuts into abandoning their traditional lip ornaments. Now Americans frowned on Aleut houses, their disdain prompting islanders to build frame structures. These, however, required coal, wood, and oil, which cost money. In the past, Aleuts had survived off the land and a system of mutual exchange. Life under the Americans tied them to a money economy. There were changes in religion, too. The Russian Orthodox Church remained on the islands, but new missionaries from other faiths came. In 1886, the Methodist Women's Home Mission Society opened an American school on the islands. It forbade students from speaking their own language. The discovery of gold on the mainland (Nome, Alaska) attracted more outsiders in 1899. Among them were New England whalers, European fishermen, and California fur seal hunters. Soon new epidemics—influenza and tuberculosis—claimed more Aleut lives.

The 20th century brought dramatic changes. Americans opened cod, salmon, and halibut businesses, hiring natives as unskilled laborers. Conservation policies limited fur sealing. In 1910, two American vessels hired 40 Aleuts who caught 16 sea otters. The next year, hunting fur seals for profit was outlawed, a ban which lasted for five years. This hurt those Aleuts who depended on sealing for income. The government declared the Aleutian Islands a National Wildlife Refuge in 1913. The people living on them, the Aleuts, suffered poverty and discrimination. On the Pribilof Islands a U.S. agent could legally drink alcohol; Aleuts could not. In 1916, islanders petitioned the government to remedy injustices. Their petition requested they be allowed to speak Aleut and reopen the Orthodox church school. With a petition came a note from the agent: "the people...are living in actual slavery" (Antonson 1985, p. 459). This was 50 years after the emancipation of African Americans.

World War II. Conditions improved, then worsened, then improved again. Trapping blue foxes, highly valued as a fashion item in the 1920s, lured new outsiders to the region and brought more employment. Meanwhile, much intermarrriage occurred between Aleut women and outsiders; single Aleut men became plentiful. In 1924, the United States awarded citizenship to all of its natives. The Aleuts won more self-government in 1934. Then World War II brought devastation to the Aleutian Islands. In June, 1942, the Japanese bombed American naval facilities in the Aleutians, inflicting casualties and taking prisoners.

The United States ordered many Aleuts to evacuate. Only those islands closest to the Alaskan mainland were exempted. To keep the Japanese from occupying the Aleuts' villages, the United States burned them and relocated the villagers. They were hustled to abandoned fish canneries, where they lived without sufficient food, shelter, or activity. Many died, among them elders who had kept alive Aleut traditions. At war's end the evacuees returned home to their destroyed villages. They recognized the loss not only of their homes but also of Aleut traditions. So they began to revive old customs, using their native language and living off the land.

New wealth? The post-War years brought dramatic change. For two centuries outsiders had controlled Aleut life. Slowly the Aleuts gained more control over their own affairs. Alaska became a state in 1958, and statehood led to the formation of the Alaska Federation of Natives. Land disputes followed. Aleuts, Inuit, and Indians claimed ownership of land they had before the advent of foreign adventurers. In 1967, the Aleut League formed, in part to win this land claim. The discovery of petroleum in 1968 gave the Aleuts, Inuit, and Indians a new opportunity to bargain for jobs. However, inexperience in politics and disharmony among the groups weakened their leaders. Few jobs were forthcoming.

Meanwhile, the land disputes were resolved. The Alaska Native Claims Settlement Act (1971) set aside 44 million acres (of 375 million total acres) for native groups. One of the native corporations elected to oversee the settlement was the Aleut Corporation. Each Aleut became a stockholder, but the Corporation brought few monetary benefits to the people. Due to their extreme poverty, many shareholders attempted to sell their stock. Other natives recalled the dangers of control by outsiders. Alarmed, they amended the Settlement Act in 1988, banning the sale of stocks to outsiders unless a majority of the stockholders approved.

Another opportunity for wealth presented itself. In 1989, a tanker brought the worst oil spill in history to Alaskan waters about 200 miles from the Aleutian Islands. There was a brief infusion of wealth as the responsible party, Exxon Corporation, paid Aleuts high wages for cleaning up the spill. They used the wages to purchase television satellites, motor bikes, and similar luxuries. Meanwhile, the clean up interfered with native efforts to live off the land. The next winter, smokehouses in the region stood empty of fish.

Culture Today

Economy. Aleuts today often divide their time between jobs taken to earn money and the old activities of hunting and fishing for survival. At least for part of a year, the people take jobs for pay in fur seal or fishing concerns, in a regional Aleut Corporation, or in the tourist industry. Mostly unskilled, the positions available to them are limited. Their unemployment in 1980 was estimated at ll percent.

The Aleuts cannot simply revert to their old ways of hunting and fishing to satisfy their needs. There has been overkilling of sea mammals in Alaskan waters. To preserve wildlife, new laws (the Marine Mammal Protection Act and the Endangered Species Act) limited the hunting and fishing done by outsiders. The restrictions did not apply to the Aleuts. Over time these laws produced positive results. By 1980, the fur seal population had grown to about 1.7 million. Aleuts on the Pribilof Islands depend on income from the fur seals. Along with the old market for sealskin, there have been new demands for seal carcass used as dog food and crab bait. Still, hunting fur seals is a subject of controversy; scientists have supported limited hunting.

The fisheries process seafood—salmon, cod, and crab. While they hire outsiders more often than natives, many Aleuts turn to employment in fishing and canning plants. The fishing industry as a whole is regarded as a main source of employment. Husbands hire themselves out as fishermen on seafaring ventures, which furnish seasonal employment. Wives take jobs in canneries to earn additional income. On the island Atka, fishermen leave home to work for pay six months a year. The other six months they hunt reindeer, seals, and sea lions back on their own island for family subsistence.

Family life. Aleut marriages and divorces occurred without ceremony at first. In contrast to family life among outsiders, male-female relations were casual and permissive. Wife loaning occurred: Aleut husbands might temporarily lend a wife to an honored guest. Both men and women could marry more than one partner. In most cases, partners could not afford two families. The Russian missionaries introduced reforms. Alarmed at the permissiveness, they chided not only Aleuts but also Russians for illegitimate families they had on the islands.

Aleut families today live in their own separate houses. Once an entire village took responsibility for child rearing: the women raised infants and girls; uncles, not fathers, trained boys. Now fathers raise their sons, perhaps as fishermen. By age 11 or 12, boys spend their summers at sea. Girls of the same age take charge of the household, after learning the duties of a fisherman's wife from their mother. When a woman works in a cannery, household duties fall to her daughters. Such a family pattern describes some areas of the Aleutian Islands in the late 20th century. As in the past, though, habits vary with the village.

A new variable is the degree to which families enjoy present-day conveniences—supermarkets, appliances, American clothes, and canned foods. Replacing the bidarkas that served Aleut and Russian hunters so well in the past are plywood boats with outboard motors. Exposed to such inventions, young Aleuts often lose interest in hunting for survival. Yet their alternatives remain scarce.

Education. When the Russians left the Aleutian Islands in 1867, they closed the local schools. The Alaska Commercial Company opened two schools in 1870 under United States rule. Slowly more American schools appeared, and native women became teachers. Educated outside the Aleutians, Katherine Dyakanoff Seller, for example, returned to teach on Atka Island. Under the Organic Act (1884) Alaska promises education to all children without regard to race. Today several regional school districts are largely under Inuit or Aleut control. Aleut parents favor both elementary and secondary education. However, in the late 20th century not all islands can provide their children with both. Students on Atka attend a two-room schoolhouse. (Except for the Aleut language, subjects are the same as those taught elsewhere in the United States.) Education on Atka ends at grade eight. Then students travel off the island to board at a high school. Some never return.

Language. The Aleut language is a major branch of what has been called the Eskimo-Aleut family of languages. No longer mutually intelligible, the Aleut and Eskimo languages are thought to have become distinct from each other by the year 1,000 B.C. Aleuts on the various islands spoke different dialects of their own language. Once the Russians arrived, they quickly became bilingual. Their early teacher Father Veniaminov noted how aptly they learned the Russian language, which is still used today in Russian Orthodox religious services. Otherwise, the people speak English or Aleut.

Religion. Originally the Aleuts believed that creatures, places, and objects had a soul force. Spirit-powers directed nature. Religious leaders called shamans communicated with the spirits for the people. They were ritual specialists who strove to avert or remedy disasters on behalf of the village. Villagers themselves observed rituals in an effort to control their environment. After wounding a whale, a hunter secluded himself and fasted for three days, imitating the animal's sighs and groans to make it die and float ashore.

Russian missionaries such as Father Veniaminov convinced the Aleuts to adopt Christianity. Remaining on the islands after the American takeover, the Russian Orthodox Church is still the religion of some Aleut islanders. Other Aleuts now belong to American Protestant churches.

Arts. Early Aleut art appears on practical or religious objects. One such object is the funeral mask. In early times, Aleuts preserved the body of an important villager. They stuffed the dead body with dry moss, dressed it perhaps in fur skins, then wrapped it in matting. The mummy bundle was placed in a dry cave in a cradle. Discovered in burial caves, wooden masks survive as an example of their art. The Aleuts also carved masks to represent religious spirits. More practical were spoonlike dippers, which they carved, and then etched with geometric shapes or human and animal figures.

Aleut women are most renown for sophisticated basketry. Using finely split grasses, the women wove some of the most expertly crafted baskets in North America. A basket had up to 1,300 stitches per square inch; its surface quality compared to linen cloth. For decoration, the women added geometric designs and floral patterns. Aleut women now weave these traditional baskets for sale. Buyers have paid 100 to 500 dollars for a single basket.

In oral literature, the Aleuts had nonfiction tales, fables, myths, and songs. Among characters in their myths were the Outside Men. They were described as villains who lived in the mountains and would kidnap Aleut males. If families set food outside for the Men, they could avoid harm. In the Central Aleuts, myths were told about the raven, a trickster who could empower humans to kill whales.

The Aleuts held public performances. These featured theaterlike dramas, as well as song and dance. Here are lyrics from parts of an old Aleut song about hunting (Black 1984, p. 182-183).

As I was going along [paddling along, proceeding], looking
around, I saw a beast, the sea lion, surfacing smartly;...

Going on [I went on] and coming close, shot at him, but failed
to drive home the dart [failed to place the dart into him]....

I followed him and shot at him, but was not able to do him
any harm, and only spoiled the points of my darts.

I kept looking behind me, looking for someone, but saw no one;
If I had someone with whom to cry, as I felt like crying....

Aleut performers also re-enacted hunting episodes in short dramas.
Beginning gently, dances involved a violent build up.

Culture blend. Today's Aleuts form one group, made up of anyone who
descends from the first dwellers on the Aleutian Islands. A dozen or so Aleut
villages exist in the late 20th century. For leadership, they no longer rely on
their *toion* and elders. These old local leaders have been replaced by a village
council, a school board, and the mayor. Yet Aleuts still observe old traditions
along with customs they have adopted from outsiders. Their culture today is
a mix of Aleut, Russian, and American customs.

For More Information

See these reading materials:

Antonson, Joan M. and Hanable, William S. *Alaska's Heritage.*
Anchorage: The Alaska Historical Commission, 1985.

Morgan, Lael. "Atka, Rugged Home of My Aleut Friends." *National
Geographic*, October 1974, pp. 572–583.

Contact these organizations:

Aleut Corporation, 2550 Denali Street, Anchorage, Alaska 99501.

Aleutian/Pribilof Islands Association, 1689 C Street, Anchorage, Alaska
99501.

AMISH
(a´mish)

A religious group of German and Swiss ancestry that
still observes customs of 19th century rural society.

Population: 87,000 (1989).
Location: United States (primarily Ohio, Pennsylvania, and Indiana);
Canada (mainly Ontario).
Language: German, English.

Geographical Setting

Amish settlements in the United States.

Although they are spread through 20 American states, 75 percent of the
Amish live in Pennsylvania, Ohio, and Indiana. Before immigrating to North
America, the Amish were scattered throughout Europe. Areas of
Switzerland, France, and Germany tolerated clusters of Amish individuals,
but the people suffered persecution for their religious beliefs. Seeking land to
farm and freedom of worship, some 500 Amish settled in Philadelphia,
Pennsylvania, in the 18th century. Several thousand more Amish migrated to

North America in the 19th century, landing in New Orleans, then traveling up the Mississippi River to Ohio. Part of this tide, the migrant Christian Nafziger led his followers to Ontario, Canada.

The Amish population in North America grew, spreading westward on the continent in search of fertile farmland. Meanwhile, the early settlements in Pennsylvania, and Ohio, became Amish strongholds. Southeastern Pennsylvania has been a center of Amish America for over two and a half centuries. Here the Amish hold rich farm and timber land east of the Appalachian Mountains, watered by the Susquehanna River. Wherever possible, the people maintain pasture land, too. They are one of the most productive farming societies in North America today. Lancaster County, Pennsylvania, their first area of settlement, has been described as a garden spot of the nation.

Historical Background

Origin in Europe. Many Protestant sects had appeared in Europe by the 1700s, some of whom held radical Christian beliefs. One such sect, the Mennonites, refused to take oaths, perform military service, or hold public office. The Amish were an offshoot of this sect. In both groups, members wanted only to till the soil and to be away from the rest of humankind.

There was disagreement within the Mennonite sect. Jacob Ammann, a Swiss Mennonite bishop, split from the main body of Mennonites in the late 1700s. Mainly he differed from them about *Meidung*, the practice of avoidance or shunning. Ammann advocated complete avoidance of persons who disobeyed the doctrines. He believed transgressors should be warned, then shunned if they refused to change. In other words, people should neither eat nor keep company with offenders, be they husbands, wives, sons, or daughters. Ammann founded the sect that is named after him (the Amish) based on his beliefs. Already the Mennonites practiced adult baptism. Newborns were not Mennonite; rather they could be baptized into the faith upon reaching adulthood. While the Amish continued this practice, they added other rituals particular to them. Amman introduced foot washing, recalling the act as described in the New Testament to symbolize the washing of a person's soul. He also attached great importance to simple clothing, condemning fashionable dress. Unlike the Mennonites, who wore garments with buttons, the Amish used hooks and eyes. The Amish, then, led stricter lives than the Mennonites.

Migration to North America. Both groups migrated to the United States and Canada. The periods of heaviest migration occurred from 1727 to

1770 and from 1815 to 1860. In the 1700s, some 500 Amish arrived. They voyaged over on ships such as the *Charming Nancy*, embarking on a journey that was anything but charming. Crowded together like herring, the passengers endured unsanitary meals and a foul stench, often dying enroute to America. Because Pennsylvania welcomed religious outcasts (see QUAKERS), the Amish settled there first. Related families set up house near one another. At first, they did not divide themselves so strictly from the non-Amish.

By the 1770s, the strength of the Amish had been shaken. Their young began to marry out of the faith and the War of Independence in America threatened their religion further. Opposed to military service, most Amish refused to fight in this war, though they agreed to pay the war tax. Fellow colonists considered them traitors, and several Amish were jailed. After the war, a steady stream of followers converted to other religions. The Amish must have looked on this loss with dismay, but the group rallied in the next century.

A new wave of Amish migrated to North America in the 1800s. Nearly 3,000 followers arrived between 1815 and 1860, occupying areas such as Ohio, Indiana, Ontario, and again Pennsylvania. Christian Nafziger began the Ontario community, traveling from New Orleans to Pennsylvania on foot, then to Ontario by horse. Ontario's Amish began settling there in 1823, farming their own 200-acre plots. They continued coming to Canada for the next 50 years. Meanwhile, the Amish of Lancaster County, Pennsylvania, organized the first formal settlement there in 1843. Until then, clusters of families had lived scattered among the non-Amish, but now they withdrew more completely from outside society. Their isolation increased until the dawning of the American Civil War.

19th century conflicts. The Amish experienced conflict with the outside world and among themselves in the 1800s. Despite their isolation, they were drafted by the North and by the South during the Civil War. The Amish refused to fight, since their religion was opposed to bearing arms. In the North, they were exempt from military duty if they paid a fee. The Conscription Act of 1864 dismissed conscientious objectors from armed service in exchange for 300 dollars. The South insisted that conscientious objectors fight or be treated as deserters. Some Amish draftees hid, others fled. If caught, they were forced into either the army or jail.

The Amish have steadily refused government money. A few served in the Civil War, then repented and rejoined the faith. Their service in the war entitled them to a military pension. A deliberate decision to refuse such pensions was made by the group as a whole at the *Diener-Versammlungen*.

Held by the Amish to settle their own differences, this was a series of conferences attended by members of the group from 1862 to 1878. Only partially successful, the conferences led to a basic split in Amish society after 1878.

There was the strictly conservative low church and the less severe high church, whose members relaxed the rules. Many degrees of Amish developed between the two extremes. Formed in 1881, the Old Order retained early traditions. Its members upheld horse-and-carriage travel, plain dress, and the German dialect. Middle churches that made small changes joined the Mennonites. Named for Moses Beachy, the Beachy Amish formed in 1926. They permit automobiles, meeting houses for preaching, and daily use of the English language. The New Amish formed in 1966, relaxing rules on telephones and tractor-driven farm machines but protesting tobacco. Unlike the Beachy, the New Amish still forbid automobiles and meeting houses.

World Wars. While splits among Amish groups continued into the 20th century, the people were affected by world events. Some of them moved to western Canada around the turn of the century, settling in the province of Alberta. With World War I came hostility from other Canadians and Americans toward the nonfighting, German-speaking Amish. The Amish opposed military service of any kind in the war. However, America's Selective Service Act and the Canadian Military Service Act demanded duty in noncombat roles at least. After June 1918, 60 percent of the Amish American draftees received farm work assignments. A number of draftees suffered jail sentences for refusing to participate in this war. Others escaped the American draft by migrating to Alberta or British Columbia in Canada. World War II allowed Amish draftees to replace military duty with public service. Of Amish draftees, 94 percent served as conscientious objectors in this war.

Tradition and change. The draft continued to trouble the group from 1946 to 1976. Performing two years of noncombat duty away from home, young men drifted away from traditional Amish life. Members of the Old Order, for example, began to ride in automobiles rather than in horse-driven buggies. Permitting farm service in another Amish community, local draft boards helped some draftees avert the threat. Again a few of the men refused any option but jail. War was against their beliefs, which they had come to America and Canada to uphold. Recognizing the righteousness of the argument, neither country forced the Amish to fight.

The people, then, managed to uphold their stand on nonparticipation in war. They have been less successful in providing farms for their children. While Amish farms are highly productive, the people seek not profit but enough money to buy farms for all their offspring. In the 19th century, when acreage was abundant, the Amish could meet this goal. Now land is scarcer, and the average Amish family is still large (seven children). One tactic has been to divide a farm into small plots for the family's sons. As a result, the average size of an Amish farm has decreased. Typically over 90 acres in the mid-1800s, a plot may be a third that size in the late 1900s. Amish farms now range from 30 to 120 acres, and some young men inherit no land at all. The Amish have therefore developed new work options, which enable them to maintain their rural ways.

Culture Today

The Amish now practice many customs that were common in rural society as a whole during the 19th century. Harking back to their leader, Jacob Amman, other traditions are distinctly Amish. Basic always to their way of life have been four kinds of beliefs: closeness to nature, separation from the world, social regulations, and religious practices.

Closeness to nature. Amish work habits keep the people tied to rural life, which is a cornerstone of their religious faith. They regard themselves as stewards or caretakers here on earth, meant to engage in farming or occupations of a rural nature. Rejecting cities, they prefer labor done with the hands. Occupations other than farming employ the Amish, but they are limited to practical jobs easily performed in rural areas—carpentry, for example. Amish farmers grow a diversity of crops. Farming continually by rotating crops, they raise corn, grain (wheat, oats, or barley), and hay (alfalfa or clover). Their farms include woodlands wherever possible, and the people plant many vegetables and fruits. To meet their own needs, the Amish produce milk, cheese, cereals, and meats. They are a self-sufficient people, but will buy sugar, salt, and flour in village stores. Producing more than they consume or sell to other Amish, they market their surplus to outsiders. Once they raised tobacco to earn cash, and roughly a third of the people still do so today. Others produce whole milk and grow tomatoes, which have replaced tobacco as the highest moneymakers.

Separation. The Amish still isolate themselves from the outside world. They will not join with non-Amish business partners nor marry outside the faith. To the present they have refused to fight the larger society's wars, take its oaths, or hold any of its public offices. In these ways, they disengage themselves from the outside world. Contact is limited to selling outsiders whole milk or hiring non-Amish truck drivers, for example. The Amish make no attempt to convert others to their faith. Given the many children in a family, the population increases naturally. Baptism occurs in the late teenage years. Families raise their children in the Amish way, so they are prepared to make an educated choice about whether to join the religious community. In most cases, they do join. The Amish are an increasing population.

Just as they avoid outside business or politics, the people reject any aid offered to them by the outside world. This includes old-age and farm subsidy payments. The Amish abide by national crop-reduction programs but refuse payment for raising fewer crops. With exceptions, the group pays taxes. It is exempt from self-employment taxes in the United States, and in Canada is also exempt from the pension plan. The people practice mutual aid, raising milk houses and barns together and forming insurance societies of their own.

To consciously separate themselves from outsiders, the Amish set their watches on different time, either slower or faster than everyone else's. When the outside world switches to daylight-saving time, the Amish continue on standard time. When the world switches back to standard time, the Amish set their watches a half hour ahead. They will abide by worldly time in their limited contact with the English. (*English* is a universal term used by the Amish for "outsider.")

Social rules. Called *Ordnung*, Amish social regulations describe the acceptable behaviors in a church district. Communities agree on basics such as separation from the world, but they develop their own rules for daily living. The majority of districts in the United States and Canada agree on the following regulations. They reject high-line electricity, telephones, central heating systems in homes, and tractors with compressed-air tires. They endorse the use of horses for farming and simple clothing. Single or married, men keep their hair long, covering part of the ear; married men grow beards but do not wear mustaches. Children attend elementary school only, with some exceptions. The belief is that conveniences such as the telephone would allow the outside world to penetrate into the community and so would threaten its survival. Using the same reasoning, high school would draw children too much into the outside world.

Religion. The Amish believe that at some point in Christian history the organized church went astray. Therefore, they formed a new church to fulfill the teachings of Christ on earth. The Amish consider themselves in a suspended state between good and evil, obedience and disobedience. If they walk in the ways of Christ during their sojourn on Earth, they will achieve eternal life after death. Their commitment to this end is judged by conformity to rules. Rule breakers are shunned. Called *Meidung*, shunning requires everyone in the community, even family, to avoid the offender. For example, someone who purchased an automobile against the rules might be shunned. The offender is warned, then either abandons the objectionable behavior or is shunned. In other words, the deviant is excommunicated. No one eats or keeps company with offenders, until they admit their sins and make amends. When Amish ministers disagree, a new Amish settlement may form. Their different views on shunning have led to many such divisions.

Three types of Amish leaders—bishops, preachers, and deacons—are chosen through election and selection by lot. Highest in authority, the bishop is the *Voelliger-Diener* minister with full powers. There may be two preachers to act as ministers of the book. The deacon ministers to the poor.

The Amish draw on passages from the Bible for guidance in daily living. Since girls are not officially Amish until grown, they braid their hair. They put it up after joining the faith because of the Biblical warning that "women adorn themselves...not with braided hair" (Timothy 2:9).

Social and political organization. The group generally settles by highways close to small rural towns, interspersed among non-Amish farm families. As a rule, they organize into three geographic divisions— settlement, church district, and affiliation. A *settlement* is a collection of Amish families in the same geographic area. The largest settlements appear in Holmes County, Ohio, and Lancaster County, Pennsylvania. A ceremonial unit within a settlement, the *church district* is all the people who worship together in one farm dwelling, at most about 35 households. Finally, an *affiliation* is several church districts that practice the Amish faith in the same way. Different affiliations may appear in a settlement, since splits have produced various approaches to the Amish faith.

In American politics the majority of Amish are Republicans. They vote most heavily in local township elections.

Weekdays and holidays. The Amish workday begins by 5:00 a.m. First comes milking, then field work, lunch, and more field work. Suppertime is 5:00 p.m. Afterwards, livestock are fed, and men may return to the fields. Families go to sleep around 9:00 p.m. on weekdays, while Sunday is a day of rest. Every other Sunday, they attend a preaching service.

Conducted in an Amish home, the Sunday preaching lasts from about 9 a.m. to noon. Families take turns hosting the service, which they build their houses to accommodate. Holding 200 or more worshipers, an Amish house may have a layout that allows backless benches for the worshipers to be spread across several rooms. Hymns in the service are 16th-century slow-moving ballads, sung without music. Drawn from the book *Ausbund*, the ballads recount the tragic fate of early believers and include conversations with their executioners. The service is followed by a meal, visiting, and Sunday night singing all in the same Amish home. Quite different than the leaden sound of the ballads, Sunday night singing is a spirited rendering of 19th-century gospel tunes. The singers, young men and women, start in German, sometimes switching to songs in English halfway through the night.

Of all holidays, Christmas is the most celebrated by the Amish but not as a ceremonial event. Rather, the holiday is a family and kinship affair, without Christmas trees or Santa Claus. Individuals may exchange presents, and some groups observe Christmas for two days, after an old European custom.

A typical Amish transportation system.

Family life. Though some Amish drive automobiles, horse and buggy is the common form of transportation. Family carriages may be topless or covered by a black, white, or yellow top. Some of them have modern conveniences—battery-operated lights, curtains, or brakes. Legally they must have an orange reflector triangle at the rear. From group to group, the style of the carriage differs according to the rules of the community.

Topless carriages are often used for courting. Sunday evening singing allows young people to meet before marriage. Called *rumspringa* (running around), Amish courtship begins at age 14 for girls, 16 for boys. The process is secretive. A boy takes a girl home after Sunday evening singing and visits her every other Saturday night. Shining a flashlight on a girl's bedroom window, the boy waits for her to come downstairs and answer the door. They spend the evening downstairs, keeping each other company far into the night. The marriage is arranged by a minister or deacon, sent by the boy for the parents' consent. Then comes the Amish wedding, a joyous occasion for the whole district. It means a new home in which to hold preaching services and another family who will raise children in the Amish way. Parents provide the couple with a dowry and guests bring useful gifts—dishes, kerosene lamps, quilts, and farm tools. Clearly they intend to help the couple build an Amish household; the marriage begins with the promise of success. The Old Order seems to hold respect for a mate in higher regard than love. In Amish society, there is no divorce.

The value of respect in the household trickles down to the children, who learn quickly to honor their parents' word. In the preaching service, obedience to parents is stressed. Children learn over and over again to obey their fathers and mothers. At age 4, children are assigned chores. Young boys feed the animals and gather the eggs. Young girls help with the cooking and cleaning. Between the ages of 6 and 15, children attend school, and as early as age 16, boys become farmhands. There are two large decisions to make in late adolescence—whether to join the Amish church and whom to marry. Having married in their early 20s, a couple builds an Amish home, then retires between the ages of 50 and 70. They turn the main house and the responsibility for the farm over to a married son or daughter. The older couple moves into a second farm dwelling known as the *Grossdaadi Haus*, or Grandparents house. After retirement, a couple may continue to farm or may open a small shop of their own.

The Amish still define a woman's place as the home. Her chores include cooking, sewing, gardening, cleaning, tending the chickens, and some milking. Raising children is her main job, though. Like the men, the women work with their hands. They make rugs and quilts, sew the family's clothes, and preserve and prepare food. Quiltings are social occasions. Women can visit as they work on quilts, which they artfully embellish with embroidery. In religion, women have less authority than men. The Amish, unlike the Quakers, have no women ministers. However, Amish women have a vote in religious decision making.

Food, clothing, and shelter. Amish living quarters are similar to non-Amish homes. Typically a two-story structure, the house may be built of pale brick. Generally, there are barns, a well-kept lawn, a carriage shed, and storage buildings. Windmills are a familiar sight. Inside, the kitchen, sitting, and living room may flow as a unit to accommodate worshipers at the Sunday service. None of the rooms have electrical appliances. There may be a gas-powered refrigerator and stove, but electric toasters, can openers, hair driers, radios, and television sets are absent. No electrical wires reach from roads to houses. Telephones may skirt the public roadside but none appear in Amish houses. For entertainment, members of a family play games and read. Amish reading fare includes classics such as *Black Beauty* and newsy magazines written either by the Amish or the English.

Highly self-sufficient, the people grow much of the food they eat. Their meals are rich in fats and carbohydrates. Breakfast in Pennsylvania might consist of eggs, fried scrapple (cornmeal mush), cooked cereal, and fried potatoes. Along with every meal comes bread, butter, and jelly or apple butter. Customary dishes are chow-chow (chopped vegetables pickled in mustard) and shoo-fly pie (filled with molasses and brown sugar, which attracts flies). Influenced by the diet of outsiders, the group has adopted foods such as meatloaf and pizza. Kerosene-operated refrigerators or ice boxes keep all the foods cool, since the people forbid electricity.

The Amish are easily recognized by their dress. On the whole, Amish clothing recalls styles in rural 19th-century Europe and among the early Quakers. Women wear ankle or floor-length dresses, hemmed within eight inches from the ground. Allowing only solid colors, women may wear bright shades. Favorites in Lancaster County appear to be purple and royal blue. Along with dresses, most women wear aprons, bonnets, and shawls. The *Halsduch* is a triangle-shaped cape whose apex fastens in the back and whose two ends cross in front at the waist. In Pennsylvania, women wear a *Lepple*, or flap down the back from the waistline. It is said that the more conservative the community, the wider the Lepple will be. Such garments are attached to the waist with straightpins. Over their hair, women wear the *kapp*, or head cap. Its design (width, pleat, seams) depends on the community.

Men dress in simple dark clothes with no outside hip pockets. In most communities, they wear suspenders and hats. The strictest groups favor wide hat brims (over three inches). As in the past, men cling to hooks and eyes on Sunday coats. They now wear buttons on trousers, shirts, and sweaters, following rules on where and when buttons can be worn. Dress rules change with the community. In Mifflin County, Pennsylvania, different communities of Amish have different policies on men's suspenders. Conservatives prohibit suspenders altogether. A second group favors one suspender fastened with buttons, and a third has prescribed two suspenders that cross in back.

Amish people dress in plain clothing.

Language. The 87,000 Amish share about 125 family names. In 1980, 25 percent of Lancaster County Amish had Stolzfus as a last name. The situation inspired Amish everywhere to adopt nicknames. For example, "Strong" Jacob Yoder and "Seven Thick" Jacob Yoder identify two men. (Seven Thick had such a large overcoat that seven men got into it one Sunday.)

While they read some English, the Amish are a German-speaking people. Parents converse in German at home and begin teaching their children how to read the language. People call their dialect Pennsylvania German or Pennsylvania Dutch (referring not to the Netherlands but to the word *Deitsch* meaning "German"). Some early Amish immigrants spoke French, so a few French words crept into the dialect. In their religious books, the people use only High German, the dialect spoken in southern Germany. Transactions with outsiders demand mastery of the English language, which is achieved in school. In effect, the Amish learn three languages—Pennsylvania German, High German, and English.

Education. Today most Amish students attend private schools of their own. This was not always the case. In Pennsylvania, for example, the Amish went to public school until 1938. Then small, one-room schoolhouses were abandoned, and children from different areas were sent to larger schools. Fearing this would confuse their children with strange new ideas, the Amish opened small, older fashioned schools of their own. Most Amish children now attend elementary school (grade one to eight) and then vocational school. Providing on-the-job training, the vocational school is designed for students not old enough to obtain a work permit. It trains them in farm and domestic duties, obligating them to keep a daily journal and attend class for three hours a week. The Amish have no high school. They view it as useless to rural life. Once Amish parents went to jail for keeping their children out of high school. Then *Wisconsin v. Yoder*, a 1972 Supreme Court case, made it illegal to force high school on the Amish. They attended court, though the Amish normally will not involve themselves in government issues. A nonresistant people, they will suffer injustice without self-defense.

The Amish teach a limited number of subjects, mainly reading, writing, and arithmetic. For textbooks, they use discards from public schools or books written for the Amish, whose stories have morals about lying, for example. Pupils study German and English, and always there is recitation, or oral reading. The school teaches perhaps 30 students. Like old rural schools, it has one or two classrooms and often a rope-pulled school bell. A ball field completes the scene. Amish teachers divide the school day (8:30 a.m. to 3:30 p.m.) into four periods, 90 minutes each. Religion is not taught, but hymn singing and Bible reading begin the typical day. As for report cards, students receive as many as six each year.

Health. Though the Amish are self-sufficient in most ways, their limited education means they have no Amish doctors. They receive treatment in nonAmish hospitals. Since the Amish marry only insiders, spouses are often related. John A. Hostetler reports in *Amish Society* (1980) that only three of 1,850 Amish couples in Lancaster County are not related. Healthwise, marrying insiders has increased the incidence of genetic defects. Also known as dwarfism, Ellis-van Creveld syndrome (EVC) befalls more Lancaster Amish than outsiders. Its victims are born not only with short limbs but also with six fingers. By 1964, the Amish had reported about 52 cases, equaling the total number reported in the rest of the world.

Arts. The traditional arts are practical—quilt making, embroidery, and pottery. Since 1890, the Ohio weekly the *Budget* has been the main avenue for communication, sharing news about farms, accidents, and marriage in the

the Amish world. A newer Pennsylvania weekly, *Die Botschaft* (The Message), appeared in 1974. In this journal, the writers are Amish. Readers contribute poetry and sociable letters to its pages. Located in Ontario, Canada, Pathway Publishers is an Amish bookmaker that caters to both adults and schoolchildren. It also prints journals that examine old Amish beliefs about topics such as tobacco or women working in a farm's fields.

Amish future. The Amish have adapted to changing conditions in the outside world. Until 1960, most men were farmers. Then land grew scarce and costly. So young men took farm-related jobs. Or fathers subdivided farms, and sons ran mechanized poultry or hog barns on smaller plots. Some Amish permitted powered farm tools if they were horse driven. Pennsylvania dairies allowed milking machines, bulk tanks, and diesel coolers. Most important has been the growth of small Amish businesses. Adding to the farm income, families have opened appliance stores, bakeries, cheese centers, carriage shops, and farm equipment and repair centers. There are even Amish health-food stores. Given these businesses, the group can better meet its own needs and separate itself from outsiders in new ways. Amish trends in the late 20th century have made the people more self-sufficient and less dependent on the outside world.

By 1980, many young Amish had divided into ten gangs or groups, with names such as the Ammies and the Kirkwooders. While some groups were conservative, others grew worldly, abandoning horses and harmonicas for automobiles and electric guitars. Other young people take winter jobs in Florida, where they experiment with worldly dress and apartment life. For pleasure, adults turn to traditional activities—barn raisings, quilting bees, country auctions and rodeos. Their children swim, sled, skate, and play ball. Young and old, the majority of Amish society today remains conservative.

For More Information

See these reading materials:

Fishman, Andrea. *Amish Literacy: What and How it Means.* Portsmouth, New Hampshire: Heinemann, 1988.

Hostetler, John A. *Amish Society.* 3rd ed. Baltimore: The Johns Hopkins University Press, 1980.

Irwin, Jerry and Lee, Douglas. "The Plain People of Pennsylvania." *National Geographic*, April 1984. pp. 492-519.

Contact this organization:

National Committee for Amish Religious Freedom, 30650 Six Mile Road, Livonia, Michigan 48152.

ARAB AMERICANS
(ar'uhb eh mer' uh kins)

Immigrants from several Arab nations who have
formed a unified culture in the United States.

Population: 2.5 million (1984).
Location: United States, mainly Michigan, New York, and California.
Language: English, Arabic dialects, Assyrian-Chaldean.

Geographical Setting

■ Greatest
▨ density
▤
☐ Least density

States with greatest Arab American populations.

Though scattered across the United States, Arab American communities
today appear mostly in or near urban centers. The largest community resides
in Detroit, Michigan. Greater Detroit claimed 250,000 Arab-Americans in
1984, centered in the southeastern city of Dearborn. Among the oldest of
Arab American settlements, Dearborn was founded around 1890.

New York once had the greatest number of Arab Americans. Once they arrived at nearby Ellis Island, they joined the first successful American colony of Arabs in New York. The earliest Arab immigrants came from the eastern area of the Mediterranean Sea, an area now known as Lebanon, but then part of Syria. Syria was a province at the time, ruled by the Turks as a conquest of the Ottoman Empire. Later, it and other Arabic-speaking nations won independence, and the early Syrian migrants were joined by others from Egypt, Iraq, Jordan, and Yemen. The immigrants from Yemen constitute an exception to the Arab American preference for urban settlement. While most Arab immigrants have rejected farming, many Yemenis labor for California grape growers.

Historical Background

Cultural identity. Arab Americans are a new, emerging culture in the United States and a rapidly growing one. The term *Arab American* has only recently come into use. It refers to many but not all groups from the Middle East, excluding the Iranian and Jewish immigrants. Before World War II, officials identified the immigrants variously as Syrians, Turks, Greeks, or Asians. Not only was there official disagreement about what to call Arab Americans but they themselves did not yet share a single identity. Though almost everyone spoke Arabic, their ties were not to language or nationality but to family, village, and religion.

The pattern of immigration resembled that of other groups (see ITALIAN AMERICANS). A father or son would migrate first and then send for relatives, until whole family and village units reestablished themselves in America. Since the general area from which the early migrants came was Syria, the term *Syrians* is perhaps most legitimate.

Early migration. The pre-World War II immigrants differed greatly from the post-War stream that would follow. Mostly unlettered, the early immigrants came mainly to better their fortunes. They intended not to stay but to earn and return.

The early stream of Arab immigrants sprang from Mount Lebanon, a small Christian district in the Ottoman Empire. It began in the 1870s and continued for several decades. Driven by a poor economy and a ruinous taxation policy in the Ottoman Empire, one fourth of the population left the area. Theirs was a divided society whose members were devoted to village, family, and religion, not to nation or Empire. There were many factions, yet the different villages shared certain "Arab" traits. The family group took precedence over any individual member. Society was patriarchal—the eldest male in a family exercised strict control. Family honor depended on the women remaining chaste. Households were crowded, since they sheltered an extended family of parents, children, and relatives. Aside from fierce ties to family, the members of a village devoted themselves to religion. Whole villages shared a single faith. In general, the Syrians valued family, place of origin, and religion. They displayed fierce loyalty to their own small groups.

Migration to *Amrika* or *Nay Yark*, as Syrians described it, began in the 1870s. Held in 1876, the Philadelphia Centennial Exposition was a fair with a Turkish exhibit including a coffeehouse, exotic articles, and Syrian traders. The opportunity for trade and profit excited participants and enticed other Arabs to migrate to the New World. Almost all the original migrants were adventurous bachelors. Typically, they voyaged from Beirut to Marseilles to Ellis Island. A port of ill repute, Marseilles proved to be a perilous stop, where scoundrels conned migrants out of money.

Peddling. Better fortune awaited the migrants at Ellis Island. Almost immediately, most of the Syrians worked as peddlers, selling a variety of wares from door to door. Peddling became their niche, the dependable key to success. Since few immigrants were well-educated or fluent in English, they faced great limitations in the job market. At the same time, there was a need to funnel goods to towns and out-of-the-way farms across the nation. Syrians filled the need. While German Jews and others peddled too, Syrians became most deeply associated with the trade. A full 90 percent of the Syrian immigrants took up the trade, the men later joined by women and even children. They became a common sight on urban streets and dusty country roads, stimulating the nation's appetite for manufactured goods.

From 1880 to 1910, Syrian peddlers sold their wares across America. The business was organized. Suppliers provided the peddlers with goods, and directed them here or there. Much like the Irish barkeeper (see IRISH AMERICANS), the supplier served various functions—organizing peddlers' routes, banking their savings, providing supplies, even mediating between them and local authorities. The first suppliers built a successful Syrian colony in New York. They lived in dingy, weatherbeaten homes whose cellars were stock full of peddlers' goods, everything from cologne to carvings.

Peddling required little preparation, not even a working knowledge of English. Once a peddler learned the key phrase *Buy sumthin', Maam?* he stood ready. Most typical was a young man with a heavy suitcase (some weighed 200 pounds) bound to his back. Strapped to his chest was the *kashshi*, the notions case with its several drawers. In each hand the peddler carried a satchel. His wares consisted of ribbons, buttons, shirts, socks, suspenders, work gloves, and caps. At first the peddlers hiked their way across America. Later, some of them took to riding horses, wagons, even automobiles, which led to their peddling goods such as imported rugs.

Life on the road taught peddlers quick, hard lessons. They learned business. Making a profit was the first goal. When a supplier sold a peddler a dress for 10 dollars, the peddler sold it to a customer for 20 dollars, taking 10 dollars from the customer before releasing the merchandise. The Syrians earned a reputation for being shrewd but honest. Since peddlers planned to revisit customers, and sold items on credit, fairness was not only ethical but good for business. As for the income, a peddler could earn 40 or 50 dollars a week around the turn of the 20th century. Peddling could be depended on for a satisfactory income. Meanwhile, it exposed the Syrians to new ways. They learned to speak English quickly on the road and adopted other American habits.

Over time the sellers divided into three types. Long-distance peddlers roamed several states for six or ten months at a time. Medium-distance peddlers left home for two to three weeks. Day peddlers (women, children, the elderly) returned each night. Home base for all three was the peddling settlement. Sometimes called little Syrias, peddling settlements actually housed immigrants from other foreign groups, too. The Syrians settled in lower-class neighborhoods, scattered among these groups. Clusters of peddlers from the same town in Syria or of the same religious faith tended to settle down as a unit. In this way, they carried some of the Old World into the New.

Settlement life was anything but glamorous. Why spend money on beds, the peddlers reasoned, when their stay in America was temporary? So they typically slept on the floor of a boarding house and used orange crates for cupboards. There was a warm group life, though. The kitchen became the heart of the home, a room for sharing meals, card games, songs, and stories of hardships suffered on the road.

While peddling sounded romantic, the difficulties were great. Through snow and rain peddlers laden with heavy packs lumbered onward for 15 or 20 miles a day. They grew hungry, cold and tired. At night they sought lodging at a farmhouse, or else slept outdoors. Some peddlers who slept in their buggies froze to death. Perhaps most painful for these mustached men and long-skirted women was the loneliness. Raised in the crowded household of an extended family, they suddenly faced day after day of solitude for hours on end.

Peddling began to decline about 1900. The peddlers learned to speak English, accumulated capital, and went into business for themselves. They opened retail shops, favoring the dry goods store. Those who could not yet afford a shop went to work in industry. The Arab American community of

Detroit grew, as automobile factories attracted workers. Slowly immigrants abandoned the notion of a temporary stay in America. Instead they planted permanent roots in the nation. Its battles became theirs. During World War I, over 300 Syrians from Massachusetts alone served in the armed forces. Thereafter the Johnson-Reed Quota Act of 1924 limited the number of newcomers allowed into America. Only about 100 persons a year could migrate from areas of the Mideast. Though severe, the limitation did not bother most Arabs in America. Their families had joined them by then. Called *chain migration*, movement had followed a pattern: a man would immigrate, then send for relatives or a wife if he had one.

Christian Arab Americans. Arab Americans of the early 20th century went about their business, opening retail shops and taking factory jobs. Now that the group was here to stay, religious centers became a priority. About 90 percent of the Arabs who came to the United States were Christian. The rest were Muslims. Curiously the reverse is true in the Arab world, where the population is 90 percent Muslim.

While almost all the early Arab immigrants were Christian, they did not all belong to the same sect. Some were Orthodox, and some were Catholic. Among the Catholics, there existed several subdivisions: Melkite, Maronite, and Syriac. Since each group's members identified strongly with their religion, the divisions hindered their unifying as an all-Arab group.

Americans regarded the Christian churches of the Middle East as socially backward. Despite this view, the Arabs built Melkite, Maronite, and Orthodox churches in America. By the early 1920s, the three sects had erected 75 churches, but in time they lost over half their followers. Surrounding Americans favored the Christian churches of Europe. Different from churches of the Middle East, the Roman Catholic Church, for example, was associated with progress and prestige. Such churches won Arab converts. Also, the Arab religious sects brought to America changed on its shores. They toned down differences in their services and promoted only the most basic Arab customs (food habits, music, crafts, and warm, obedient families). Both the Orthodox and the Catholics joined with surrounding groups. Arab Catholics assimilated into the Roman Catholic system, which did not grant them their own bishops in America until 1966. Meanwhile, the Orthodox joined with the Greek and Russian Orthodox churches. As a result, the Arabic community was split even further.

Muslim Arab Americans. Fearing they would be unable to maintain their religious commitments in a non-Muslim society, Muslims did not come to America in large numbers at first. Communal prayer on Friday afternoons, for example, the month of fasting during daylight hours, and dietary restrictions would be difficult to observe. Also, American and Muslim laws differed greatly on marriage, divorce, and inheritance. A few Muslims moved to the United States despite such obstacles. They had built a *mosque*, a Muslim church, in the country by 1920.

The number of American mosques escalated after World War II. Having won independence, Arab states in the Mideast sent students to the United States for advanced training. Many of them remained in the country once their education was complete. At the same time, well-educated Arabs emigrated from their countries, causing a "brain drain" in the Arab world. It was modernizing too slowly to keep pace with their talents and continual warfare seemed to plague the region. Egypt alone lost 7,000 professionals to the United States from 1968 through 1971, the heaviest years of the brain drain. Unlike the early Syrian migrants, these newcomers came from various Arab nations. Many of them were fluent in English, well-educated, and highly skilled. The Muslim community grew, 400 mosques dotting North America by the early 1980s.

Like the Christian sects, the Muslim mosques became more like North American churches. They adopted Sunday communal prayer services for those who could not attend the customary Friday service. In America women could appear at Sunday service and teach Sunday school. For leadership, members elected representatives, who hired the *imam* (prayer leader). Such democratic leadership was not the case in the Arab world, where government-appointed ministries ran the mosques.

Arab Americans and the Arab-Israeli wars. Two Arab-Israeli wars erupted in 1967 and 1973, and areas occupied by Palestinian Arabs have existed as military zones since then. Then came civil war in Lebanon (1975-1978) and its invasion by Israel (1982). With these recent conflicts has come a large new wave of immigration to the Detroit, Michigan, area.

The wars left a lasting effect on Arabs in America. Before they had consisted of so many different groups, loyal to their religion, their family, and their village of origin. Warfare inspired them to cooperate and unify. Now they thought of themselves as a single Arabic-speaking people. This new-found identity began in reaction to the 1967 war, which had affected the Arab Americans in three ways:

1. Arab Americans grew indignant at U.S. policy on the war, feeling it unfairly opposed the Arab position.
2. After the war, new politically active Arab immigrants entered America, arousing old-time immigrants.

3. Long assimilated Americans of Arab descent were
suddenly subjected to ugly stereotypes of themselves.

Angered by the media's portraying them as either robed, ignorant desert dwellers or corrupt, overwealthy oil sheiks, Arab Americans organized in protest. They took particular offense at ABSCAM, an incident in which an FBI agent posed as an Arab sheik to expose congressmen and businessmen who would accept bribes. In the late 20th century the ethnic group has formed national organizations to maintain their identity and protect their interests. Among these is the American-Arab Anti-Discrimination Committee, organized in 1980 to fight stereotypes in media, education, business, and politics.

Culture Today

Politics. The majority of Arab Americans are described as conservative and Republican. To influence U.S. policy in the Mideast, they have formed the Association of Arab American University Graduates (AAUG) and a lobby of business and professional leaders known as the National Association of Arab Americans (NAAA). While the AAUG is located in Belmont, Massachusetts, the lobby is headquartered in Washington, D.C. Dearborn, Michigan, is another center of political activity. Its Arab Americans have held lectures on Mideastern events and contributed financial support to the wounded and homeless in the Mideast. Entering United States government, the first Arab American senator, James Abourezk (South Dakota), took office in 1980.

Religion and holidays. With the newest wave of immigrants, a type of backlash has occurred in Arab American religion. More Muslims have arrived, beginning a *reform movement* in America. The religion centers on the Arab prophet Muhammad, whose revelations provided followers with the Koran, the text on which their holy law is based. It prescribes communal worship on Fridays, which occurs in the mosque. As described, early mosques in America had become more like churches. Not only did they serve as religious centers but also as sites for fundraisers and cultural events like folk dancing. The latest wave of Muslim immigrants began to reform the faith in America by stricter observance of traditions. They aimed to purge the faith of changes adopted over the years and to revive old customs. The participation of women, for example, has been reduced. Also, the democratic election of leaders seems to have lost ground. The international Muslim World League has replaced local prayer leaders with *imans* from the Mideast. A similar throwback to earlier customs appears to have occurred in the Arab American Christian (Orthodox, Melkite, Maronite) sects.

With the Arab Muslims, new holidays came to America. *Eid al-Fitr* falls at the end of the month of fasting. At the end of *Hadji,* the pilgrimage to Mecca during which Muslims renew their dedication to God, they celebrate *Eid al-Adha.* Neither holiday is officially recognized in America, except in Dearborn, Michigan, where both receive some recognition.

Family life. Arab Americans still place high value on the family, but they now live in nuclear (parents and children) rather than extended (including relatives) family units.

Another change is an increase in women's status. In the Arab world, the family operated under the notion of male supremacy. Men were considered the stronger, wiser gender; women raised children, helped their husbands, and displayed hospitality. The role of women changed in America. During the peddling period, married men were absent from home for long stretches of time. So discipline of the children fell to the women. Moreover, they sewed or embroidered goods for their husbands to peddle, contributing to the family income. Some took jobs in garment factories. They abandoned old customs. Worn by both Christian and Muslim women, head coverings were put aside. Muslim women also abandoned the veil, the customary face covering they had worn in public.

Since many more men than women immigrated at first, the Arab Americans entered into mixed marriages from the start. The Muslims were less free to do so than the Christians. While it was permissible for a Muslim male to intermarry, authorities forbade the women from doing so. It was believed that women must abide by their husband's religion.

Children are greatly valued. Arab parents typically devote themselves to their offspring. In public, parents will display affection toward children with kisses, for example. Sons are raised to assume the role of authority in a family. Traditionally, chastity among girls has been highly valued. Daughters are taught to behave modestly.

Food, clothing, and shelter. Besides abandoning their head and face coverings, women adopted new clothing styles. They replaced their customary long skirts and tight bodices with shorter skirts and looser blouses. The most daring cut their hair. As for the men, many had worn a white collarless shirt with baggy black trousers that tapered at the ankles. A black vest and waist sash completed the outfit. It too was abandoned in the New World.

Food habits have been more resistant to change. Among the Muslims, dietary laws forbid the consumption of alcohol, pork, and improperly slaughtered meat. Muslims eat *halal,* meat from animals that are not stunned but properly butchered and bled with God's name recited when they are slaughtered. In some American cities, butchers sell *halal* meat. Otherwise Muslims use kosher (slaughtered according to Jewish law) meat, but recite a special phrase before eating it. Arab Americans have brought over recipes, which remain popular today. Two dips eaten with pita bread are *hummus* and *baba ghannouj*. Hummus is made of ground chick peas flavored with sesame seed oil, lemon juice, and garlic. Baba ghannouj is made of eggplant. Dressed with lemon juice and oil, the salad *tabbouleh* is a mixture of wheat kernels with chopped parsley, onions, tomatoes, and mint leaves. Rice and lamb are common staples. Topping off meals is coffee served Middle-Eastern style—thick and sweet in very small cups.

The Arab American neighborhood of Dearborn, Michigan includes the duplex home, tenement, coffeehouse, and gold-domed mosque, topped by a crescent moon, the symbol of the Muslim faith. In contrast to some other Arab American communities, residents here are mainly members of the working class. Most of these residents rent rather than own their homes. Along with the mosque, the coffeehouse is an Arab transplant here. It caters to men of all ages, especially those over 18. Many of them work in factories, go home for dinner, then frequent a coffeehouse to spend leisure time with male companions. The popular activities here are backgammon and card playing.

Business. At first even the automobile factory workers saved their earnings so they could purchase their own stores. While dry goods stores were most common, Arab Americans also became grocers, rug dealers, and traders in Oriental goods. Many of their children received university educations in the United States, then entered professional occupations. Among the professions, they favored careers in medicine or law.

The number of Arab American professionals has risen. A study of Detroit's Maronite community (1974) reported that 30 percent of its children were in professional fields as opposed to 2 percent of their fathers. At the same time, fewer children (52 percent) than fathers (80 percent) were in their own businesses. It is said that the south end of Dearborn, Michigan, is the heart of Detroit's Arab American community. Here it was reported that the majority were wage earners, with an average family income of 13,981 dollars in 1980. The number of unemployed (31 percent) was on the increase, partly because of the reduced need for laborers in automobile plants. It has been predicted that many recent immigrants will search for manual labor, given their background in farming.

Education and language. The early immigrants learned English quickly due to their peddling experience. Still, an Arabic-English patois, or jargon, became popular. For example, *I parked the car* became "barrakkt al-car." *We signed the paper* was "sayyanna al-baber." Arabic fell into disuse in America. The early immigrants had published over a dozen newspapers and magazines in Arabic by the early 1900s. In 1926, the *Syrian World* was the first to appear in English. American-born offspring soon grew up without learning Arabic. In the 1960s, America experienced a reawakening among ethnic groups throughout the nation. The teaching of Arabic was reintroduced at the time and continues today. Arabic is, in fact, a main language spoken by Arab residents in Dearborn, Michigan. Therefore, the Dearborn Public schools adopted an Arabic bilingual/bicultural program in 1976.

Literature. Most renowned among Arab American authors is Gibran Khalil Gibran (1883-1931). Born in Bsharri, Lebanon, Gibran moved to Boston in 1895 with his mother, who sold cloth and lace to support her four children. Gibran illustrated and wrote poems, acquiring a publisher through the efforts of a Boston settlement house. His most famous book *The Prophet*, which first appeared in 1923, is a classic of mystical poetry about the human soul. As a young man, he returned to Lebanon, where he studied Arabic literature and absorbed surrounding scenes that influenced his later poetry. Samuel Hazo is one of the best known poets of recent times. He, like other Arab American writers, treats subjects of wide appeal. For example, these lines are excerpted from "Some Words for President Wilson," a poem that reflects on the passing of a United States President (Hazo 1981, p. 10).

> He never guessed
> that he would be the final
> president to write his speeches
> out by hand.
> Or that the future he foresaw but never
> saw would happen differently
> the same and change its wars
> by number, not by name.

Other notable writers are William Blatty, Vance Bourjaily, and veteran newspaper correspondent Helen Thomas.

Heroes. Americans of Arab descent have distinguished themselves in several fields to the benefit of the public at large. Consumer advocate Ralph Nader is one example. Chief of Staff for President George Bush, former governor John Sununu is another. In the sciences, there are anthropologist Laura Nader (sister to Ralph Nader) and Dr. Michael A. Shadid, founder of America's first cooperative hospital. Interestingly, Shadid came to America at age 18 and earned money for medical school by peddling. His earnings also paid for his mother's and brother's passage to the country. In entertainment, there are award-winning actor F. Murray Abraham, comedian Danny Thomas, and disc jockey Casey Kasem. Sportsmen of Arab descent include football star Doug Flutie.

Ties to the Arab World. Like the Polish (see POLISH AMERICANS), the Arab immigrants have long demonstrated concern for taking care of their own. It has been considered dishonorable not to aid the needy in a family or community, *hasani*, or honorable, to do so. Therefore, Arab Americans organized to support the needy in their own communities. They have also contributed to the needy in their homelands, their contributions funding new churches, orphanages, hospitals, and schools in countries of the Middle East.

Other ties to the Arab world are commercial and religious. Companies who do business in Arabic-speaking nations have a demand for members of the group who have been educated in the United States and are fluent in Arabic. In religion, the Muslim World League influences U.S. Muslims. Overall, ties between Arab Americans and the Arab world are more of a personal than a political or an organized nature.

For More Information

See these reading materials:

Bushrui, Suheil. *Kahlil Gibran of Lebanon.* Gerrards Cross, Buckinghamshire: Colin Smythe, 1987.

Zogby, James, ed. *Taking Root Bearing Fruit.* Washington, D.C.: American-Arab Anti-Discrimination Committee, 1984.

Contact these organizations:

American-Arab Anti-Discrimination Committee, 4201 Connecticut Avenue, N.W., Suite 500, Washington, DC 20008.

National Association of Arab Americans, 2033 M Street, N.W., Suite 300, Washington, DC 20036.

BRITISH CANADIANS

(brit´ish cuh nay´ dee uns)

Canadians of British descent; the majority of the Canadian population.

Population: 9,785,959 (1981).
Location: Canada; British Canadians are the largest group in every province except for Quebec.
Language: English, French.

Geographical Setting

Canada is the second largest country in the world, and British Canadians live in every Canadian province. (A province is a division of the country like the states of the United States; however, it is much more independent.) Due to the size of the nation, the land on which British Canadians live is highly varied. A major geographical feature of the country is the Canadian Shield. This area includes the Hudson Bay and land surrounding it from near the Atlantic Ocean to the center of the continent and from near the Great Lakes to the far north. The Shield consists of rugged, ice-scoured rocks. In some areas it is heavily forested, in other places bacovered with re rock, and in the north it is ice-covered. Although the Shield is rich in minerals, timber, and water for generating water power, it did not attract the first settlers. East of the Shield lie low mountain ranges and then the flatter coastal land of New Brunswick and Nova Scotia. The early French settlers found this region attractive, particularly around the St. Lawrence River. More attractive land for farmers surrounded the Great Lakes and dipped between them. The early British settlers established themselves in this area. Later both British and French settlers moved west. On the western side of the Shield, Canada levels into a great plains area, then rises to the Canadian Rockies and a coastal mountain range, before falling to a plain along the Pacific Coast. Almost 90 percent of Canada lies north of the 50 degree parallel and is arctic or subarctic territory. Most of the French and British immigrants wanted to avoid this harsh climate, settling in the strip of land that stretches from the Atlantic to the Pacific just 200 to 300 miles north of the United States border.

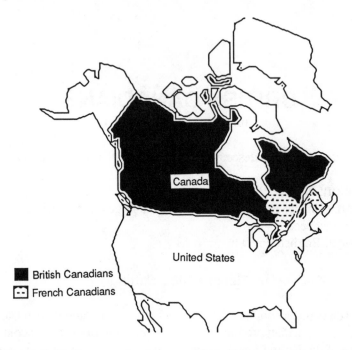

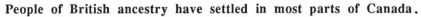

People of British ancestry have settled in most parts of Canada.

Historical Background

Early British exploration. Early in European exploration of the Americas, both the French and British laid claims to the north. In 1497, Italian-born John Cabot led an English expedition to Newfoundland. Thirty-seven years later, Jacques Cartier landed on the tip of the Gaspé Peninsula at the mouth of a large bay leading to the St. Lawrence River and claimed the land for France. While the French moved their settlements west along the St. Lawrence waterway, the British were establishing their colonies south in what are now Massachusetts and Virginia and exploring to the west and north. The struggles between the two powers in Europe found their way to the Americas. As early as 1613, English troops from Virginia attacked the French settlement of Port Royal. In 1629, a British fleet attacked and conquered the French at Quebec. A 1632, treaty (St. Germain-en-Laye), returned Quebec to France, but competition between the two countries continued. Throughout the 1600s, French explorers like Radisson, Groseilliers, Joliet, and Marquette traveled west to the plains area of Canada and south to the Mississippi River.

By the 1700s, the French had realized the importance of controlling the Great Lakes and the Mississippi to claim the continent. The British, who had been moving west as well as north, also saw the strategic importance of controlling the Great Lakes. Skirmishes between the two countries resulted first in the Treaty of Utrecht (1713) in which the French renounced all claim to Hudson Bay, most of Newfoundland, and Acadia except for Isle Royale (Cape Breton Island). Acadia then became Nova Scotia, some of its residents moving to Louisiana (see CREOLES).

British rule. In Europe in the mid-1700s, France and England were engaged in the Seven Years War. This erupted in America as the French and Indian War in 1754. By this time, the French were greatly outnumbered by the English. Fort after French fort around the Great Lakes and the St. Lawrence River was captured by superior English forces. Finally, the English won Quebec in a siege followed by an attack, and a year later English troops entered Montreal. The Treaty of Paris in 1763 gave England all the French territory east of the Mississippi River except for two small island fishing bases. At this time there were only 60,000 French settlers in the Americas.

The English governors expected this small number of French people to blend into the growing number of English in Canada. Instead, Catholicism, customs, and language united the French, making them resistant to assimilation. Acknowledging this division, the British government's Quebec Act of 1774 recognized the Catholic Church and its right to collect tithes, allowed French communities to be governed by French civil laws, reinstated the old feudal land ownership pattern of the French, and expanded the Quebec territory under a French-style appointed council.

Canada and the United States. By 1776, the United States had entered the picture, and American soldiers were attacking Quebec. The French in Quebec refused to help the English in this battle for Quebec or in any other struggles between the British and the Americans. In 1783, the Definitive Treaty of Peace divided the territory that is now the northeastern United States and southwestern Canada between the United States and the British colonies in Canada. The United States' vision of expanding farther north ended in the War of 1812, which finally established British control of the land north of the Great Lakes. This war also unified the Canadians as a people; they began to build a separate identity. Because their transportation along the St. Lawrence River had been threatened by the war, the Canadians decided to build an alternate water way. They dug a 123-mile canal from Kingston to Ottawa. Later, as added protection, the capital of Canada was moved to Ottawa.

French/British conflict. Between 1815 and 1850 nearly 800,000 British immigrants moved to Canada. About 100,000 of these settled in Nova Scotia. The rest settled in the Great Lakes region. French and British communities developed in the east with French Canadians occupying the Upper Province (Quebec) and the British occupying the Lower Province (Ontario). By an 1841 agreement, these two regions and others farther west united under a single legislature with each province represented equally. In 1867 the British North America Act defined Canada as a confederation of independent states; it became a British commonwealth nation, separate from Great Britain but with a governor who would speak for the British crown. The French and Métis (French-Indian people), however, demanded separate freedom. By 1870, these people had won the right to retain the French language and their church-run school system. The differences continue today, with Quebec frequently threatening to withdraw from the Canadian confederation (see FRENCH CANADIANS).

Ethnic dominance. Ninety percent of the people of Ontario are of British descent, and this percentage holds roughly for the other Canadian provinces except for Quebec (80 percent French) and New Brunswick (39 percent French). In the 20th century, many ethnic minorities have peopled Canada. The French remain the most significant minority, but there are also many Germans and Asians. However, because of the large preponderance of British Canadians, we usually think of them when describing Canadian life.

Culture Today

In many ways, Canada has preserved ties to its British past. English place names such as London, Edmonton, Alberta, and Victoria attest to the British link with Canada. The English language of Canada preserves British spelling as in *theatre, colour, connexion, cheque,* and *defence,* and also in the use of some distinctively British words (such as *marks* instead of "grades"). A major holiday is called Dominion Day, recalling Canada's former status as a dominion of the British Commonwealth.

Economy. Today's British Canadians are as varied as their land forms. They are business people in Toronto, farmers on the plains, miners in the north country, and operators of tourist attractions throughout the country. The economy of Canada is changing. Once largely dependent on agriculture and living comfortable rural lives, most British Canadians are moving to the cities to share in the growing manufacturing and service economy of the country. .

British Canadian engineers designed the Canadian Railroad.

Many British Canadian workers helped build the railroad.

British Canadians were the major developers of the Canadian Railroad.

Arts and literature. Although reluctant to accept the idea, British Canada shares much of its cultural development with the United States. Canadians read many American books, listen to American music, and watch mostly American television programs and movies. But Americans watch Canadian entertainers nightly as well. Peter Jennings, an ABC newscaster, is British Canadian. So are Hank Snow, a country singer, and the very popular singer Ann Murray. Norman Jewison, producer of *Fiddler on the Roof* and *Moonstruck*, is Canadian. The list of British Canadian actors known in both countries is large and includes such personalities as Glenn Ford, Walter Pidgeon, Raymond Burr, Lorne Greene, and Michael J. Fox.

Both Canadian and American children enjoy books by British Canadians such as Lucy Maud Montgomery, who wrote the classic *Anne of Green Gables* series, which takes place in eastern Canada. Other British Canadian authors popular in both countries are Stephen Leacock, Brian Moore, and Arthur Hailey. In poetry, Margaret Atwood has written about the Canadians. Her poetry reflects her belief that Canadians are bound to each other by a will to survive, and she has recently become a very popular novelist with bestsellers like *The Handmaid's Tale.*

One event that perpetuates the link between Canadian and British culture is the Shakespeare Festival in Stratford, Ontario. The festival, in which Shakespearean and other classic plays are performed, first occurred in 1953. Canadians who lived in Stratford wanted to start an artistic tradition comparable to those in Europe. So they organized and financed the project, and Canadians peopled the cast, crew, and audience. The festival has been a resounding success, attracting performers and theatergoers from around the world. It has helped to develop a native Canadian theater community, which was virtually nonexistent before the festival began.

Canadians generally are wary of becoming Americanized. To protect Canadian culture, the national government has created a fund for cultural development. Among the projects funded by the government is a National Film Board, which supports Canadian-made movies. A number of these have been marketed in both Canada and the United States. Through the National Film Board of Canada, Canadians have created their own version of the "Oscar" award for excellence in film—the Genie Award.

Recreation. Chris Haney and Scott Abbott, two British Canadians, invented the popular game *Trivial Pursuit.* James Naismith, is given credit for the invention of modern basketball, although its exact origin is a matter of controversy.

One recreational activity that is distinctly Canadian is the sport of ice hockey. Canadian players dominate the National Hockey League in the United States, and the sport is far more popular in Canada than in the United States. Played on an ice rink, this team sport consists of players on skates trying to land the puck, a small flat cylinder, into nets on either side of the rink. Equally popular with French and British Canadians, the sport has been referred to as the "national religion" of Canada. Millions of Canadians watch the Saturday night hockey telecast every week, and hockey players are national heroes.

The Canadians' enthusiasm for hockey extends to amateur players as well. It is the most popular and competitive sport for boys (as in many American sports, girls are not encouraged to play) from elementary school through college. Hockey is a fast-moving and violent sport; people who cringe at American football are likely to be shocked by Canadian hockey. Fans often become violent as well, swarming the ice after victory or defeat. As the national obsession, hockey is a unifying force for a people divided by geography and ethnicity.

Heroes. Terry Fox was a track star in the early 1980s who was stricken with cancer. As his last activity, Terry set out to run from one Canadian coast to the other to raise money for cancer research. He collapsed and died at Thunder Bay in Ontario in 1983. A monument in his honor stands in that city, and a popular film was made of his efforts. Terry raised several million dollars for cancer research before he died.

Religion. The majority of British Canadians who express a religious preference belong to one of three Christian churches. Forty-seven percent of all Canadians profess to be Roman Catholics. However, more than half the Roman Catholics are French Canadians. The greatest percentage of British Canadians are members of the Anglican Church of Canada or the United Church.

Government. Canada is a wealthy nation but small in population compared to the United States. In order for the Canadian economy to prosper, it must at the same time preserve its local market and become a major world trader. An example of the steps taken to preserve the Canadian market is the "Canadian Content" guideline for radio and television that defines the number of Canadian actors and film or sound workers necessary to make a program Canadian.

The Canadian government presides over a confederation of independent provinces. The central government of the confederation is at Ottawa in Ontario Province, which is 90 percent British Canadian and reflects the British heritage. The legislative branch consists of a House of Commons as well as a Senate. There is a cabinet of managers of various governmental functions, but this cabinet is called by the British name, Privy Council, and is responsible to the House of Commons. The head of government is a prime minister. All acts of this government are approved by the royal governor.

Working with the provincial governments, the Ottawa parliament provides a nationalized medical service that furnishes inexpensive medical service to all Canadian residents and an excellent educational system.

Education. Education in Canada is regulated by each province. In French Canada the state supports both public and parochial schools. In Ontario, which is predominantly British Canadian, only public schools receive governmental support. At a higher level, the government also supports renowned universities such as the University of Toronto and the University of British Columbia.

British and French Canadians today. Drawn together by a mutual distrust of the more populous United States, Canadians, both French and British, consider themselves Canadians first. The bond between the two has been strengthened by a national interest in the French language. French language schools have helped to make 16 percent of all Canadians bilingual. However, the French Canadians do not have English language schools, which is typical of their attitude toward British-Canadian culture, and some French complain that the schools are "little butchers of French." Serious tensions exist between French and British culture in Canada. However, many Canadian politicians view bilingualism as a bond to help unite the two groups.

For More Information

See these reading materials:

Thompson, Wayne C. *Canada 1989*. 5th rev. ed. Washington D.C.: Stryker-Post Publications, 1989.

Walz, Jay and Audrey. *Portrait of Canada*. New York: American Heritage Press, 1970.

Watson, Jessie and Wreford. *The Canadians: How They Live and Work*. North Pomfret, Vermont: David & Charles Inc., 1977.

Contact these organizations:

Ministry of Culture and Communications, 77 Bloor Street West, Toronto, Ontario, Canada M7A 2R9.

Ministry of Municipal Affairs, Recreation and Culture, 747 Fort Street, Parliament Buildings, Victoria, British Columbia, Canada V8V 1X4.

CHEROKEES

(cher´ uh kees´)

An American Indian tribe of the Southeastern United States.

Population: 121,000 (1989 est.).*
Location: United States (Oklahoma and North Carolina).
Language: English, several Cherokee dialects.

*Official tribal count based on certified ancestry; 1980 U.S. Census count of 232,000 includes everyone who identifies self as Cherokee.

Geographical Setting

There are Cherokee reservations in Oklahoma and North Carolina. Most Cherokees live off the reservations.

Around 1650, the Cherokees formed the largest Southeastern tribe in the United States, including about 22,000 members. They controlled a vast territory, some 40,000 square miles in the Southern Appalachian mountains, parts of present-day North and South Carolina, Virginia, Tennessee, Georgia, and Alabama. Much of the territory consisted of mountainous, forested terrain with numerous streams. The Great Smokey Mountain chain sat in one area of Cherokee settlement; the Blue Ridge Mountain chain divided two additional sites.

In the late 1830s, the Cherokees were pushed off their land to an area west of the Mississippi River, known first as Indian Territory and later as the state of Oklahoma. Officially, the United States now recognizes three divisions of the tribe: the Cherokee Nation of Oklahoma, the United Keetoowah Band (also in Oklahoma), and the Eastern Band of Cherokees. The largest group, the Cherokee Nation of Oklahoma (104,000), is commonly referred to as the Western Band. Located in the old Cherokee territory of North Carolina, the Eastern Band forms the next largest group (10,000). The Keetoowah Band (7,000) occupies northeastern Oklahoma. Other, unofficial Cherokee groups appear in areas of the country such as California, Georgia, and Missouri.

Historical Background

Legend has it that the Cherokees lived first in the Great Lakes area, then migrated to the Southeast because of warfare with Delaware and Iroquois tribes. In 1540, the DeSoto Expedition visited Cherokee country in the Southeast, its explorers becoming the first Europeans to contact these Indians. The explorers came and went, leaving the Cherokees to pursue their traditional lifestyle for the next 150 years.

Early life. The Cherokees prospered in the Southeast, building 64 communities, divided into Lower Towns, Middle Towns, and Upper Towns. Due to the rugged geography, variations developed in everyday customs. Townspeople everywhere spoke Cherokee, for example, but different dialects of the language appeared in the various areas.

Different settlement patterns appeared from region to region, but certain tendencies can be described. The Cherokees lived in over 60 towns and villages, each housing 350 to 600 inhabitants. Their settlements usually faced streams, and a cluster arrangement was common. At the center of town stood a council house, a granary and a communal food garden. Spreading out from the center was a cluster of homes, constructed of poles and bark or wood siding. Homes could be dome-shaped, with mats plastered with clay over the inner and outer walls. A sweathouse sat near the dwelling. Pouring water over its heated stone floor created steam, a curative against evil thoughts and disease. The Cherokees surrounded their settlements with a stockade of sharp, closely set poles to keep out wild animals and enemies. In fact, the log cabin and fort idea of colonial pioneers may stem from the Cherokee settlement plan.

Five-year-old Cherokee boy performs a traditional tribal dance.

In addition to common house styles, the Cherokees shared some basic habits in food and dress. For clothing, men wore breechcloths and buckskin shirts; women wore calico skirts and short jackets. Both men and women clad themselves in leggings and moccasins, decorating their footwear with porcupine quills. Men hunted deer, bear, and buffalo for meat, or fished for seafood. Meanwhile, women raised corn, beans, squash, and sweet potatoes, preparing dishes such as cornbread and corn cakes. Wild fruits and chestnuts, foods that grew in natural abundance, supplemented the daily fare.

The different towns shared religious, social, and political habits. The people regarded the sun as their chief deity. The red of sunrise symbolized bravery and was worn by the Cherokees to signify their status as the sun's children. Socially, they divided themselves into seven clans: the Kituwah, Wolf, Deer, Bird, Holly, Paint, and Long Hair. The Cherokees had no central government, which would later frustrate whites in negotiations with them. Instead each town relied on a head man and a council of elders. Some large settlements had a war chief, who assumed control in times of conflict.

Participating in the selection of chiefs, women commanded high respect in Cherokee society. The wife of a chief could speak in her husband's absence at a council meeting, and settlements had a separate Women's Council. In the family, the wife owned the home and the planting fields. A new husband moved into his wife's family dwelling, and Cherokee children belonged to the clan of their mother.

Colonial America. Regular contact with the Europeans began in 1673, traders from the southern colonies coming to the Cherokees for slaves and deerskins. In exchange, the Cherokees acquired European kettles, axes, mirrors, guns, and rum. The Indians quickly replaced traditional ways. They abandoned the bow and arrow for firearms and adopted the metal hoe. Clothing styles entered a transitional phase between native attire and everyday wear of the poor white farmer. Adopting calico dresses, colorful hunting shirts, turbans, and shawls, the Cherokees still wore feathers, and moccasins. Business thrived. The traders were receiving 50,000 skins a year from the Cherokees by 1708, and one million a year by 1730. Then smallpox devastated the tribe, with half the Cherokee population perishing in 1738. Another outbreak around 1750 cost many more lives. Thereafter, the population decreased due to unnatural causes.

The Cherokees supported the English in white people's wars, but when provoked, the Indians would turn on their allies. In 1754, the French and Indian War erupted. The Cherokees supported the English, but in 1756, some English colonists ambushed and killed two dozen Cherokees. Offered a 15-pound reward for every Indian scalp, the colonists failed to differentiate between their Indian allies and enemies. Beginning to view all frontiersmen as the enemy, the Cherokees retaliated, burning cabins and killing whites.

Revolutionary War. The Cherokees supported England in the American Revolution, a stand they took in self-defense because the Patriots seemed to have an insatiable hunger for land. The American-Cherokee War of 1776 broke the military power of these Indians, making them harmless enemies. Colonial militias burned Cherokee towns, cut down their corn, and killed the townspeople or drove them into the woods. Planning to destroy the Cherokee tribe, Virginia and Carolina colonists scalped the dead warriors, South Carolina paying 75 dollars a scalp. Though crushed, the Cherokees would conduct raids against the colonial settlers for the next 10 years.

Sequoia and his alphabet.

Sequoyah's alphabet. Despite efforts to destroy them, the Cherokees survived and flourished as an impressive society. In 1789, President George Washington adopted an Indian Policy. Teach English to the Indians, transform them into farmers, and divide up their land, for only as self-supporting individuals would they be treated as full and equal citizens. The Cherokees were caught in a paradox—they felt pressured to adopt some white ways in order to preserve their tribal identity. Throughout history, they would struggle to incorporate new ways yet retain old ones.

Rebuilding their war-torn settlements, the Cherokees made advancements that earned them a reputation as one of Five Civilized Tribes (Cherokee,

Creek, Choctaw, Chickasaw, and Seminole). A missionary school appeared in Cherokee country in 1801, after which one-room schoolhouses sprung up across their frontier. In 1809, Cherokee councils began holding trials to resolve disputes instead of leaving enemies to exact blood for blood. A system of law enforcement took effect, Indian sheriffs keeping the peace throughout Cherokee country. From 1809 to 1821, an Indian named Sequoyah labored to invent an alphabet for the Cherokee language. The Cherokees made quick use of his 85-letter alphabet, learning to read and write. In 1827, the group established a nation modeled after the United States, adopting a written constitution, courts, and a system of representation. They elected John Ross principal chief of the Cherokees east of the Mississippi River and located their capital at New Echota, Georgia. In 1828 they issued a newspaper in their own language, the *Cherokee Phoenix*, developed by Elias Boudinot.

Removal to the West. Meanwhile, whites introduced a new Indian policy— removal. Its goal, to move Indians west of the Mississippi River, was first championed by Thomas Jefferson. Jefferson negotiated the Georgia Compact (1802), purchasing all Georgia's claims to western lands for 1,250,000 dollars and a promise to rid Georgia of Indian claims to its territory. This set the new policy in motion, but Indian removal took three more decades to accomplish. Andrew Jackson became its primary advocate. Ironically, the Cherokees fought alongside a man who became their archenemy. Several hundred Cherokee warriors fought with Jackson in the 1813–14 Creek War. If the conflict spread, they reasoned, Cherokee country would be ravaged once again. So they helped Jackson defeat the Creek Indians at the Battle of Horseshoe Bend, wearing two feathers in their headband and a deer's tail on their backs so he could identify them as Cherokees.

President Jackson and the Cherokees. Jackson considered treaty making with Indians absurd and vigorously pushed for their removal to the west. When he became President in 1828, his plans for the Cherokees inspired the following comment from an old warrior named Junaluska: "If I had known that Jackson would drive us from our homes...I would have killed him that day on the Horseshoe" (Collier 1973, p.53).

By this time, many Cherokees had moved from towns to log cabins, where they lived much like their white neighbors. Most tended small farms, although some of these Indians farmed hundreds of acres. Being Southerners, they purchased black slaves and built large brick houses for themselves. The Cherokees had a slave code, forbidding marriages between Indians and slaves. It also prohibited slaves from owning property.

Meanwhile, the Cherokees themselves amassed a great deal of property. It was reported that they owned 22,000 cattle, 7,600 horses, 10 sawmills, 62 blacksmith shops, 31 gristmills, and 2,488 spinning wheels in 1826.

The 1830s proved disastrous for the Cherokees. Congress passed the Indian Removal Bill (1830), making relocation of the Indians west of the Mississippi River an official goal. In Georgia, lawmakers created Indian Codes that crippled Cherokee rights. Gold was discovered on Cherokee land in Georgia, and these lands were confiscated from the Indians. They could be imprisoned for speaking against removal, said the Codes, and could not testify in court against whites. Pony Clubs, vigilantes on horseback, set fires on Cherokee land, foreshadowing black history (see AFRICAN AMERICANS). Becoming a national issue, Cherokee mistreatment in Georgia upset U.S. senators and was addressed in the Supreme Court. The 1832 case *Samuel A. Worcester v. The State of Georgia*, held that Indian tribes were subject to federal, not state, laws. Still, the Indians faced a federal policy of removal.

An internal split among the Cherokees complicated matters. The majority of the Indians sided with Chief John Ross, who wanted to remain in the Cherokee homeland. A minority, led by John Ridge, preferred to make a treaty with the United States for new lands in the West. In 1835, without the approval of the Ross group, Ridge signed the Treaty of New Echota, exchanging the Cherokee homeland for 15 million dollars and land in Indian Territory (Oklahoma). The U.S. government decided to hold all Cherokees to the treaty, sending General Winfield Scott to oversee their removal. An observer described the process (Thornton 1987, p. 116):

> Under Scott's orders the troops were disposed at various points
> throughout the Cherokee country, where stockade forts were erected
> for gathering in and holding the Indians preparatory to removal.
> From these, squads of troops were sent to search out with rifle
> and bayonet every small cabin...to seize and bring in as prisoners
> all the occupants...Men were seized in their fields or going along the
> road, women were taken from their wheels and children from their play.

Trail of Tears. About 1,000 Cherokees escaped into the hills; these fugitives later became the Eastern Band. The vast majority, about 17,000 Cherokees, were rounded up and removed in 1838, traveling along what became known as the Trail of Tears. By foot, on horseback, in wagon, and in boats, 13 groups of a thousand or more Indians made the arduous journey west. They trudged through several states in the trek to northeast Indian Territory. Deaths occurred daily due to cold, accidents, and diseases such as whooping cough.

Upon reaching their destination, more died of starvation or sickness in the first year after their arrival. Most Cherokee families suffered the loss of a loved one; Chief John Ross had a wife who perished on the journey. Altogether, an estimated 8,000 Cherokee Indians may have died as a direct or indirect result of the Trail of Tears.

The Civil War. Conflict between the majority Ross and minority Ridge groups added dozens of murders to the Cherokee death toll from 1839 to 1846, the strife ending with a treaty signed in Washington, D.C. The people recovered. By 1859, population and prosperity were on the rise once again. Cherokee country in Oklahoma had 32 public schools, 100,000 acres in cultivation, and 240,000 head of cattle. The Cherokee Nation exported 50,000 head of cattle a year, over a million dollars worth, to the East.

On the heels of prosperity came another setback, the Civil War. Chief John Ross took a neutral stand on the War. However, the South promised the Cherokee an Indian nation in America if they supported the Confederacy. Ross felt forced to abandon his neutral position and support the South. The Cherokee leader Stand Watie led one Confederate battalion, and John Drew formed a regiment of Cherokee Mounted Rifles. To their credit and discredit, Colonel Drew's mounted Cherokees and Colonel Watie's dismounted Cherokees fought valiantly in the Pea Ridge Campaign. Newspapers of the day made much of their scalping and mutilating many of the Union dead.

Actually, the Cherokees were divided on the Civil War, and fought on both sides. Warriors who supported the North included the Keetowah Society, full-blooded Cherokees who battled alongside Union troops with corn husk in their hair. The Cherokees had their own civil war in progress, allies of the North pitted against allies of the South. Composed of Creeks, Cherokees, and Seminoles, two regiments helped invade Indian territory in 1862. They captured Chief John Ross, taking him to Washington, D.C., where he befriended President Abraham Lincoln. In 1863, Ross broke his alliance with the Confederacy, freed his slaves, and declared allegiance to the United States. Stand Watie's Cherokees, however, remained in the Confederacy until war's end. Losses mounting on both sides, 7,000 Cherokees perished in the five-year war.

Tribal vs. U.S. control. Again the Cherokees began the tired tale of rebuilding. The Civil War left Indian Country in ashes, its aftermath bringing railroads and more land losses. The Atlantic and Pacific Railroad spread across Cherokee country in 1872, leaving white settlers there. Towns sprang up at train depots, and marriages occurred between whites and the Cherokees. Due to white demands for acreage, the United States ordered the

Indians to sell some grazing land (the Cherokee Outlet). Congress passed a series of laws in the 1890s that would upset tribal authority and land ownership. An 1897 act made all tribal laws subject to veto by the President of the United States. The Curtis Act (1898) provided for the breakup of tribal lands in Indian territory, extending the Allotment Plan to this area. This plan divided tribal lands into individual plots—160 acres for a family, 80 acres for an adult, and 40 acres for a child. The Curtis Act also proclaimed that tribal governments would dissolve after issuing allotment deeds and ending tribal business.

20th century revival. In 1907, the government of the Cherokee Nation ceased to exist, so the Cherokees organized into various groups to make sure their voices would be heard. The groups sought national charters from the U.S. government, which began appointing the Cherokee chief. The policy of allotting tribal lands to individuals continued. Its goal, to transform the Indians into small farmers, failed. Many of the Cherokees raised cattle and hogs. By the 1920s, this type of small farming had declined, and the standard of living followed.

The population included both full-blooded Cherokees and individuals of mixed ancestry. Early white traders had settled among and intermarried with the Cherokees, as had missionaries. When whites flocked to Oklahoma, more intermarriage occurred. Mixed-blood children mastered white customs and the English language, assuming responsibility for tribal interests. Becoming a minority, full-bloods lost their tribal influence and retreated to the eastern Oklahoma hills. There they supported themselves cutting wood, hunting game, and cultivating small gardens. In 1966, the full-bloods rallied in support of old ways. Young men hunted for food out of season without a license. John Chewie was arrested but not convicted for the offense. Called the Five County Cherokee Movement, a full-blood society began reviving old ways. They established a Cherokee newspaper and a local radio program. Their efforts led to the formation of the Cherokee Community Organization for dealings between the outside world and full-bloods. Having formed this organized link with outsiders, about 11,000 Cherokees live in full-blood settlements today, speaking little English and observing traditional ways.

The more numerous mixed-bloods have largely assimilated with surrounding American culture. Their tribal structure has resurfaced, though. Relaxing its authority in the 1930s, the United States allowed tribal governments to reorganize. Various Cherokee groups sought national recognition, and it was given to the three divisions of Cherokees today (Cherokee Nation of Oklahoma, United Keetoowah Band of Cherokee of Oklahoma, and Eastern Band of Cherokees). The United States appointed the

Cherokee principal chief until 1970, when Congress approved their popular election. In 1983, the Cherokee Nation elected Wilma Mankiller, the first woman chief of a major Indian people. Her election recalls the strong position held by women in early Cherokee society.

Culture Today

Distribution. The distribution of many Indian tribes in the late 20th century parallels 19th-century reservation sites. Most Cherokees are centered around Tahlequah, Oklahoma, or on the reservation in North Carolina. The total Cherokee area in Oklahoma is about 92,000 acres. Slightly more than half this territory was allotted to individuals in the Cherokee Nation of Oklahoma; the rest is tribally owned. The Cherokee Reservation in North Carolina is 56,573 acres of tribal land. In the 1980s, the Cherokees on Oklahoma's reservation outnumbered those on South Carolina's by about eight to one.

Education. As early as 1801, Moravian missionaries (a Protestant sect brought over by Germans) opened a school in Cherokee country. The Moravians coaxed the Indians to adopt white ways but made no attempt to learn the Cherokee language. A mistrust developed. Advocating education before Christianization, the Presbyterians began winning Cherokee converts. Education became a main focus of the tribe, the Cherokees viewing it as an investment in self-protection. With education, they thought, they would be able to safeguard their own interests. By 1826, some 18 schools had appeared in Cherokee country. The missionaries encouraged the Cherokees to read and write, admiring their ability to grasp new ideas. In 1881, the Society of Friends (see QUAKERS) opened some schools, which proved so successful the federal government took them over, overseeing them through the Administration of Indian Affairs.

The picture grew less bright in the 20th century, with few Cherokees ever completing high school. The schools, students complained, provided vocational classes taught in English, not Cherokee. Some 1909 U.S. government inspectors found them in deplorable condition, dirty and rundown. Full-blood Cherokees have grown disillusioned in Oklahoma. By the 1970s, the typical full-blood dropped out of school after five years. There are, however, various routes to obtaining an education for those Cherokees who want it. In the Eastern Band, some of the students attend reservation schools while others prefer local white schools or adult education classes.

Religion. Much is secretive in Cherokee religion. In early times, the people selected young males (called *Adawhi*, or Medicine Men) who became privy to these secrets. A spiritual revival in 1811 called for a return to original religious rites and the removal of whites from Cherokee land. While this spiritual resurgence frightened whites, it faded in the tumult of the 19th-century wars. Today, most of the Cherokees belong to Christian churches, but many of them still participate in traditional religious ceremonies.

Family life. Living conditions vary with location. In the Oklahoma Ozarks are some 70 settlements of full-blooded Cherokees. Each contains from 10 to 35 households, whose central meeting place is often the local Cherokee Indian Baptist Church. In North Carolina, log and frame structures have prevailed for much of the 20th century. Cooking was done in fireplaces or on wood-burning stoves until Quakers began a program of rural electrification. An Indian group, Qualla Housing Authority, began improvements in 1962. By 1990, their efforts had resulted in 1,200 newly owned homes and 127 rental units.

Given the great loss of life in Cherokee history, grandparents often raised children. Some 13- and 14-year-old girls became pregnant, the grandparents tending these great-gramdchildren, too. The multigenerational household became commonplace. With the building of new houses in North Carolina came the breakup of the extended family household. A community of new houses sprang up near a rebuilt older one, though, with family members still living close to one another.

Traditionally, women have been the property holders and farmers in Cherokee society. The importance of hunting, warfare, and diplomacy, the male arenas, decreased greatly. Labor replaced hunting for late-19th or early 20th century Cherokee men. However, jobs paid little, and the husband's role as major contributor to the household was upset. This placed extra stress on Cherokee marriages from 1880 to 1950. Especially during the Prohibition Era, when trade in liquor was illegal, Cherokee laborers resorted to alcohol. They opened moonshine businesses, earning high profits by producing corn whiskey from the 1920s to the 1930s. In the 1950s, a rekindling of Indian arts and crafts and a growing tourist trade provided new sources of income. These trends have had a positive effect on family life, husbands regaining status through new economic contributions to the household.

Occupations. The renewed interest in Indian handicrafts provided jobs. Marketing goods to outsiders, Weaver's and Basket Associations fashion homemade woolens and baskets. Despite this boost, in the early 1970s the average Oklahoma Cherokee family earned only 2,000 dollars a year. Most full-bloods were unemployed; the women took housework for white neighbors. Social workers provided a monthly check, which the full-bloods relied on more than farm income or low wages. There are businesses in Oklahoma that hire Cherokee laborers. Phillips Products, which produces plastic pipes, has employed a majority of Cherokee workers; their lack of education has qualified them mostly for low-paying, not supervisory, jobs.

In North Carolina, the Eastern Band of Cherokees relied on farming for their livelihood as late as the 1940s. The traditional *gadugi*, or work company, continued here, too. The gadugi was a voluntary association, a type of labor gang that would farm each member's land in succession. While details changed, such work-sharing groups persisted until the 1960s. Wage labor overtook farming in the second half of the 20th century. Today's Eastern Cherokees take jobs in businesses that serve the local population, or in logging and tourism.

Government. The Eastern Band is governed by a constitution, an elected chief, and a 12-member tribal council. In Oklahoma, the Cherokees are governed by an elected chief and a 15-member tribal council. A new constitution took effect here in the 1970s. It defines a Cherokee by ancestry, not degree of Indian blood. A Cherokee who furnishes proof of ancestry may enroll in the Nation; enrollment entitles members to an array of benefits from education grants to housing and food plans. Greatly outnumbering full-bloods (who are only 13 percent of the Cherokee population), the mixed-bloods direct the tribal government in Oklahoma. In dealings with the U.S. government, the Cherokee Nation of Oklahoma represents not only Cherokees but also Delaware, Shawnee, and other Indians.

A number of Cherokees have participated in American government. Among them are Robert Owen, one of the first U.S. Senators to be elected after Oklahoma became a state (1907). Another renown Cherokee, N. B. Johnson, became Chief Justice of the Oklahoma Supreme Court and won the Freedom Award as most distinguished Indian in the United States.

Arts and recreation. Cherokee handicrafts include basketry, weaving, and carving. In the 20th century, several artists have won high acclaim. Bill Glass, Jr., received the 1975 Jerome Tiger Memorial Award for his work in ceramics. Joan Hill has won 234 prizes for her traditional and contemporary paintings.

Cherokee literature includes legends, correspondence, and chants. Based on history, one legend celebrates an Eastern Band hero named Tsali. It takes place during Removal to the West, on a day when Tsali's wife was supposedly mistreated by her captors. Tsali, the legend claims, retaliated for the mistreatment by killing one of the captors. He then fled into the hills with his family, joining other Cherokees who had escaped Removal and lived in hiding there. The army promised to leave the escapees in peace if they handed over Tsali. Resolving the matter, Tsali preferred to surrender rather than be hunted down by his own kind. He is now remembered in *Unto These Hills*, an outdoor drama that portrays the origins of the Eastern Band.

The Cherokees enthusiastically embraced the alphabet invented for them. Immediately, letter writing began. It is said that some young men abandoned archery, hunting, and fishing to write letters for entertainment. Others traveled long distances for the express purpose of sending letters. More seriously, leaders like Chief John Ross corresponded with personages such as Abraham Lincoln. Such letters now exist as valuable historical documents.

The Green Corn Festival was an annual event to celebrate nature's goodness in ripening the corn. Traditionally, the greatest athletes competed in ball-play at this festival. Each player held a pair of sticks with a braided pouch at one end for the ball. The object of the game was for one team to send the ball beyond the other team's goal 12 times. Through the years, ball-play has survived as one of the major Cherokee customs. Also performed at the festival was the Green Corn Dance, a ceremony conducted to aid cultivation. The Cherokees, in fact, developed a collection of dances and chants for various purposes. Love chants, for example, were performed to attract mates (Kilpatrick 1965, p. 18).

> Ha, then! You women of the Seven Clans!
> Ha! Now it has surely become time!
> All of you have just come to put White Eyes into me.
> All of you will not be able to glance elsewhere.
> It will be my body alone upon which all of you will be gazing.

To the early Indians, *put White Eyes into me* meant "look at me longingly." *Seven Clans* referred to the whole Cherokee nation, harking back to their beginnings as a people.

For More Information

See these reading materials:

Collier, Peter. *When Shall They Rest? The Cherokees' Long Struggle With America.* New York: Holt, Rinehart and Winston, 1973.

Finger, John R. *Eastern Band of Cherokees 1819–1900.* Knoxville: University of Tennessee Press, 1984.

Contact these organizations:

Eastern Band of Cherokees. P.O. Box 455. Cherokee, North Carolina 28719.

Cherokee Tribe. P.O. Box 948. Tahlequah, Oklahoma 74464.

CHEYENNE
(shai an´, shai en´)

A peace-loving American Indian people of the Plains.

Population: 15,000 (1988).
Location: United States (Montana, Oklahoma).
Language: Cheyenne, English.

Geographical Setting

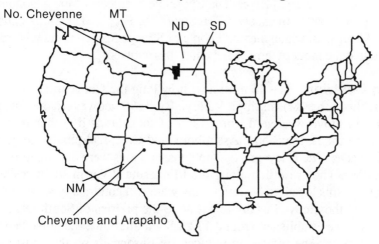

There is Cheyenne land in Montana, North and South Dakota, and New Mexico

The Cheyenne Indians have lived in three main ecological environments during their history. European explorers first met them in the upper Mississippi Valley (mostly in southeastern Minnesota), on the edge of the Eastern Woodlands. The Cheyenne began traveling westward from here about 1690. Before 1700, they settled in the prairies of southwestern Minnesota. In the middle of the 18th century, they gradually left these settlements, becoming nomads. They traveled the valleys and plateaus of the

Great Plains in search of bison, ending up in two main locations. A northern group settled in western Nebraska, eastern Colorado, and Wyoming (the capital of Wyoming is named Cheyenne); a southern group settled in southwestern Nebraska, western Kansas, and southeastern Colorado. Today, the Northern Cheyenne live on the Northern Cheyenne Indian Reservation in Lame Deer, Montana. Many Southern Cheyenne live in Oklahoma, where there used to be a Southern Cheyenne reservation. Thousands of other Cheyenne live in cities and rural areas across the United States.

Historical Background

First encounter with Europeans. The Cheyenne were first noted by the explorer LaSalle in 1680. A group of them came to his camp (now a part of Illinois) to offer to trade with him. At that time, the Cheyenne lived in what is now southeastern Minnesota and southwestern Wisconsin, around the head of the Mississippi River. The Cheyenne, members of the Algonquin language group, called themselves *Tsistsistas*, the People. The Sioux called them the *Shahiyena*, which means "People of Strange Speech," and it is from this word that the modern term "Cheyenne" has evolved.

Moving westward. We do not know how long the Cheyenne had been living in the upper Mississippi Valley. By 1690, however, they were beginning to move westward, forced out of their lands by other Indian tribes. These tribes, the Sioux, Assiniboin, and Cree, had purchased guns from Europeans. The Cheyenne had no guns, and thus were dislodged from their territory. They resettled along the Minnesota River in southwestern Minnesota. In this location, however, they were still continually at war with the Sioux, so they moved again, this time to the prairies of South Dakota, where they were established around 1725. Soon after this, the horse began to spread through the region, introduced by Europeans on the coast and moving west as Indians traded them from tribe to tribe. By 1780, the horse was a regular part of Cheyenne life, used in both hunting and warfare.

Westward to the Plains. Two main forces caused the Cheyenne to move even farther west. One was the continued hostility of surrounding tribes such as the Chippewa and Sioux; the permanent villages of the Cheyenne were too vulnerable to their attacks. The other was the diseases that the European fur traders had brought with them. Lacking the antibodies to fight diseases like smallpox and measles, entire villages could be annihilated by germs to which the Europeans were immune. The close-living style of these villages aggravated the spread of disease.

The Cheyenne began to leave their villages in the middle of the 18th century. The advent of horses made it possible for them to give up their villages and take up a nomadic way of life on the Plains. By 1830, the agricultural lifestyle of the villages was completely replaced by the hunting lifestyle of the nomads. The tipi had replaced the village.

During the 1800s, the Cheyenne divided into two groups: Southern Cheyenne living near the Arkansas River and Northern Cheyenne living near the Platte and Yellowstone Rivers. In 1840, the Southern Cheyenne made peace with the Comanche, Kiowa, Kiowa-Apache, and Arapaho, uniting with them against the European invasion of the Southern Plains. The Northern Cheyenne allied with the Sioux.

The buffalo hunt. The Cheyenne hunted bison in every place they lived. Before the move to the Plains, an entire band of 50 to 100 people would participate in the hunt. They would build a corral at the end of a ravine or the bottom of a steep cliff. Then the medicine man would say special prayers for the success of the hunt and the young men would search out a herd. When a herd was located, the entire band armed themselves and hid on either side of a path leading toward the corral. The fastest runner among the young men sang to the herd in imitation of a calf. Once the herd started to move toward him, he ran down the path. As the buffalo moved down the path, the hidden men made noise and drove them into the corral, where the men killed them.

Once the Cheyenne acquired horses they no longer needed this elaborate hunting procedure. A small group of mounted braves with bows and arrows could easily bring down enough buffalo to supply the band. The hunter would ride his horse up to the right side of a running buffalo and direct his arrows into its ribs. With horses, the band could also easily kill a surplus to have buffalo robes for trading.

Societies and family life. The Cheyenne had many societies for both social and communal needs. Among the women, the *me e no ist st* (she sews on quills) society was very important. Women in this group were known for decorating ceremonial headdresses, clothing, tipis, saddles, bags, and shields with porcupine quills. The long quills were soaked until flexible, flattened, and then appliquéd to the leather surface. In the 19th century, beadwork replaced quillwork. European traders brought small glass beads which were incredibly popular with Indian artists, since many more designs were possible with beads than with quills. Also, porcupines, and thus their quills, were becoming more difficult to find. Many artists combined quills and beads.

Among the men's societies were groups who were camp police, soldiers, great hunters, and fast runners. The camp police had great power. They were known to whip even high-ranking offenders, especially if the offense regarded a buffalo hunt. Members of the Fox or Coyote Society had great cunning and the ability to run long distances. Other societies acted as judges regarding the laws of the tribe and enforced those laws.

Family structure was an important component of Cheyenne life. Courtship could take three to five years and involved special dances. After marriage, the couple would live near the wife's mother. The family men hunted as a group under the leadership of the oldest active husband, and the women cooked as a group in his wife's tent. An extended family included the head man and his wife or wives, her sisters and their families, and daughters and their families.

Children learned adult activities very early, with boys riding by five or six and girls gathering water and wood at the same age. By their early teens boys had gone on their first buffalo hunt. In honor of this step toward manhood, their fathers gave horses to poorer families and their mothers would provide feasts. Girls had special coming-of-age ceremonies when they reached puberty. Lasting several days, the rituals involved seclusion and special lessons from older women, and they culminated in a feast. Children and adults played games including a form of lacrosse called *oho knit* (knocking the ball), which took place on a field about 200 to 250 yards long. They used curved sticks and a flattened ball made out of deer hide, playing the game either on foot or mounted, like polo.

Religion and philosophy. Among the Cheyenne, all life was centered on the relationship between the individual, the community, and the cosmos. Special rituals were performed to uncover universal truths and help people understand their own life. Medicine men used their ritual knowledge to cure illnesses and improve the fortunes of the tribe.

The main Cheyenne god is Heammawihio, "the wise one above." The Cheyenne saw him in different parts of the universe: the Sun, the Moon, the Morning Star, the Evening Star, and so on. According to Cheyenne legend, Heammawihio had lived with them long ago and had taught them about agriculture, hunting, and fire before ascending to heaven, where the Cheyenne would join him when they died.

The binding forces that tied everything together were the Maiyun. Searching for understanding of this idea was a basic part of every Cheyenne's life. According to Cheyenne tradition, Sweet Medicine went to the Sacred Mountain in South Dakota and talked to the Maiyun. They gave him four sacred Medicine Arrows, which symbolized the spiritual health of the tribe, and they taught how to honor the arrows and keep the tribe healthy. Another hero, Erect Horns, went to the Sacred Mountain to find out how to bring relief to his people during a famine. The Maiyun taught him the Sun Dance and told him that performing it would help end his people's distress.

The Cheyenne used the Sun Dance to help them find individual and community vision. In the summer, bands gathered and erected a pole. People tied offerings to it and men and women danced around it or stared at it with trance-like concentration for hours. Young men would shove leather strips through their flesh and tie them to the pole, then hang until the flesh tore and they were free. A form of self-sacrifice, this torture was voluntary. Men did it to obtain the pity of supernatural spirits and achieve good fortune in the future.

The Cheyenne believed the earth was held up on a pole like the one used in the Sun Dance. According to their legends, the Great White Grandfather Beaver of the North was gnawing on this pole, and when he got all the way through the world would end. This is why the Cheyenne would not eat or kill beavers; they hoped that the Grandfather Beaver would gnaw more slowly if they pleased him.

Warfare. Historically, the Cheyenne were a peaceful group who tried to avoid great conflicts with other tribes. But like all Plains Indians, they raided for horses and defended their territory. Capturing horses or taking a shield or a gun was viewed as a brave deed. But even braver was "counting coup" on an enemy warrior: touching him, either with a hand or a special stick. The warrior who touched the enemy was accorded more honor than the one who actually killed the man. Up to three warriors could count coup on the same person, receiving credit according to the order in which they touched him. Scalping among the Cheyenne was chiefly ceremonial. A piece of scalp the size of a half-dollar might be taken by a youth to prove his manhood.

Interaction with settlers. The coming of white men forced the Cheyenne to change. Their trading and farming activities brought them into contact with settlers and immigrants who did not understand or appreciate their life. There were many confrontations and small battles. However, instead of open warfare, which was not in the Cheyenne tradition, the Southern Cheyenne, along with several other Plains Indian tribes, signed a treaty with the U.S. government in 1854. In this treaty the Indians were guaranteed a free territory of 122,000 square miles which settlers could cross but which would remain Indian land. As compensation for the passage of the immigrants, the Cheyenne and Arapaho were to receive 50,000 dollars a year for ten years. However, passing wagon trains killed game and the Indians retaliated by attacking the settlers. By 1857, it was full-scale war. The 1858 gold rush in Colorado brought more whites into contact with the Cheyenne. These miners and settlers wanted the Indians removed from the land so that they could move in safely. This time the government said that the Cheyenne would have to forfeit more territory, stop hunting completely, and become farmers on a small reserve. The compensation was 450,000 dollars. The Cheyenne refused to move and the war escalated.

In 1864, a militia officer and Methodist minister, John M. Chivington, led an attack on a band of friendly Cheyenne gathered under military protection at Sand Creek in eastern Colorado. Chivington's party killed and mutilated men, women, and children, among them seven chiefs who were in favor of peace. One chief, Black Kettle, tried to stop the attack with a white flag of surrender and an American flag, but the massacre continued. Black Kettle escaped with other members of the band only to die four years later in another surprise attack led by Lieutenant George Armstrong Custer.

The Dog Soldiers. After Sand Creek, many young men and their families decided that peace with the whites was impossible. They left their bands and joined a group called the Dog Soldiers. Before this, the Dog Soldiers had been a military society advocating raiding. With new members they could defend their own territory and came to be known as "hostiles." This term included all Indians living in the area, Cheyenne and Sioux. The Dog Soldiers fought whites and tried to keep the main groups of the Cheyenne from signing treaties. After many were massacred at Summit Springs in 1869, the Dog Soldiers lost much of their power.

Territorial disputes. By the 1870s, most of the Southern Cheyenne had signed a treaty accepting reservation land in the Indian Territory of Oklahoma. But in 1874, 30-year-old Quanah Parker, a chief of the Kwahadi Comanche, led 700 Comanche, Kiowa, and Cheyenne against a band of 30 white buffalo hunters. Armed with large bore guns, the hunters had been killing up to 200 buffalo in one day. Under the terms of the 1867 Medicine Lodge Treaty, the principal tribes of the Great Plains had been granted inviolate reservations where they were to live and hunt in peace. The buffalo hunters ignored the boundaries and hunted at will. Between 1870 and 1874, they almost eliminated the buffalo; by 1900 the 100 million buffalo who had roamed the western plains had been reduced to 1,000. Parker and his warriors battled with the hunters for three days. But the hunters held them off and the Indians only killed three whites.

The Northern Cheyenne allied with the Dakota (Sioux) at the end of the Civil War in an attempt to enforce treaty borders and oust white forts built in violation of the agreements (see DAKOTA). They were a part of the victorious force that wiped out Custer's Seventh Cavalry at the Battle of the Little Big Horn, also known as Custer's Last Stand. Ultimately defeated along with the Sioux, the Cheyenne were forced onto a malaria-infested reservation in Oklahoma in 1877. A group of the Northern Cheyenne in Oklahoma escaped and were brutally massacred by the army after being recaptured and held at Fort Robinson. When reports of the outrage reached the American public, a separate reservation for the Northern Cheyenne was demanded and finally established in Montana.

Economic difficulties and relocation. In 1880, the Southern Cheyenne on the reservation in Oklahoma faced famine because their land was infertile and the bison had been wiped out. Under a new series of laws concluding with the Dawes Severalty Act in 1887, each male Indian head of family was given ownership of a plot of land which could not be sold for 25 years. All remaining reservation land could be bought by the U.S. government. The government purchased 3.5 million acres; the Cheyenne and Arapaho got 500,000 acres. The land allotted to the Indians by the whites was not suitable for farming, and they lacked the capital to begin ranching. The reservation was gone. Many of the Indians leased their land to ranchers who defaulted on the leases but eventually purchased the land at low prices. The tribal and extended family relationships that supported the Indians were undermined by the enforced separation through land allotments.

The Northern Cheyenne fared better and were able to maintain more tribal land ownership. This enabled them to continue tribal customs and provide support for members of the group when they needed it.

Ghost Dance. Late in the century, the Cheyenne, like many other tribes, were searching for something to give them hope. They turned to the Ghost Dance (see DAKOTA SIOUX). Cheyenne delegates traveled by train to the Walker Lake Ghost Dancing. There they watched the Dance and spoke to Wovoka, its Paiute founder. They took what they learned back home to the bands. Most of the Cheyenne adopted the ritual, which promised the return of the bison and prosperity for all Indians. The Cheyenne used the Ghost Dance as a vision-producing ritual, but by the end of the century it had been banned by the government as dangerous to the peace of the reservation.

By 1910, all of the old tribal chiefs and war chiefs were dead and the reservation agent selected new chiefs from men he could control. He saw that they adopted white religion, clothing, and marriage customs. These men then lost credibility with the tribe and had no power to govern.

Recent history. In 1934, the U.S. government passed the Indian Reorganization Act, which allowed tribal governments to be formed as corporations with constitutions and tribally elected councils. This was the first step in returning control over their lives back to the Indians. The Cheyenne and the Arapaho formed such a corporation together. Then, in 1935, the Society of Chiefs was established. This band of leaders and people in positions of authority meets to discuss tribal concerns. The Cheyenne-Arapaho are still governed by this tribal council.

In 1947, the Indian Claims Act allowed tribes to sue for payment for lost lands. After innumerable delays, the Cheyenne-Arapaho federation received 15 million dollars. However, conditions for the Southern Cheyenne in particular remained bleak.

Also after World War II, the Northern Cheyenne embarked on a program of buying all Indian land that came up for sale. John Woodenlegs of the Northern Cheyenne provided the leadership that enabled the tribe to implement this ambitious program. In general, the Northern Cheyenne have been more successful economically and culturally than their Southern cousins.

Culture Today

Food, clothing, and shelter. Before their nomadic phase, the Cheyenne lived in permanent villages. Their housing consisted of "earthlodges," homes made of soil, grass, and wood. The Cheyenne were primarily agricultural, farming tobacco, maize, beans, and squash and hunting buffalo in the Black Hills. When they became nomadic, the easily transportable tipi became the standard housing. Though the women continued to plant fields of maize and beans in river-bottom land, returning to harvest the crops when they were ripe, the nomadic Cheyenne were primarily hunters.

Cheyenne tipis were known for their outstanding beauty. They were decorated with beadwork, quillwork, and painted illustrations of mythological and religious ideas as well as the personal badge or symbol of the owner. The women erected and cared for the tipis and were considered their owners. At least four poles held up the tipi, and up to 18 skins formed the "walls." The fireplace was in the center; a hole was left at the top for smoke to exit. The entrance, which faced east toward the rising sun, had flaps which could be closed during bad weather. There was little furniture, but sometimes they used backrests made of woven willow sticks and a tripod.

Women were responsible for tanning the skins that the male hunters brought home. They made tipis, buffalo robes, and clothing from the tanned skins. Men wore loincloths and fringed leggings with knee-length shirts over them. Women dressed in leggings and tube-shaped sacks that reached below the knees. Everyone wore moccasins.

Once the Cheyenne lived in tipis on the Plains.

The women also stripped the carcasses of meat and smoked or dried it. Some of the dried meat was pounded together with melted fat, bone marrow, and dried cherries, including the pits, to make *pemmican.*

Much of the Cheyenne wealth came from their active trade in buffalo robes for food and manufactured goods. They developed strong ties through intermarriage with white traders and established camps near trading posts. After the camps were made, the women began farming while the men continued to be responsible for hunting.

Today, raising cattle is a major occupation among the Northern Cheyenne and they have a tribal herd. Their modern houses face east, toward the Sacred Mountain, just as their tipis used to.

Among the Southern Cheyenne, substandard housing, extremely high unemployment, and welfare dependency are the norm. The Cheyenne have become fairly acculturated. Their food and clothing habits are like those of other Americans in their area; the prolonged courting rituals of the past have been replaced by elopement. Certain elements of Cheyenne culture persist, however, such as the people's religion and language.

Traditional clothing of the Cheyenne.

Religion. Many Cheyenne continue to believe in Heammawihio and the Maiyun. They make pilgrimages to the Sacred Mountain, *Nowah wus*, in South Dakota in their search for wisdom. The Sacred Arrows of the Cheyenne are still maintained by a Sacred Arrow Keeper according to the rituals given to the Cheyenne hero Sweet Medicine centuries ago.

The Peyote Cult is another Cheyenne religion. It was formulated late in the 19th century and is an active force in many tribes. The rituals include prayers, songs, drumming, and the eating of peyote, a cactus that causes hallucinations. Like the other religions, it is a search for a vision of truth.

In Medicine Mountain, Montana, there is a stone monument at least 200 years old called the Medicine Wheel. It is a flat arrangement of stones that may be a sundial used to calculate when to build medicine lodges for the Sun Dance. (Stonehenge in England is believed to be another such sundial.) Many Cheyenne visit the Medicine Wheel today and leave offerings of handkerchiefs, tobacco pouches, or feathers hanging off the fence that surrounds it.

Family and social life. Traditional Cheyenne keep the extended family structure intact in their living arrangements today. Related families may occupy two or more houses in the same block, across the street, or back to back in urban areas, or in compounds in rural areas. Every June the more traditional families hold annual ceremonies. During the two-week festivals everyone tries to speak Cheyenne, respect the old religion, and honor ancient laws. In some areas a modern-day Sun Dance is performed. The offerings are frequently lengths of brightly colored fabric. Just as the old Sun Dance required the offerings to remain on the pole at the mercy of the elements, the modern Sun Dance pole is abandoned at the end of the ceremony. Each year the chiefs, priests, and headmen draw together thousands of Cheyenne for powwows and other ceremonies on reservations in both states.

Today the military societies work to continue the spiritual and religious life of the Cheyenne. The Dog Soldiers have been especially active in the area and provide leadership for the entire tribe.

Political economy. Because of the close link between the earth and Cheyenne, they are very environmentally aware. About 56 percent of the Northern reservation sits atop a huge coal deposit, and the Cheyenne have been offered a great deal of money to lease the land to a mining company, but they have refused to do so. Cheyenne who lead the opposition to strip mining speak of the problems of dislocating people living there and allocating the revenue. Also, these Cheyenne have seen the effects of strip mining elsewhere in the country and want no part of it.

Arts. Like many Indian tribes, the Cheyenne have been very successful in the decorative arts. Historically, the Cheyenne expressed themselves artistically on items that were part of their daily lives: clothing, bags, and later saddles and tipis. The move to nomadism meant that art would have to be small and transportable, leading to such items as beautifully beaded pipes. Decoration of skins was a way of pleasing the dead animal; it would prevent the animal's revenge and hopefully maintain its goodwill. Women were known for abstract geometric designs, especially when beads became popular, while men tended toward more naturalistic portrayals, painting stories onto buffalo hides. When the Cheyenne moved to reservations, it resulted in more freedom for decorative artists. There was no longer a need for every belonging to be practical or easily transportable, and because of high unemployment many people had time on their hands. This resulted in artworks like enormously heavy, intricately designed beaded dresses, meant for display and not use.

Some Cheyenne artists are well-known in other areas of visual art. Dick West, an educator and historian, is best known for his paintings. They are detailed, historically accurate renditions of preindustrial Cheyenne life. Archie Blackwell is also well-known for his paintings of the rituals and customs of Cheyenne life, especially the Sun Dance.

Combining the American literary tradition of authors such as Nathaniel Hawthorne with the dream theories of Carl Jung, Lance Henson has found a way to express Cheyenne philosophy in poetry in his book *Keeper of the Arrows* (Velie, 1979).

For More Information

See these reading materials:

Grinnell, George Bird. *The Cheyenne Indians*. Lincoln: University of Nebraska Press, 1923.

Moore, John H. *The Cheyenne Nation*. Lincoln: University of Nebraska Press, 1987.

Contact these organizations:

Museum of the Plains Indians, P.O. Box 400, U.S. Highway 89, Browning, Montana 59417.

Southern Plains Museum, 749 Highway 62 East, Anadarka, Oklahoma 73005.

CHINESE AMERICANS
(chi neez´ eh mer´uh kins)

Americans whose ancestors lived in the People's Republic of China, Taiwan, or Hong Kong.

Population: 812,000(1980).
Location: United States, primarily the West Coast and Northeast.
Language: English, Chinese (mostly Cantonese and Mandarin dialects).

Geographical Setting

There are Chinese American communities in the large cities of the West Coast and in Boston and New York.

San Francisco was the greatest Asian immigrant port and remains the center of Chinese American life. Between 1860 and 1880 about 80 percent of Chinese in America lived in California. (Nearly all adult males, they formed perhaps 25 percent of the work force there.) At the end of the 19th century the Chinese began moving east, mining in Western states and establishing

Chinatowns in New York City and Boston. After an initial period of rural work in mines and on the railroads, they became a largely urban group. This urban tendency has continued to the present day.

Historical Background

Early discoverers. An ancient Chinese text, the *History of the Liang Dynasty*, recounts the discovery of the "Kingdom of the Fusang" by Chinese Buddhist missionaries in the fifth century. The recent discovery off the California coast of 30 anchor stones, with manmade rope holes and Chinese lettering, supports the idea that the "kingdom" was actually North America, in which case the Chinese would have preceded Christopher Columbus by over a thousand years. The Chinese did launch expeditions just before Columbus' time, from which the stones might date. In more recent times, a handful of Chinese merchants, carpenters, and servants are reported to have been in Philadelphia around 1785. Perhaps 50 such Chinese came to the East Coast before 1849, including several students. The most important of these was Yung Wing, who arrived in America in 1847 at age 19. In 1850 he entered Yale, graduating in 1854 to become influential in early commercial and diplomatic relations between the two countries. Yung Wing helped organize the Chinese Educational Mission of 1872 to 1881, which brought 120 students from China to Connecticut. The Mission brought 30 youths per year, who would train in America for 15 years before returning to China to benefit their own society.

The "Coolie Trade." Beginning in the 1840s, thousands of Chinese contract laborers called *coolies* were brought not to North America but to Latin America on crowded, unsanitary ships often after being abducted or lured by false promises. Very few survived the harsh voyage and the virtual slave labor that followed. In 1862, the United States outlawed the transportation of Chinese contract laborers, workers under obligation to work for a fixed period of time. Actually meaning "those who do bitter work," the term *coolie* as used in the American West described Chinese immigrants generally, and it took on connotations of slavery or servitude.

Gold Rush prosperity. The first significant Chinese immigrations to America—the coolies cannot be considered immigrants, since many came against their will—began with the California Gold Rush of 1849. Opportunities abounded not only in the mines but also in the huge labor and service markets produced by prosperity.

Young men voyaged across the Pacific on ships whose conditions varied. On some, the Chinese voyagers crammed into narrow bunks, three to an airless cargo hold. Many died under such conditions. Still, the migrants came, enticed by tales of quick riches, joining the tens of thousands of other immigrants who had journeyed to North America.

Records show approximately 300,000 Chinese entries from 1849 to 1882, 90 percent of them men. Voyaging back and forth, many immigrants entered more than once. Perhaps 150,000 to 160,000 individuals came, mostly from the southern coastal region of Guangdong (Kwangtung), which was beset by natural disasters and armed uprisings against the Imperial government. Chinese or American agents might loan an immigrant 50 dollars to pay for passage, extracting a promise of a fourfold or 200-dollar repayment at a later date. Others borrowed from family, friends, or a long-established credit system called *hui*. Leaving wives and children in China, they intended to make a fortune of 500 to 1,000 dollars, then return to their villages and families. The very word for "immigrant" in Chinese means "sojourner," or person who arrives for a temporary stay.

Miners. The Chinese were persistent and hardworking miners, often tackling abandoned sites that others left as used up. Having mined gold overseas for 50 years in Borneo, the Chinese had developed mining technology (such as the water wheel, which allowed them to drain rivers). Chinese miners came to the New World specifically to mine, unlike many white immigrants who had already settled in America when the cry of "Gold!" broke out. Three Chinese are recorded as having arrived in gold country one month after the first nugget was discovered at Sutter's Mill in 1848.

The Chinese miners started in California, then moved to other states in the West. By 1870, they made up about 60 percent of miners in Oregon and Idaho and were active also in Washington, Nevada, Montana, and Colorado. Along with the well-known pans, they wielded pack-axes, sluice boxes, and water wheels which became known as "China pumps." They often walked to the mines or rivers, carrying huge loads, while white miners rode there. The Chinese slept in caves, in the open, or in abandoned huts or tents, washing in streams. On guard against the bandits that preyed on the camps, they stuck together. Most of them spoke little if any English.

Railroad workers. In the 1860s, the Central Pacific and Union Pacific companies were racing to complete the transcontinental railroad. As construction lagged, agents in San Francisco contracted to supply the Central Pacific with groups of Chinese workers. By 1869, when the two coasts finally linked by rail, the company had hired between 12,000 and 15,000 Chinese.

Chinese workers were paid about three-fourths of the wages their white coworkers earned and had to supply their own room and board. Usually the agents advanced food and a cook, subtracting each worker's share of the cost from his pay at the end of the month. A Chinese railroad worker could expect to save perhaps 20 dollars per month. He faced 12-hour days of strenuous, often dangerous labor, clearing land, leveling roadbeds, blasting rock, and digging tunnels. Among the high ridges of the Sierra Nevada, Chinese were lowered in wicker baskets to place tunneling charges in cliffs. They would light the fuses and hope to be pulled away before the charge exploded. Other Chinese workers built trestles in 10- to 20-foot snow drifts. Accidents were common: ropes broke, or the men were caught in explosions or avalanches. Perhaps 1,200 Chinese died before the railroad was completed.

Entrepreneurs. Chinese merchants accompanied the laborers, investing in retail and manufacturing operations that served both Chinese and white communities. They owned laundries, grocery stores, and restaurants or made shoes, textiles, and cigars. In 1876, for example, Chinese cigar factory owners in San Francisco employed 7,500 of their countrymen. Other Chinese laborers began as gardeners, farmers, and fishermen. By the 1870s, Chinese made up 80 percent of the workers in the Columbia River's salmon canneries. Others worked for California growers, harvesting wheat and, after completion of the railroad, more perishable products for Eastern markets. They often turned to farm work after the mines or rails, making important contributions to American agriculture. A few developed new varieties of rice or introduced crops such as celery to large markets. One horticulturalist, Ah Bing, developed in Oregon the popular hybrid cherry that still bears his name; another, Lue Gim Gong of Florida grew the first frost-resistant oranges, on which the Florida citrus industry was founded.

Anti-Chinese discrimination. At first, the Chinese were welcomed by officials and employers in California. In 1851, Governor John McDougall urged "further immigration and settlement of Chinese—one of our most worthy classes of newly adopted citizens—to whom the climate and character of our land are particularly suited" (Daniels 1988, p. 35). Chinese workers were praised for their stamina and ability in the mines, on the railroads, and in the fields. Wherever they excelled, it seemed, they encountered the hostility of whites, who objected to their "unfair" practice of working longer hours for lower pay. These whites quickly attributed Chinese success in America to subhuman attributes. As early as 1852, white miners in California called for immigration barriers against "these burlesques of humanity" (Daniels 1988, p. 33). In 1862, the big labor unions started Anti-Coolie Clubs, reflecting a movement which would gain popular force as the boom economy of the West slowed. In 1869, with the transcontinental railroad completed, over 10,000 unemployed Chinese made their way to the already depressed labor market of California. Anti-Chinese agitation spread from San Francisco as far east as North Adams, Massachusetts, where 75 Chinese strikebreakers caused a popular uproar in 1870. The movement culminated in the Chinese Exclusion Act of 1882, which banned the entry of Chinese laborers for ten years. The Geary Act (1892) extended the ban for another ten years, and a 1904 exclusion act extended the ban indefinitely. Meanwhile, other laws tried to limit the number of Chinese already in America. In 1888, Congress passed the Scott Act, denying reentry to some 20,000 immigrants who had been visiting China. The labor unions remained at the head of the anti-Chinese movement until the early 20th century, when they began to admit Chinese members.

Society of bachelors. Several interconnected factors delayed Chinese assimilation. First, Chinese immigrants retained especially strong ties to the mother country, sending back money and visiting regularly. They clung to the "sojourner" mentality longer than other groups—as shown by the Scott Act's catching such a large number as 20,000 out of the country in 1888. Next, because these "sojourner" immigrants kept wives and children in China, they produced no second generation to speed assimilation. As late as 1920, women comprised only 10 percent of Chinese in America. Third, this "bachelor" lifestyle gave rise to support systems that further discouraged assimilation.

The support systems were based on regional and blood ties. The basic unit was the *huiguan*, a social group originally formed by merchants in China, who banded together with others of their region to protect their interests. Merchants also led the huiguan in America. Called companies, they grew to encompass anyone from a particular region. The earliest were started in San Francisco in about 1851: the Kong Chow Company, the Sam Yup Company, and the Sze Yup Company. In the 1860s, the six huiguan of San Francisco united to form the Chinese Consolidated Benevolent Association (CCBA), or Chinese Six Companies. The Six Companies founded branches in other cities, as far east as New York and Boston, looking after Chinese interests during the period of exclusion, 1882 to 1943.

Clan associations whose members shared the same ancestor were also strong. In China, the members of a given village often shared blood ties.

They tended to work and settle together. In America, one clan often dominated the Chinatowns in smaller cities: for instance, the Moy Clan in Chicago, the Chin clan in Denver, and Yee clan in Pittsburgh.

On a smaller scale than the Six Companies were the secret illegal societies called *triads* or *tongs*. In China the societies resisted an unpopular government. In America, the press exaggerated the activities of the tong. They were said to be associated with opium, gambling, and prostitution rings With few legal institutions in the American West, the tongs grew into mafialike organizations.

Craft guilds were also transplanted from China. Responding to the hostility of American labor, they flourished in the cigar, shoe, and garment industries. All these organizations were male-oriented in China. Among the nearly all-male Chinese in America they became even more so.

Exclusion period. After the Exclusion Act of 1882, the population of Chinese in America dropped from about 125,000 to just over 60,000 in 1920. This drastic decline makes the Chinese unique in the history of immigration to the United States. The Chinese Exclusion Act forbade the entry of laborers, but did not apply to merchants, students, citizens by birth, and the children of citizens. These individuals were exempt from the act. Usually the children of citizens were sons—often "paper sons," fraudulently claimed, especially after the 1906 earthquake in San Francisco destroyed immigration records.

The "bachelor" society continued through the exclusion period, growing even more pronounced. Often, men had come to America intending to send for their wives in China once they had amassed some fortune. The Exclusion Act denied entry to these men's wives, too (unless the men were merchants).

From Pearl Buck to Pearl Harbor. Events in China took on great significance for Chinese Americans in the 20th century, contributing much to their relations among each other and with the larger, mostly white community. When Japan invaded China beginning in 1931, American perceptions of China and the Chinese began to change. Americans saw China as the "underdog" to Japan's "aggressor." Also changing American perceptions was the author Pearl Buck with novels like the *The Good Earth*. Winning Pulitzer (1932) and Nobel (1938) prizes, she popularized a sympathetic image of the Chinese peasant.

Chinese Americans had responded to Japan's invasion of China with money and soldier power. Set up in Oregon and California, flying schools trained young men like Arthur Chin (Chin Suey Tin) as fighter pilots for China. After the Japanese attack on the American Navy at Pearl Harbor,

Hawaii, in 1941, America and China became allies against the Japanese. (Chinese Americans ultimately contributed about 25 million dollars to China in the war against Japan. A number of them joined the war effort even before Pearl Harbor, including 33 young pilots from Oregon.)

Recent immigrants. The ten-year period (1931-41), from the invasion of China to Pearl Harbor, marked a turning point in how Chinese Americans were perceived in America. During World War II, over 12,000 Americans of Chinese descent served in the U.S. Army. The Exclusion Act was repealed shortly thereafter (1943). Alien wives of citizens became eligible for citizenship without limit. Nearly 10,000 Chinese women immigrated in the eight years following World War II.

In the 1960s, American-born students of Chinese descent joined other minority groups in protesting racial injustice. The decade saw some gains. The Immigration Act of 1965 eliminated anti-Asian discriminatory quotas. Male-female ratios gradually balanced as immigration continued into the 1980s. By 1980, the Chinese were the largest Asian American ethnic group.

Ties to China. The influx of recent immigrants, the slow adoption of American ways, and family members left behind have long kept Chinese Americans tied to events in China. Sun Yat-sen, Nationalist leader of the 1911 Revolution, gained much of his support from the Chinese in America. The 1911 Revolution marked a turning point for them. Men stopped wearing their hair in the *queue*, a long pigtail, imposed by Manchu emperors as a sign of submission. Women began to mix more freely with men in public. American clothes gained popularity. In the optimistic early days of the Republican government many returned to China. Others contributed money to their native regions. In the 1920s, the Nationalists in China faced bitter opposition from the Communists. Unrest led to a surge in illegal immigration to the United States. When the Communists won control of mainland China in 1949, many Americans severed their ties to the homeland. Others continued to support the Nationalists, who had been forced onto the island of Taiwan. Meanwhile, Taiwan took advantage of the anti-Communist climate in America during the 1950s to strengthen its ties to Chinese groups in the United States.

Both Peking and Taiwan continued to court Chinese-American sympathies throughout the 1970s and 1980s, holding summer camps, study tours, and seminars. Taiwan's government lost credibility by its failure to allow democratic institutions; ground that was won by Peking in 1980s' reforms was lost in the shock and anger that followed the massacre of student demonstrators in China at Tiananmen Square on June 4, 1989.

Today, Chinese Americans wait to see what course events will take after the death of the Communist leader Deng Xaioping.

Culture Today

A Chinatown in the early 1900s.

Chinatowns. After the Chinese Exclusion Act of 1882, discrimination drove immigrants away from farms, mines, and other areas. Many of them gathered in one section of San Francisco, forming the city's Chinatown. Moving into other major cities, they developed more Chinatowns in the country.

Residents provided their own police protection and educational institutions in these Chinatowns. They created a self-contained community with shops, restaurants, schools, and homes. Not everyone lived in the community. Owners of large businesses, upper class Chinese lived elsewhere. So did middle-class owners of small businesses. Working as waiters perhaps, lower-class immigrants lived in Chinatown. Fortune tellers, barbers, and doctors all plied their trades there. Chinese opera provided leisure-time activity, as did games of Chinese chess and mahjong (played with dominolike tiles). Besides these legitimate activities, there were opium dens, gambling houses, and brothels, institutions that harmed the image of the Chinese in America. Various Chinese organizations fought to eliminate the criminal element. Chinatowns now serve as colorful tourist attractions, while continuing to offer a haven for the recent immigrant. Some of the smaller ones have closed down altogether, and new satellite Chinatowns have developed in major cities. These are urban pockets, like Elmhurst in New York, where the Chinese congregate. Housing in these satellite communities is usually superior to the low-income dwelling in a Chinatown.

Food, clothing, and shelter. New York's Chinatown has spread to the Lower East Side, once home to other immigrant groups (see JEWISH AMERICANS). A low-income family might live in a five-story walk up apartment here. Rent is generally reasonable, but units are in disrepair. There is a middle-income housing project in New York's Chinatown, too. Called Confucius Plaza, the project contains an elementary school, stores, offices, and 750 co-operative apartments.

Chinese Americans maintained their customary diet from the mining camps to Chinatowns until recent times. What they couldn't grow, they imported: bamboo shoots, rice, pork, sausage, and dried foods (fruit, fish, oysters, abalone, seaweed, and mushrooms). Agents for the railroad gangs hired Chinese cooks, who kept kettles on the boil for frequent cups of tea during the day, which the men drank from little cups without handles. Until the postwar period, most whites knew Chinese food only as chop suey and chow mein, which were actually American versions of Chinese dishes. Beginning in the 1960s, however, Chinese restaurants became popular options for Americans in general. This popularity, along with the broader regional mix of immigrants from different areas, widened the range of cuisines. Besides the familiar Cantonese, restaurants now offer Sichuanese, Hunanese, Peking, Northern Chinese, Mongolian and Formosan dishes.

At first, Chinese immigrants dressed quite distinctively. Laborers wore coarse, wide-legged pants, cotton tunics, broad-brimmed straw hats and sandals or wooden shoes. A merchant dressed in gowns and silk caps with cloth shoes. The proper Chinese woman—these were mostly the wives of merchants—wore distinctive dress, too. At the turn-of-the century, she might have appeared in a long, pleated and brocaded skirt, a short satin jacket, and all her jewelry, including ornaments in her hair. Such delicate costumes became a style of the past as assimilation progressed in the 20th century.

Women. As with traditional dress, the public separation of men and women gradually disappeared. The ancient practice of binding a woman's feet to impede their growth also disappeared. But in the 19th century, the few Chinese women who had immigrated to America faced new evils. They often fell into the clutches of kidnappers who used them for illicit purposes. Chen Cong, a Seattle merchant, lost his new wife to kidnappers in 1866. After years of trying to track her down, he finally had to abandon the search.

There were heroines among the Chinese American women, too, individuals like Lalu Nathoy, an Idaho pioneer whose courage and skill in nursing twice saved her husband's life. Less dramatically but just as purposefully, Leah Hing earned her license as an airplane pilot in 1934 and worked as an instrument mechanic at a U.S. air base during World War II.

Women often remained subordinate to men despite such achievements. The writers Jade Snow Wong and Maxine Hong Kingston depict the frustration of growing up female in the Chinese America of the 1930s to the 1960s. In her 1945 book *Fifth Chinese Daughter*, Wong describes girlhood in a family whose culture put men first. Maxine Hong Kingston's 1976 autobiographical novel *The Woman Warrior* recounts the sexual and racial prejudice encountered by a young Chinese American woman. Beginning in the 1970s many Chinese women shared in or benefited from the feminist movement: educated, middle-class and largely American-born, they shook off traditional roles. Such women include television journalist Connie Chung, Republican Party activist Anne Chennault, and California politicians March Fong Eu and Lily Lee Chen. Other women have fared less well, many working in Chinatown sweatshops under conditions hardly better than those of Chinese men over 100 years ago. Even these women, though, often benefit from a rise in status due to life in America.

Business. In the traditional Chinese family, status progressed downward from grandparents to males to females. Women gained prestige in America because they found jobs, sometimes more easily than men. Often women landed factory work in the garment industry. Over half the families in New York's Chinatown now have someone working in this industry.

Chinese American men have concentrated in restaurant work. Laundry businesses mushroomed, too. Typically, a man had to settle for employment beneath his qualifications. A doctor might become a factory or restaurant worker. If he therefore experienced dissatisfaction in work, he could take comfort in the promise of a better future for his children.

Politics. Men derived some status from their role in voluntary organizations. These have given the Chinese a political forum. The people organized political groups, social service groups, family groups, and trade associations. One political body, the Organization of Chinese-Americans was formed to advance the rights of the minority in the United States. The Chinese Consolidated Benevolent Association (CCBA) has acted as a type of governing body in Chinatowns. Often their residents have regarded the CCBA president as their mayor. A social service group, the Chinatown Planning Council formed to address the needs of newcomers to New York in the 1960s. It operates day-care centers and programs for the elderly. Trade associations include the Chinese Hand Laundry Alliance. Highly structured, the old family associations extend to kin. An association's members have numbered in the hundreds and even thousands. These family groups continue to exist, but they have weakened with the passage of time. One of their main purposes has been financial aid to the members.

Family life. Obedience was stressed in the Chinese American family; children learned to be passive and respectful. They grew up sharing rooms and possessions with their parents, an arrangement that fostered a strong sense of interdependence and belonging. Rather than arrange for a babysitter, Chinese parents would bring children to social gatherings such as parties or the theater. Children quickly became used to interacting with adults. When they reached marriageable age, matches were often arranged between clans. For Chinese Americans, such traditions have conflicted with individualism.

Sometimes children would precede their mother by a year or more in joining their father in the United States. They would be exposed to American ways in school. By the time their mother arrived, their behaviors may have changed. Usually, both parents—unassimilated father, recently arrived mother—maintained traditional ways at home. Tension arose when it came time for a child to marry. Perhaps an oldest son wished to wed a white girl, but his parents objected. He might feel obligated to search the Chinese community or even visit China to find a Chinese sweetheart. In all likelihood, the youth would feel torn between his ingrained parental respect and his American individualism.

Education and values. Parents expected and received high achievement from Chinese American children in school; a student's performance reflected on the family's honor. As the second generation grew in the 1930s and 1940s, Chinese communities across the country set up schools for Chinese language and culture. The organization the Chinese Six Companies ran the oldest one, the Chinese Public School in New York. Opened in 1908, this school boasted over 100 students by 1933. Such schools were often destined to disappear. Many of them closed when assimilation gathered speed after World War II.

Recent years have seen the development of bilingual education for the Chinese in public schools. Serving the flood of newcomers among other students, New York initiated one such program in 1975. Chinese American children have performed most strongly in mathematics and the sciences. Generally, they score the highest of any ethnic group on Scholastic Aptitude Tests in these subjects. The 1980 census showed the Chinese to be the best-educated group in America.

Though many Chinese students succeed in education, the students have experienced conflicts in adjusting to America. Their struggle to succeed in a new language is a common immigrant trial. Less commonly, Chinese students and their families also struggle with the difference between old and new values. Chinese tradition, for example, has encouraged a type of formality. Unlike other groups (see ITALIAN AMERICANS), family members do not outwardly show affection. Individuals sacrifice their own desires for the good of the group, and mental abilities rank more highly than physical prowess. Clashing with American values, such beliefs created inner tensions. The old attitudes have changed over time.

The arts. The most popular Chinese-American literary figures have been the female writers Jade Snow Wong and Maxine Hong Kingston, whose works are mentioned above. Both have written autobiographical best sellers, dramatizing the Chinese American experience for a wider audience. In her 1975 book *No Chinese Stranger,* according to historian Roger Daniels, Wong "reflects a communal change in attitude, a change brought about, at least in part, by an increasing sense of security about the place of Chinese Americans in our national life" (Daniels 1988, p. 328). Eleanor Wong Telemaque, who wrote the novel *It's Crazy to Stay Chinese in Minnesota* (1978), won the Manhattan Borough President's Award for Excellence in the Arts.

In the dramatic arts, playwright Frank Chin created works about the barriers still encountered by Chinese Americans. Yuet Fung developed a film on Chinese hand laundries in America, *Eight Pound Livelihood.* Another of her subjects has been Chinese restaurant workers and their struggle to unionize. (Apparently one out of six Chinese in America work in the restaurant business, many of them for meager pay and no benefits.) Released in 1976, a television miniseries, *Gam Saan Haak, Gold Mountain Guest,* revealed the role Chinese played in building the American West. In the music world, singer Yi-kwei Sze and composer Wen-chun Chou have won renown. Him Mark directed an exhibit of his group's ethnic experience, *Chinese of America 1785 to 1980,* which was presented across the United States.

Religion. The three main Chinese religions, Buddhism, Taoism and Confucianism, continued to be practiced by most Chinese Americans well into the exclusion period. By the 1920s, however, these faiths began to give way to Christianity. Christian organizations had always been among the main white champions of the Chinese American population. Many converts refused to give up their traditional beliefs, even while attending Christian worship. The Chinese cultural background rejects the Christian concept of exclusivity. Buddhism, Taoism, and Confucianism can all be practiced simultaneously. Some Chinese in America added Christian elements to the mix, often in an attempt to assimilate. Unlike other groups in America, the Chinese have not centered their communities around any religious organization. Religion appears to be an individual rather than a group concern. There is no congregational worship in popular Chinese faiths.

In the 1980s, a large Buddhist Temple
was built near Los Angeles.

Holidays. The New Year Festival requires those who still observe old religious rites to visit a public temple. Fairly recent additions for the Chinese Americans, Buddhist temples in their communities are often store-front establishments. The Chinese New Year is a three to five day celebration falling between January 20 and February 19. Its highlight is the Golden Dragon Parade (the dragon, it is believed, wards off evil). Much visiting is done during the several day celebration, and businesses close. At the end of the holiday, *hoi nien*, a ceremony opening the year is performed.

Diversity. The Chinese American population nearly doubled between 1970 and 1980, contributing to an increase in crime in America's crowded Chinatowns. Less violent than in the past, tongs still exist and youth gangs have appeared. The Chinese have fallen victim to new tensions in America, too. Mistaken for Japanese, Vincent Chin was beaten with a baseball bat by an unemployed automobile worker in 1982. Chin died of the injuries.

At the same time, Americans of Chinese descent have excelled in various fields. In 1983, Harry Lee, a Sheriff of Jefferson Parish near New Orleans, won the AMVETS Silver Helmet Award, an American Veterans of World War II, Korea, and Vietnam award for distinguished service. I.M. Pei is a renowned architect. Three Chinese American physicists, Chen-ning Yang, Tsung-dao Lee, and Samuel Ting, have won Nobel Prizes. In space science, astronaut Taylor Wang flew on the 1985 space shuttle STS 51B. Computer manufacturer An Wang ranked fifth on *Forbe's Magazine*'s list of the richest 100 people in the United States. In skating, Tiffany Chin has won worldwide recognition. This great diversity perhaps helps explains the new security about the place of the citizens of Chinese descent in American life.

Meanwhile, America itself has become more diverse due to the Chinese. Acupuncture is now a treatment in its medical establishment, for example, and self-defense techniques such as kung fu enjoy widespread popularity. The California Bungalow was strongly influenced by Chinese or oriental-style buildings. As with other immigrant groups, their native culture helped shape American society while they became adjusted to it.

For More Information

See these reading materials:

Chen, Jack. *The Chinese of America*. San Francisco: Harper and Row, 1980.

Daniels, Roger. *Asian America: Chinese and Japanese in America since 1850*. Seattle: University of Washington Press, 1988.

Contact this organization:

Organization of Chinese Americans, 2025 Eye Street N.W., Suite 926, Washington, DC 20006.

CREOLES
(kre´ols)

Descendants of the original French or Spanish settlers in Louisiana, who may be all white or mixed-bloods from unions with African blacks.

Population: 100,000 (est. 1986).*
Location: United States (mainly Louisiana, Texas, California, and Illinois).
Language: English, French, French Creole.

*Estimated for Louisiana Creoles; population elsewhere unknown.

Geographical Setting

Major Creole population area.

Creole culture began in Louisiana territory before it belonged to the United States. Centered in New Orleans, Creoles also settled northwards towards Natchez and eastward near the Cane River. Clusters lived by the intersection of the Missouri and the Mississippi rivers, too. Some 10,000 refugees fled from Haiti first to Cuba, then to Louisiana in 1809, almost doubling the population there. Meanwhile, Americans from the East Coast pushed westward into the territory. An American community appeared in New Orleans. The older Creole community remained supreme for a time, but the decades after 1830 transformed the French and Spanish settlement into an American city, similar to others in the United States. Changes increased with the Civil War. Thereafter, many Creoles moved to southeastern Texas, where they settled in the "golden triangle," an area bounded by the three towns Port Arthur, Beaumont and Orange. The 20th century brought more migration. After the two world wars, Creoles moved to Chicago, Illinois, and to the Los Angeles or San Francisco areas of California. The majority remained in Louisiana, where today's community confines itself to New Orleans.

Historical Background

The French. Named Pierre le Moyne, the first French man arrived in 1699 at the site of New Orleans. There was nothing but muddy ground at the time, so he rested by a small bayou (marshy body of water) near the Mississippi River. Nineteen years later, his brother Jean Baptiste Le Moyne would build a settlement in the area. His builders began *La Nouvelle Orléans* (New Orleans) in 1718, situating the settlement below the level of the Mississippi River. They faced difficult land conditions—a flat, marshy, forest-covered plain infested with mosquitos and flooded for perhaps eight months a year. On one side was the river; on the other, swampland. The climate was hot and wet.

Planned by engineers, New Orleans grew from a square to a rectangle with three arteries to hold all the settlers. The French and then the Spanish controlled the entire Louisiana territory in the 18th century. French rule lasted from 1718 to 1768, attracting more men than women to the settlement, along with their African slaves. Early society fell into three classes—the whites, the slaves, and the *gens de couleur libre* (free people of color). Physically, the free people of color showed signs of racial mixture—light-skin and straight hair, for example. This three-class society continued for over a century, the existence of both free people of color and slaves separating it from other societies in North America.

Free people of color enjoyed the same rights as whites in French Louisiana with some exceptions. A free man of color could own property. However, he could not vote or hold public office. It was illegal for free people of color to marry a white person or inherit a white person's possessions. On documents, they had to label themselves f.m.c. and f.w.c. (free man or woman of color). Still, owning real estate enabled a few of the men to earn fortunes of their own. As Louisiana grew, so did its free class of colored persons. French law allowed masters to manumit, or free, their slaves. According to the *Code Noir* (Black Code) of 1724, a master who was 25 or older could exercise this right. Frenchmen often bestowed freedom on mixed-blood children whom they fathered and on their mother if she was a slave.

The Spanish. Spain ruled Louisiana from 1768 to 1803, but customs of the colony continued in much the same way. Like the French, the Spanish governed with a relaxed hand, allowing a master aged 20 or older to free his slaves. There was an increase of free people of color in the colony. Meanwhile, more French-speaking settlers arrived due to two migrations. Expelled from Nova Scotia in Canada, white French-speaking Acadians (called Cajuns) made their way to southern Louisiana in the late 1700s, with over 1,600 Cajuns arriving in 1785 alone. They were peasants, so they built farms, away from New Orleans. The other tide of French-speaking immigrants preferred the city, and nearly doubled the population of the colony. From 1789 to 1810, a slave revolution in Saint-Domingue (later called Haiti) drove planters out of that French colony. Planters of white and mixed blood fled the revolution with their slaves, stopping in Cuba and the eastern United States before settling in Louisiana. Coming from Cuba in 1809–10, the largest wave of these refugees numbered 9,059, including 2,731 whites, 3,102 free persons of color, and 3,226 slaves. The revolt had destroyed aristocratic life in Haiti (as the Civil War later would in the United States), so white, black, and mixed-blood members of the old society retreated to French Louisiana.

The Americans. Some years earlier, in 1803, the United States purchased Louisiana. Spain had returned the territory to France by then, so President Thomas Jefferson bought it from Napolean Bonaparte, sending James Monroe to seal the bargain. Perhaps the greatest real estate deal in history, the Louisiana Purchase cost the Americans 15 million dollars. The land it bought them would later became part of 15 states. After the cotton gin was invented in 1793 and sugarcane proved highly profitable, Americans moved into the colony. There was a clash of cultures. French Louisianans and their slaves kept their distance from the newcomers, calling them *Méricains Coquins* (American rascals). Proud of their French and Spanish blood, old-time Louisianans considered themselves a more advanced people.

Whether they were white, free people of color, or black slaves, they used the term *Creole* to advertise their heritage and to set themselves apart from the Americans.

The *Creoles*. European countries began using the term *creole* when they first colonized areas of the New World. Referring to children of Portuguese, French, or Spanish settlers born on the new shores, the term separated them from colonists who were foreign born. Taken from the Portuguese *crioulo* or the Spanish *criollo*, the word means "native," "to be born," or "to create." Its spelling in French is *creole*. The term came to have a broad meaning in Louisiana. First, French-speaking whites (of either French or Spanish descent) used the term *Creole* to distinguish themselves from Anglo-Americans. Whites who entered into unions with slaves or mixed-bloods called their offspring *Creoles of color*. Suggesting a mix of racial origins, the expression referred mainly to people of French or Spanish *and* African blood. Over time "of color" was dropped. Racially mixed people were simply called *Creole*, a name that also applied to whites.

The Creoles have historically been a self-conscious group, perceiving themselves as an ethnicity and ardently maintaining a separate identity. White Creoles of Louisiana viewed themselves as a social elite and felt superior to the Cajuns, whom they considered to be backward peasants.

It must be remembered that Creole society was steeped in French and Spanish, not English, traditions. With the Franco-Spanish traditions came certain expected behaviors. Men, for example, had great authority; a woman learned to accept their whims. There was a rigid class system. In descending order, it included gentlemen, tradesmen, small farmers, and those with African blood. This bottom class was further categorized, according to the degree of mixed blood in a person's veins: People who were 1/16th, 1/8th, or 1/4th black occupied the same category, called octoroon. Beneath the octoroons were mulattos (1/2 black), griffes (3/4 black), and sacatras (7/8 black). Where blacks fell in this system determined their place in Louisiana society. People of color who were free enjoyed privileges that would be denied them in other states. In nearby Southern states, an individual with any portion of African blood was simply considered black. In Louisiana, the law allowed persons of mixed blood to reach unparalleled wealth and status. Creoles of the Cane River colony, in particular, boasted many prosperous members.

Creoles vs. Americans. Life was quite different under the Americans than it had been under earlier rulers. After the Louisiana Purchase, an attempt to replace French dances with English dances ended in riot. One woman protested that the Spaniards ruled for 30 years and never forced the Creoles to dance the fandango. Neither did they want to dance the American reel or the jig. For 80 years, the Creoles fought against Americanization. They absorbed several foreign groups—German, Swiss, Irish, and many Spanish—but they locked horns with the Americans. The American preoccupation with work and money clashed with the Creole devotion to the *joie de vivre* (joy of living). At the same time, the Creoles upset the Americans. New Englanders were scandalized by the Creole concern for pleasure. They viewed the Creole gentleman's custom of kissing someone on both cheeks as foolish and disapproved of his business and personal habits.

In Creole society, a man's status depended not only his color but also on his occupation. No gentleman would engage in work done with the hands. Instead he might become a planter, lawyer, doctor, or broker in cotton or sugar. Gentlemen were idle much of the time, yet always seemed busy. They took fencing lessons, hunted, courted ladies, or sipped coffee and sherry for hours at the local cafés, which had gambling tables. The Creoles also played billiards, opening close to 40 billiard parlors by the 1830s.

Creole gentlemen had a code of honor. At the slightest offense, they would challenge the culprit to a duel. The duelists fought with a saber, rapier, or sword, usually ending the duel after the first drawing of blood. Begun by the upper class, the art of dueling spread to the middle class. The goal of defending one's honor was lost in the process, swords were sometimes exchanged for pistols, and the fighting became a dangerous thirst for vengeance.

White men outnumbered white women in French Louisiana. So relationships with women of color became the custom. They continued first under Spanish and then under American rule. Marriage between the groups—whites, free people of color, and slaves—was against the law in Louisiana after 1807. So instead of marriage the white man and free woman of color had an arrangement. Called *plaçage*, the arrangement was formal. The gentleman settled on payment with the girl's relatives, perhaps a house or 1,000 dollars. The girl was his mistress, and the settlement was insurance should he ever leave her. Famous for her beauty, the quadroon (1/4 black) was commonly selected for such an arrangement. She gained respect in Creole society, a house of her own, silk dresses, and jewels. Should the gentleman later decide to marry a white woman, his mistress could open her own business, run a lodging house perhaps. Her gentleman might not abandon her even if he did marry. Instead she might be treated like a second wife, the gentleman still providing for her and any children they had. The number of Creole girls involved in plaçage was mostly limited to the attractive, the educated, and the fair-skinned. Many had straight, dark hair, which they tied in a *tignon*, or kerchief, in the manner of their African ancestors. During Spanish rule, governor Estéban Miro ordered the wearing of the tignon by free Creole women to signify their lowly status and to decrease their beauty in comparison to white women. They had to accept the order, but fashioned tignons of fine silk with jewels, then tied them artfully to enhance their appearance. The Americans had these women continue their practice of wearing the tignon.

At the time of the Louisiana Purchase, the Creoles outnumbered the Americans by seven to one. The gap was quickly closing, though, as sugarcane and cotton drew in settlers in droves. Louisiana became a state in 1812. Against the rising tide of American newcomers, the Creoles fought stubbornly to defend both their language and customs. Parents refused to speak English or enroll their children in public school, educating them in France or at private Creole schools instead. Elderly Creole gentlemen met at the Café des Ameliorations, scheming to return the city to the French. In government, the younger Creole gentlemen won some control. Nine of the 15 governors from 1812 to 1860 came from the Creole sector of society. Described as the quintessential Creole gentleman, Bernard Marigny remained in the state legislature for some 28 years. Such tactics went far to preserving the Creole community, which would survive two 19th century wars.

19th century wars. The War of 1812 dragged on to 1814 before approaching New Orleans. It pitted the British against Americans who fought under the lanky, 48-year-old Kentucky general Andrew Jackson. Upsetting New Orleans whites, he commanded the city to raise a militia of Creoles of color. The militia was raised, and its men fought in the Battle of New Orleans January 8, 1815. Already the Treaty of Ghent had ended the war, but news of it failed to reach New Orleans in time. Hundreds died in the battle, Creoles and Americans uniting to win a brilliant victory. Jackson praised the militia of color warmly for their valor, though his relations with the Creoles worsened due to the events that followed.

For a time before the Civil War, the Creoles continued to control life in New Orleans. They flourished under the Americans from 1815 to 1830, outnumbering them in that year by two to one. In the next decade, however, this vigorous Latin (Franco-Hispanic) center of life in Louisiana changed into a busy American metropolis. English, not French, became the language spoken on the streets. Immigrants moved into the *Vieux Carré,* the French Quarter, and Creoles moved out.

Still, individuals continued to prosper. Many Creoles amassed wealth in real estate. Norbert Rillieux made his fortune by inventing an improved sugar-refining process. Patented in 1843, his method for evaporating liquid from sugarcane to isolate sugar would be used in modern industry. Misfortune beset all Creoles of color, though. Harsh laws had been passed against all people of color by the 1840s. The United States declared anyone with African heritage as black, relegating all shades to the same status. In response, some Creoles of color fled to Haiti. Those who remained suffered increasing restrictions. In 1855, a law required free Creoles of color to carry a permit when walking through town. Louisiana outlawed manumission, or the freeing of slaves, in 1857. To some Creoles, this presented no problem. A count in the sugar territory showed 201 Creoles and 290 Americans each owning 50 or more slaves in 1859–60.

The Creoles were divided on the issue of the Civil War. If the South won, it was thought, Creoles could maintain their special status. If the North won, there was the attractive hope of gaining freedom once everyone was treated alike. The war drew Creoles closer to other Americans through combat. In 1861, Louisiana joined the Confederacy against the North. Creoles of color supported the South, inspired by their own spirit of independence. They could not stomach the idea of English-speaking Northerners controlling their state. So they fought for the South. Some 1,500 Creoles helped defend New Orleans before it fell to Union troops in 1862. In the Southern cavalry, the Creole Chargers were part of a regiment that pursued the enemy from Baton Rouge, Louisiana, into Mississippi. The regiment surrendered in 1865. In the infantry, the Creole Guards had to surrender that year too. Of their regiment's 1,321 foot soldiers, 252 had been killed. Other Creoles meanwhile joined the Union cause.

The Civil War changed Creole life. Suddenly all blacks were free. The war had leveled differences between free people of color and slaves. There were only blacks and whites. White Creoles and white Americans banded together against the blacks. In 1873, they formed the Parti Blanc, or White League, to return white supremacy to Louisiana. It was evidence of Louisiana's transformation from three racial classes into two. Meanwhile light-skinned Creoles of Color attempted to *passen blanc* (pass into white society). They had been afraid of losing their higher status and now they feared discovery. Once consulted proudly, birth records in St. Louis Cathedral held evidence of partly African blood. Stories mounted. One man destroyed the record of his octoroon grandmother to protect his daughter. In another case, a woman sued a neighbor who said she had black blood. She showed no traces of such blood, but the evidence led the state Supreme Court to judge the neighbor correct. The woman, Toucoutou, was upbraided in song by fellow blacks (Crété 1978 p. 141).

Ah! Toucoutou, yé conin vous	Ah! Toucoutou, they're wise to you
Vous cé tin morico	You're just a nigger wench:
Na pas savon qui tracé blanc	There is no soap so white, for true,
Pou´ blanchi vous lapo.	You're sooty skin to blench.

While the war created an identity crisis for Creoles, it cast them into positions of leadership among freedmen, too. Creoles, unlike slaves, had education and some experience with freedom before the war. Given these advantages, they fought for the vote in Louisiana, helped form its Republican party, and contributed to a new state constitution. Four Creoles served as state senators between 1868 and 1888. A refugee from Haiti, Dr. Louis C. Roudanez, published a newspaper, the *New Orleans Tribune*. Never before were there such opportunities. Creoles of color were welcome in schools—New Orleans University, Straight University, Southern University, and Leland College.

Freedom was sweet but brief. New segregation laws sent blacks back to their own schools in the late 19th century. A group of Creoles formed the *Comité des Citoyens* (Citizens' Committee) to fight the new laws. One member, Homère Plessy, protested a law requiring blacks to ride special street and railway cars. The Supreme Court ruled against him in *Plessy v. Ferguson*. Handed down in 1896, the ruling made it legal to separate races in public places as long as the facilities were equal. An era of Jim Crow laws began (see AFRICAN AMERICANS). How did the Creoles of color react to segregation? Some moved out of the South, rejecting black life there. They settled in the North and passed as whites if their skin was light. Others migrated to California or Sonora, Mexico. In short, they joined white society or integrated with black Americans. The majority remained in Louisiana, facing discrimination as Southern blacks.

Change. From 1910 to 1939, Creoles changed neighborhoods. They left the French Quarter, or *Vieux Carré* (Old Square). Moving uptown or scattering into other parts of the city, they also began to speak more English than French. They mostly withdrew from politics, becoming active again before World War II, along with other American blacks. After the War, Creoles joined blacks in the fight for black rights. Creoles began to surface in the NAACP (National Association for the Advancement of Colored People) and CORE (Congress of Racial Equality). Creole lawyers defended civil rights suits. Meanwhile, more people migrated. Some 20,000 Creoles and blacks moved to Los Angeles, California, in the 1940s and 50s, to an area there that became known as little New Orleans. Back in New Orleans, the heightened pride of black Americans inspired Creoles to look at their own heritage. Citizens of the 1960s recognized their first home, the old French Quarter, as the heart of the city. City planners worked to preserve houses and to revive the Quarter's early spirit.

There is a saying that old traditions die hard. In the case of Creole concern with skin color, the saying seems apt. A 1970 law in Louisiana claimed anyone with 1/32 black blood was black. In 1982, 48-year-old Susie Phipps went to court to have herself declared white. Phipps' case revealed the injustice of the law itself, so in 1983 it was repealed. The new generation of Creoles takes pride in being black, even those who could pass for white. In New Orleans, high-school students call themselves black, not Creole. It seems the people *are* blending into larger society. Yet they maintain a Creole identity due to traditions kept alive to the present.

Culture Today

The term *Creole* now refers mostly to people of French or Spanish and African descent in Louisiana. The label is used loosely today, though, even by Creoles. Rather than people's heritage, it may refer to their speech or looks.The vast majority of today's 100,000 Creoles descend from Creoles of color. In 1976, an estimate of white Creoles suggested a population of 5,000. Physically, white Creoles tend to have milky or light olive skin, pitch black hair, and a short stature. Black Creoles may have a mix of features—dark skin and straight hair or curly hair and fair skin. The Creole beauty grew famous for her mysterious, deep-set eyes.

Business. Creoles now hold positions in many different fields from insurance to law and entertainment. Once they were confined to certain jobs. Reputed for high-quality work, the free men and women of color were skilled craftspeople. They excelled as artisans. Men became barbers, shoemakers, and tailors. Women worked as hairdressers, seamstresses, and midwives. Turning their homes into small factories, families rolled cigars. Even Creole slaves performed skilled labor; owners rented them out by the month or year and they earned money for themselves by working overtime. In the early 20th century, oil refining and rubber manufacture drew Creoles to Texas in search of jobs. The jobs were new, but in the tradition of skilled Creole labor.

In New Orleans today, Creoles of color prefer jobs that require more training. Still associated with them are fields they once controlled: carpentry, plastering, cabinetmaking, cigar manufacturing. Men become construction workers; women take jobs in clothing and cigar factories. However, young Creoles aspire to jobs in the professions. An 1850 survey showed that most of the men became carpenters. In a 1961 survey, Creoles ranked *priest* as a first job choice, *doctor* as second, and *carpenter* as twelfth. The skilled craft, carpentry, had moved down in the spectrum. As for white Creoles today, many find jobs in education. They became planters, lawyers, doctors, priests, educators, military officers, or clerks in the past, rejecting jobs that would require them to work with their hands. When poverty forced white Creole women to do hand sewing after the Civil War, they insisted on working at home to avoid being seen.

Home life. Creole living quarters have ranged from the simple raised cottage to the great plantation house. Some of the early mansions have been restored. Originally they were long, low structures with wood and brick frames. Stuccoed walls in yellow or white were topped by a sloping roof, and there were covered balconies. Houses stood above ground level to escape the murky delta. Inherited from the Spanish was a taste for simple, somber furnishing. The Great House had a drawing room for social occasions and a sitting room for the family. Along with brick fireplaces, the rooms had wooden floors covered with straw matting and simple mahogany or perhaps walnut furniture. In each bedroom was a canopy bed with a large mirrored armoire (cabinet). The huge dining room was equipped with silverware, china, and crystal for entertaining guests. A two- to four-room cabin sheltered two families of Creole slaves. When the plantations were subdivided after the Civil War, blocks of houses appeared. Whites lived on blocks by the old mansion, blacks by the slave cabins. Since the two areas were close by, to some degree the neighborhood was racially integrated.

Different Creole house styles have appeared inside the city. First occupied by Creoles, the French Quarter of New Orleans is 100 blocks with various buildings. Creoles built their finest hotels, townhouses, cafés, and shops here. Famous for its lacy iron balconies, the brick townhouse stood one to three stories high with a colored stuccoed front. Again the ground floor was often raised above street level. Creoles also built low brick and wood houses in the Quarter, and simple plankwood cottages. A typical house would have two front rooms with French glass doors that opened onto the sidewalks. In the Quarter, too, buildings are now being restored. Creoles, though, have moved uptown and elsewhere. Now many families occupy contemporary-style living quarters. The homes are generally modest, since there are less than a dozen upper-class Creole families left in New Orleans today.

Family life has been central to Creole survival. Extremely close-knit, Creole families regarded it as their duty to shelter widowed cousins or orphaned relatives. The family's master was the father, a loving parent and generous husband. No matter what other relationships he had in his life, he ate meals at home and brought his wife to the theater and balls. Plantation owners gave their sons bachelor quarters near the main house, small octagonal structures two stories high. They entertained women here, marrying within their own class. As for race, white Creoles did not marry Creoles of color. Marriage between the races was against Louisiana law from 1807 to 1972, except for a brief period after the Civil War.

A Creole wife was expected to devote herself to the family. Before the Civil War, she often had eight to ten children. Young women began their search for a husband by spending an evening at the *Théâtre d'Orléans*. Young men in the audience surveyed the women and requested her father's permission to call on the girl of their choice. It was common for middle-aged men to marry girls in their teens. An example is 60-year old Don Andrés de Almonester who married 16-year-old Louise de la Ronde. During the engagement, an older female chaperoned the couple. The father gave the man a dowry, as much as 40,000 dollars. Before the ceremony, the man presented his fiancée with a wedding basket—lacework (a fan, handkerchiefs), a cashmere shawl, and jewels. Weddings took place at St. Louis Cathedral in the late afternoon.

Some customs of the past continue in family life today. Now the Creoles have debutante balls for young ladies to come out into society and begin their search for a husband. Families are still large, but many mothers work. In the immediate family are parents, children, and possibly a grandparent or an aunt. Family members are close among themselves and with relatives. As for newborns, they are welcomed at christenings with feasting and dancing. Creole hospitality extends to strangers too. The people in general are described as a lively, warmhearted group.

Food. Spicy and well-seasoned, Creole cooking is a mix of French, Spanish, African, and Chocktaw Indian elements. *Gombo*, a stewlike soup, is the most original Creole dish. The gombo (okra plant) is its basis and it can include just about any meat or seafood—ham, oyster, chicken, crabs. Gombo is thickened with *filé*, or powdered sassafras leaf, and served on dry rice. As a soup, it serves as a first course. Gombo, crawfish tails, roast capon, fried artichoke, green salad, and ground pecan cake with cream make an old-style meal. For beverages, coffee and cognac are served. Loaves of French bread accompany Creole dishes. Other specialties are turtle soup, bouillabaisse, and *jambalaya* (smoked bacon, shrimp, crabs, onions, ham, tomatoes, rice, and red pepper). Jambalaya has been especially favored by people of the Mississippi Delta. Among the poor, rice and red beans is a common meal.

Religion. White or black, Creoles are Roman Catholics. Women traditionally attend Church faithfully, while men do so sparingly. Much has been made of the voodoo religion in Louisiana. Some of the refugees from Haiti brought along voodoo, a cult that combines Catholic and African beliefs. Voodoo was rejected by most Creoles, though, who remained staunchly Catholic. Two Creole women, Sainté Dédé and Marie Laveau, became famous voodoo leaders, but they were the exception. Still strong Catholics, the people continue to consecrate major events in church and to educate their children in church schools.

Education. From the start, Creoles supported private education. They preferred tutors or French schools. Gentlemen's sons frequently attended universities in France, where they studied medicine after graduation. Back in Louisiana, church schools taught French history, manners, embroidery, and music more often than science. Ursuline nuns often trained the girls; Jesuit priests, the boys. Educated in separate schools, the students learned to become young gentlemen and ladies. As for college, many of the parents felt it lured their children away from Creole life. Their attitude to higher education has changed. Creoles still frequent private schools, but they now view college as highly desirable. Located in New Orleans, St. Augustine High School has a student body made up largely of black Creoles. Some 90 percent of its graduates in recent years continue on to college. A school that educates black Catholics in New Orleans, Xavier University has primarily been attended by Creoles of color. Over the years, their level of education has risen and its focus has changed. Now students prepare for professions in larger America, not roles in Creole society. Classes are taught in English, not French, though it is a school subject.

Language. English entered Louisiana along with the Americans in 1803, but the Creoles continued to speak French. They clung to the language for over a century, finally adopting English after World War I. Still in their speech, however, is a sprinkling of French words. *Bamboucher*, "to have a good time," surfaces whenever Creoles gather for a *bon temps*, or good time. In early Louisiana, there were three varieties of French—standard French, Cajun, and Louisiana Creole. The Creoles spoke only standard French.

Cajun was a French dialect brought to Louisiana by the Cajun people from Nova Scotia. Also known as Gombo or Congo, Louisiana Creole was spoken by African slaves. It grew from their need to communicate with other slaves and slaveowners. Originally they spoke many different African languages. To communicate, the slaves created a simplified French. They shortened sentences, discarding some words and changing others (*monsieur* became *michié*). African terms entered into the language, making it an Afro-French dialect. In short, it became a *creole* (the word *creole* sometimes means "a language that grows from two other languages"). So soft and musical were the sounds of this new language that lower class whites adopted it and some words crept into upper class speech. For example, *Gombo*, which came to mean "mixture," was used like *Louisiana Creole* as a name for this Afro-French language. Curiously, the people who spoke Louisiana Creole were not, in fact, the Creole people. White and black Creoles spoke standard French. Devoted to the language, they tried to speak it as perfectly as possible. Creoles now speak standard English. While they feel strongly connected to blacks today, they mostly avoid speaking Black English.

Clothing. The Creole preference for proper standard English echoes their attachment to standard French in the past. In both cases, the people show concern for proper behavior. This also influences the way they dress. For years, their attire was formal. Young men wore jackets and ties, young women white gloves and hats. Gentlemen, too, wore gloves and hats. By day, women wore cotton or muslin gowns, changing to satin and silk by night. They carried the ever-present fan, made of feathers, lace, ivory with pearl, or palm leaves. Although these habits have largely been abandoned, many older white Creoles continue to dress quite formally. Young people today wear blue jeans in the fashion of other black and white children.

Holidays—Mardi Gras. Black and white Creoles appear in formal clothing at Mardi Gras balls. Meaning "fat Tuesday," *Mardi Gras* is the day before the serious religious period Lent. It ends the season Carnival, a time of fervent merrymaking. By 1766, Mardi Gras was already a custom in Louisiana, but the celebration took shape over the following years. A group of young Creoles staged the first parade in 1827. Having just returned from Paris, they recalled festivities there, banging pots, singing, and blowing horns as they marched through New Orleans in outlandish costumes. Over a decade later, in 1839, floats became part of the parade. These have become the public parts of the holiday that anyone can see.

Mardi Gras is also a private affair. Crowds watch parades, but the people of New Orleans attend private balls. From early times, balls have enjoyed wide popularity in New Orleans. The first for free blacks was the Quadroons' or Blue Ribbon Ball. Held in public ballrooms from 1809 onward, it was attended by women of color and white men. Black men appeared only as servants or musicians. The music was set to French dances—the waltz, the cotillion, the quadrille.

Balls for black Creoles have changed since then. Today some 20 balls are held for them annually. They are exclusive events—only the invited attend. Each is organized by a social club, a Mardi Gras organization known as a *krewe*. Formed in 1894, the Original Illinois Club is the oldest krewe for Creoles of color. Its founders were skilled craftsmen, then the highest class of the group. A more generally black krewe is the African-named group Zulus. Several balls present debutantes. With an escort, they walk onto the dance floor and curtsy one by one. The balls begin on King's Day, which features a King Cake. Hidden inside is a bean or doll. Whoever gets the slice that contains it becomes king or queen of the next week's party.

Arts. The early Creoles had a passion for entertainment from dancing to gambling to theater. Beginning in 1791, a small acting troupe from Haiti performed plays first in outdoor tents and later at Saint-Philippe Theatre. Well-loved and in constant use was the French Opera House with its 805 seats. Free people of color owned boxes at the Opera House, too. In short, the Creoles were patrons of the arts.

Probably the most renowned Creole artists were musicians. There were some writers. In 1843, Armand Lanusse started a magazine, *L'Album Littéraire;* he himself wrote one of its short stories, a melodrama about a beautiful quadroon. Then came an anthology of Creole poems *Les Cenelles*, or *Holly Berries*, in 1845. Both works were by Creoles of color, among the first black writings to be published in North America. A white observer of Creole society, George Washington Cable wrote *Old Creole Days*, a book of stories about the people. He wrote about disreputable characters and so was deeply resented by the living Creoles. People everywhere read his stories and thought all Creoles behaved in an unseemly way. Noteworthy in Creole folklore are proverbs and metaphors, sometimes adopted from slaves. A man who spent too much time at home was *un encadrement*, a doorframe. A mother who sang her children's praises drew the comment *Tout macaque trouve son petit joli*, or every monkey thinks its young one pretty. (Hearn 1885, p.36)

Music has long been considered an acceptable career. Beginning as a predominantly French sound in Louisiana, Creole music became a French, an African, and a West Indies blend. A funeral tradition developed. En route to the cemetery, a marching band would play solemn music. The journey back was accompanied by upbeat, lighthearted tunes in keeping with the belief that the departed was now in the promised land. Called ragtime, the music and its improvisations moved to dance halls and cafés. Credit for helping to produce the first jazz music goes to Creoles, who merged French love songs with black musical sounds such as the blues. Besides Jelly Roll

Morton, notable Creole jazz artists have included Kid Ory, Sidney Bechet, and Alphonse Picou.

Creole la-las, or zydeco, can mean a style of music, a syncopated two-step dance, or the event where they take place. The music is a mixture of Cajun, Afro-American, and Afro-Caribbean sounds. For instruments, the musicians use an accordion and steel vest (a rub board, or *frottoir*). Amédé Ardoin and Adam Fotenot are legendary Creole accordionists whom people have walked miles to hear. Clifton Chenier's band added Rhythm and Blues to the music after World War II, gaining wide recognition. In the 1990s, Queen Ida and the Bon Temps continue the Louisiana sound of the la-las and its house parties, which have grown and moved to social halls.

For More Information

See these reading materials:

Crété, Liliane. *Daily Life in Louisiana 1815-1830.* Translated by Patrick Gregory. Baton Rouge: Louisiana State University Press, 1981.

Haskins, James. *The Creoles of Color of New Orleans.* New York: Thomas Y. Crowell, 1975.

Judge, Joseph. "New Orleans and Her River." *National Geographic,* February 1971, pp. 151-187.

DAKOTA (SIOUX)
(duh ko´ ta sue)

A group of American Indians who once dominated
the Great Plains; commonly called Sioux.

Population: 64,000 (1985).
Location: United States (Minnesota, Missouri, Nebraska, North and
South Dakota, Montana, Wisconsin, and Wyoming); Canada (Alberta,
Saskatchewan, and Manitoba).
Language: Siouan languages, English.

Geographical Setting

Once they roamed over the Northern Plains.
Now the Sioux own 16 reservations in the North.

Not native to the Great Plains area, the Sioux moved there from the
Great Lakes region. Spreading across the Plains, the Sioux formed three
regional subgroups. The largest subdivision, the Tetons, lived on the
western Plains. Smaller Sioux subdivisions occupied territory on the middle
Plains and eastern Plains. The Sioux tribes flourished through the mid-
1800s, dominating life on the northern Plains. At their height, their territory
stretched from the Rocky Mountains in the west to the Mississippi River in
the east and from the Arkansas-Red River divide in the south almost to the
Saskatchewan River in the north. By the late 1800s, disputes with whites
had severely reduced this territory. Most of today's Sioux live on 16 U.S.
reservations: eight in South Dakota; two in North Dakota; four in Minnesota;

one in Nebraska; and one in Montana (shared with the Assiniboines). Canada has 15 Sioux reserve lands: five in Alberta; five in Saskatchewan; and five in Manitoba.

Historical Background

Migration and differentiation. Before 1735, the Sioux occupied permanent villages, hunting forest animals and farming on a limited basis. There were no horses northeast of the Missouri River, where they lived. Tribal warfare and scarcity of game forced them west across the river around the mid-1700s. By 1796, the Sioux had adopted horses and guns, though they still used bows and arrows for hunting, since muskets proved difficult to reload on horseback. Contact with whites came to a climax in the next century. The Sioux would keep their own records of forthcoming events, using *Winter Count*. This was a Sioux method of painting figures on deer skin to record momentous events.

In 1804, the explorers Meriwether Lewis and William Clark encountered the Sioux in South Dakota. The Louisiana Purchase in 1807 brought more whites into Sioux territory. Both the War of Independence and the War of 1812 found most Sioux supporting the British against the Americans. A treaty in 1815 finally declared peace between the United States and the Dakota, or Sioux Indians. Murderous violence ensued, making this peace treaty meaningless. The first half of the 1800s saw the rise of the Sioux, their power and wealth increasing as they adopted the horse and gun. Many bands moved onto the Plains and developed a nomadic lifestyle in pursuit of the buffalo herds. Intertribal warfare increased. Sioux bands raided other tribes for territory and horses, defeating Kiowa, Cheyenne, and Pawnee Indians between 1805 and 1843. The raiding led to a value system in which status depended on defeating enemies. It also extended Sioux territory.

Seven nations of Sioux spread across the western, middle, and eastern Plains. On the eastern Plains was a collection of Sioux nations known as the Santee (the Mdewakanton, Wahpekute, Sisseton, and Wahpeton). They called themselves *Dakota* after their dialect of the Sioux language. Tribes in the middle Plains were the Yankton and the Yanktonai. Their dialect uses an *n* instead of the *d* of the Dakota, so they called themselves *Nakota*. Farther west and to the south lived the largest group, the Teton. In their language, the *d* of the Santee is replaced by an *l*, so they called themselves *Lakota*. These were the seven Sioux nations, or council fires. The Teton were subdivided into still smaller groups, including the Brulé, Blackfoot, Hunkpapa, Miniconjou, Oglala, Sans Arc, and Two Kettle.

Food, clothing, and shelter. For the numerous Teton Sioux, life revolved around the horse, the buffalo, and trade. The Teton ate buffalo meat, made buffalo skin robes, and used the hide to construct portable tipis for homes. As they followed the buffalo, the people would set up temporary villages in two sets of concentric circles. Men hunted buffalo, then brought them into camp, where they were transformed into goods. Stripping carcasses of meat, women prepared *pemmican*, a food made by pounding together dried meat, melted fat, bone marrow, and dried cherries, including the pits. From the beast's hide, they designed not only buffalo robes but also tipi liners. Men sometimes painted lifelike designs inside the robe, while women decorated garments with geometric designs. At first, the women used quills, but in time beadwork supplanted the quills. Women used beaded designs to decorate dresses and moccasins. In men's wear, the shirts and leggings had moccasins. Men tied their hair into two braids they kept behind the ears. War bonnets had meaning. There was a long trail of eagle feathers on a headdress called the shave horn war bonnet, for example. It symbolized the collective deeds of men who followed a certain war leader. Through prowess in battle, a warrior earned the right to wear the bonnet.

Family life. In Sioux society, the group was more important than the individual. From birth, children learned not to cry because the sound might reveal the whereabouts of the band to an enemy. Babies received a second set of parents at birth, relatives or friends of the natural parents. In infancy, a boy was cared for by his second mother so that his birth mother would not dote on him at the expense of her relationship with her husband.

Boys did not address their mother or sister directly after they reached the age of seven. At puberty, they underwent a ceremony for passage into manhood. Wearing a breechcloth and moccasins, they were escorted to a barren hill. They would neither eat nor drink, fasting to strip away the superficial and to prepare for a vision. During his fast, the future war leader Crazy Horse had a vision that told him he would not die because of a bullet. He would grow into a great warrior. First named Curley, Crazy Horse inherited this last name from his father after distinguishing himself in battle.

From age six or seven, girls lived under the watchful eye of an old woman. Even when they encountered boys on the water path, an old one was near. Her presence, however, would not prevent a boy from playfully shooting an arrow through a girl's waterskin, or the girl from chasing him and rubbing his face in the dirt. At puberty, Sioux maidens had ceremonies too. They retreated to an isolated lodge, then joined a feast to celebrate their passage into womanhood.

A young man moved into a young woman's tipi to form a family. They started the household with a bed, a cookstove, and an Old One. It was Sioux custom for every household to include an older person, who respected the couple enough not to give unasked-for advice. If the couple was unhappy, divorce was possible. Since the tipi belonged to the woman, she would simply throw out her husband's belongings to sever the relationship. A man could also throw away his wife, but more ceremonially at a dance. He would toss a "give-away stick" toward another man, thereby appointing him to take care of the wife for a time.

Once Crazy Horse fled with another man's wife, a love he had courted in his boyhood. Her husband shot Crazy Horse, and the whole incident tore at the unity of his tribe (the Oglala). Only wounded, Crazy Horse brought back the woman, his father gently reminding him that a warrior should never place his own happiness above the common good.

Societies. The Sioux created many societies that took responsibility for maintaining order, training warriors, and so forth. Among the Oglala, for example, there were medicine societies, a chief's society, and the camp police. Among women's societies was one for skillful tipi makers and another for expert quill workers. Not everyone belonged to society. Still, these societies had enough members to keep order in a Sioux community and to provide for its welfare. While the camp police might stop younger men from conducting an unauthorized raid, the chief's society cared for the tribe's poor, especially its widows and orphans.

The societies not only organized life in the community, they also perpetuated Sioux values. Proving oneself by enduring deadly danger was a common value. Reserved for older, unmarried boys, the Kit-fox society had its members sing the following verse (Lowie 1954, p. 101):

I am a Fox.
I am supposed to die.
If there is anything difficult,
If there is anything dangerous,
That is mine to do.

The Sun Dance. The Sioux thought all living things were spiritually connected. They called this idea *Wakan Tanka*. The world, it was believed, began in harmony, and humans were obligated to maintain this harmony. Shaman, or medicine men, communed with the spirits, and the people themselves went on vision quests to receive spiritual guidance. They thought it important to heed the visions. Otherwise, the sacred powers would be offended. The Sioux defined *Wakan Tanka* as the sum total of all sacred powers. They organized these powers into four divisions—Sun, Sky, Earth, and Rock. Regarded as the superior power, the Sun controlled human courage, strength, generosity, and loyalty.

The Sun Dance occurred in many Plains Indian societies. It was a time when the roaming bands of a people like the Sioux gathered together for ceremony and trade. Volunteering to participate, men performed the dance. The volunteers sought a cure for a relative's illness, perhaps, or a vision that would solve an ongoing problem. The ceremony itself rested on the notion that all things come forth through hardship. Sacrifice, it was thought, would right disharmony in the world, and the dancers would win favor from the spirits in the future.

The ritual took several days. It was a four-part ceremony, including the capture of the warriors, skewering the warriors, their captivity, and deliverance from captivity. It was considered both an honor and an obligation to perform the Sun Dance. Captives were tied up, and subjected to voluntary torture. Inserted into the chest or back, wooden skewers pierced their bodies. Leather ropes were fastened to the skewers and the top of the Sun Lodge, leaving the dancers dangling in the air until the skewers broke their flesh free and the ritual ended.

Chief Sitting Bull performed the dance in 1876, gazing directly at the sun all the while. He had a vision in which he foresaw many soldiers falling upside down into a Sioux camp. A short while later, battle broke out between warriors and United States soldiers in the valley of Little Bighorn.

Sioux vs. whites. The Sioux earned a reputation as fierce warriors. Their primary objectives in battle were revenge, horse stealing, and personal glory. More important than killing an enemy was "counting coup," that is, touching the living enemy with the hand or a special stick. It was also important that the raiding party lose no men. Scalping was common, especially among the Teton. The warriors believed that taking an enemy's scalp killed his soul, thereby preventing it from reaching the spirit world.

Though there was intertribal warfare, the Sioux did not mount strong resistance against whites until they came onto the plains and began killing the buffalo. Thereafter, the fighting grew furious, with the Sioux engaging in some of the most brutal white-Indian wars of the late 1800s. Many whites crossed the Plains during the California Gold Rush. Confrontations erupted, leading to intervention by the U.S. military. Meeting with the army in "councils," the Sioux signed several treaties. The Fort Laramie Treaty of 1851, for example, guaranteed safety to travelers on the Oregon Trail in exchange for promises made to the Indians. Such treaties were mostly ignored in the coming decades.

The next 25 years found the Sioux and whites almost continually at war. Most famous during this period was Red Cloud's War (1865–1868). Using guerrilla tactics, Red Cloud harassed U.S. soldiers for a few years before the army admitted defeat and removed some illegal forts they had on Sioux territory. Chief Red Cloud made a new treaty that said his band's land could be entered only by the Indians' consent. Red Cloud then led the band onto a reservation. Disagreeing with the move, some warriors fled to the hills.

Little Bighorn. Two chiefs, Sitting Bull and Crazy Horse, led Sioux who refused to give up the nomadic life. Their final battles became the War for the Black Hills. In 1876, the discovery of gold drew a rush of white miners to the Black Hills. The army ordered the Indians out of the region where gold had been found. They refused. In a series of eight battles, the issue resolved itself.

The Indians won the Battle of Little Bighorn. Full of self-confidence, General Custer misjudged their strength. He pitted about 600 U.S. soldiers against some 1,500 Sioux and Cheyenne warriors. Crazy Horse and his companion Gall fought with a vengeance. The soldiers had killed five members of Gall's family early in the battle, which filled him with fury. He began killing his enemies with a hatchet.

Custer himself led about 210 of the men against the Sioux, but was defeated in about an hour. The Sioux victory was temporary. Within a year the Army had forced most of the Sioux onto reservations. One band after another was overpowered and forced to surrender. They were placed on South Dakota's Rosebud Reservation under Spotted Tail or on the Pine Ridge Reservation under Red Cloud.

Crazy Horse surrendered and died in 1877. As his boyhood vision had foretold, he was not killed by a bullet but, rather, was stabbed by a bayonet during an attempt to escape prison. His death became a picture record, part of an 1877 Winter Count. Sitting Bull and his band fled to Canada, then returned and surrendered in 1881. The power of the Sioux was broken.

Reservation agreements provided food rations for ten years. During this time, the

Crazy Horse dies.

reservation superintendent encouraged the Sioux to adopt white-style frame houses and send their children to boarding schools. The authority of old leaders was undermined. New leaders who reported to the superintendent gained control, and the tribal councils were ignored. The ten years of food rations ended during the harsh winter of 1889. Crops failed, and the buffalo were nearly extinct. Suffering mounted. Threatened by starvation, the Sioux Indian bands stood ready for any promise of relief.

Traditional dress of the Sioux.

The Ghost Dance. In 1888, Wovoka, a Paiute Indian prophet, began preaching about a new dance that would bring back the prosperity of the Indians. Called the Ghost Dance, it was a vision quest involving men, women, and children. They were to join hands in a circle and dance, singing songs all night for as many as five consecutive nights. Wovoka taught that the Indians had to live in harmony with each other, avoiding the ways of the whites. In the end he said, the dance would restore their precious natural resources, especially the bison. At the same time, dead Indians would be resurrected and a new happy existence for all Indians would follow.

In the fall of 1889, the poverty-stricken Pine Ridge reservation sent a delegation to Wovoka to learn about the Ghost Dance so that it could relieve their suffering. The delegation, Short Bull and Kicking Bear, visited a holy man, who showed them an image of their departed relatives and then explained the vision (Erdoes and Ortiz 1984, pp. 481–482).

> "You have seen it," he told them, "the new Land I'm bringing. The earth will roll up like a blanket with all that bad white man's stuff, the fences and railroads and mines and telegraph poles; and underneath will be our old-young Indian earth with all our relatives come to life again."

Short Bull and Kicking Bear returned home and began performing a dance to roll up the earth and resurrect the dead. They added a dimension to the dance, Ghost Shirts that they said would make them immune to the white man's bullets. Suspecting the Ghost Dance was the beginning of an uprising, the U.S. Indian agent prohibited it. Tribal leaders endorsed the dance, though, and it continued. In the winter of 1890, as conditions worsened, more Sioux began to dance. They asked Sitting Bull to join them. Fearing what would happen if the war chief came, the army ordered his arrest. Sitting Bull, his 17-year-old son, and six warriors were killed while resisting this arrest.

Wounded Knee. The army also ordered the arrest of Big Foot, a proponent of the dance. He began to lead his band to the Pine Ridge Reservation to join Red Cloud and the other chiefs who wanted peace. Met on the way by remnants of the Seventh Cavalry, Big Foot was forced to surrender. He was ordered to camp at Wounded Knee Creek, and the next morning a detachment of the cavalry entered the camp to disarm the Sioux. A gun discharged into the air (some say Black Fox shot at a soldier), and fighting broke out. The army outside the camp began firing heavy artillery. In the ensuing massacre an estimated 350 Sioux met their deaths The investigation that followed concluded that there had been no real threat of a Sioux uprising.

Shifting government policy. From 1890 on, the Sioux fell victim to shifting government policy. First they were confined to reservations, next the reservations were broken up, then the government supported reservations again.

In 1887, the Dawes Act broke up reservations and allotted parcels to individuals. The government purchased land left over after a tribes' territory was allotted. Ranching worked for a few Indians, but many more became entangled in land deals with whites. The Indians were encouraged to earn money by leasing their lands to whites. When cattle prices fell abruptly, whites failed to pay for their leases, and the Indians could only sell their parcels to survive. Once the land was sold, they had nothing left. The Indian Reorganization Act of 1934 put an end to further allotments. New reservations were formed.

Recent history. Following World War II, in which many Sioux distinguished themselves, the Sioux nations experienced new threats against their lands. The Pick Sloan Plan, a government project, resulted in the building of dams on several Sioux reservations. The project destroyed the Indians' timberland and 75 percent of their wild game supply, and it uprooted 600 Sioux families. Completed in 1966, the dams eliminated a self-sufficient economy in which the Indians could provide for themselves by living off the land. They shifted to a cash economy, and began to participate strongly in American politics. Helen L. Peterson and, later, Vine Deloria, Jr., led the National Congress of American Indians, a movement that united different Indian peoples to tackle their common problems. Sioux Indians joined the Poor People's March on Washington, D.C., and Russell Means formed the American Indian Movement (AIM), an organization for Indians living off reservations.

In 1973, Russell Means developed a protest on the site of the original Wounded Knee massacre. About 250 Indians protested local housing, a recent murder, and poor reservation conditions. For 71 days they held both the site and the nation's attention. Their aim was to force the government to honor its 1868 treaty with the Teton, which had made all of western South Dakota a Sioux reservation. The siege ended with two Indians dead and few concrete accomplishments, but tremendous national publicity. One especially tragic result was the murder of Anna Mae Aquash, a Micmac Indian supporter (see MICMAC). However, the incident did bring some benefits. After Wounded Knee, Indians everywhere demanded more control over their own affairs.

Culture Today

Reservation life. Early reservation life provided little satisfaction. Tipis were replaced by log houses, and then by prefabricated housing. Meanwhile, the Sioux had virtually no control over their own destinies. The Bureau of

Indian Affairs drafted tribal constitutions and approved all tribal decisions. Then, in the 1950s, the government encouraged Indians to relocate off the reservations again. In the 1970s it finally accepted their right to self-management and self-government. Many of the Sioux Indians had remained on reservations during the 20-year interim.

Most of the Sioux continue to live on reservations. The lands are a combination of tribal holdings and parcels that were allotted to individuals under the Dawes Act. The sizes of the reservations vary. While the Rosebud Reservation spans only 978,230 acres, Pine Ridge covers 2,778,000 acres. Another variable is tribal government. A 22-member council governs at Rosebud; Pine Ridge has a 32-member council. In dealings with the United States, the council's president is regarded as head of the tribe.

Sioux life is similar to that of other Americans. The Indians eat the same foods, though they maintain some early habits. There are Sioux Indians who still eat choke cherries and dried corn, for example. Except on special occasions, the people dress like other Americans, mostly in blue jeans and t-shirts. They train for jobs and seek employment like everyone else in the country.

Cattle ranching and meat packing are two of the businesses at Pine Ridge, and Rosebud has a factory that manufactures kitchen cabinets. Most reservation business owners are whites, however. Some Sioux have been trained as carpenters, plumbers, welders, or electricians, but these laborers often cannot find work. Unemployment is high. In 1969, it reached 50 percent at Rosebud and Pine Ridge and has since risen to 80 percent on some Sioux reservations.

A reservation earns a collective income from tribal enterprises and from land leases. On Pine Ridge, the income is about 570,000 dollars annually, earned mostly by grazing permits. It is a meager sum in relation to tribal needs. Pine Ridge reported 12,000 Indian residents in 1980. Dividing this population into its income provides the tribe with less than 50 dollars a year for each of its members. Recent U.S. budget reductions have worsened the situation. At Pine Ridge, lack of funds reduced the hospital staff and medical care in the late 1980s. Some 75 percent of the residents on the reservation suffered from eye problems that went untreated.

Arts. Traditional art forms are a source of income for the Sioux. Reservation life has given women an opportunity to perfect old designs and to create new items, such as intricately beaded baby cradles. Among individuals, Sioux painter Oscar Howe has won the Waite Phillips Trophy for outstanding contributions to American Indian Art. Howe explained Sioux picture writing. It occurred during a ceremony in which a narrator would describe a historical event while an artist painted it in front of an audience. Contact with whites early in this century gave Sioux artists new ideas and motifs to use in their work. In 1939, Henry Standing Bear, a Sioux chief, asked the sculptor Korczak Ziolkowski to carve a statue of Crazy Horse in honor of Indian heroes. Ziolkowski agreed, and, in 1947, began work on Thunderhead Mountain in South Dakota's Black Hills. He decided to carve the entire 600-foot granite mountain into a monument of Crazy Horse on horseback with his arm outstretched and finger pointing. Ziolkowski worked until his death in 1982. His family then continued the carving, which they predict will be finished in 2,150.

In literature, two widely-read Sioux authors have been Dee Brown, who wrote *Bury My Heart at Wounded Knee*, and Vine Deloria, Jr., who wrote *Custer Died for Your Sins*. Such books have given voice to past generations, revealing wrongs that were inflicted on American Indian peoples.

Religion. Most of today's Sioux have adopted Christian beliefs, but some maintain the old religious customs. First outlawed in 1881, the Sun Dance, skewers and all, was openly revived in 1958, and continues in the present day. Dancers are not as universally admired by the Sioux as they once were, now that many have adopted Christianity. Traditionalists still regard the Black Hills as the sacred home of Wakan Tanka; the hills also remain the burial ground of their dead and the place where visions originate. The old quest for a vision, *hanble cey* ("crying for a dream"), continues today. To obtain such a vision, a few Sioux have formed the peyote cult, which features the chewing of the hallucinogenic plant peyote. They belong to the Native American Church. Many more Sioux belong to various Protestant and Catholic churches. Old symbols join new ones in these churches. At Pine Ridge, images of the peace pipe, the buffalo, and Jesus Christ have shared the altar.

Education and recreation. During the 1970s and '80s, the Sioux were able to gain control of the schools on their reservations. Head Start programs were set up under local control. For the first time they could teach tribal history and culture. Like other minority groups, however, the Sioux strive not only to keep their culture alive but also to equip their children with the tools that will allow them to succeed in the greater world. In the 1980s, the average level of education for adults on the Rosebud and Pine Ridge reservations was grade nine. Encouraging higher education, Oglala Lakota College opened in 1971. Females get an eagle feather at graduation; males receive a medicine wheel.

In American sports and recreation, the Santee Sioux Charles Eastman (writer, teacher, and physician) helped found the Boy Scouts of America in the early 1900s. Later in the century, an Oglala Sioux became a hero for the entire nation. Billy Mills won a gold medal in the 10,000-meter race of the 1964 Olympics after an accident during the race had placed him 20 yards behind the leader. In winning, he set a new world record.

Values. At Pine Ridge, the Red Cloud Arts and Crafts Guild teaches old techniques for drying meat and using quills and feathers for decoration. Such traditional behaviors mix with newer ones as Sioux attend college and adopt other nonnative ways. One of these new ways is working through government channels to address grievances. The Sioux lawyer Kurt Blue Dog argued before Congress in the 1980s on behalf of tribes who wanted compensation for land taken illegally. While tribes won new payment, the Sioux have disagreed about accepting it. Some of them protested their tribal government's acceptance of payment for the Black Hills, saying it would forfeit their right to that sacred region

Today's Sioux aim to materially improve the conditions under which they live without violating old values. In 1987 Wayne Ducheneaux proposed accepting high-level radioactive waste for disposal on the Cheyenne River Reservation. The U.S. government was offering large sums to any takers. The reservation rejected the proposal, citing the Sioux's long-standing devotion to the harmony of the earth. Such Indians aim to harmonize old and new ways. A current concern is how to capitalize on resources under reservation land, such as coal and oil, without destroying the earth.

For More Information

See these reading materials:

Dog, Mary Crow. *Lakota Woman.* New York: Grove Weidenfeld, 1990.

Jordan, Paul. "Ghosts on the Little Bighorn," *National Geographic,* December 1986, pp. 787-813.

Contact these organizations:

Oglala Sioux Tribe, Box H, Pine Ridge, South Dakota 57770

Rosebud Sioux Tribe, P.O. Box 430, Rosebud, South Dakota 57570.

ENGLISH AMERICANS

(ing´glish eh mer´uh kins)

Americans whose ancestors came from England.

Population: 23,748,772 (1980).
Location: United States, every region (highest proportions in Utah, New England, and the Appalachian Mountain regions).
Language: English.

Geographical Setting

Plymouth

Jamestown

Settling first in the Chesapeake Bay area, English Americans spread through New England.

Beginning in the 1600s, English men and women established colonies along the eastern coast of what would become the United States. They settled in four main areas at different stages during the colonial period: the coastal areas of present-day Virginia and Maryland (1607); Massachusetts and New England (1623); the Delaware Valley and Middle Atlantic states (1675-1725);

and the Appalachian and surrounding regions of western Virginia, Tennessee, North Carolina, and Kentucky (1700s).

Although the English continued to come to the United States in the 1800s, other immigrant groups surpassed them in numbers. Still, English laborers and farmers swelled both industrial centers of the East and communities of the ever-expanding western frontier. Some of the English established agricultural communities in Midwestern states, such as Illinois and Indiana. In the 1900s, English immigrants to the United States have favored states with large urban centers, such as Massachusetts, New York, and California.

Historical Background

Legacy of colonialism. As the first European settlers in what would later be the 13 original United States, the English established the country's cultural, commercial, religious, and legal institutions. For nearly 200 years, until American independence, steady immigration from England reinforced these institutions, despite a decrease (from 90 percent in 1690 to 49 percent in 1790) in the proportion of the population born either in England or of English descent. Dutch, German, French, and other early immigrants established communities that preserved their own old ways, thus leaving their mark on the American patchwork, but English ways provided the context into which these immigrant peoples were absorbed. For this reason, assimilation has been easier for English immigrants than for many other immigrant groups.

Jamestown and Virginia. On January 29, 1607, the English established their first colony in the new world. They called the tiny settlement Jamestown, in honor of King James I. Led by Christopher Newport, the colonists were unprepared for survival in their strange new environment. Mostly members of the English elite, they considered manual labor, such as digging, planting, cutting trees, and building, beneath them. They expected to find large amounts of gold, as the Spanish had done in Mexico, and were not equipped with strategies for survival. For food, they relied on the Indians and on supplies from England. Many perished in the first few years. Not until John Smith took command in 1609 did the settlers begin taking steps to comfortably feed and house themselves. Prosperity did not come until the late 1610s, when John Rolfe began cultivating and exporting the profitable cash crop tobacco, the high price of which attracted energetic and practical men to join the colony. The Virginia Company of London controlled the settlement until 1624, when King James dissolved the company. He made Jamestown a crown colony, to be ruled by a governor whom the king himself would appoint.

Model for the South. For the first 35 years of its existence, the colony of Virginia (which extended from present-day New York to Georgia) remained a poorly organized and rough outpost. By 1642, its population was only around 8,000, mostly young, single men with a collective reputation for unruliness. Over the next 35 years, however, during the governorship of Sir William Berkeley, a cohesive society developed that would dominate the future of the South. Berkeley, a fierce supporter of King Charles I, encouraged immigration among his fellow Royalists, many of whom came in the 1650s, after the defeat and execution (1649) of Charles I by the Puritans in the English Civil War. These defeated "cavaliers," or gentlemen soldiers, came mostly from southern England, the heartland of Charles' aristocratic support. They established large plantations on Virginia's best land, providing a model for future development in later southern colonies such as Maryland, the Carolinas, and Georgia. Their families became Virginia's ruling elite, supplying local and national leaders for generations to come. Presidents Thomas Jefferson, George Washington, and James Madison all descended from these old families, as did General Robert E. Lee.

More numerous in this period of heavy migration were those of lower social rank. Over 75 percent of the Virginia colonials came as indentured servants, agreeing to serve a term of four years labor in exchange for passage from England to America. Like the elite, people from this group came mostly from the south of England. These unskilled laborers often continued in domestic service after their terms ended. Nearly all of the servants were young men, with 96 percent between the ages of 15 and 35. Many worked off their debts in the tobacco fields of the plantation owners, who also began using black slaves brought from Africa by English ships. A plantation economy based on slave labor and a narrow range of crops—first tobacco and later tobacco and cotton—quickly developed. These crops were exported to England. Because of this economic connection, until the American Civil War England had a stronger influence on the South than on any other region in the United States. The latest English fashions, for example, were quickly adopted by the plantation-owning elite. In New England, despite the region's name, English settlers became independent sooner.

Puritans. Beginning in 1620, 13 years after the founding of Jamestown, a very different migration took place to Massachusetts and to neighboring areas in the north. Like the Virginia migration, this one was both spurred by political events in England and dominated by emigrants from a specific region. Before the Puritans overthrew the English monarchy in 1649, causing the exodus of their enemies the Royalists, they were subjected to persecution for their beliefs. Around 21,000 elected to leave England for Massachusetts during the years 1629 to 1640. This "great migration," as it is called by historians, established the core of New England's Yankee ancestry. The Puritans established the first colonies in the Northeast, founding Plymouth in 1620, Massachusetts Bay in 1630, Connecticut in 1635–1636, and Rhode Island in 1636. Although nearly every English county was represented in the new settlements, about 60 percent came from a region in the east of England, known as East Anglia.

Unlike the Virginia colonists, the Puritans came mostly in family groups and were thus more evenly balanced in terms of age and sex. Furthermore, many of these families were related to one another. Virginia immigrants had been divided into upper-class elites and lower-class servants, but the great majority of Puritan immigrants belonged to the commercial middle class. They were artisans, merchants, and prosperous farmers, many from the lively market towns of East Anglia. Very few needed to indenture themselves to pay for their passage to America.

In England, religion and politics were closely connected, for the monarch was also the head of the Anglican Church. Thus, by opposing Anglican religious practices, the Puritans also threatened the political power of the Crown. The great migration coincided with the most severe attempts of King Charles I to make them conform to Anglican practice. Although the Puritans expressed their religious ideas in political terms, those ideas were originally very personal in nature. They believed that the world was a battleground for the forces of good and evil and that life was a constant struggle—a personal struggle—to avoid being ensnared by evil. Men and women had to be constantly alert against sin to avoid eternal damnation. This harsh view of the world gave rise to a stern morality that became the hallmark of the New England Yankee, the descendant of the Puritans. An aim of the migration was to supply an environment free from the temptation of elaborate Anglican church ceremonies. Like their own ceremonies, Puritans were simple and austere.

The Puritans multiplied in the New World. From the 21,000 who had arrived by 1640, their descendants numbered 100,000 in 1700, and over one million by 1800. In the 1600s, they settled throughout southern New England, moved north and east in northern New York, Vermont, and Maine in the 1700s, and then headed west in the 1800s to found cities such as Chicago, Cleveland, Denver, Salt Lake City, and Seattle.

Backwoodsmen from the borderlands. The third contingent of settlers from England was a religious group called the Quakers, who settled in the Delaware Valley. For an account of the subculture they developed in the Valley, see QUAKERS. The fourth and last major group considered here came from northern Ireland and the border regions of northern England. After immigrating, most of them struck off into the wilderness of the Appalachian Mountains. They migrated during the 1700s, until American independence in 1776. Less ethnically homogeneous than emigrants from southern England, they were a mix of English, Scotch, and Irish. People who lived close to the border between England and Scotland were more similar to each other than to other English or Scots. The border itself had often shifted over the centuries, as the kings of England and Scotland warred against each other. To further complicate matters, many of the border people had migrated to northern Ireland, where they were called "Scotch-Irish" or "Anglo-Irish."

The border people were rough and ready, used to life under conditions of warfare and poverty. In the 1700s, social change in these regions led to widespread unrest. Landlords began to exploit their tenants ruthlessly, evicting many from their homes. Throughout the 1700s, the rural population rose up in a series of rebellions. Famine and disease added to the turmoil. Spurred by these harsh conditions, the border people fled to America, some 250,000 arriving before independence curtailed immigration. They came mostly to Philadelphia, where their size and alien ways alarmed the Quakers. Quaker leaders encouraged them to move farther inland. There, they would act as a buffer between the Quakers and the Indians.

West with the frontier. Thus, the border people of the old country became the frontiersmen of the new country, moving into the Allegheny Mountains of western Pennsylvania, the Appalachian Mountains of western Virginia, and the Blue Ridge Mountains of southern Virginia and the Carolinas. The descendents of these backwoodsmen moved with the frontier as it extended west, settling Arkansas, Missouri, Oklahoma, and Texas in the early 1800s, then pushing on to New Mexico, Arizona, and California. Some became colorful leaders, pioneers like Daniel Boone and Sam Houston. Other famous descendents of these immigrants include major political figures such as Presidents Andrew Jackson (known as "Old Hickory" for his toughness) and James Polk ("Young Hickory").

Environment and early subcultures. Regional environments played an important role in shaping the distinctive early American cultures in Virginia, New England, and the Appalachian area. In Virginia and Maryland, early settlements were clustered around the huge Chesapeake Bay. This superb natural harbor was surrounded by rich farm land and offered access to many major rivers. In all, 48 navigable rivers fed into the bay, making it possible for early Maryland and Virginia planters to load tobacco and other export goods straight onto cargo ships from their plantations.

The warm climate offered a long growing season. However, the heat and humidity also made the many shallow swamps breeding grounds for diseases like typhoid, dysentery, and malaria. Death rates among the early colonists soared, encouraging reliance on African slaves. These factors combined with the settlers' attitudes to create the Virginia plantation society (see AFRICAN AMERICANS), which in turn influenced the entire social structure of the South.

In New England, a short growing season and land of inconsistent quality dictated that settlers establish small family farms rather than large plantations. New England was colder in the 1600s than it is today—the Puritans arrived during a period that meteorologists call the "little ice age," when rivers froze solid and violent blizzards were common. The cold inhibited disease among the whites and led to a significantly lower death rate than in the South. Believing that "idle hands tempt the devil," the Puritans found the invigorating climate conducive to a busy lifestyle. (A European visitor joked that Puritans developed the rocking chair so they could remain active while sitting down.) In keeping with this philosophy, manufacturing joined small farms in the area. Communities like Waltham, Massachussetts, saw some of the first cotton mills in America. From 1770 to 1830, England's emigrants included some trained manufacturers whose expertise brought the industrial revolution to America. New England then contributed to this revolution in its own right, developing new techniques (power-loom weaving) in factories with better working conditions and more efficient procedures than their British counterparts of the time.

In Appalachia as well, environment and immigrant culture were well-suited to each other. The relative isolation of mountain communities meant that the border people, who organized themselves primarily by clans (or extended families), were able to preserve their way of life to a higher degree than other groups. Fertile and moist soil provided ready sustenance through farming, allowing the proud and independent people to be self-reliant. Their warrior tradition also contributed to their survival, when they clashed with Indian tribes (Cherokee, Choctaw, Creek, and Chickasaw) that inhabited the area. Today, the Appalachian people maintain perhaps the strongest and oldest traditions of all English-descended groups. Many of their ballads, for example, can be traced to the border regions of 17th-century Britain.

Immigration in the 1800s. After a pause in immigration between American independence and the War of 1812, the English continued to come to America in greater numbers than before. However, their cultural impact lessened as they were joined by an ever-increasing number of other immigrant groups. Perhaps 225,000 of the English came during the first half of the century. About half the adult male immigrants were craftsmen and skilled workers. A mass of textile workers came, mostly lowly hand-loom weavers. Among them were a few men equipped with the latest skills, acquired in England, pioneer of the world's industrial revolution. Others brought with them the latest techniques in the manufacture of household items such as furniture, glassware, and jewelry. One-quarter were farmers, and only one-tenth, laborers. These immigrants tended to come with their families, and favored the Middle Atlantic states of Pennsylvania and New York.

Around 1850, the patterns of immigration began to change. Increasing mechanization at the workplace—largely a product of transplanted English techniques—led to a higher demand for unskilled workers. Fewer came with their families. By the late 1880s, almost two-thirds were laborers, miners, and construction workers. Many of the unskilled workers were probably sojourners, single men who intended to return to England when they had made some money. Those who remained settled mostly in the mining and industrial areas of the Northeast, Midwest, and West. Altogether, about 600,000 English immigrants arrived in the second half of the century, outnumbering the earlier group by more than two to one.

Ties to England. Relations were not always warm between England and the United States in the 1800s. Remaining tension from the Revolutionary War erupted in the War of 1812, and English support for the South in the American Civil War resulted in more distant ties towards the end of the century. However, shared efforts in two world wars, as well as the gradual passing of world leadership from Great Britain to America, gave rise in the 1900s to what leaders on both sides of the Atlantic have called a "special relationship."

At the same time, the percentage of English immigrants to the United States began to decline. Recent immigrants to the United States include highly educated professionals, who came in the 1960s and 1970s, when England was suffering an economic recession. Because this reduced the intelligentsia in England, this exodus was referred to as the "brain drain." Families have again immigrated in high proportions. This recalls the pattern of the early 19th century. Neither then nor now, however, have major groups immigrated as they did in the pre-Revolutionary period. It is the legacy of those first major groups that so deeply influences American life today.

George Washington

John Adams

Abraham Lincoln

Eli Whitney (cotton gin)

Frank Lloyd Wright

The Wright Brothers' airplane

Many English Americans are well known today.

Culture Today

Food, clothing, and shelter. English Americans are not a distinct people today. Rather they have been the dominant ethnic group, whose customs have most greatly affected the development of a mainstream American culture. The early settlers left traces that have survived to the present day.

Southern cooking, for example, drew on the eating habits of the English gentry from whom the early Virginians were descended. Roast beef and wild game such as venison, quail, and partridge graced Virginia tables, as did the oysters and waterfowl that abounded in and around the Chesapeake Bay. Planters grew traditional English vegetables and fruits, such as asparagus and strawberries, but they also ate native plants, like potatoes and tomatoes. Fried chicken had its origins in recipes of the English south, where frying was a popular way of cooking. Similarly, the brick ovens of New England produced dishes—for example, pies and baked beans—that reflected a strong tradition of bakery in East Anglia.

Clothing also revealed cultural origins and attitudes, particularly in New England, where the stern Puritans brought with them a preference for drab, "sadd colours." This preference is still apparent today in, for example, the school color of Harvard University, which is a subdued, deep purple. Many New England Yankees still prefer dark, autumnal colors in their daily dress. In the days of the Puritans, subdued clothing was required by law, and violators faced stiff penalties. Black or gray, considered too distinguished for the ordinary citizen, was reserved for church leaders. As stated in a 1638 list of approved colors, everyone else could dress in hues like liver color, tawny, russet, purple, and French green (Fischer 1989, p. 140). Puritan apparel included leather leggings, woolen leggings, woolen jerseys, and often black steeple hats.

Like their East Anglian forefathers, New Englanders built simple wooden structures for their shelters. An example is the "Salt Box House" a square-frame structure with two stories in front and one in back. Wood continues to be the favored building material for houses in New England. In the South, grand plantation mansions reflected the tastes of the wealthy aristocrat. Brick, which became popular in England in the late 1500s, was favored for these large and spacious homes. In England, the size of bricks was regulated by royal decree, and Virginians tended to follow the English standards. During the reign of Charles I, for example, the approved size was exactly 9 by 4 3/8 by 2 1/2 inches. In the Appalachia region, settlers at first built British-style border dwellings of earth and stone, but these tended to erode in heavy rains. The settlers soon adopted the more convenient and weatherproof log cabin, which was introduced by Scandinavian immigrants. Using the abundant native timber, the log cabin soon became the most popular frontier home. Such housing styles still appear in the nation today.

Family life. Attitudes toward the family were equally varied. In New England, the family was considered the chief expression of a pious existence. The important Puritan idea of a covenant, or contract, between God and the individual was extended to "wives, children, and servants..." (Fischer 1989, p. 70). A well-disciplined family reflected the order of the individual's soul. Accordingly, children were strictly raised, instilled with respect and obedience. Disobedient children were subjected to public punishment: for example, a child who whispered had to wear a wooden bit, tied around the neck and placed between the teeth, from which hung a sign saying "he whispers."

While New England households were small, those in Virginia included servants, visitors, stepchildren, lodgers, tutors, and other boarders. The large plantations were self-supporting communities. Unlike New Englanders, who relied on town life, many Southerners depended on their home for work and entertainment. Southern culture thus came to emphasize a relaxed, hospitable domestic climate, in which travelers were welcome and relatives often came for extended visits. The South continues to cherish this tradition of hospitality.

The border people who settled the inland mountains brought their traditions of clan loyalty with them, in which "kinfolk" settled close to each other and maintained their line through intermarriage. The immediate family was large: three or four generations lived together in a single small cabin. These nuclear families were supported by the extensive clan network, which offered protection in what could be a violent and dangerous world. Such networks continue today in the more isolated mountain areas. An Appalachian woman describes a clan in the early 1900s: "All the children in the district are related by blood in one degree or another. Our roll call includes Sally Mary and Cripple John's Mary and Tan's Mary, all bearing the same surname; and there is besides, Aunt Rose Mary and Mary-Jo, living yon side the creek. There are different branches of the Rogers family—Clay and Frank, Red Jim and Lyin' Jim and Singin' Jim and Black Jim Rogers—in this district, their kin intermarried until no man could write their pedigree" (Fischer 1989, p. 667).

Clans also perpetuated a darker aspect of the border tradition, the blood feud. Such feuds pitted clan against clan in violent conflict that often went on for generations—sometimes until no one could remember its origins. Most famous was the feud between the Hatfields and the McCoys.

Politics. In contrast to those who perpetuated feuds, English immigrants set up government structures in America. They modeled Congress after the British parliament, creating two lawmaking houses in the United States. The United States Constitution, was a product of experience with British law and government and the colonial experience in America. During and after the revolution, some patriots became champions of equal rights for women. One was Thomas Paine. Shortly after the revolution, a book that had appeared in England, *A Vindication of the Rights of Women* by Mary Wollstonecraft, made its way to the United States. The fight for women's rights would continue over the centuries to come, spurred continually by the women's movement in England. In 1840, the World Anti-Slavery Society held a convention in London that excluded women. Elizabeth Cady Stanton and Lucretia Mott (see QUAKERS) were there. Influenced by English women's leaders of the day, they laid plans for an American Women's Rights Convention at Seneca Falls (1848). Alice Paul spent a year working with British women's rights leader Emmeline Pankhurst in England, then began the Woman's Party in America. Founded in 1914, it revived interest in women winning the right to vote in American elections. England granted women this right in 1918; America folowed in 1920.

Fine arts and crafts. Early American artists and writers found inspiration in European models, looking especially to English masters in their respective areas. At first their efforts were mostly imitative, but soon after independence a distinctively American style emerged. In the decorative arts, Paul Revere (best known for his midnight ride) was a silversmith whose skill rivaled that of anyone in London; Jonathon Gostelowe and Thomas Affleck could equal the best English cabinetmakers. Furniture made in America followed classic English patterns, though often more substantial in its lines. The first American potters could not match the delicacy of England's Josiah Wedgwood, however, and American porcelain continued until the late 1800s to suffer from a dearth of highly skilled craftsmen.

American painters quickly achieved distinction. The first major artist to achieve an independent American style was John Feke, born on Long Island in the early 1700s. Other native-born artists refined this style, which distinguished them from the English-born who worked in the colonies. The most notable of these early American-born painters were John Greenwood, Benjamin West, and John Singleton Copley. Later artists such as Gilbert Stewart and Charles Willson Peale continued the tradition, firmly establishing the context in which American art would develop over the next two centuries.

Literature. American literature was slower to establish itself. Well into the 1800s, American publishing houses issued mostly reprints of popular English works. As late as 1828, the writer James Fenimore Cooper (1789-1851) complained, "Compared to the books that are printed and read, those of native origin are few indeed" (Peach 1982, p. 6). Cooper himself became the father of American literature, writing a set of popular novels, known as the Leatherstocking series. Legend has it that reading a story of English country life to his wife, he boasted that he could write as well and tried. Reacting to British writers and influenced by them, Americans gave birth to a distinctly American literature. For example, Nathaniel Hawthorne (1804-1864) examined life in an early Puritan community in his classic *The Scarlet Letter*. His subject matter is purely American, but he was influenced by Sir Walter Scott, the most popular British author of the day. In the short story and longer prose, Washington Irving (1783–1859), became the most popular writer of his time. He created a sense of American folk life through tales like "Rip Van Winkle" and *A History of New York by Diedrich Knickerbocker*. America's poets responded to the Romantic movement in England, giving their own verses a special twist. Walt Whitman (1819–1892) published *Leaves of Grass* in 1855. Written in free verse, his poems began a new style of poetry that was a type of declaration of independence from English conventions.

Entertainment and recreation. Surviving to the present day are ballads that came to the Southern Appalachians with the Scotch Irish. They concern family feuds, love gone awry, maidens in distress. In some old ballads, the immigrants would change English characters and locations, giving them American names. Once *broadside ballads* were the rage in England and America. The broadside was a ballad about an event of the day, a newspaper of sorts. Printed on a single sheet of paper with a simple woodblock illustration, it might concern a criminal, a natural disaster, or romantic love. Two patriots, Benjamin Franklin and Thomas Paine, were song and nonfiction writers. Also a printer, Franklin published "Lovewell's Flight," a broadside about an ambush and a massacre of some white bounty hunters who had gone after American Indian scalps. Thomas Paine's most popular ballad, "In a mouldering cave" was about a general who died in action. He wrote it before he left England, then created more ballads in America. They all paled, however, beside his pamphlet *Common Sense*, which popularized the idea of total independence from England. It outsold every writing in America for the next 130 years. Other English immigrants of the time introduced the fiddle to America and the reel, a popular dance that was set to music. Baseball, which began in England, was brought over by 18th century immigrants, too.

In theater, North America's first professional actor was 20-year-old Anthony Aston, a vagabond from England whose acting career in America began in 1703. Early English American actors performed to a greater or lesser welcome in the colonies, depending on location. Puritan New England was, of course, opposed to such frivolity. The first theater was built around 1720 in Williamsburg, Virginia, where the governor, Sir William Berkeley, was himself a playwright. Opening in Williamsburg in 1752, the English immigrant Lewis Hallam has been hailed as America's first great stage actor.

He starred in *The Merchant of Venice*, a Shakespeare play. For the most part, American theatergoers adopted English taste. Actors presented the latest plays from London and the old favorites. The most popular playwright in colonial America was William Shakespeare: *Richard III* and *Romeo and Juliet* were his most performed plays. *George Barnwell*, by George Lillo, was next in popularity. This play concerned a young man's drive to steal and murder for an unethical woman. As in England, early plays in America were followed by a short afterpiece. The most popular involved the character Harlequin, his bumbling servant Clown, and Pantaloon. Father to a fair maiden that Harlequin loved (Columbine), Pantaloon kept interfering with the young couple's courtship.

Language. It is sometimes said that England and America are two countries divided by a common language (because of the differences in speech and vocabulary that evolved). One might also say that they are two countries in which a common language was divided, for many American usages retain old forms. Current in England when the earliest colonists emigrated, words that fell out of use in the old country survived in the new. Many of these were regional variations that came with certain groups of settlers—expressions common in East Anglia, for example, that survived in Puritan New England. American regional accents show the same influences. Thus, the "Yankee twang" which makes *yesterday* into *yistidy* and *daughter* into *darter* reflects origins in a speech still found in remote areas of East Anglia. Where Yankees clipped syllables, Virginians added them: *daughter*, for example, became *duh-owtuur*. These and other speech patterns of the South are well-grounded in southern England of the 1600s, as are the words *bandanna, skillet, innards, lick* (as in "beat"), and even *moonshine* for "homemade liquor." They are still used today in some parts of America but have long disappeared from common usage in England. Similar examples abound in New England and especially in Appalachian speech.

No sooner had the colonists declared independence than were lexicographers at work defining "the American language." The greatest figure in this process was Noah Webster (1758–1843), who published *Grammatical Institute of the English Language* 1783–1785. Later, Webster published his *American Dictionary of the English Language* (1828), which became the authority on American English.

American English is a dynamic language. Ethnic groups in the nation have contributed to its growth, as has regional variation. Today speech ranges from the cultured drawl of Boston's old families to the Black English of urban centers. The language, however, remains rooted, in the words that crossed the Atlantic Ocean with the first English Americans.

Values. White English Protestants occupied most of America's first neighborhoods and grounded them in their own values. Many of them were dedicated to work, material success, rational thinking, and individuality. Since they began with these values, they did not need to adopt them. However, life in America encouraged the growth of new values: a concern for organizations over the individual, for example, and the weakening of Puritan discipline to allow for more pleasure. English Americans adjusted to these new values, in the same way that some of the other immigrant cultures did. Finally, English America consisted of different groups—Puritans, Quakers, Virginia planters, and New England factory workers. Not all of them shared the same values. From the beginning, the English Americans brought diversity into the New World. Later immigrants simply added to the mix of American culture.

For More Information

See these reading materials:

Bailyn, Bernard. *The Peopling of British North America.* New York: Alfred A. Knopf, 1986.

Fischer, David Hackett. *Albion's Seed: Four British Folkways in America.* New York: Oxford University Press, 1989.

Wright, Louis B. *The American Heritage History of the Thirteen Colonies.* New York: American Heritage Publishing Co., 1967.

FILIPINO AMERICANS

(fil´ eh pee no eh mer´ uh kins)

Americans whose ancestors lived in the Philippine Islands.

Population: 782,000 (1980).
Location: United States, mainly the West Coast and Hawaii.
Language: English, Ilocano, Tagalog, Visayan, Spanish.

Geographical Setting

Nearly half of all Filipino Americans live in California, mostly in the largest cities.

The Philippine archipelago consists of about 7,100 islands between Taiwan and Borneo in the Pacific Ocean. Most of the Filipinos who moved to the United States left these islands in one of three waves. From 1903 until the 1930s, small groups of students attended universities across America. Between 1907 and 1934, larger numbers of unskilled laborers came to Hawaii and the West Coast, eventually concentrating in cities such as Honolulu, San Francisco, and Los Angeles. More recently, the 1965 Immigration Act enabled a still larger and more varied group to immigrate, including professionals and their families. Though some settled in urban areas of the East and Midwest, most continued to favor the West Coast and Hawaii. New York and Chicago have notable Filipino communities, but nearly half of America's Filipinos live in California. By 1980, the Filipinos had grown to be one of the largest Asian groups in the United States, second only to the Chinese. The influx of new immigrants continues into the 1990s.

Historical Background

From colony to country—the Philippines. Discovered by Ferdinand Magellan in 1521, the Philippines (named for Spain's King Philip II) were a Spanish colony from 1565 to 1898. Spain brought Roman Catholicism to the Philippines. Adopting the religion, most islanders would remain Catholic to the present day. After America's victory in the Spanish-American War of 1898, the islands passed into United States control. In 1946, U.S. President Harry Truman declared the Philippines independent. The new country maintained a democratic government until 1972, when President Ferdinand Marcos declared martial law and seized dictatorial power. Marcos was ultimately overthrown by a bloodless "people's power" revolution. At its helm was successful Presidential candidate Corazon Aquino, whose electoral victory Marcos had attempted to deny.

Early contacts with America. Excellent sailors and shipbuilders, Filipinos accompanied early exploratory expeditions along the California coast and later helped Franciscan missionaries establish their chain of coastal missions. Though little is known about them, a group of Filipino seamen settled around 1750 on the coast of what would later become Louisiana. Other Filipinos, wealthy landowners and students, traveled widely, visiting both Europe and America in the 1800s.

By the 1900s, the Philippines were under United States control. In 1903, the U.S. government began to sponsor Filipino students who wished to attend American colleges and universities. The first group of 100 "pensionados"—so called because of the pensions they received—was selected from 20,000 applicants. Chosen from the middle and upper classes, they studied mostly in professional subjects, such as engineering, agriculture, and medicine. The students lived with American families.

It was hoped that the pensionados would return to promote democratic values in the Philippines. They did, in fact, contribute much to its agriculture, education, business, and government, but they provoked hostility from Filipinos, who viewed them as snobbish, and from American administrators, who thought they had "forgotten their place" in society.

When the program ended in 1910, perhaps 250 students had graduated from American schools. These early students inspired many others to come independently. By 1938, according to one estimate, almost 14,000 had enrolled in U.S. schools. These independent students faced obstacles—for example, language problems and high costs of living. Some persisted, working as "houseboys" or in hotels and restaurants to support themselves. Many eventually graduated from American universities, but others abandoned their hopes and settled for low wages as unskilled laborers.

Hawaii and the West Coast. Beginning in 1907, plantation owners in Hawaii began recruiting Filipino laborers to work in their sugar-cane and pineapple fields. Filipinos replaced Chinese and Japanese workers who had been imported before them (see CHINESE AMERICANS and JAPANESE AMERICANS). Most field hands signed contracts that guaranteed free housing and payment of their passage back to the Philippines. They worked ten-hour days for six days a week, earning two dollars and forty cents a day in 1925. They cultivated the fields, cut the cane, and loaded it into wagons in the hot, humid climate. Between 1909 and 1931, the years of heaviest migration, about 110,000 Filipinos entered Hawaii. Of these, perhaps half remained. Most of the rest returned to the Philippines, and about 18,000 proceeded to the mainland, where they settled on the West Coast.

A larger number of Filipinos moved directly from their homeland. Immigration to the mainland began later than that to Hawaii, climaxing in the 1920s. Arriving in San Francisco, an immigrant male might be met at the dock by relatives who had preceded him. They would give him a place to stay, a job possibility, or advice on American ways. If the new immigrant lacked such a support network, he was often prey to unscrupulous characters. Labor agents and contractors, white and Filipino, would attempt to sign him quickly, before he had a chance to find more profitable work. Many Filipinos engaged in "stoop work"—the same sort of low-paying labor they had left behind in the Philippines. They harvested vegetables such as asparagus, lettuce, and sugar beets. Gangs of 30 to 120 men labored for contractors who bid against each other to the growers. The competition kept wages low, usually 20 to 40 cents an hour.

By 1930, perhaps 50,000 Filipinos had come to the mainland. Though most worked in the fields of California, smaller numbers joined the merchant marine or found employment in the salmon canneries of the Northwest. Most Filipino work was seasonal, and during lulls the workers would return from the countryside to larger cities like San Francisco, Los Angeles, or Seattle. A heavily male population (14 men for every woman in 1930), they became a transient group with few property owners or entrepreneurs.

Anti-Filipino discrimination. Like the Chinese and Japanese before them, Filipino workers aroused hostility from whites, who resented their willingness to take on unpleasant jobs for low wages. As jobs grew scarce in the Depression, white labor unions sought to curtail Filipino immigration. They were supported by whites against marriage between Filipinos and white women. Vigilante groups formed in California communities, and violence often erupted. Under pressure from the unions and other exclusionists, Congress passed legislation in the mid-1930s designed to stymie Filipino immigration. The Tydings-McDuffie Act of 1934 limited the number of immigrants from the Philippines to 50 a year. The act brought immigration to a virtual standstill. In 1935, Congress passed the Repatriation Act, which offered Filipinos free transportation back to the Philippines.

Ambiguous legal status. Filipinos were denied both citizenship and the protection of a foreign consulate. At the beginning of World War II, their status as U.S. "nationals" but not citizens made them ineligible for the draft. Some obtained citizenship in order to get around this provision, and the First Filipino Regiment formed as a result. Most had to wait until 1946, the year of Philippine independence and the Filipino Naturalization Bill. Signed by President Harry Truman, the bill made members of the group eligible for U.S. citizenship. Discrimination continued, despite the bill. California and other states maintained laws against miscegenation, or intermarriage. Filipino men were not allowed to marry white women in California until 1948, when the state's Supreme Court declared miscegenation laws unconstitutional.

Postwar growth. In the first 20 years after World War II, Filipino immigration steadily increased, though numbers remained small. Perhaps 80,000 arrived altogether, averaging under 2,000 a year. Mostly they came after serving in the U.S. Navy, whose installation in the Philippines is headquarters for the Pacific Fleet. Citizenship came after three years in the Navy, during which Filipinos were largely limited to work in the mess halls. Servicemen brought their families to America after the war, the Filipino population nearly doubling from 1945 to 1965 and totaling about 160,000.

The next decade the population doubled once again. From 1965 to 1974, more immigrants arrived from the Philippines than from any other country except Mexico. In contrast with earlier patterns, women made up half the Filipino immigrants after 1965. Furthermore, many of the immigrants were educated, roughly two-thirds belonging to the managerial or professional ranks. In 1985, the U.S. Population Reference Bureau estimated the Filipino American population at 1,051,600, an increase of 34.8 percent in just 5 years. Today, Filipinos continue to be one of America's fastest growing Asian communities.

Culture Today

Professionals—teachers, accountants, engineers, and doctors—make up high percentages of the Filipinos who immigrate. Often they have been trained in the United States, and in most cases they find employment in their chosen fields. A 1985 survey indicated that the majority of immigrants were content with their new lives, though a few had encountered discrimination, especially during the first five years (Denton 1986, pp. 136-42).

Language. Filipinos share little sense of national identity, probably due to the separate islands on which they lived. Instead, they group themselves by linguistic background. Filipinos speak eight or nine major languages and over 80 dialects. The immigrants to the United States fall into three main groups. Two of these originate from the large northern island Luzon: the Ilocanos, who make up the largest immigrant group of Filipinos in the United States; and the Tagalogs, whose language, renamed *Pilipino*, became the official one of the Philippines in 1946. Near the island Luzon are the smaller Visayan islands. They supply the third immigrant group, known as Cebuanos, who speak Visayan. In America, the three groups—Ilocanos, Tagalogs and Cebuanos—tend to settle separately and keep to themselves.

Kinship support. Within linguistic groups, family or kinship alliances further fragment the immigrant community. Family is the traditional basis for social organization, and familial relationships lay the main claim on a Filipino's loyalty. In the most traditional families, marriages represent alliances between clans. The adoption of honorary family members known as *compadres*, a child's godparents, cement ties between adults. The traditional outlook dictates subordination of individual desires to the desires of the group. Disagreement is frowned upon, as is personal ambition. Such customs fade, however, as families assimilate.

Immigrants have always had strong ties to relatives in the Philippines, sending back money regularly or assisting a relative in immigrating. In the early days, this might mean putting the new arrival in touch with a reliable labor contractor and providing a bed for the first few weeks. Since 1965, naturalized citizens have been able to claim relatives under the new immigration laws; these relatives then receive priority treatment.

Education. Members of this ethnic group generally possess high educational attainment. According to the 1980 census, 75 percent of Filipinos age 25 and over are high school graduates. About 37 percent have at least four years of college or university education.

In the recent past, the educational picture was less optimistic for young, American-born Filipinos than it was for the foreign-born. Estimates placed the dropout rate from high school in California at about 25 percent in 1980, and college enrollments for this group were also low.

Labor. Filipinos, like other Asian workers, were mostly excluded from the American labor movement until after World War II. Hawaiian unions were quicker to admit Filipinos than those on the mainland, where California growers resisted unionization of laborers until the 1960s. Around 1960, however, two groups arose that would revolutionize California agriculture: the Filipino-dominated local of the Agricultural Workers Organizing Committee (AWOC), led by Larry Itliong; and the National Farm Workers Association (NFWA), led by César Chávez. In 1965, Itliong's AWOC struck 33 San Joaquin valley grape growers. The issue was the workers' pay. Eight days into the strike, Chávez's NFWA joined the cause. Attracting wide public sympathy, the strike lasted seven months. It ended in the merger of the two unions as the United Farm Workers Organizing Committee, and the recognition of this union as sole bargaining agent for most agricultural workers in California.

Politics. Because such a large proportion of Filipino Americans (66.3 percent in 1980) is foreign-born, their political interests lie with events in the Philippines. Most of the post-1965 immigrants left the Philippines during the reign of Ferdinand Marcos, either out of fear of political persecution or, more commonly, out of a desire for greater economic freedom. As the Marcos regime became more oppressive, Filipino Americans played an ever-greater role in organizing resistance to the dictator. Several Filipino groups formed. These groups lobbied Congress to stop U.S. aid to the Marcos regime and urged a redefinition of the relationship between the two countries. With the assassination of Marcos' main political rival, Benigno Aquino, in 1983, Marcos faced increasing popular unrest. Corazon Aquino, widow of the slain leader, galvanized support among Filipinos in both the Philippines and America. As Marcos' power base eroded, Filipinos in America became bolder. Opposition groups publicized the plights of political prisoners and the occurrence of torture and assassination in their homeland. Cultural awareness dawned, as the activists used songs, poetry, and skits to express solidarity against the Marcos government. The song "Ang Bayan Ko" (My Country) became the movement's anthem.

Bound up in this anti-Marcos movement was a feeling of cultural independence from the United States, which had heavily supported Marcos. Filipinos of the post-Marcos era have grappled with the question of a strong U.S. military presence in the Philippines. In 1985, 91 percent of Filipinos questioned thought the bases should remain in the Philippines. In the Philippines themselves, however, opinions have been more sharply divided.

Growing unity. Filipino and Chicano efforts against growers in the 1960s, along with the anti-Marcos movement of the next two decades, produced more unity among Filipinos in America. In 1969, the Californians formed the Filipino-American Political Association. Headed by Larry Itliong, the association focused on human rights. In 1970, the Filipino-American Coordinating Committee addressed the old problem of fragmentation. A coalition of some 30 groups, the committee focused on the poor and elderly and on politics.

Yet the multiplicity of Filipino groups remains. One Filipino scholar (Pido 1985, p.107) suggests that of all the groups in the United States the Filipinos are riven by the most intraracial discord and factionalism. As immigration continues into the 1990s, the newcomers are likely to reinforce existing conflicts. The difficult task of the Filipino American community, it seems, will be to achieve unity without sacrificing cultural identity.

For More Information

See these reading materials:

Cordova, Fred. *Filipinos: Forgotten Asian Americans*. Dubuque, Iowa: Kendall/ Hunt Publishing, 1983.

Denton, Frank H. and Villena-Denton, Victoria. *Filipino Views of America: Warm Memories, Cold Realities*. Washington: Asia Fellows, Ltd., 1986.

Contact this organization:

Filipinas Americas Science and Art Foundation, 1209 Park Avenue, New York, New York 10128.

FRENCH CANADIANS

(french cuh nay' dee uns)

Canadians of French descent

Population: 6,200,000 (1981).
Location: Canada: Quebec Province (80%of the population) and New Brunswick Province (39%), with lesser numbers throughout Canada.
Language: French, English.

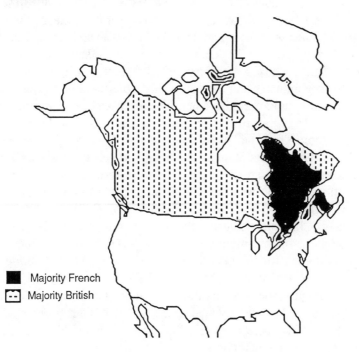

■ Majority French
[⋅⋅] Majority British

Geographical Setting

While French Canadians live throughout Canada, they form the most sizeable groups in the provinces of Quebec and New Brunswick. Quebec is Canada's largest province; it extends for 1,200 miles north to south and residents there experience a wide range of soils and climates. Much of this large province lies on the Canadian Shield. This is a massive rock shelf scraped by ancient glaciers, now a harsh mixture of brush and forests. At the lower western edge of this shield sits Toronto, population three million and the center of British Canada. On the eastern edge lie the metropolises of French Canada: Montreal (slightly smaller than Toronto) and Quebec, the city that is the capital of Quebec Province. The territory of the Québécois ranges from mild-wintered farmland in the south to an area of perpetual frost in the north. In this difficult environment, French Canadians have hunted and planted farms since the early 1600s.

Historical Background

Early French exploration. French explorers came early to the Americas. In 1534, Jacques Cartier was sent by the king of France in search of gold. Cartier established a base on a peninsula near the entrance to the bay that joins the St. Lawrence River and the Atlantic Ocean and claimed the land for France. During the next 70 years, few Frenchmen settled in what was called New France. Those who did were adventurers, who proceeded to establish a fishing industry and fur trading with the Indians. Not until 1604 did the French attempt to establish a permanent settlement on an island they called St. Croix. They named this settlement Acadia. A year later some of these pioneers moved to Nova Scotia and settled in a community named Port Royal. In 1608, the explorer Samuel de Champlain visited the Acadians and decided that both of the small settlements were too exposed to possible enemy sailors and to the weather. Moving deeper into the St. Lawrence River basin, Champlain established the town of Quebec. Here, some distance inland, Champlain felt that the people could live in freedom and peace. Although the three communities were to suffer from the elements and from Iroquois raiders for the next 50 years, they were the beginning of a French nation in North America that lasted for 150 years. Leaders such as Dollard des Ormeaux, the Marquis de Tracy, and Madeleine de Verchères fought the Indians and eventually made peace as the Indians became heavily outnumbered. By 1698 there were 13,000 French settlers in New France and only 2,000 nearby Indian neighbors.

Religion followed the settlers in the form of Jesuit missionaries who came to this part of America in 1625. These priests brought the dominant French religion, Catholicism, to the French-American settlers. By 1642, the church had established a mission for the Indians in what is now Montreal. This was to become the second French town in the New World. The priests also established a pattern of church schools that was to last through centuries. In 1635, they built the first Jesuit school in Quebec. The Catholic Church was to become a dominant religious, social, and economic leader.

French rule. In 1663, the French king Louis XIV made New France a royal province and appointed a governor to act as his representative. A second leader, the intendant, was appointed to manage day-to-day affairs. A bishop directed church, missionary work, and education.

Jesuit priests established an educational system that endured through the 17th century, and the Church vigorously constructed church buildings. By 1750, there were more than 100 churches lining the St. Lawrence River. In the early days of the royal province, the Catholic bishop François Laval was so powerful that no governmental decisions were made without him. Governor, intendant, and bishop vied for control of the people.

Another divisive force stemmed from King Louis' plan for encouraging settlers. As in old France, land was awarded to military leaders and men of wealth. They ruled their territory in feudal fashion, bringing farmers from the old country to work the land for them. However, feudal rule in Canada was not as strong as in France because Canadian land was plentiful. It was easy for peasants who were ill-treated by their *seigneurs* (feudal lords) to run away and start farms for themselves or to follow the fur or fishing trades. One result was that the French in America were never able to establish a strong and unified central government.

From 1663 to 1672, the government of France subsidized immigrants to the new world. Consequently, 6,700 immigrants settled the land around Quebec and Montreal by 1672. Even though the government ended its support of the immigrants in that year, the population grew steadily until there were about 60,000 French people in the new world in 1760, when the land was lost to the British.

In the early 1700s, the British and French skirmished frequently over land boundaries. The French had sent fur traders into the west and had settled Louisiana. They felt they needed the Ohio territory for easy communication with these outposts. The British were determined not to allow France to settle in Ohio. In 1754, the British sent troops from Virginia under a young leader, George Washington, to discourage the building of French forts. Washington was defeated, and so were other British efforts to gain French land. In 1755, British tensions over disputes with the French grew so intense that the British who controlled the old Nova Scotia/New Brunswick areas (known then as Acadia) chose to expel some 10,000

Acadians from their homes and scatter them through the colonies. This action was taken even though the Acadians had already pledged to remain neutral in the French and British disputes. Some of the Acadians found their way to Louisiana where they became the Cajuns of today (see CREOLES).

British rule. The British were finally victorious in a siege of Quebec and a battle for Montreal. In 1763, the Treaty of Paris awarded the British rights to all the French land in North America. The British attempted to Anglicize the French in Canada but to no avail. Language, habits, and religion bound the French, and they resisted all efforts to transform them into English settlers. By the 1770s, it was clear that the French would maintain their own language and religion. The Quebec Act of that period gave the French civil and religious freedom, but the British clung to the idea of a single English language and tried to abolish French. French Canadians were given menial jobs, treated as lower-class citizens, and ruled by a British governor and legislative council. In 1837, came the first French rebellion against such actions. Led by Louis J. Papineau, a party of French began to revolt against the British authorities, but the royal government suppressed this uprising.

The United States and Canada. By the 1800s, another force, the United States, had entered the territorial disputes. During the War of 1812, the British and the Americans attempted to seize land from each other. Americans captured and burned the British capital at Toronto (then York) and the British responded by burning Washington, D.C. Determined never to have the line of travel between Toronto and Montreal endangered again, the Canadians hand dug the 123-mile Rideau Canal between Kingston and Ottawa. Completed in six years, this was such a large undertaking that it gave Canadians of all ethnic backgrounds some sense of unity as a nation.

Independence. Uneasiness between British and French Canadians persisted. The British proposed a federation. French Canadians and British Canadians would each have local control of their affairs and would share the national government. In 1867, this federation plan became law and the Canadian nation was created. The French controlled Quebec Province, the British, Ontario Province. The French gained more influence in the national government than in the past. This was confirmed when Wilfrid Laurier became the country's first French Canadian prime minister in 1896. Still, many French Canadians felt dissatisfied. English was still the official language of the country. The French experienced discrimination in jobs, government, and management.

Quiet Revolution. In the mid 1900s, Jean Lesage organized a "Quiet Revolution," a movement to defend French Canadian rights. Some French Canadians advocated complete independence from the rest of Canada. This position gained momentum with a visit from Charles de Gaulle, who seemed to encourage French independence. The dispute erupted into scattered violence. In 1969, Prime Minister Pierre Trudeau led the government of Canada to pass the Official Language Act, making French and English both official Canadian languages. Today, 16 percent of all Canadians speak both languages. Although the movement for French independence continued to have some supporters, it was weakened. Even though the Québécois call their provincial government the "national" government, they demonstrated their solidarity with all Canada by rejecting a vote for independence by a three to two margin in 1980. Nevertheless, dispute over official recognition of ethnic differences continues. In 1981-82, Canada approved a revised constitution against the wishes of the Parti Québécois, which was in power in Quebec at the time. Quebec never ratified this constitution because it did not recognize Quebec as a special or independent province.

Debate over bilingualism continues as well. The prime minister of Saskatchewan, a mostly British Canadian province, proposed to repeal the bilingual laws, and Quebec's Premier Bourassa, who had previously signed the bilingual agreement, decided to outlaw the use of English on outdoor commercial signs in Quebec.

Today the French Canadians consider themselves as Canadians and have little association with the people of France. The French spoken in Canada is quite different from that spoken in France. Canadian French has adopted many English words, so the Québécois talk about *le hamburger, le potate, le brake drum*..... Also, French Canadians take pride in the unique architecture of Quebec and in their rising economic level as they make increasing use of the water power and natural resources available from the Canadian Shield.

Culture Today

Food, clothing, and shelter. The first French farmers settled in New Brunswick and Nova Scotia, the land they called Acadia. They built simple, often one-room, houses of rock and plaster, whitewashed inside and out, and with steeply pitched, thatched roofs. The roofs changed through the years to cedar shingles or iron. As recently as the 1950s, many French Canadians lived in these simple farmhouses. While there remain a few symbols of these homes in the Acadia region today, most French Canadians have given up simple farm homes for stone and concrete houses and apartments in Quebec, Montreal, and smaller cities. (Whereas in 1900 three-fourths of all Québécois were farmers, today only one-third of them live in rural areas.) Housing varies with the region. A home in Montreal is often a narrow, deep, stone building with a chimney at one end where the walls of the house extend above the roof. Quebec residents build homes of stone or wood. Frequently, they are heated by a central fireplace whose chimney extends above the steep gable of the roof. Walls of these homes are often low and solid with dormer windows.

Clothing, too, varies with the locale. People in Montreal and Quebec wear suits, pants, and dresses like their European relatives. In New Brunswick and Nova Scotia, though, one still finds men wearing pants, a long-sleeved shirt covered by a vest, and a cap.

The cuisine of the French Canadians reveals their mixed heritage. There are roughly two types of French Canadian cooking. One originated in the countryside and is indigenous to Canada; the other is found in the cities and is strongly influenced by French cuisine. Rural, or regional, cooking tends to be heavy, with plenty of meat, pastry crusts, and maple sugar. Beef and pork are crucial to French Canadian cooking, as are spices. On the other hand, the urban cuisine is similar to that of sophisticated French restaurants in America: coq au vin, crème caramel, and so forth.

Maple syrup and maple sugar are regional specialties of Canada and particularly Quebec. Made from the sap of the maple tree, they are used to flavor desserts from cakes to candies to ice cream. Of course, maple syrup is also a favorite on pancakes. Canadian maple syrup is quite different from the syrup that many Americans enjoy on their pancakes, however. Most American varieties contain little or no real maple syrup, which is an expensive delicacy made only in certain northern states such as Vermont. Canadian maple syrup is completely pure. It is less sweet and has a more woodsy flavor than American syrups.

Cheeses are another popular Canadian delicacy. One family in Quebec has been making a certain cheese, called *Fromage Ile d'Orléans,* in the same way since 1679.

Religion. Like their language and history, the Catholic religion binds French Canadians to one another. Most of them belong to the Roman Catholic Church. Many homes contain small shrines to the Mother Mary, and many French Canadians attend church, where they are strongly influenced by local priests and bishops. This, too, has been changing in recent years. Until 1962, religion directed the education of Québécois. Then, as part of what is known as the Quiet Revolution, the schools fell under the direction of the government and fewer and fewer French Canadians spent parts of their Sundays in church. Pope John Paul II lamented the change, claiming that Quebec had become a "dechristianized society." As part of the ferment of the 1960s many beliefs about politics, religion, and economics have been questioned.

Education. The change in the educational system established a continuum of primary, secondary, pre-university and university institutions. The curriculum changed in the 1960s from a total emphasis on language, philosophy, and literature to a program in which these subjects were balanced with math, computer science, business, and other courses designed to bring Québécois closer to the needs of today's working world. Perhaps as a result, French Canadians are now beginning to take more active roles in politics and in industry, and the income of this once poorer people has begun to rise toward the level enjoyed by British Canadians.

Arts and recreation. Before the late 1800s French Canadian literature consisted mostly of folktales and folksongs of their French ancestors. Later writings have perpetuated the themes of French spirit and independence that formed the basis for early stories. Not until 1904 did a French Canadian, Benjamin Sulate, attempt a history of the people in *Histoire des Canadiens-Français*.

Traditions in the other arts have persisted through the changes in the society. Religious themes remain dominant in artistic expression. The Ursuline nuns of the Catholic Church began one artistic tradition— embroidering leaves, fruits, and geometric patterns on a wide array of materials. Originally, these embroideries decorated church altars and some clerical vestments. One Catholic sister, Jeanne Le Ber, spent 19 years in chapel dividing her time between devotions and needlework.

Poetry, too, was first associated with the church. A group of poets known as the School of Quebec wrote religious and patriotic verse in the 1800s. A well-known poet of this era was Léon-Pamphile Lemay. More recently poets such as Anne Hébert have turned to other subjects, writing about the human soul or comparing the hardships and joys of rural and city life. Roger Lemelin and others write popular realistic novels.

The city of Quebec is the home of a summer drama festival that promotes French Canadian theater. Montreal supports a famous symphony orchestra and Les Grands Ballets Canadiens.

Ice hockey, the most popular sport in Canada, is a French as well as a British passion (see BRITISH CANADIANS).

Quebec Province today. Recently Quebec Province has begun to seriously reconsider seceding from Canada. Since voting against it in 1980,

Quebec's economy has prospered and French Canadians have dramatically improved their economic and social status. They are no longer second-class citizens in Canada. This prosperity has made secession a real possibility: because French and not British Canadians now control major Quebec corporations, secession is economically feasible. Many of these Quebec businesspeople see independence as economically desirable. Also, the French Canadians' separate cultural identity, rather than disappearing over time, has been strengthened by the self-conscious cultivation of French Canadian language and culture.

Separatist sentiments came to a head in June 1990, when two Canadian provinces, Manitoba and Newfoundland, failed to ratify a constitutional amendment called the Meach Lake accord that would have recognized Quebec as a "distinct society" within Canada. This accord, designed by Prime Minister Brian Mulroney and the leaders of the ten provinces, was an attempt to placate Quebec after the 1981-82 disagreement over the constitution and to keep the Canadian nation together. Many Canadians, however, were uncomfortable with the special status that they thought this accord would confer on Quebec.

Canada may have lost its last chance at keeping the economically and culturally important region of Quebec within its boundaries; however, it remains to be seen whether separatist sentiments will result in action. For now, the French Canadians are waiting.

For More Information

See these reading materials:

Watson, Jessie and Wreford. *The Canadians: How They Live and Work.* North Pomfret, Vermont: David & Charles Inc., 1977.

White, Peter T. "One Canada—or Two?" *National Geographic,* April 1977, pp. 436–465.

Contact this organization:

Center for Research on French-Canadian Culture, Lamcoureaux Hall Room 274, 145 Jean-Jacques Lussier Street, Ottawa, Ontario, Canada KIN 6N5.

GERMAN AMERICANS
(jer´ man eh mer´ uh kins)

People of German ancestry who are citizens of the United States.

Population: 5,300,000 (1983 estimate of Americans born in Germany or having parents born in Germany).
Location: German Americans live in all of the 50 states but are most heavily represented in Pennsylvania, Wisconsin, and the Midwest.
Language: English, sometimes German.

Geographical Setting

The earliest German immigrants to the United States were mostly farmers. They had come from an agricultural economy in Germany, and were at ease with the land they found in Pennsylvania, the Carolinas and the Northeastern states. Later, more schooled people began to move to America, and some German Americans began to build towns of their own or to populate the already existing cities. Today, the geographical setting for the German Americans is the setting of Americans everywhere.

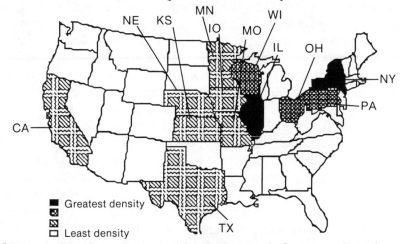

States with the greatest populations of German Americans.

Historical Background

The First Germans in America. The earliest visitor to America from Germany is said to be the foster father of Leif Erickson. About 1000 A.D. this man, Tyrker, joined the Norse pioneers who explored Nova Scotia and New England. In fact, Tyrker is said to have wandered from the party somewhere in what is now New England and become lost. While lost he discovered a grape vine and was so excited about a vine like those at home that he named the place Vineland.

Certainly, the role of Germans in America had begun by 1507. In that year, word about the new world had reached Martin Waldeschmüller in Freiburg, Germany. Waldeschmüller suggested that the new world be named after Amerigo Vespucci, the explorer who claimed to have discovered the American continent in 1497.

Immigrants from Germany were among the first settlers in America. By 1607, they had found their way to Jamestown (in Virginia), and had become farmers—sometimes working for hire to farm land owned by the Anglo-Saxon pioneers. By 1608, German craftsmen had migrated to America and begun such industries as glass blowing. They proved so much more effective in dealing with the Indian inhabitants that the British landowners, in envy of the German work habits and honesty in Indian dealings, had given their German neighbors the derisive label of "damn Dutch." In fact, the Germans were nearer the Dutch settlers of New Amsterdam (New York) in language and work habits than to the British. So as many as one third of the early immigrants to the New Amsterdam area were German. By 1620, skilled craftsmen from Germany had erected sawmills in the new world and, by 1653, able German farmers had begun to develop tobacco plantations.

One famous immigrant from the city of Wesel on the Rhine River was instrumental in building New York. Peter Minuit bought much of the land around Manhattan Island from the Indian residents in 1626. By 1689, a German immigrant, Jacob Leisher from Frankfurt, had become the second governor of the colony at New York. In that same year, German settlers began to build the city of Germantown in Pennsylvania—a city later to become part of Philadelphia. By that time German skilled workers had become weavers, vintners, carpenters, locksmiths, shoemakers and tailors in the new society along with many other occupations. However, these early German immigrants had been dominated by princes in the old country and had little interest in political activities in the new world. Some found little difference in the new world dominated by British immigrants. A 1728 journal describes the plight of early German immigrants: "The immigrants are all examined as to whether any contagious disease be among them. The next step is to bring all the new arrivals in a procession before the city hall and there compel them to take an oath of allegiance to the king of Great Britain." (O'Connor 1968. p. 22.)

German eagerness for a new land was the result of the turmoil in European Germany in the 1600s through the 1800s. Beginning with the Thirty Years War (1618-1648) the people of Germany were pressed first by Bohemians, then Swedes, then Spanish followed by the French and Bavarians. The 1707 Spanish War of Succession brought new oppression to the area. In that year, Joshua von Kochesthal brought 60 smiths, weavers, and carpenters to the new world. That was followed in 1709 by 500 Germans who first fled to Holland, then to England. These Germans were seen by Indian visitors to England who gave them land near what is now Philadelphia. The same year saw 600 families immigrate to the Carolinas and 3,000 to New York. Unable to care for so many living in destitute circumstances, the governor of New York hit upon the idea of sending 2,000 Germans upstate to make pitch and tar for the growing colony. Of those who remained in New York City, an orphan, Peter Zenger, eventually became publisher of the *New York Weekly Journal*. This newspaper led the way in advocating reforms in government, taking such strong positions that Zenger was thrown in jail in 1735. Thereupon, his wife took on the publishing duties and became the first woman publisher in America.

A German state in America. Many of the German immigrants to America had come from near-feudal princedoms in Europe or had felt the heavy hand of rule by dictators from other countries. So, much of their early actions in the new world were rejection of organizations that threatened their independence. They held to their own language, and many had dreams of an independent German country in the Americas. As early as 1738, newspapers in the German language were published in the colonies. In that year, a man named Sauer began *Der Hoch Deutche Pennsylvanische Geschichtschreiber* in Philadelphia. It was followed in 1762 with *Wöchentliche Philadelphische Staatsbate*. As the numbers of immigrants increased, the number of German-language papers increased. By 1818 there were fourteen prospering newspapers for German readers.

Religious oppression was common in Europe in the 1700s, and the German Americans were reluctant to be dominated by any single religious leader. Germans were responsible for the organization of a wide range of religious groups in the Americas: sects such as Ephrata (predicting the imminent end of the world), Mennonites, Dunkards (so named because of their insistence on Christian baptism by immersion), Lutherans, United Brethern, and the German Reformed Church.

German Americans in the Revolution. Their own oppression in Europe also made many German immigrants wary of the British crown. In May of 1776, Germans formed their own regiment to serve under George Washington. This regiment distinguished itself in battles at Trenton, Princeton, and Brandewine. Gerhard Augustin Steuben was credited with much of the organization and training of the American troops. Alexander Hamilton credited him with having "introduced into the army a regular formation and exact discipline." Other German officers played important roles in the American revolution. Peter Mühlenberg commanded the Eighth Virginia Regiment, while Nicholas Herkimer led troops to the borders of Canada to hold the British in the north. Following the war, Mühlenberg served the new country as a congressman.

Immigration in the 1800s. German immigration was small in comparison to that from some other European countries at first, but grew to exceed even the immigration of the Irish by the mid 1800s. Until 1800 German immigration ranged from 200 to 2,000 a year. By the years 1832-1837 this annual movement had risen to 10,000 to 25,000 each year, and in the early 1850s Germans fled Prussian aggression and religious oppression in Europe at the rate of 500,000 each year. The growing numbers of German Americans resulted in two very different actions. Some Germans held to their dream of a German state on the American continent. But the numbers of immigrants resulted in spreading the Germans across the continent and resulted in more blending of Germans with other immigrant groups.

German Immigration by Year			
1830	6,761	1870	787,468
1840	152,454	1880	718,182
1850	434,626	1890	2,452,970
1860	951,667	1900	505,152

Germans in Europe held their own rebellions in the early 1800s, and tasted freedom for a short time. When the Prussian armies reasserted their power over Germany in the 1840s, some of the leaders of the rebellions migrated to the United States. They became known as the 48'ers, a small group of intellectuals very different from the farmers that had come to America earlier and established themselves as land owners. These newcomers sought to build independent German republics in Texas, Missouri, and Wisconsin. Their ideas did not gain strong acceptance among the German farmers who had already become successful in the new world. Eventually, the movement for a German state faded. However, German traditions remained strong. Better students were sent to Germany to attend universities. Between 1815 and 1850, 137 of these students returned to become professors in the beginning American universities.

German Americans in the West. German Americans led settlers to many parts of the continent. Daniel Boone, who spoke German but was of English ancestry, helped settle Kentucky as did Germans like Stoner and Harod, who left their names on towns in the territory. Conrad Weiser and Christian Post led Moravian settlers into the Ohio Valley. John Jacob Astor settled the community that carries his name in Oregon. John Sutter started the gold rush to California. Heinrich Hilgard was president of the Northern Pacific Railroad that helped tie the East and West by rail. By 1840, 10,000 Germans had settled in New Orleans.

The Civil War. By the beginning of the Civil War, Germans had spread into all occupations and all states. The majority of them were anti-slavery and strongly in favor of a unified democratic nation. One hundred seventy-six thousand Germans joined the Union Army—nearly one-fifth of all the Union soldiers in the war. General Sigel, a German, was chief of staff of the Union Army led by General Sherman. Another German, Carl Schurz, had fled Germany to prevent imprisonment for leading rebellious acts. As he escaped, his best friend was captured. Schurz planed a one-man invasion to free the friend and carried it out successfully. In the United States, Schurz became a lawyer and a political leader. He campaigned for Lincoln's election to the presidency and was an adviser to the president until Lincoln's assassination. Following the war, Schurz became a senator from Missouri and led the congress in acts to give full citizenship to blacks and to provide reparations that would restore the South.

Industrial developers. After the Civil War, German Americans, always enjoying strong reputations as farmers, began to lead in industry as well. Familiar names today such as Heinz (canned foods), Spreckels (sugar), and Steinmetz (electric power companies) illustrate German success in industry. There were others: John Roehling, who designed the suspension bridge, Andrew Carnegie (steel), and J. M. Studebaker (automobiles).

Politics. Germans also became more active in politics. By 1857 German socialists had begun a communist party in the United States. In 1877, Germans started a Socialist Labor Party that was effective to the end of the century. Some Germans still clung to the idea of a German state, and many still tended to settle in their own communities and to read German newspapers.

World War I. When World War I began, there were two and a half million German immigrants in the United States and another nearly four million born in the United States of parents who were born in Germany. Their interest in preserving their own culture, the German record of independence in language, religion, and politics, and their family ties to European Germans led to American German resistance to becoming involved in the war. This resistance to American participation in the war was led by a German organization, the German-American Alliance. While most German Americans were quick to place their allegiance with America, a few actively opposed American participation and refused to obey the draft of soldiers. These factors also led many Americans to distrust their German neighbors. As one result, the teaching of the German language was banned from schools in 26 states, and German-owned stores were stoned in many American cities. German introductions to American society underwent name changes to avoid the German stigma. Sauerkraut became known as liberty cabbage, for example, and the frankfurter became a hot dog. Still, the leader of American forces in World War I, General John J. Pershing was of German ancestry and many German Americans distinguished themselves in battle. Three of America's flying aces in this war were German Americans: Eddie Rickenbacker, Frank Luke, and Joseph Wehner.

A result of World War I was the beginning of the disintegration of a separate German-American identity. Two hundred seventy-eight German publications survived to begin again after World War I, but by 1930 there were only one hundred seventy-two remaining. World War II reinstilled some distrust of German Americans by other citizens, but the actions of the European German state were indefensible to many. For a time, German Americans sought to preserve their identity and to avoid further involvement with Germany through such organizations as the Nonpartisan Alliance. But a new and influential organization of German Americans, the Steuben Society, was organized to thoroughly Americanize the people of German ancestry. Their work was aided by a slowdown of German immigration to the United States.

Hitler and the Nazis. By 1925, Adolph Hitler had taken power in Germany and was determined that Germans outside Germany would never again oppose the fatherland. Hitler organized propaganda campaigns to elicit support from German Americans but was not very successful. In 1936, a strong German American Bund was organized and threatened to increase its importance as a Hitler propaganda outlet under its leader Fritz Kuhn. However, Kuhn was imprisoned. Despite the organization of such political bodies as the American Nazis, who still remain active although small in number, the final assimilation of German Americans began as these citizens of the United States found it impossible to join their European relatives in the Hitler ideals. German exiles to the United States formed an impressive brain trust that advanced American technology in a number of fields such as rocketry. Werner von Braun led American scientists and German exiles in this field. When World War II finally involved the United States, German Americans for the most part did not hesitate to choose the American side. After the war there was little that would distinguish German Americans from other white Americans of European ancestry, except for some social clubs.

Today. In the 1950s and 1960s there was a new influx of immigrants from Germany. A new openness in Europe along with a sharing of U.S. and West German troops, led to new bonds between European Germans and their U.S. counterparts. This interest in ancestry pervaded the United States after the 1976 centennial celebration and has resulted in student exchanges, inquiries about ancestors overseas, and cultural exchanges between the two countries. Still, most German Americans consider themselves to be Americans; the hyphenated term is no longer widely used.

Culture Today

Family life. The first German Americans were farmers and Protestants fleeing a Europe of oppression. They were strongly religious and scrupulously honest with all people. Daily Bible reading was common. The father was the ruler of his household, and everyone in the family was supposed to help with the work of the house or farm. It was this work ethic that set the early settlers apart from their colonial neighbors. Their hard work and honesty earned them a good rapport with their Indian neighbors. Through the centuries since the first settlers, German families have continued to be strongly united, and German Americans have continued to be known for their intense work habits. Later German immigrants to the United States brought with them a strong interest in education. The German point of view is that through hard work and learning, the person can achieve almost any objective.

A page from an old German Bible.

Food and shelter. German food tends to be simple and plentiful. Meat, potatoes, and coarse bread, along with cabbage dishes, stews, and pastries are still the menus for German-American families today. German butchers brought new kinds of sausages to the American diet. Today, such foods are so much a part of American diets that we do not identify them as "German-American." Foods such as sauerkraut, frankfurters, liverwurst, and streusel are food names from the German language. Dark bread, a German staple, can be found in most supermarkets.

The first Germans in America survived by building houses of whatever material was available. In the first years, many German immigrants lived in homes dug out of the earth and covered over with wood and more earth. Later they would build sturdy houses of wood and brick not distinguishable from those of other immigrants. Today, homes of German Americans are as variable as those of any other Americans.

Business leader, John D. Rockefeller

President Eisenhower   Rocket expert, Werner von Braun

Dwight Eisenhower, Werner von Braun, and John Rockefeller were German Americans. Kindergarten is a German school addition.

German contributions to American culture. A review of German names among those with major achievements would tend to verify this point of view. German Americans have excelled in almost all fields of work. H. J. Heinz in food manufacture, Claus Spreckles (the sugar baron), and Frederick Weyerhaueser (lumber), J.M. Studebaker (automobiles), Henry Hilgard (railway developer), Werner von Braun (rocketry), Margaret Fuller and Theodore Dreiser (literature), Dwight D. Eisenhower (politics), Ernstine Schumann-Heinke (not a German but generally associated with German

Americans in music), Admiral Chester Nimitz, and many others brought German values and arts to America. But the influence of German Americans on the American culture is not totally reflected by these German-American leaders.

Germany's influence in America. In the 1800s, European Germans, under independent princes (the Spanish, French, and Prussians) were world leaders in education and thought. Great philosophers such as Goethe, Kant, and Hegel led world thought in new directions. German scientists gave rigor to the new scientific methods of test and verification. Long leaders in music, the music of Germany spread throughout the world. Americans seeking sound educations often visited Germany to study. American writers such as John Greenleaf Whittier, Henry David Thoreau, Herman Melville visited Germany and brought back ideas for their own writing. Philosophers like Josaiah Royce and John Dewey studied German writings and applied them to their teaching and study in American universities. In the 1890s, G. Stanley Hall studied in Germany and brought the new experimental psychology to America. The result of all this exchange has been that much of German culture has been integrated into the general American culture today.

Literature. German Americans have from the first been interested in literature. German language newspapers were among the first in America. Benjamin noted that of the first six newspapers in Philadelphia, half were in the German language. Perhaps the most famous German language newspaper publisher was Joseph Pulitzer, a German-speaking Hungarian who migrated to the United States just before the end of the Civil War. He worked for German newspapers until he was able to save enough to buy the English language *St. Louis Post-Dispatch*. Later he would buy the *New York Morning World* and become one of the country's leading journalists. Today, Pulitzer prizes are awarded for distinction in journalism.

Today. The difficulties of World War I and World War II brought the decline of German language use in America, and a reduction in the number of social and political organizations of German Americans, so that today there is little to identify as a purely German-American culture. However, the influence of German thought has become a major part of the general American culture, and Americans of German ancestry continue to contribute strong leadership in every field of endeavor.

For More Information

See these reading materials:

Heubener, Theodore. *The Germans in America.* Philadelphia: Chilton Company, 1962.

O'Connor, Richard. *The German Americans..* Boston: Little, Brown and Company, 1968.

Totten, Christine M. *Roots in the Rhineland..* New York: German Information Center, 1983.

Pochmann, Henry A. *German Culture in America..* Madison: University of Wisconsin Press, 1961.

HOPI
(ho´ pee)

The westernmost of the pueblo-dwelling Indian groups of New Mexico and Arizona .

Population: 8,500 (1987 est.).
Location: Northern Arizona.
Language: Hopi.

Geographical Setting

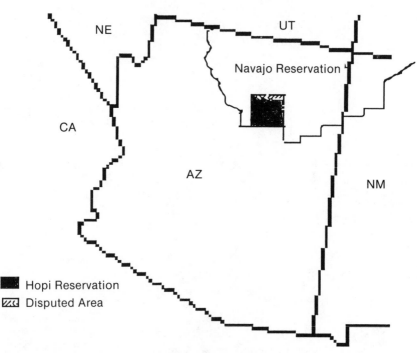

Hopi Reservation
Disputed Area

The Hopi Reservation in Arizona is surrounded by the larger Navajo Reservation.

The northeastern section of present-day Arizona, southwestern Colorado, and northwestern New Mexico is a high plateau carved by canyons worn over millions of years by the Colorado, Little Colorado, and San Juan Rivers. Here canyon walls rise almost perpendicularly from the stream beds in canyons that are narrow and long. Rainfall is scarce, and the seasons are harsh in this country where the most abundant natural resource is rock.

This region is also the home of the Navajo Indian; the Hopi Reservation is surrounded by that of the Navajo. Hopi people live in old and newer towns of a few hundred or a few thousand inhabitants. Their towns are built on the bluffs overlooking the deep canyons. Hopi farmers plant their crops in the canyon floors and travel up and down each day to tend the crops. Only on the canyon floors is there enough moisture to supply crops such as corn and squash.

Historical Setting

Origin. Little is known about the origins of the Hopi people. Their own stories tell of being born far beneath the earth and rising through three worlds finally arriving at this the fourth world. The land of today's Hopi people was inhabited before 300 B.C. by bands of hunters who searched the canyons for food. About the fourth century A.D. the people of the region were introduced to corn and became farmers. At first these ancient hunters and farmers lived on the canyon floors and used the many caves in the canyon walls to store their food. They built pit dwellings, carved out caves covered with logs and mud, and became proficient in the art of basket making. These were the old people, the Anasazi. About A.D. 500 the Anasazi (see ANASAZI), who may have been the ancestors of today's Hopi, began to make pottery. Still later, they discovered the bow and arrow. Despite their accomplishments, by 500 to 700 the old people had begun to disappear. Taking their place were people whose language was related to the Shoshone languages and whose culture contained elements of Aztec origin. The new people, arriving about the year 1000, built houses of stone and mud in the canyons, then in the caves in the canyon walls.

Spanish explorers. When the Spanish began to explore the Southwest in 1540, they found the great cities hanging abandoned from the cliff faces. They also found nearly 20,000 people living in communities of stone buildings from central New Mexico to northern Arizona. In 1540, Francisco Vásquez de Coronado entered New Mexico from Mexico and marched north in search of the "seven cities of Cibola," where there were reputed to be large quantities of gold. Reaching the seven Zuni communities in northern New Mexico and not discovering gold, Coronado sent Pedro de Tovar along with horsemen and a Franciscan priest, Juan de Padilla, farther west and south, where they found seven more cities, those of the Hopi. The Hopi people, whose name means peaceful, had long told a stories of a white diety, Pahaña, who would someday visit among his people. So their early attitude was that a god had arrived in the person of Juan de Tovar. But de Tovar's demeanor soon convinced the Hopi that he was not the god of their stories. In the spirit of the Hopi, de Tovar was given food and lodging in the villages and then sent on his way. The Hopi joined the pueblo dwellers in a revolt against the Spanish in 1680. In New Mexico, church buildings were destroyed, as the Pueblos regained their old ways and religions.

Navajo. Shortly after the Spanish arrived, the Hopi encountered a new threat to their way of life. Bands of marauding fighters and hunters came to Hopi land. At first these people were fed and housed temporarily by the peace loving Hopi, but finally the visits became too long and threatening and the Hopi villagers armed themselves and drove off these first Navajo. The Hopi were visited again by Europeans in 1583, when Antonio de Espijo passed through the land in search of gold.

Spanish rule. Not until 1598 did the Spanish send soldiers again, this time under the leadership of Juan de Oñate. Having won submission of all seven of the Hopi villages, de Oñate paved the way for new Catholic missionary work among the Hopi. Missionaries arrived in 1629 and proceeded to build a series of missions: San Bernardino in the village of Awatovi, San Miguel in the Hopi principal city, Oraibi, and San Bartolomé in the village of Shongopovi. The Hopi resented the attempt to sway them from their own religious beliefs and the construction methods of the Spanish priests. Workers were sent to bring huge logs for the mission construction, sometimes dragging the logs as far as 40 miles through the canyons. Stone was quarried and carried to the building sites by Hopi workers. Reluctant or incapable workers were sometimes publicly beaten, much to the embarrassment of the villagers.

So in 1680, when their New Mexico neighbors living in pueblos along the Rio Grande River rebelled, the Hopi joined them. The missions were destroyed, the priests killed, and the Hopi returned to their old life of peace. However, the Spanish came again and reconquered the Hopi villages. Missionary work proved futile except in one Hopi village, Awatovi. So strong was the Hopi rejection of the Catholic religion, that the other chiefs met at Oraibi and decided that Awatovi must be destroyed. Hopi legend tells how the different clans divided the chores and plotted the massacre. In the evening, when Awatovi men were all gathered in the *kiva*, a large pit room used for religious purposes, warriors from the other villages threw burning materials into the entrance in the roof of the kiva and covered it. The men of Awatovi were killed by the fire and smoke. Some women and children were also killed, others taken for slaves. The message was clear. No Catholic missionaries were wanted in the Hopi villages, and none came for nearly 100 years, until 1775. The churches were never rebuilt. However, fearful of Spanish revenge for the uprising against them, the Hopi abandoned the six villages in the canyons and rebuilt them on points of the mesas overlooking the canyons 600 feet below. One village, Oraibi, was already established on a mesa, having been in existence since the 1300s. No Spanish punitive retaliation occurred, however, and the Hopi were left to their old ways until 1775, when Catholic priests again unsuccessfully tried to convert the Hopi. Then in 1832, the Spanish came again and began to reform the Hopi people.

American rule. When the territory came under American rule (1848), the Hopi, still disturbed by their break with their peaceful traditions, were among the most peaceful acceptors of American rule. Schools were provided. Children were taken from their parents to attend these boarding schools, led by white people, where even the Hopi language was forbidden. The Hopi way of life began to fade. The people had long lost their interest in pottery making, when at the beginning of the 20th century a Tewa woman, Nampeyo, who had married a Hopi man began to revive the ancient designs and to create beautifully crafted pottery. Since then, pottery making and jewelry making have been revived among the Hopi.

Recent disagreements with Navajos. The feuding of their first encounters smoldered among the Hopi and Navajo, even though some Navajo had been taken in and cared for in Hopi villages when white settlers and soldiers came to northern Arizona. As the Navajo increased in numbers, they claimed more and more of the land that the Hopi once had enjoyed. Eventually, Navajo land surrounded the Hopi villages. In 1937, the United States government ruled that the Hopi were entitled to exclusive use of 630,000 acres and could share another 1,800,000 acres with the Navajo. But neither side was satisfied by this edict and feuding continued. Finally, in 1970, the Indian Claims Commission ruled that the Hopi should have been paid for the 1,800,000 acres of their land they were forced to share with the Navajo. Still, the issue was not resolved and tensions mounted in regions where Hopi people had lived for centuries. Again in 1986, the United States government took judicial action to try to resolve the issue by forcing some Hopi to move from land claimed by the Navajo. The Hopi see the Navajo claims and government intervention as a threat to their way of life. Another threat to the Hopi way was the discovery of coal on the Indian lands. Known to be there throughout much of this century, coal mining in a commercial venture after World War II created jobs away from the family home and farm for many of the young Hopi.

Today Hopi relations with the outside world are guided by a tribal council headquartered in the community once known as New Oraibi but now called Kykotsmovi by the residents.

Culture Today

The Hopi village of Walpi.

Isolation. The disputes with their Navajo neighbors and their historical disillusionment with Christianity, particularly with Catholic missionaries, has helped to isolate the Hopi and perpetuate their old ways of life. Not until recent years have they begun to find jobs outside their farming communities and to develop their skills as artists for a wider commercial market.

Today, the Hopi people live in 12 villages; 11 of them are located on three great mesas overlooking valleys that cut through the Hopi Reservation.

Their villages are Old Oriabi (the oldest Hopi village), Kaikochomovi (located on the canyon floor), Hoteville, and Bacabi, all of which are located on what is known as Third Mesa. Sungopovi, Shhipaulovil, and Mishongnovi along with the Hopi Cultural Center are located on Second Mesa. Hano (a Tewa village), Walpi, Sichomovi, and Polacca (on the canyon floor) are located on First Mesa, the easternmost mesa. The village of Moenkopi is 40 miles northwest of Old Oraibi.

Water. Hopi tradition is regulated by their religion as well as the land and weather. Perched atop three high mesas, the Hopi villages overlook wide valleys where corn and some cotton are grown. However, water is scarce. There is little rain, but when the rain does fall, it often falls in torrents flooding the valleys. The water quickly sinks into the dry sand leaving trickles of streams and shallow pools from which the Hopi draw water for home use and for irrigation. In recent years, this water supply has been augmented by water trucked into the villages by the residents. A pickup truck carrying a large water container is a common site in northern Arizona.

Kachinas

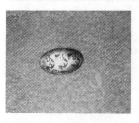

Overlay silverwork   Nampeyo pot

Examples of Hopi arts and crafts.

Food, clothing, and shelter. In this environment, the Hopi plant mounds of maize in June and rely on the summer rains to prepare the September harvest. Men tend the crops, but more and more, these men go out of the village to find jobs such as carpenters, coal workers, painters, and masons. There is now a Hopi cultural center along the main highway through the Hopi land. Here craftsmen produce excellent jewelry of silver and stone.

This Hopi girl wears the traditional dress and hair style.

Women stay in the village to make baskets, create pottery, cook and maintain the home. Their houses in old Oraibi, the oldest of the Hopi towns, are made of stone cemented into place. Mostly, homes are small single rooms or may have divisions for cooking and sleeping. Newer houses are made of wood frame and other building materials as are houses in other places in the Southwest.

Maize is the traditional staple food. Hopi women produce many different dishes from maize. One food that is well-known is *piki,* a tissue-paper-thin bread made of cornmeal and baked on a red-hot rock slab. More conventionally shaped breads are also baked and often covered with beans, chili, and meat to make a sort of Hopi "pizza."

Women on the Hopi Reservation enjoy bright-colored blouses with full, long skirts. Men today mostly wear western white clothing of blue jeans, long-sleeved shirts, and wide-brimmed hats. Both men and women enjoy silver and stone (mostly turquoise) jewelry.

Economy. Many Hopi men work as laborers on government projects or in neighboring towns and ranches, but each man also works in the fields, growing corn and squash. A typical Hopi workman might work at a job for someone else for eight hours, return to his own field to weed and tend the crops, then spend some evening hours socializing with other men in the *kiva,* a separate room or building for men. The men work the fields but they do not own them. Hopi society is matrilineal. Land is held by the village as common land but is divided among the women. In the villages, blocks of small, flat-roofed houses are built around plazas or squares around the home of the eldest woman of the family. This pattern is irregular in today's villages, but in the time of the first Spanish visits, they reminded the visitors of the plazas and squares in their own cities.

Language. The Spanish called the people of the canyon lands Pueblo people, thinking of the Hopi, Zuni, and the people living in the pueblos of New Mexico as of a common origin. However, the Hopi language is not related to the languages of the New Mexico pueblo people. The origin of the Hopi is unknown. Hopi stories deal with this unknown. Folklore tells how the first Hopi were born in another world far beneath this one. Through successive periods, the Hopi people migrated through two other worlds, eventually coming to this the fourth Hopi world. Here the Hopi share the world with the animals and plants, and therefore need to respect the animals. The ruler of the underworld, Masau'u is but one of many gods and spirits of Hopi religion. Masau'u, the god of Earth and Fire, is often portrayed bearing a basket of food to remind the people that it was he who gave the Hopis their most ancient foods.

Religion. In each Hopi village, a dug-out shelter called a kiva is built. This is a meeting place for the men of the village and a center for religious activity. Hopi religion is complex and much of it is secret. In the harvest season it centers around celebration of the food plants that give their lives to feed the people. The harvest season's religious festivals end with initiation of the children of the village into adulthood.

December through July is the time for religious celebrations involving the *kachinas*. The significance of the Hopi kachinas is difficult to describe in other languages. Kachinas may be symbolized by figurines in the homes, or as living costumed dancers in the religious ceremonies. They do not represent gods, nor are they always representative of human ancestors. The kachinas represent a larger spirit of the Hopi. Some are treated as powerful guardians bearing gifts of rain, crops, animals, and prosperity. Some play double roles, acting as messengers to the gods and as lesser dieties themselves. *Ahola* is such a kachina. Impersonated by a human dressed in mask, costume, and paint, he ritually opens the kivas to welcome other kachinas when they return to the Hopi villages. The Hopi believe the kachinas reside in the mountains near Flagstaff, Arizona. Legend has it that the kachinas were once frequent visitors, amusing the villagers when they were sad or lonely, teaching them to hunt, and bestowing gifts upon them. One story is that at one time the spirits were offended because they were taken for granted so they left to live in the mountains near what is now Flagstaff, Arizona. As a departing gesture, they taught ceremonies to a few of the Hopi and showed them how to make masks and costumes. The few Hopi charged with continuing the religious tradition also guard sacred sites scattered throughout a much larger land the Hopi once inhabited, reaching as far as the Grand Canyon. Periodically, the trusted Hopi visit these sacred spots and hold private ceremonies involving the use of corn meal and the leaving of gifts to the Holy People.

Impersonators wearing these masks and costumes are believed to be transformed into the spirits themselves. Other villagers receive the benefits of supernatural association by owning *kachin-tihus,* small, doll-like, sculptured effigies of the spirits. Often these kachin-tihus are crafted by Hopi fathers and uncles for the religious instruction of the children. Almost all kachinas are regarded as benevolent, but there are a few ogres, whose role is to admonish children when they misbehave and remind them to practice the rules of life that bind the Hopi. The early figurines that represented these spirits were block-style carvings with little motion. Over the years the style has become more naturalistic so that kachin-tihus now show kachina dancers in motion.

Another major feature of Hopi religion is dance. There are corn dances, snake dances, eagle dances, and dances in which other animals play significant roles. Perhaps the dance that is most well-known outside of the reservation is the Snake Dance, a rain dance held in late August in Mishognovi and Shongnopovi on alternate years. In this dance, Hopi men dance while working with live snakes. A typical dance includes 30 to 40 performers—all costumed men. They are often accompanied by six kachina maidens, actually men dressed as women. Dances are performed to the music of drums, rattles, bull roarers, flutes and whistles—Hopi musical instruments. Many of the Hopi dances have been witnessed by outsiders, but in recent years, these outsiders have mistreated or stolen fetishes, objects used in the ceremonies, which the Hopi consider sacred. Sporadically, the dances have been closed to outsiders because of this disrespect.

HOPI CEREMONIAL CALENDAR

KACHINA SEASON (Celebrations involving kachinas; held during Winter Solstice—Dec. 21 to mid-July)

January	February	March	April	May	June	July
Kiva Dances	Powamuya (Bean Dance)	Kiva Dances	Plaza Dances	Plaza Dances		Plaza Dances

NON-KACHINA SEASON (Mid July to Winter Solstice)

July	August	September	October	November	December
Niman	Snake or	Women's Society Dances		Wuwtsim	Soyalangw
Home Dance	Flute Dance			Tribal Initiation	

There are celebrations and rituals from the cradle to the grave in Hopi society, beginning with a ceremony in which the paternal grandmother names a newborn child at the age of 20 days. Later boys are initiated into various societies as an entry into adulthood and are then eligible to participate in the religious dances. The religious societies are presided over by a heirarchy of priests and chiefs. Priesthood is handed down to children by a mother's brother in keeping with the matrilineal organization of the people. In a matrilineal society, property and rights within the society are often handed down from generation to generation through the women's lineage.

Government. Hopi religious societies are composed of clans, each clan with particular responsibilities in the society, and each associated with an animal or other part of nature. There is the bear clan, beaver clan....The Bear clan ranks the highest because its ancestors are thought to have been the first to emerge from the underworld.

Until forced to unite in recent years by outside pressures, the Hopi had no central government. Politics was left entirely to the village, whose chiefs remain the "keepers of tradition." Each village is headed by a council. This group of leaders, with one as the village chief, was the only representative government in the past. Now the federal government has devised a tribal council in order to deal with the Hopi as one unit. The council elects a chairman who is, at least in dealings with outside groups, the chief representative of the Hopi people.

Today. Closed into their own world by their complex religion, unique language, and reluctance to welcome new ideas, the Hopi are gradually being drawn into the larger society of the United States. Young people are more often leaving the villages to seek their fortunes in other communities, and the elders struggle to preserve the old Hopi ways. Thus, in recent years the Hopi struggle to preserve their traditions has grown more difficult. Tourists flock to the most famous Hopi ceremonial dances, sometimes disturbing the Hopi tranquility. In their struggle to maintain their independence, the Hopi insist that visitors take no pictures and record no sounds on the reservation without permission.

For More Information

See these reading materials:

O'Kane, Walter Collins. *The Hopis*. Norman, Oklahoma: The University of Oklahoma Press, 1953.

Wright, Barton. *Hopi Kachinas*. Flagstaff, Arizona: Northland Press, 1977.

IRISH AMERICANS

(i´rish eh mer´ uh kins)

Americans whose ancestors were born in Ireland.

Population: 10,337,353 (1980).
Location: United States (all regions).
Language: English, Irish brogue, Gaelic.

Geographical Setting

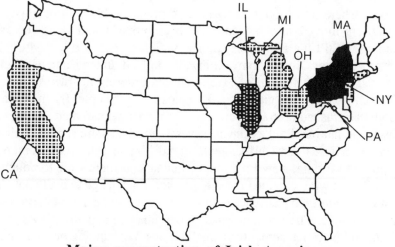

Major concentration of Irish Americans.

Though once the Northeast was the region most heavily populated with Irish Americans, over the years this group has become fairly evenly distributed through the United States. One route of entry brought them first to Canada, which counted 669,685 residents of unmixed Irish descent in 1986. However, the vast majority immigrated directly to the United States or moved on to America after their arrival in Canada. They became an overwhelmingly urban people, preferring America's cities to its farm areas. New York, Philadelphia, Boston, Chicago, and San Francisco proved to be favorite cities. As a rule, the immigrants would form their own enclave in a city, Irish towns growing within the larger metropolises. The largest contingency settled in New York, whose population continues to include the greatest share of Irish Americans today.

Historical Background

Hibernia. The history of the Irish Americans begins in Hibernia, the name given to Ireland by the Romans who ruled it. Roman power was waning in the year 432, when Saint Patrick converted many of the Irish to Christianity. After the Normans conquered England, they moved on to Ireland in 1169. They conquered Irish territory, beginning to dominate the people, a condition that would last for over 700 years. There followed an enslavement of the Irish by the English, which is remembered bitterly in story and song.

The feud blossomed into a religious war under England's King Henry VIII (1509-47), who moved to replace Ireland's Catholic Church with his own Anglican Church. The Irish resisted, doggedly insisting on remaining Catholic. Therefore, England seized Irish property. Plantations appeared, and settlers moved into the country to colonize it and tame the Irish "heathens." Still the Irish resisted. The violence escalated in 1649, when England's dictator Oliver Cromwell invaded Ireland. In the name of religion, Cromwell conducted a war of extermination, ordering his men to execute 2,800 Irish soldiers and citizens at Drogheda, for example. By the time all Ireland was crushed (1652), over a third of its people had died due to wars, disease, and famine. Sold as slaves, several thousand were sent in chains to the West Indies. Cromwell's agents urged him to sell Irish women for transport to Virginia, New England, or Jamaica, as there were too many in Ireland. Those who remained faced a grim lot. England passed a Penal Code of laws that said Irish Catholics could not vote, serve on a jury, carry a gun, or go to college. The Catholics had to pay taxes to support the Anglican Church, and their punishment for small crimes was hanging or banishment. So thousands of them left. If they couldn't afford passage to North America, they became indentured servants. That is, for the price of passage they sold themselves into service for a wealthier colonist for two to four years, after which they could pursue their own fortunes in the new land.

Immigrants. The Irish arrived in large groups from about 1717. By 1870, close to 3,300,000 Irish immigrants had arrived in North America. They came to the continent in two general phases. Before the potato famines of the

1800s, many Protestants from Ulster, Northern Ireland, settled in America. They were clearly Irish, but their ancestors had originally come from Scotland to Ulster. Calling themselves Scotch-Irish, they used this heritage to shed the stigma that was later attached to the pure Irish. Back in Ireland, a famine in 1740 claimed 200,000 Irish lives. Then the linen trade flagged, inspiring more movement to North America.

Franklin and the Irish. Benjamin Franklin, in particular, encouraged this movement. Reputed as excellent soldiers throughout the world, the Irish fought in the French, Spanish, and German armies. The Irish brigade had won great fame in the French army, carrying its own flag into every battle. Franklin traveled to Ireland in 1771 to secure some of these fierce fighters for the American cause. Four years later, on May 10,1775, the Second Continental Congress dangled America before the Irish as a home of safe refuge from the English.

The Revolutionary War. The Irish upheld their reputation in America, individually and as a group. Irishmen such as Captain Samuel Howard took active part in the Boston Tea Party, dressing as Mohawks and dumping the tea into the harbor. A corps of riflemen, mainly Irish, formed in June, 1775. Dressed like Indians, they wore leggings and moccasins decorated with beads and porcupine quills. Their white-or-brown linen hunting shirts had fringes and their wampum belts held a knife and tomahawk. Fighters for the Revolutionary cause, they were feared by the Loyalists for their deadly aim. Irish sailors were equally formidable, winning the first naval battle of the Revolution at Machias Bay (June 12, 1775) under Jeremiah O'Brien. O'Brien went on to fight more battles by sea until he was captured and shipped to Mill Prison, England. From there he escaped, then settled in Maine. Captain Molly fought too, beginning a tradition for Irish women in America. After her husband fell from a gunshot wound, she took over, firing his cannon on the advancing enemy. The deed, General Washington thought, was deserving of rank, so he dubbed her *Captain.*

For a brief 50 years after the Revolution, the Irish enjoyed a respected role in American society. A dynasty of sorts began with the most important Irish Catholic family of early America, the Carrolls of Maryland. Already in 1688, Charles Carroll had distinguished himself in politics as the Attorney General of Maryland. His grandson Charles Carroll became the only Catholic to sign the Declaration of Independence. A daughter of this Charles, Mrs. Richard Caton, became the first lady of high society. The Irish came to America with experience in politics from Catholic Associations they had formed to repeal the Penal Code back in Ireland. Therefore, men such as the first Charles Carroll rose to the forefront, becoming Attorney General of Maryland in 1688. Education and oral arts—poetry, speechmaking, storytelling—had also been highly valued in Ireland. In the new country, journalist Matthew Carey, who had fled Ireland after writing articles against its government, began the *Pennsylvania Herald* in 1784. Robert Adrian became a leading mathematics professor at Columbia and other American universities.

Famine years. Then came Ireland's series of potato crop failures beginning in 1822 and its Great Famine of 1845–47. Some one million people starved to death or died of related diseases in the Great Famine. Close to one and a half million others made the perilous journey to America in the decade that followed. Mostly from Southern Ireland, this later tide of immigrants was generally unwelcome. They were peasants with a reputation as a poor, hard drinking, quarrelsome lot, and an unpopular religion— Catholicism. Without skills, these newcomers would work for less money than other laborers. So they competed for jobs, and taxes rose because they increased the need for poorhouses. With the immigrants came new housing problems. They built rickety shanties or crowded into slums like the Five Points District in lower Manhattan. Full of tenements and noisy saloons, the district sheltered a whole family in one multipurpose room.

Riots. Anti-Irish, anti-Catholic riots began. In Charlestown, Massachusetts, in 1834, a mob burned the Ursuline Convent, forcing out 12 nuns and 60 students. Riots erupted ten years later in Philadelphia's Irishtown. Here 3 churches were destroyed, 200 homes burned, 30 people killed, and 150 more wounded in the street fighting. Less violently, New England businessmen sought workers for hire, saying "No Irish Need Apply." The backlash peaked in 1854 when the Know-Nothing Party began winning elections. A secret party, its members claimed to "know nothing" when asked about their group. They preached against immigrants and Catholics, then died with the coming of the Civil War.

The Irish rioted in New York City's 1863 draft riots, burning and looting to protest a law that allowed wealthier citizens to buy their way out of the army for 300 dollars. A number of Irish-born Northerners spoke against abolishing slavery, arguing that it was hypocrisy to champion freedom for blacks when there was so much poverty among whites in New York.

The Civil War. Once in the army, however, the Irish displayed an eager willingness to fight that did much to elevate their image in the nation. General Thomas F. Meagher placed a newspaper advertisement summoning

100 young Irishman to a company attached to the 69th Regiment. Known as the "Fighting 69th," the Irishmen charged into battle at Bull Run with bayonets and a green silk banner, stripped to the waist in the July sun of 1861. Thirty eight died. Still, the unit went on to lead the attack at Antietam in 1862, then dispersed after heavy losses at Gettysburg. Some 150,000 Irish-born served the North in the war, including General Philip H. Sheridan. Roughly 85,000 served the South, including the Emerald Guards of Alabama and Stephen Mallory of Jefferson Davis's Cabinet. The Irish gained a new image. Instead of unruly ruffians, they were considered a staunch-fisted, freckle-faced group with tremendous courage. The last quarter of the 1800s became a time of achievement.

Progress. Socially, the Irish who immigrated in the late 1800s were a young group, mostly under 35 years of age. Some 75 percent could read and write English, but their lives as peasants in Ireland left them ill-prepared for city life. They came to Lowell, Boston, Philadelphia, Chicago, San Francisco, their fortunes depending somewhat on the community. In California, the group seemed to have a golden touch in real estate and mining, which gave rise to the expression "the luck of the Irish" in the late 19th century. In San Francisco, they experienced more financial success than anywhere else. Peter Donahue, for example, founded the city's first iron foundry and manufactured its first streetlights. He earned four million dollars before his death, gifting his wife a coach made entirely of glass.

Elsewhere the Irish were more likely to work in a foundry than own one. Lowell was a Massachusetts mill town, where Irish factory hands earned low wages. Along with textiles, they manufactured the traditional Irish shawl for pennies. Women in Boston and Philadelphia earned as little as nine cents a day for making shirts. Other Irish women and men worked as house servants (gardeners, grooms, cooks). Mostly, though, they served as a massive unskilled labor force whose hard work transformed towns into cities. Streets and sewers were largely built by Irishmen. They did dangerous work, hard physical labor. In the 1820s, many built the Erie Canal. Then came the 1860s and the backbreaking laying of tracks for a transcontinental railroad. The Irishman joined forces with the Chinese for three dollars a day. A song of the era says "Poor Paddy works on the railroad," using Paddy for Irishman. In the 1890s, the Irish went on to build skyscrapers. Through the years, the Irish staffed volunteer fire companies and the police. Over one third of New York City's police at mid-19th century were Irish-born.

Since much of their work was dangerous, men died early, often by their late 30s. Accidents and injuries were the main cause of deaths in the 1880s. Widowed women became a familiar sight in Irishtowns.

City life. The Irish formed their own tightly-knit towns within the larger city. Here lived the early Irish businessmen—the blacksmiths, the grocery-store owners, the saloonkeepers. The home, the church, and the saloon became familiar centers of life. More than a drinking place, the saloon was a center of community activity. It doubled as a meeting center for political parties, unions, and societies. Mothers often bore their children at home in the shanty or tenement room, and families ate their meals together here.

Parishes, or neighborhood church districts, appeared in Irish areas of settlement. Using their own money, residents built the Catholic church—often a red brick building with a square tower. Catholic schools included instruction on life in Ireland. The Irish Catholics preferred such academies to public schools, where students read from a Protestant Bible. There were only enough Catholic schools for a small number (35 percent in the mid-19th century) of students, and many could not attend because they had no funds for tuition. Still, a system of Catholic schools appeared through the college level. A mainly Irish student body attended Notre Dame, so the university's athletic nickname became "The Fighting Irish."

A strong system of material and emotional support existed in the Irish community. If the father of a household died early in life, the family worked together for the survival of the unit. Young children remained in school but sold papers or ran errands for money at age five or six. A 12-year-old boy might take a full-time job hauling freight. Neighbors helped. For instance, widows received donations from surrounding homes. Similarly, old timers aided the new immigrants. They held "kitchen rackets," welcoming parties, on Saturday nights and then helped the newcomers find jobs.

Politics—Tammany Hall. As members of a larger society, the Irish sometimes resorted to violence. Mine bosses paid no heed to miners' complaints against low wages or forced buying at company stores. So the Molly Maguires, a small, terrorist group of Irishmen, murdered nine managers in 1874–75. Working undercover, an Irish-born detective tracked down 19 culprits. They were tried, then hung.

Two hundred New York Irishmen stormed Tammany Hall, the headquarters of Democrats who excluded the Irish from politics early in the century. Windows as well as noses were broken. After this incident, the Irish played a pivotal role in Democratic politics in New York. William Marcy Tweed, a Tammany boss of Scotch-Irish ancestry, bribed politicians and robbed New York's treasury. The Irish-American lawyer Thomas Addis Emmet brought Tweed to justice in the courts.

The Irish were mainly Democrats. They organized political "machines," groups whose leaders, or bosses, controlled politics in large cities of the North and Midwest. Part of the machine, block captains served as a boss's agents in the different neighborhoods. They promised the residents jobs and help with government in exchange for their votes. For example, a boss might get a city to build new bridges, which created jobs for construction workers. As the 19th century progressed, the Irish grew powerful in government and law enforcement across the country. In 1860, John G. Downey became the first Irish-born governor of a state, California. In 1873, the first Irish-born political boss, "Honest John" Kelly, took over Tammany Hall. Lee McNelly led the Texas Rangers in an 1875 war against raiders who were stealing some 200,000 cattle a year.

Sports and Religion. Aside from politics, boxing and the Church were fields in which the Irish could and did excel in the 19th century. In 1853, Irish-born John Morrissey won America's heavyweight championship. The prizefighter John L. Sullivan became as famous for boasting about his skill as displaying it. His name was John Sullivan and he could "lick" just about anyone. Raised in a Boston tenement, he remained heavyweight champion until 1892, when he lost a 75-round bare-fisted fight to Irishman James J. Corbett. Corbett came from San Francisco. Called "Gentleman Jim," he represented a new breed of "lace curtain" Irish. The term refers to middle-class Irish who struggled to overcome the image of a quarrelsome, hard-drinking people, the image associated with the "shanty Irish." Though their grandmother may have lived in a Central Park shanty, the "lace curtain" Irish had achieved some financial success. Now they wanted to climb the social ladder, if possible back up to the level of the great Carroll family of earlier days.

The Catholic Church was an area in which the Irish reached the highest rung on the ladder. Irish and Germans competed for leadership in it, and the Irish won. By 1886, of 69 bishops, 35 were Irish American and 15 were German. Two Irish American leaders of the Church, James Cardinal Gibbons and Archbishop John Ireland, directed its growth. Becoming active in daily life, the Church opened orphanages and hospitals as well as schools. It has been regarded as the most binding tie in Irish America. The Church served as a bridge, encouraging the Irish to build lives in a new land while bringing them the old, familiar religious traditions.

Ties to Ireland. Like the Church, the cause of Irish freedom from England bonded Irish Americans together. There were more Irish in America than Ireland, and Irish American organizations (the Fenians, Clan na-Gael) acted to liberate those back in the home country. America was Ireland's base of operations. Aside from loyalty to the cause, many Irish Americans felt other Americans would only respect them after they undid their disgrace as a conquered people. In 1921, the war between England and Ireland ended. England agreed to create an Irish Free State in the south, leaving Northern Ireland under its rule. The agreement plunged Ireland into guerrilla warfare in 1972. There were Irish Americans who shipped weapons to the rebels. More generally, their identity as a group had begun to wan. Now many took a more active interest in their cultural roots than they had in the recent past.

In the early 1900s, Irish farmers left farms such as that on the left to start a new life in American apartments (right).

Culture Today

The Irish American mix. In the late 20th century, Irish Americans have been less visible as a group than in earlier years. A cause is their success as individuals in larger society. Also by 1960, they were more likely to marry someone of non-Irish than Irish heritage, thereby dampening the ethnic influence.

Business. Irish Americans gained power in arenas beyond politics, the Catholic Church, and boxing rings. Individuals distinguished themselves in business, building on a tradition set by earlier Irish Americans. Cyrus Hall McCormick had revolutionized farming by inventing the reaper (1834) and William Kelly had patented a steel-making process (1857). After taking a meat-packing job at age 14, Michael Cudahy developed refrigerated meat and founded a meat-packing company that controlled much of America's livestock. Later, Henry Ford introduced the first standard automobiles (1908).

The Irish Americans furthered the growth of labor unions, too. Involving the Church in daily affairs, Cardinal Gibbons won support for the nation's first union movement, the Knights of Labor. At its head was Irish American Terence V. Powderly. After its demise Irishmen formed the majority of teamsters, dockworkers, and builders in the American Federation of Labor. Women participated, too. Mary Harris Jones helped organize Industrial Workers of the World in 1905. Supporting poverty-stricken coal miners, Mother Jones, as she was called, was often jailed for her activities. Irish American George Meany led the joint AFL-CIO (Congress of Industrial Organizations) until his death in 1979.

Holidays. From their largest union, the Brotherhood of Carpenters, came Peter J. McGuire's 1882 proposal for the American holiday Labor Day. St. Patrick's Day (March 17) was first an Irish celebration. The belief is that St. Patrick was a bishop who converted the Irish to Christianity after being sold into slavery by outlaws in his youth. He is linked to the shamrock, whose three leaves he used to explain the Trinity. Infecting non-Irish Americans, St. Patrick's Day celebrations became a national event. New York City staged a grand parade that has continued to the present.

Minority relations. As the largest minority and the first to speak English, the Irish served as path breakers for other groups. After John F. Kennedy became the first United States Irish Catholic President, he appointed the first Italian American Cabinet member (Anthony Celebrezze), the first Polish American Postmaster General (John Gronouski), and the first African American housing agency director (Robert Weaver). There was a tradition of conflict, too. The Irish competed against the Italians for jobs, houses, and church rule. Regan's Colts, an Irish athletic club, attacked blacks moving into Chicago's Irishtown after World War I, and there was an earlier attempt to bar blacks from Catholic schools. In the 1930s and 40s, fierce street fighting broke out between the Irish and Jews in New York City

Language and Mr. Dooley. Back in Ireland, the people's gift for words had spawned classics by native writers such as Jonathan Swift (*Gulliver's Travels*) and George Bernard Shaw (*Pygmalian*). They carried the gift to America, where their words affected the language and their works attracted worldwide attention. As a conquered people, their own language, Gaelic, had been supplanted by English in the 19th century. In America, they spoke brogue, an Irish variety of English.

Finley Peter Dunne began in 1803 to write newspaper sketches about an Irish saloonkeeper named Mr. Dooley. In brogue, Dooley discusses life with a patron, Hennessy. On one occasion Hennessy reflects on his life in America. (Fanning 1987, p. 179).

"...I've lived a misspent life," he says. "I niver give care nor thought to th' higher jooties iv citzenship,' he says. "Mebbe," he says, "I had to wurruk too hard,"....

Mr. Dooley became a 20-year feature in American newspapers.

Theater. The 1930s and 40s were decades of accomplishment for Irish American writers and actors. Playwright Eugene O'Neill won the Nobel Prize for Literature in 1936. Before him, the Irish had contributed greatly to American theater, in minstrel and musical shows. George Primrose originated the softshoe of the minstrel show, combining elements of African and Irish American dance. With Tony Hart, Edward Harrigan produced a series of musicals about Irish Americans. Included in their last plays were songs about the newly rich.

Harrigan also acted, displaying a talent that escalated him to stardom. By 1910 he had been upstaged by a master of romantic and musical comedy, George M. Cohan—a singer, dancer, and playwright. *The Song and Dance Man*, a 1920s Broadway hit, told the story of Hap Farrell, a second-rate variety actor who considers himself the best in the world. Later, Gene Kelly starred in *Pal Joey*, a play based on short stories written by John O'Hara. The actress Laurette Taylor is often remembered for her role in *Peg O'My Heart*, a play about an Irish girl in an English family who turns out to be the true lady of the family. Irish American John Ford rose to fame as a director of motion pictures, and James Cagney as an actor in gangster roles. (In fact, real Irish American gangsters appeared after the prohibition of liquor, and the

Hudson Dusters were an infamous gang of New York Irish boys.) Other notable Irish American actors included John Barrymore and John Wayne.

Novels and news. In the 1930s and 40s, the novels of F. Scott Fitzgerald and James T. Farrell escalated Irish American writers to fame. While Fitzgerald (*Great Gatsby*) is celebrated for his superb talent, Farrell (Studs Lonigan trilogy) has been hailed as a spokesperson for Irish America. His novels portray the working class. Aged 15, the boy Studs jams his hands in his pockets and sneers at circumstances: "'Well, I'm kissin' the old dump goodbye tonight.'"

Farrell was not the first Irish American writer to deal with social issues. Before him came the novels of Stephen Crane (*Red Badge of Courage*, 1895.) Also, poet John Boyle O'Reilly (1844–90) had written articles in the Boston *Pilot* defending blacks and Jews. Newspaperwoman Nellie Bly (Elizabeth Cochrane) exposed the misery of tenements. Starting a tradition for Irish American women, her career led to the comic strip "Dixie Dugan."

Comics. Comics, too, became a forum. There was "Bringing Up Father" by George McManus, a strip about Irish Americans. Jiggs is a business man whose wife nags him to leave behind the warm, friendly past and climb up the social ladder to the future. Addressed to a more general audience, "Pogo" by Walt Kelly commented on American politics and social life. "Dick Tracy" by Chester Gould was pure detective entertainment.

Heroes—the military and politics. In real life, soldiers and politicians have continued as Irish American heros. Irish American John Barry has been dubbed Father of the United States Navy. After his feats in the Civil War, General Philip Henry Sheridan became Commander in Chief of the United States Army. The "Fighting 69th" reappeared in World War I. General John O'Ryan and Colonel William "Wild Bill" Donovan served in this war. Donovan went on to head America's first intelligence agency during World War II.

The record in politics is more mixed. Alfred E. Smith was a political hero. To the Irish, government service is the highest calling and officials are judged by the ideals they further. Smith fought for social reforms—workman's compensation for injured laborers, fire escapes, sprinkler systems, no child labor, and equal pay for women teachers. He served as New York's governor for four terms, becoming the first Irish Catholic nominated for President in 1928. Though he lost, Irish Americans acquired powerful federal positions soon after. Frank Murphy became Attorney General and Joseph P. Kennedy an ambassador to London. Both were appointed by President Franklin Delano Roosevelt. Kennedy's case seemed to be a landmark appointment: an ambassador of Irish Catholic heritage was sent to England. With the advent of Joseph Raymond McCarthy in the 1950s came a black period in politics. He whipped the country into a scare that America was secretly being undermined by communists. McCarthy accused and had the Senate interrogate a host of Americans, causing much injury to their careers. Some Irish politicians—Senator McMahon, for one—fought his scare tactics. Others supported McCarthy, while many avoided him. In 1954, he was censored for improper conduct, and the scare fizzled out.

James Daley

John Kennedy

Irish immigrants became leaders in public services, then rose to be important political leaders.

Six years later, in 1960, the Irish experienced what might be called a green period in government, a beginning. The nation elected John Fitzgerald Kennedy, the first Irish Catholic President. Over the centuries the American Irish had worked for power in society, and now it was theirs. Society had accepted them. Then Kennedy died under the fire of an assassin's bullet. Killed in 1963, his time in office had been turbulent. He faced grave issues—Civil Rights riots, for example—that he took very seriously. Yet he displayed an Irish sense of humor and gift for words (Adler 1964, p. 58).

> I used to wonder when I was in the House how President Truman got into so much trouble. Now I'm beginning to get the idea....

Later leaders include Robert Kennedy, a candidate for President in 1968, when he too was shot. Also Mayor Richard Daly governed Chicago until his death in 1976, and Tip O'Neill served as Speaker of the House until his retirement in 1987.

Tradition today. Irish Americans as a group have become less visible in the second half of the 20th century. In sports, Irish boxers faded after James Braddock lost the heavyweight championship in 1937. The group had displayed a strong presence in baseball too, with greats such as Cornelius McGillicuddy (Connie Mack) of the Philadelphia Athletics. Today they have fewer ballplayers. The traditional sports—hurling and Irish football—continue. Much like field hockey, *camánaíocht*, or hurling, has teams that use broad-bladed sticks to drive a ball into a goal. Irish football has been described as a mix of soccer and rugby.

Other traditions survive today. At annual gatherings known as the *feis*, people in old Irish dress perform dances. New York has Saint Patrick's Day parades, replete with floats and banners, which preserve ties to Ireland, too. Customary dishes such as corned beef and cabbage have become part of the daily American diet. Within the Irish American family, trends continue. Children of Irish-born immigrants still marry later than other foreign-born groups.

Change has occurred in religion. Presently, the role of the Catholic Church seems weaker than it once was in the daily life of the people. Irish Americans formed only 17 percent of the total Church membership in the 1970s. However, they still exercised a large measure of control, since at the same time 50 percent of the bishops were Irish Americans.

Called the Waterfront Priest, Father John Corridan, kept alive one of the finest of Irish American traditions. He became a champion of the common people, the longshoremen. Father Corridan died in 1986, after the New York Waterfront Commission was established for the longshoremen's protection.

For More Information

See these reading materials:

Callahan, Bob, ed. *The Big Book of American Irish Culture*. New York: Viking Penguin, 1987.

Cooper, Brian E. ed. *The Irish-American Almanac and Green Pages*. New York: Pembroke Press, 1986.

Contact these organizations:

Irish American Cultural Institute, 2115 Summit Avenue, Box 5026, College of St. Thomas, St. Paul, Minnesota 55105.

An Claidheamh Soluis—The Irish Arts Center, 553 W. 51st Street, New York, New York 10019.

ITALIAN AMERICANS
(i tal'yen eh mer' uh kins)

Americans whose ancestors were born in Italy.

Population: 6,883,000 (1980).
Location: United States, mainly the Northeast.
Language: English, Italian American, Italian.

Geographical Setting

Areas of greatest Italian American population.

The majority of today's Italian Americans live in the northeastern United States. Next in population is the North Central region, then the West, and lastly the South. Some 90 percent live in cities rather than rural areas, favoring New York, Boston, Philadelphia, San Francisco, and New Orleans.

The first immigrants came from northern Italy, but the greatest number came from southern Italy and the island Sicily. Bound for New York, many of these later migrants remained in this city. Most Italian Americans today trace their ancestry to the later migrants. Their mass-migration around 1880 had far-reaching effects. A century later, in 1980, New York still claimed more Italian Americans than any city in the nation. However, their location within cities had changed. Italian Americans no longer occupy separate neighborhoods, as they once did. While a few churches and grandparents remain in their old areas, the people now reside mostly in the suburbs or in working class neighborhoods.

Historical Background

Early explorers. Italians greatly influenced early American history. The explorer Christopher Columbus sailed for Spain in the late 1400s but was born near Genoa, Italy. Amerigo Vespucci, from Florence, Italy, made four voyages to the New World (1497, 1499, 1501, 1503). America takes its name from him. Arriving in New Orleans in 1774, the Italian fur trader Giuseppe Maria Francesco Vigo became a hero of the American Revolution. Vigo used his wealth and knowledge to help conquer the Northwest Territory, then died penniless.

Jefferson and Mazzei. Probably the most notable of the early Italians was Filippo Mazzei. Friend to Thomas Jefferson, Mazzei arrived in Virginia in 1773. Together, Jefferson and Mazzei wrote articles calling for political freedom. It was Mazzei who made the statement *Tutti gli uomini sono di natura ugualmente liberi ed indipendenti* (All men are by nature equally free and independent). Aside from his efforts in politics, Mazzei worked as a scientist in America. He planted flowers, fruits, and vegetables then unknown in the New World. Jefferson was so impressed by Mazzei's accomplishments that he encouraged more immigration from Italy.

The 1800s. The 1800s began a century of accomplishment for Italian Americans in art and science. In 1805, Jefferson imported 14 musicians from Italy to begin the United States Marine Band. An Italian American, Antonio Meucci claimed to have built the first telephone in 1849, but he reportedly was too poor to register the invention. Sometimes called the "Michelangelo of the United States Capitol," Constantino Brumidi came to decorate this government building in 1855. He worked on it for the next 25 years, creating the first fresco in the United States ("Cincinnatus at the Plough"). Also in the mid-1800s, Italians brought opera to the country, beginning the Cuban Havana Opera Company under Luigi Arditi.

The Civil War years increased the status of the group. Italian Americans contributed to the war effort on both sides. Fighting for the North, an Italian

Legion was formed with outstanding soldiers such as General Enrico Fardella and Count Luigi Palma di Cesnola. A noteworthy soldier for the South was Decimus et Ultimus Barziza.

Immigration from Italy was fairly limited until the late 1800s. Before then, immigrants from northern Italy had migrated to America. The discovery of gold in California in 1849 attracted many of these immigrants to the West. There they worked as merchants, shopkeepers, grape growers, and wine makers. Other immigrants spread throughout the country. By 1860, a few Italian Americans appeared in every state.

Italy in the late 1800s was a collection of small states that operated separately rather than as a unified country. Especially in southern Italy, people endured miserable lives. Without land of their own, they farmed large estates using old-fashioned hand plows, hoes, and spades. Their homes were single-room hovels without windows or chimneys. Furniture consisted of a bed, a chair, and a wooden chest. For food, the *contadini* (peasants) ate mostly pasta and cornmeal, growing potatoes and corn as their staple crops. Peasants typically earned from 16 to 30 cents a day. They hoped for a better future when the provinces of Italy became united, but these hopes were quickly dashed. When Italy became unified in 1870, the Northerners seized control. Finding themselves without power or land, many southerners and Sicilians left. Some nine million of these Italians streamed over the ocean to North and South America in search of a better life.

Drawing Italian men to North America were the *padroni*. Otherwise known as labor agents, padrones combed Italy for men to send to America, or recruited the men when ships docked in North America. The padroni then sent them wherever industry demanded a large supply of labor on short notice. A padroni would promise immigrants steady work at high wages, taking a commission of one to 15 dollars from each of them.

Settlement. Since Italy only united as one country in 1870, people had little time to develop loyalty to the nation. They divided loosely into the northern Italians and the southern Italians. Close to Europe, the northerners lived in a comparatively intellectual, urban environment. They felt superior to the many poor, uneducated southerners. In both regions, though, the strongest ties were to local areas, such as Genoa, Naples, and Sicily. People thought of themselves as Genoans, for example, rather than Italians.

After the immigrants settled in North America, ties to their place of origin remained strong. In New York, Italians from Naples lived on Mulberry Street, while Sicilians settled on Prince Street, and Italians from Calabria lived on Mott Street. Omaha, Nebraska had two colonies of Italians, Calabrians on the west side and Sicilians on the east side. From Calabria,

Antonio Santa had moved to Omaha, becoming a foreman for the railroad. Thereafter, he persuaded friends and relations to join him, finding them jobs on the railroad. The Sicilian community developed in similar fashion. In the 1890s, the Salerno brothers opened a shoe repair and grocery in Omaha. Their chance of success would be greater, they thought, if there were other Sicilians in Omaha to use their services. So they persuaded their old neighbors to migrate to America, opening a boarding house for the newcomers.

The division of Italians into subgroups in Omaha was typical. It was as if small areas of Italy moved to areas of America, due to a process of *chain migration*. First a man immigrated. Then he attracted others from the same home area.

Daily life. Flocking to cities, Italians and other immigrant groups (see POLISH AMERICANS) filled a great need. The nation was thirsty for laborers to build canals, lay railroad tracks, dig trenches for its sewers, and so on. Trained only for farming, most of the Italians took unskilled jobs. In New York, three of every four Italians worked in manual labor during the 1880s. They tended to scatter among different industries, taking jobs as day laborers or railroad workers. They also became organ grinders, barbers, waiters, bartenders, longshoremen, and construction workers. In 1904, the construction workers helped build Manhattan's Grand Central Terminal for the daily wage of dollar and a quarter.

Most Italians abandoned farming when they came to America, although a few ran a successful farming colony in Byron, Texas. Some late-1800 migrants became farm laborers. Mostly Sicilians, they were treated like blacks. Plantation owners lynched or publicly whipped Sicilian farm hands for suspected wrongdoing. They earned the same wages as blacks—75 cents to a dollar for a 12 to 16 hour workday. During sugar season, a farm hand could earn 30 to 45 dollars a month, a fantastic sum when compared to earnings in Italy.

Some Italians succeeded in truck farming and fruit growing. In New Orleans, the farmers sold high-quality produce in the city, controlling its vegetable market. In California, they began as tenant farmers, saving their earnings and often forming partnerships to purchase farmland. They grew vineyards and produced wine, San Francisco's Italians becoming the most prosperous in the United States.

The men migrated to America first, then sent for the women of the family. Joining the labor force, these women worked mostly in industry. They manufactured artificial flowers, silks, lace, candy, paper, and cigars. Italian American women became the largest group of female garment workers by 1910. The women formed over a third of the work force, outnumbering Jewish women in the occupation. Outside industry, women contributed to the family in several ways. Italian women of New Orleans sewed clothing by hand, then sold it in the French Market. For their own use, they raised artichokes, squash, tomatoes, and strawberries on vacant city plots that they called *la terra benedetta* (the blessed land).

Italian neighborhoods developed, often near rail yards at the edge of town. Housing at first was quite dismal. People lived in basements, garrets, converted stables, or warehouses. In the Five Points section of New York, residents occupied barracks-type tenements, a tenement sheltering up to 50 families. In Louisiana, men and boys as young as ten crowded into one-room shacks that stood on stilts. They ate bread and water, summing up their daily life with a rhyme: *acqua e pane, vita di cane* (water and bread, a dog's life).

The Mafia. Most Italians, then, were hardworking immigrants. Yet Americans thought of them as gangsters. Along with the swarm of newcomers from southern Italy and Sicily came an image of them as *mafiosi*, or criminals. The image was mostly undeserved, since the majority were law-abiding peasants. Back in Italy, there was indeed a Mafia. Sicilian landowners had started the Mafia as a secret force to protect themselves against looters and foreign powers. It was not a gangster movement at first. However, by the 1800s, the Mafia in Italy had deteriorated into criminal bands.

Only a minority of these criminals immigrated to America. But as these Italians were convicted for organized crimes, their reputation infected many innocent Italians. The people as a whole were considered a lawless bunch,. and suffered from this stereotype for generations to come. For most of the 1800s, the image of Italians as artists had outweighed the image of them as rogues. By 1891, the tables were turned.

Americans became convinced of the existence of a single Italian American crime cartel. A Mafia (organized crime) scare swept the country. Some Italian Americans did participate in organized crime, but the existence of a cartel remains questionable (Iorizzo and Mondello 1980). Nonetheless, the Mafia was accused of heinous crimes, and innocent Italians suffered because of it. Angry townspeople blamed the murder of David C. Hennessy, a New Orleans police chief, on the Mafia. Italians killed Hennessy, they said, for investigating crime among the Sicilians there. Authorities arrested the alleged culprits. Later, some of the townsmen took justice into their own hands, shooting ten of the accused in jail. An eleventh victim was hung. Of the 11, three had already been found innocent, three were involved in an officially declared mistrial, and five had not yet been tried at all.

Sacco and Vanzetti. Fear of Italian crime swept the country. The Immigration Act of 1924 placed a yearly quota of 3,845 on incoming Italians. Meanwhile, there was the case of Nicola Sacco and Bartolomeo Vanzetti, two Italians accused of killing a paymaster and a guard in a shoe factory. Apart from their Italian heritage, the two were also anarchists, people who believed in no type of government. Sacco and Vanzetti were tried, found guilty, and executed in 1927. Before his death, Bartolomeo Vanzetti made a final statement in court (LoGatto 1972, p. 55).

> Well, I have already say that I not only am not guilty of these
> crimes, but I never commit a crime in my life...I am suffering
> because I am a radical and indeed I am a radical; I have
> suffered because I was an Italian, and indeed I am an Italian.

Crime in the early 1900s was not limited to the Italians. There were Australian gangsters (the Sydney Ducks) and Irish criminals (the Plug Uglies). Creoles and Jews each formed gangs, too. Some of the Italian American criminals earned notorious reputations—Paolo Vaccarelli, Lucky Luciano, Jim Colosimo, and Al Capone. It is argued, however, that these gangsters were a product of life in America, not Italy. After the 18th Amendment outlawed the making, selling, or transport of liquor in 1920, it became highly profitable to engage in organized crime. The Amendment was repealed in 1933. Afterwards gangs turned to illegal activities such as gambling and the narcotics trade.

World Wars. In World War I, some 300,000 Italian Americans are estimated to have served in the United States Army alone. The Sacco and Vanzetti affair followed close on the heels of the War and labeled Italian Americans as communists. Soon after, events leading up to World War II labeled them as Fascists. Many Italian Americans applauded Italy's leader Benito Mussolini at first for tackling problems such as the Mafia in Italy. Opposing views developed in Italian American communities. In New York, parading Fascists and anti-Fascists locked horns on Memorial Day, 1927. Two died in the tumult. In the 1930s, new exiles from Italy, such as symphony conductor Arturo Toscanini and scientist Enrico Fermi, arrived in America. With them came evidence that turned others against Mussolini. In 1941, after the United States entered World War II, Italian Americans fully supported its military effort against Italy. An estimated 550,000 members of the group served in the American armed forces during the war. At the time several hundred thousand Italians in the United States were not yet citizens. The suspicious government called them enemy aliens at first, but in 1942 the enemy alien status was removed. By the war's close, valiant Italian American soldiers had earned 12 Congressional Medals of Honor and ten Navy Crosses. Marine Sergeant John Basilone held off the Japanese at Guadal-canal for three days, won a Medal in 1943, then died at Iwo Jima.

Meanwhile, Italian American citizens brought honor to the group in other fields of endeavor. Arturo Toscanini won unparalleled fame as conductor of the Philharmonic Symphony Society of New York. Mayor of that city, Fiorello H. La Guardia began slum-clearance programs and raised health standards there. Enrico Fermi received the Nobel Prize for his experiments in radioactivity. Along with men such as Albert Einstein, Fermi went on to develop the atomic bomb. Congressman Peter W. Rodino succeeded in making Columbus (an Italian) Day a national holiday in 1967.

Economic success. By 1970, close to 90 percent of all Italian Americans lived in cities of the Northeast. They had a century-long history in the region, settling mainly in Philadelphia, Boston, and New York. All three cities had been sites of conflict between Irish and Italian immigrants, who competed for living space and jobs. Arriving at Pennsylvania coal mines in 1894, 150 Italians faced gunshots from Irish strikers. Similar disputes occurred in Boston and New York. Conflict continued into the 20th century, but has eased with economic success.

As individuals and as a group, Italian Americans experienced success in business during the 1900s. By 1915, far fewer Italians lived in the downtown ghettos. The ambition to own housing catapulted many of them into the suburbs and drew them away from unskilled labor. Amedeo Obici founded Planters Peanuts in Virginia (1905), becoming known as the Peanut King of America. The labor leader Luigi Antonini organized garment workers (1916), bettering their working conditions. Two Sicilians bought bananas from Honduras, their business methods earning them great respect. By the 1960s, their Standard Fruit and Steamship Company (the Vaccaro-D'Antoni corporation) was the nation's leading importer of bananas. A 1963-64 study found 48 percent of all Italian American workers employed in skilled and professional jobs. By the 1980s, the majority of Italian American families had moved into the middle class.

Culture Today

The Italian mix. Becoming an Italian American has been a two-step process. It first involved a blend of the different groups of Italians and then a larger mix of Italian and American ways. Immigrants from Northern Italy felt superior to the Southern Italians and the Southerners, in turn, to the Sicilians. Furthermore, each village group—for example, immigrants from Sicily or Genoa or Naples—tried to remain separate from all other Italians. In fact, many spoke their own dialect and did not understand other immigrants. *Piatto* meant "dish" in one dialect; *plat* meant "dish" in another.

Life in America brought the different Italian groups into daily contact with one another. They worked together, sent their young children to school together, attended the same church (the majority are Catholics). They began to cooperate. An Italian American language developed, combining standard Italian, its dialects, and English. *Storo* meant "store," *pichnicco* "picnic," *grosseria* "grocery." Neither Italian nor English, the language was called Itaglish.

The Italian American mix. As for the larger mix of Italian and American ways, children contributed to its achievement. There was strong resistance among the Italian Americans to education at first. Parents viewed children as economic assets. They added to the earning power of the family. Back in Italy, they helped with the farming. In keeping with this tradition, immigrants from southern Italy and Sicily had their children work rather than attend school. As a result, 54 percent aged 14 and over had not yet learned to read by 1910. Families continued to encourage child labor into the 20th century. A 1919 study counted 91 percent of Italian-American New York girls over the age 14 working for wages. At 14, attendance ceased being compulsory, so children withdrew from school and went to work.

In their spare time, older children and adults could acquire some education from Italian mutual aid societies. These societies also furnished health care for a small monthly sum (once 25 to 60 cents). The largest, the Order of Sons of Italy, began in New York in 1905. Today it has some 100,000 members, and other Italian American societies have since developed. Examples are the Italian-American Cultural Society (established 1957) and the National Organization of Italian-American Women (established 1980).

As a second generation of Italian Americans came of age, attitudes changed. Children moved out of old neighborhoods, spoke English, and sent their offspring to public schools. By the 1940s and 1950s, the children preferred American ways. World War II helped reduce differences between immigrant groups. Roughly 550,000 Italian Americans served in the armed forces during this war, strengthening their ties to the U.S. and to fellow soldiers with different backgrounds. The army, then, joined with the schools and the ethnic self-help organizations in easing the mix of Italian and American ways.

Food habits. The new mixture of Italian and American ways influenced daily life. In the 1940s there were *latticini* food stores, which specialized only in fresh Italian cheeses, and there were pasta shops, which made nothing but fresh pasta. Later, these were replaced by supermarkets and delicatessens. The group grew to enjoy American as well as Italian meals.

At the same time, Italian foods such as minestrone soup, chicken cacciatore, and spaghetti entered into the everyday American diet. Though Italians from different areas had became mixed, their recipes were still tied to specific places—for example, *Minestrone alla Genovese* (vegetable soup, Genoa style) and *Pizza Siciliano* (Sicilian pizza). There were many southern Italian restaurants, featuring spicy dishes with tomatoes, and a small number of northern Italian restaurants with their lighter-tasting sauces.

On holidays, Italians feast on dishes such as *pasta ca' muddica* (spaghetti in sauce made of bread crumbs, celery, and cheese). A family feeds strangers on St. Joseph's or St. Anthony's Day, believing they may be saints themselves.

Family life. In similar fashion, some traditions in family life remained. Other habits changed. Ties to the extended family have weakened over the years. Whereas relatives were once seen weekly, they now often have contact with one another only on special occasions. Also, new immigrants tend not to work in family-owned businesses anymore.

Back in Italy, families were physically demonstrative. It was important to show love and affection. Children hugged their fathers. Hosts raised their arms, greeting their guests in a gesture of warmth. These habits have continued, as has the closeness of the small nuclear family. After following a group of Italian American Catholics, one study found that 87 percent of the children still visit their parents weekly.

Also, very few of today's families place their old people in nursing homes, and divorces are rare. Respected members of the group state their own observations about growing up in the Italian American family. According to psychotherapist Aileen Riotto Sirey, the mother-son bond is the strongest (Cateura 1987, p.109). The author Gay Talese explains that he writes about father-son relations because that is where the conflict in the

Italian American family is (ibid, p. 71). By tradition, the father dominates the family.

An Italian American family in the 1930s.

Paul Campisi compared the family in Italy to first- and second-generation Italian families in America (Nelli 1983). He found, that in the middle of the century, a family in Italy educated young women for marriage. In America, the first-generation family gave young women some schooling but also educated them for marriage. The second-generation family changed even more, encouraging broad schooling for a young woman. Her individual achievement took precedence over the family. In keeping with this finding, Italian American women now swim in the mainstream of American professional life. Eleanor Cutri Smeal, three-time president of National Organization of Women, and Geraldine Ferraro, the first woman to run for United States Vice President (1988), are two notable examples.

The arts. Beginning in 1880, an Italian press in America published the daily newspaper *Il Progresso*. It continues today and has been joined by other papers. The nonfiction writer Giovanni Schiavo has written works such as *Italian-American History* (2 volumes, 1947 and 1949). In poetry, labor leader Arturo Giovannitti (1884-1959) wrote verse while in prison.

Poet John Ciardi (1916–1986) wrote for children and adults. His work includes a collection of verse that he calls "Poems from Italy" (Ciardi 1984, p. 22):

Nona Domenica Garnaro sits in the sun
   on the step of her house in Calabria.
There are seven men and four women in the village
who call her Mama, and the orange trees
fountain their blooms down all the hill and valley.
No one can see more memory from this step
than Nona Domenica.

In music, the group has furthered opera in America through singers such as Ezio Pinza and Rosa Ponselle and again through Philharmonic Symphony conductor Arturo Toscanini. Composer Gian-Carlo Menotti won a 1955 Pulitzer Prize for "The Saint of Bleeker Street." Another award-winning composer is Henry Mancini. Highly regarded vocalists include Mario Lanza, Dean Martin, Frank Sinatra, Perry Como, and recent popular singers such as Madonna (Madonna Louise Ciccone). They uphold an early tradition. Reputed as fine musicians, the immigrant Italians were readily hired in this profession. In art, cartoonist John Fischetti won a 1969 Pulitzer Prize. Frank Stella has achieved fame as an abstract painter.

An early actor, Eduardo Migliacco Farfariello (Little Butterfly) wrote and performed character sketches based on life in New York's Little Italy. In motion pictures, examples are Academy Award winning directors Vincente Minelli and Frank Capra. Acclaimed screen stars include Al Pacino.

Movies about Italians first contributed to prejudice against them. Gangster films of the 1920s, such as *Little Caesar,* featured Italian American thugs. Chico Marx of the Marx brothers mimicked Italians in the movie *Cocoanuts*, which suggested they were an ignorant group. Such images spread to other media. *Wanted Comics* told its 1948 readership that young Italian immigrants brought organized crime to America.

The media upset its own earlier stereotypes of Italian Americans in the 1970s. In the movie *Serpico*, an Italian American detective fought crime. The clever Lieutenant Columbo performed the same task on television. In Marvel Comics, there was a superhero with an Italian name—Pietro.

Heroes and holidays. Also countering the damaging stereotypes were real life success stories. In sports, Joe Di Maggio became baseball's Home Run Champion (1937, 1948). Some still regard his consecutive-game hitting streak, 56 in 1941, as the most unbreakable record in sports. Yogi Berra won baseball's Most Valuable Player Award (1955), then coached the New York Yankees to the World Series (1964). Angelo "Hank" Luisetti dazzled basketball fans with one-handed shots he kept making on the run. In football, Brian Piccolo became College Scoring Champion (1964), Ed Marinaro won the Heisman Memorial Trophy (1971), Coach Vince Lombardi entered the Hall of Fame (1972), and auto racer Mario Andretti drove the fastest lap ever (1966).

Arturo Toscanini

Jimmy Durante

Joe Dimaggio

A. P. Giannini

From tenant to bank owner—some famous Italian Americans.

Other fields have Italian American heroes as well. Credited for much progress in education is Dr. Leonard Covello. In East Harlem, New York, he configured public schools for Italian American students that fostered pride in their heritage and language. Law and government had their champions, too. Just as Mayor Fiorello La Guardia fought corruption in New York, United States attorney Rudolph Giuliani later tackled organized crime in America.

Born in Genoa, Christopher Columbus continues to inspire pride in the people. Columbus Day, October 12, has been an important holiday to Italian Americans. Already by 1869 they celebrated with floats, drum and bugle corps, sharpshooting contests, and a staged landing of Columbus's ships, the *Pinta, Niña,* and *Santa María.* Other holidays commemorate religious heroes, who are patron saints of places in Italy. Celebrated on September 19, the Feast of San Gennaro, for example, honors the patron saint of Naples, St. Januarius.

Religion. Italian Americans remain mostly Catholic today, and many are active observers. However, the group has few bishops in proportion to its numbers. It seems to accept Irish hegemony in the Church. Religion among the Italian Americans seems to be both a personal and social affair. Individuals ask St. Joseph, foster father of Jesus, to aid them in time of need—illness, for example. In thanks for recovery, they build an alter to him on St. Joseph's Day. St. Anthony's and St. Januarius's Day (the Feast of San Gennaro) inspire religious and carnival-style celebrations. Outside of Christmas, most religious holidays are not family affairs. Several are social events, though. From different areas, Italian Americans descend on New York City for the main festival of the year—The Feast of San Gennaro. A six-day event, it features fireworks, booths, even Ferris wheels.

Ties to Italy. While there is an ever greater mixture of Italian and American ways, certain customs remain. One is the habit of putting food on the table when a guest walks into the house. Another is the expression of love in the family. Ties to Italy remain strong. Italy's government was active in the welfare of the immigrants, setting up a health clinic for them in New York in 1910. The immigrants, in turn, provided for friends back in Italy. Joseph Battaglia, for example, began a grocery and produce business in America. He employed workers in Italy, having his olive oil made there, then shipped to Pittsburgh for sale. Today's Cultural Society sponsors speakers from Italy to promote traditions. Confused by the early stereotypes, many of the Italians in America once felt shame because of their ethnic heritage. Now there is a new pride in being Italian American.

For More Information

See these reading materials:

Cateura, Linda Brandi. *Growing Up Italian: How Being Brought Up as an Italian-American Helped Shape the Characters, Lives, and Fortunes of Twenty-four Celebrated Americans..* New York: William Morrow, 1987.

Gallo, Patrick J. *Old Bread, New Wine: A Portrait of the Italian-Americans.* Chicago: Nelson-Hall, 1981.

Contact these organizations:

Italian-American Cultural Society, 2811 Imperial, Warren, Michigan 48093.

National Italian American Foundation. 666 11th Street N.W., Suite 800, Washington, DC 20001.

Rudolph Valentino and other Italian Americans became famous actors.

JAPANESE AMERICANS
(jap´ eh neez´ eh mer´uh kins)

Americans whose ancestors lived in Japan.

Population: 716,331 (1980).
Location: United States, mainly the West Coast. About one-third of the U.S. population lives in Hawaii.
Language: English, Japanese.

Geographical Setting

CA

Hawaiian
Islands

Most Japanese Americans live in California or Hawaii.

Four-fifths of North America's Japanese live in the United States, the greatest two centers being Los Angeles and Honolulu. Additional groups reside in other Pacific urban centers (San Jose, San Francisco, and Seattle) as well as throughout the agricultural areas of central California.

After World War II, many Japanese Americans decided to settle in Western and Midwestern states such as Illinois, Colorado, and Utah. Chicago, Illinois, has the largest population of Japanese Americans east of the Rockies. The disruption of the war years also sent smaller numbers to virtually every region of the United States.

Historical Background

In the 1850s, Japan was just starting to emerge from a 250-year period of isolation from the West. Beginning in the 1600s, it had been ruled by the great Tokugawa dynasty, whose *shoguns* (military leaders) used isolationist policies to strengthen their political control. In the 1700s, the isolationism began dissolving as Japanese scholars began to take an interest in the West and in the British colonies in America. By 1853, when Commodore Matthew Perry arrived in Japan with a fleet of U.S. warships to negotiate a trade agreement, books about the United States had been widely circulated in Japan. A treaty was signed in 1854, setting the stage for the first small groups of Japanese immigrants to America. These immigrants, who would begin arriving in 1869, became known as the *Issei*, meaning first generation. Their sons and daughters who were born in America are called *Nisei* (second generation), and the third generation are known as *Sansei*.

Immigration. Early relations between Japan and America were important to the course of Japanese immigration because the Japanese government kept track of the numbers of immigrants and of how they were perceived and treated. This was especially true in the beginning stages, when many Japanese came to Hawaii and the United States for short-term economic reasons, thinking they would earn money and return to Japan. In 1868, the last Tokugawa shogun fell. He was replaced by the Emperor Meiji, who recognized the need for Japan to take her place in the industrial world. As Japan joined the industrial revolution and discarded the old feudal traditions, many Japanese men—especially those from the *samurai*, or warrior class— were left without a role in society. It was in such an atmosphere of social and political turmoil that Japan permitted the first emigrations to Hawaii in 1868 and to California in 1869.

Early Japanese in Hawaii. The American planters who dominated the independent monarchy of Hawaii first imported Chinese laborers under low-paying, five-year contracts. When these contracts ended, the plantation owners looked around for laborers to replace the Chinese. The owners recruited 150 Japanese in 1868 under a three-year contract in the cane fields. Accustomed to city life, the new laborers were unhappy and ineffective working in the fields. After intervening in a dispute over wages and conditions, the Japanese government forbade such emigration. The episode led the government to take an active role in managing emigration, which resumed in 1886, but with stricter controls.

Over 60,000 Japanese lived in the Hawaiian islands by the turn of the century. Like the Chinese, many Japanese immigrants had gone into business for themselves. The Japanese had a relatively easy time fitting in to the already racially diverse mix of people in Hawaii. They multiplied, and by 1920, at over 100,000 strong, they made up 43 percent of the population. Life for the immigrants would be more difficult on the mainland.

"Lost Colony." The first Japanese to settle on the American mainland were unlike those who would follow. Instead of searching for better economic conditions, they apparently fled political persecution. One group had definite connections to the fallen Tokugawa dynasty. This is the "Lost Colony of Wakamatsu," a small group of 27 farmers, tradesmen, and samurai. Located near Placerville in Northern California, the colony did not survive for long. The plants brought over by the colonists (such as mulberry trees for silk farming) failed to withstand the long journey and dry California soil. The colonists left only a few traces, one of which was discovered on a tombstone near the site in the 1930s: "In memory of Okei, died 1871, age 19 years, a Japanese girl."

Taming the soil. With the renewal of immigration in 1886, many Japanese men headed for West Coast cities in search of work. The greatest period of immigration was in the years 1890-1920, when the Japanese men replaced Chinese laborers on farms or as Western railroad workers. Later, many of these immigrants concentrated in coastal urban areas, setting up grocery stores, rooming houses, and restaurants. Others became farmers, raising fruits and vegetables on land that had earlier been barren.

The farmers often came in groups, lured from agricultural areas of Japan by promises of plentiful labor. At first working for established white farmers, the greatest number picked fruit or vegetables for long hours and low wages. Eventually some saved enough money to lease or buy a few acres and set up their own farms, frequently in areas that others had considered infertile. The story of one such Issei, K. Ikuta, is told in a 1921 report to California Governor William B. Stevens. Other farmers, the report reads, had spurned the alkaline soil of the Sacramento Valley, but a Japanese named Ikuta decided to raise rice there. After years of hardship, he conquered the difficult soil and grew the first commercial rice crop in California.

Though few were as successful as Ikuta, his willingness to struggle with difficult conditions was a common characteristic among these Issei farmers.

In the early part of this century, they introduced crops such as grapes, strawberries, tomatoes, celery, garlic, lettuce, and citrus fruits to many areas. By 1909, it was estimated that nearly 40,000 Issei worked at some aspect of farming in the United States, nearly three-fourths of them in the valleys of central California.

Those Issei who did not become independent farmers usually settled in West Coast cities: Los Angeles, San Francisco, Seattle, Tacoma, Portland. There, an Issei who was penniless could appeal to systems like *tanomoshi*. A financial self-help system, tanomoshi was a pool of money used for loans or credit. An immigrant could rely on it for a few dollars until he found work washing dishes in a Japanese restaurant or sweeping up for an Issei grocery store owner. Many small businesses were financed by tanomoshi loans. Another way Japanese helped each other was by recognizing people from the same *ken* (political region of Japan, much like a state or province). Outside of family, the highest obligation an Issei could have was to someone from the same home area, a *kenjin*. Kenjin tended to settle together and help each other in business, either by patronage or training. If an Issei opened a grocery store, for example, his first customers would be kenjin. He, in turn, would supply money and training to help his kenjin open their own stores. Common in Japanese communities, such support systems arose not only out of the culture's natural cohesiveness. They served also as a defense against barriers to success (such as boycotts by whites).

Small businesses and railroads. Since most of the Issei had been farmers in Japan, many preferred to embark on different careers in their new environment. They can be roughly divided into three groups of about 10,000 (1909) each: domestics (gardeners, dishwashers, and hotel and restaurant workers), owners of small businesses (grocery stores, restaurants, and rooming houses), and railroad workers. Competing with Native Americans (see TLINGITS), another 8,000 Issei worked in the Northwest salmon canning factories and lumber mills. Still others labored in the Western mines of Utah, Nevada, and Colorado.

Anti-Japanese discrimination. These occupations offered limited opportunities for advancement. Even the Issei who owned small businesses served only the Japanese community, in which competition was fierce. They quickly found that they were not welcome in the larger white community, which was itself mostly made up of immigrants. Like the blacks and Chinese before them, the Japanese were physically "different," so outsiders could easily discriminate against them.

Many Issei grew prosperous in agriculture, their prosperity inspiring fear and hostility among the whites. Under pressure from such "nativists," who played on fear of Japan as a new world power, the national and state governments passed a number of discriminatory measures. The Supreme Court upheld a law allowing only "free white persons" and those of African descent to become citizens. Asians such as the Issei could not acquire U.S. citizenship.

In the "Gentlemen's Agreement" of 1907, Japan agreed to limit emigration to the United States. As a result, the number of immigrants fell sharply and continued to decline. Then, in 1913, the Alien Land Act made those who could not become citizens ineligible for ownership of land, and limited their leases to three years. (This law, aimed specifically at Japanese, did not stop them from working farms, however, because many transferred ownership to their children, who were citizens by birth.) Finally, in 1924, Congress passed an "Exclusion Act," which prohibited the immigration of those who could not become American citizens. Many historians believe the act helped militarists in Japan gain power, which ultimately led to Pearl Harbor and U.S. involvement in World War II. Years after the war, in 1952, the Issei finally gained the long-awaited right to acquire U.S. citizenship.

"Picture brides" and the arrival of the Nisei. Mostly men, the first wave of immigrants looked to Japan when they had established themselves enough to think of marrying. The more prosperous traveled back to their homeland and returned to America with Japanese wives. Arranged by friends or family, many other marriages involved partners who had seen only photographs of each other. A man often married a woman from his own home area or village. Even if they came from the same home area, there were often disappointments on both sides. The "picture bride" sometimes had higher expectations of her husband's position and wealth than turned out to be the case. Generally, her husband would greet her at the dock in anxious anticipation. The wife's assimilation began almost immediately. She would typically discard her kimono for a tight-fitting corset and exchange her sandals for narrow, high-laced shoes.

The arrival of Japanese women forced the Issei men, often migrant workers, to settle down and take on the responsibilities of family life. Soon these couples began having children—the Nisei, or second generation, had arrived.

For many of the Issei, life in the United States was an unbalanced mixture of Japanese and American ways. They would adopt Americanisms reluctantly. Issei workers learned only enough English to get by on the job. They ate Japanese foods (rice with fish or vegetables, tangy *tsukemono* pickles, noodles in broth). Also, they celebrated the Japanese New Year at parties held by their *Kenjin-kai*, the association made up of people from the same home area, their kenjin. A Kenjin-kai New Year's party was a boisterous reunion, full of Japanese singing, dancing, and *sake* (rice wine).

As with the Issei, life for the Nisei was a mixture of Japanese and American ways. For the Nisei, however, the mixture appears to have been more balanced. They learned English at school and spoke Japanese at home. While peanut butter and jelly became standard lunch foods, dinner consisted of rice eaten with chopsticks. Some Issei organized Japanese language schools for their children to attend after regular school. However, many of the Nisei resented these schools, gaining little if any knowledge of Japanese by adulthood.

Parents raised their Nisei children to respect authority, work hard in school, and act as conscientious members of society. Excelling as students, Nisei often attained university education or professional training. Still, they encountered many of the same problems as their parents. Discrimination had forced the Issei parents to rely on other Japanese immigrants for work, yet when they did they were considered alien and unassimilable.

Now the Nisei encountered the same prejudice and were more troubled by it because they felt American. A Nisei with an engineering degree might have to settle for a job pumping gas. As for the professionals, a Nisei doctor or lawyer was restricted to practicing within the Japanese community. Conditions had improved, but only slightly, and for both Issei and Nisei the hardest test loomed ahead.

World War II and "Relocation Centers." On December 7, 1941, Japan attacked Pearl Harbor, Hawaii, headquarters of the American Navy's Pacific Fleet. The United States declared war on Japan, joining forces with England, Russia, and their allies. America had entered World War II. Japanese Americans felt shocked and frightened. How would the war affect them? At first, several government leaders counseled restraint: don't mistreat Japanese Americans because of something they had no share in, cautioned congressmen such as Jerry Voorhees of California and John Coffee of Washington.

Since the Japanese Americans lived mostly among themselves, other Americans had little familiarity with them. In the tense and frightened days after Pearl Harbor many thought that Japanese Americans might welcome and aid an invasion of the West Coast by Japan, or that there might be spies among them preparing to send information "home" or sabotage the war effort.

Newspapers and West Coast government leaders began calling for evacuation of Japanese Americans from the coastal states. By this time, most Japanese Americans were Nisei, U.S. citizens by birth, but those who called for evacuation ignored the citizens' rights. From the beginning, high-level military advisers told Congress that chances of an invasion were nonexistent. Exhaustive searches and interviews produced no evidence of Japanese American disloyalty or espionage. In fact, during the whole war there was not one example of treason. All the same, about three months after Pearl Harbor, the FBI began rounding up Japanese Americans, both citizens and Issei. The United States contained over 125,000 Japanese Americans by this time, and about 112,000 of them lived in the three coastal states (California, Oregon, Washington). Nearly all of them—over 110,000—were uprooted from their homes and sent inland to "relocation centers" built by the Army. The worldly goods they had so painfully amassed had to be sold off cheaply or left behind when they relocated to the centers. Ten relocation centers appeared in Western states with names like Manzanar and Tule Lake.

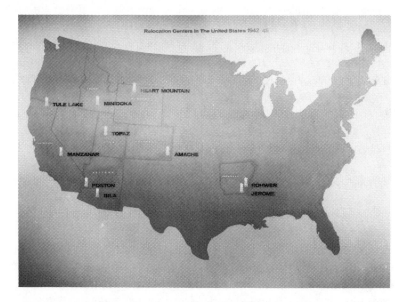

Life in these centers, sometimes called concentration camps, was uncomfortable and tedious. The camps consisted of hundreds of low, black tar-paper barracks surrounded by barbed wire and armed guards. Often located in deserts, the cheaply assembled huts were dusty and hot. Family life was difficult in the camps—everyone ate together in huge mess halls and showered in stalls that were usually far away, a trudge through dust, mud, or snow. Relocation had been so hasty that few of its proponents had considered what to do with the Japanese Americans placed there. Therefore, the Japanese had to organize themselves in the camps. Makeshift schools were set up, and representatives were elected to convey suggestions, requests, and grievances to the authorities. At Tule Lake and elsewhere, camp members held demonstrations against their unfair treatment. Housewives did their best to make the huts homelike and comfortable. In time, many of the men obtained leave to work in groups for local farmers. There was a high demand for the men's labor since other farmhands had been drafted to fight the war.

Japanese American Citizens League. "Relocation" was a terrible shock to the Japanese. They felt hurt and angered by their treatment and by the perception that they might be disloyal. German and Italian Americans, they pointed out, had not been treated this way. Internally, there were arguments over how they should respond as a group. Some reacted with hostility, but others felt that loyalty demanded they cooperate and wait until they could prove their patriotism, though such proof should be unnecessary. Among the advocates of cooperation were leaders of the largest and most influential Japanese American association, the Japanese American Citizens League (JACL). Its dynamic leader Mike Masaoka, who at first fought against evacuation, explained his eventual acceptance of it (Hosokawa 1982, p. 151):

> ... we feared the consequences if Japanese Americans refused to cooperate, and the Army moved in with armed troops and even tanks to eject the people forcibly from their homes. At a time when Japan was still on the offensive and apparently winning the war, we were afraid that the American people would consider us traitors....

Nisei war heroes. Masaoka urged Washington to allow Nisei to fight the war. Issei soldiers had served with distinction in World War I, and a few Nisei were actually serving even then, though some had been dismissed and interned in the camps. Eventually the Army agreed and established a Nisei regiment, the 442nd Regimental Combat Team, which would become one the the most highly decorated regiments in the history of the United States Army. It suffered brutal losses, especially in the famous campaign to rescue the Lost Battalion in the Vosges Mountains of France in October, 1944. Survivors of the Lost Battalion gave a silver memorial plaque to their Nisei rescuers. One of the Nisei soldiers, Private Sadao S. Munemori, won a posthumous Congressional Medal of Honor for leading a one-man assault against machine gun positions, and then sacrificing his life by diving on top of a hand grenade that landed among his companions.

Over 3,000 Nisei served in the Pacific theater as part of the war effort against Japan. Those who spoke Japanese proved especially valuable to intelligence operations by translating Japanese radio messages and interrogating Japanese prisoners of war. Many, such as Staff Sergeant Kenny Yasui, were discharged from the Army after Pearl Harbor. Allowed to re-enlist as a linguist, Yasui served in Burma, where over a loudspeaker he urged Japanese soldiers to surrender. Yasui and three others swam out to an island on which the enemy was entrenched, captured 16 Japanese soldiers, and transported them back on a raft. Nisei servicemen such as Yasui shortened the war by months. Awarded the Silver Star, Yasui became a Japanese American war hero. Fellow Americans recognized the Nisei contribution to the war as outstanding. Whether or not proof of their loyalty was needed, the Nisei made heroic sacrifices that contributed greatly to diminishing prejudice against them.

Redress. In the 1970s, the Japanese American community launched an important campaign for redress, that is payment for the suffering and losses incurred during the war years. Lasting into the 1980s, this movement became highly controversial among Japanese Americans themselves. While many supported it in principle, some dismissed it as too late to compensate those who had so long ago lost their homes and belongings or their lives. A lengthy period of debate, both in Congress and among Japanese Americans, resulted in the passage of a redress bill in 1988. Set at 20,000 dollars per person, payments were scheduled to begin in 1990. Estimates suggested that some 60,000 evacuees, about half the original total, would remain alive to receive the payments at this time.

Culture Today

Immigration from Japan to the United States continues, though in less significant numbers: 30,000 arrived in the years 1961 to 1976, for example, and immigration declined in the 1980s. Meanwhile, American citizens of Japanese descent have become more universally middle class.

Though the upheaval of the war scattered Japanese Americans to new regions of the United States, the majority returned to the familiar West Coast states to rebuild their lives. Many barriers to advancement toppled after the war, allowing the group to join the mainstream of American life. Japanese Americans distinguished themselves in school and in business. By 1990, over a third of the men occupied professional or managerial positions, compared to 4 percent in 1940.

Food, clothing, and shelter. Assimilation, the adoption of American ways, increased across the different generations. As described, the early Issei clung to Japanese ways as much as possible in America. They ate traditional foods in their new environment. The importance of agriculture, both in Japan and America, meant that vegetables have always played a central role on the Japanese table. Flavored with soy sauce, vegetables combined with rice exemplify a customary dish. The people sometimes pound rice into *mochi*, a sticky sort of dough that can be shaped into little buns. Seafood has always been central to the cuisine. *Sushi*, Japanese dishes centered around seaweed, rice, and raw fish, recently gained popularity in America. Presently, it is served in Japanese restaurants across the country. Japanese recipes have been retained, the people adding more dishes to and taking other ones from the general American diet as generations passed.

Issei arrivals quickly adopted American dress habits. Farm workers or gardeners wore straw hats, work shirts, dungarees, and boots. Women who picked crops tied a scarf over their hats for added protection. As soon as the men could afford it, they bought themselves formal suits, high-collar shirts, derby hats, and walking sticks. Their wives purchased billowy dresses and graceful hats. Nisei children typically wore khakis or jeans with canvas sneakers.

Housing depended on location and time period. An Issei contract laborer occupied an unfurnished room or a cot in a barracks house provided by his employer. Others rented space in an Issei-owned rooming house, or occupied the spare room of a relative or kenjin. As the Issei became more established, they would rent or buy more spacious houses in cities, or build bigger homes on their farms. Today most Nisei and Sansei families live in mixed neighborhoods in West Coast cities or suburbs, though "Little Tokyos" still provide a comfortable environment for recent immigrants.

Little Tokyo. The Japanese formed their own subcommunity in cities such as Los Angeles, California. Known as Little Tokyo, its history in this city showed rapid growth during the 1920s and 1930s. Fellow immigrants welcomed newcomers here. Elsewhere they faced foreboding signs: "JAPS KEEP MOVING. THIS IS A WHITE MAN'S NEIGHBORHOOD." (Murase 1983, p. 50). The early homes in Little Tokyo, small wood-frame structures, gave way to large brick buildings by the 1920s. During World War II, when the Japanese relocated, blacks settled in Los Angeles's Little Tokyo for a time. By the late 1940s, though, Little Tokyo had revived its

Japanese flavor. Changes have come with the passage of time. Now the district has a 16-story apartment building for senior citizens, a shopping mall, a Buddhist temple, and the six-story Japanese American Cultural and Community Center.

Religion. Nearly all the Issei arrived as Shinto Buddhists, but most converted to Christianity as they adjusted to life in America. Christian organizations such as the Japanese Gospel Society in San Francisco often helped them find work and learn English. Before World War II, segregated Christian churches catered to Japanese Americans only, but after the war an effort was made to eliminate such churches. The Buddhist churches that have survived in America retain links with those in Japan, and through them many Nisei and Sansei children gain exposure to Japanese ways. On a Buddhist holiday such as the *Bon Odori*, kimono-clad celebrants dance down the street to the rhythm of drums and the light of lanterns.

The arts. Drama has played an important part in the development of Japanese culture. Virtually every Issei community staged its own amateur productions of *kabuki* plays, traditional dramas with stylized music and dance. Also performed by Nisei and Sansei children, these plays often reinforced customary values such as devotion to one's parents. Theaters such as the Nippon Kan in Seattle became centers of Japanese culture. Today, however, these theaters have mostly disappeared.

With a large concentration in Los Angeles, Japanese Americans developed a notable presence in movies and television. The most famous early actor was Sessue Hayakawa, who appeared in the Academy-Award winning postwar film *Bridge on the River Kwai* (1957). Later, the Nisei actor George Takei became known to millions as Sulu, helmsman of the starship *Enterprise* on the popular TV series "Star Trek."

There were Japanese-language newspapers published in Los Angeles, San Francisco, and Seattle for the Issei. Kyutaro Abiko introduced the first English section in 1925, in the paper *Nichi Bei*. A year later he started the *Japanese American Weekly*, which acquired a Nisei readership and gave Nisei writers a chance to be published. Later, the *Pacific Citizen* became the voice of the Japanese American Citizens League.

Business. Because the Issei, like the Chinese before them, took lower-paying jobs than whites, they encountered hostility and rejection from organized labor. Both Issei and Nisei were barred from joining the unions that controlled crafts such as painting, plumbing, and carpentry. So they were forced to work for nonunion employers, which only caused more hostility. Barriers were broken in the late 1930s, when the Japanese could finally enter American labor unions.

Today Japanese Americans participate not only in labor unions but also in professional associations. The major role played by Japanese technology in America's auto industry and other businesses has inspired new prejudice. While most of it has been nonviolent, one case ended in death. Vincent Chin, a Chinese American mistaken for a Japanese American, was beaten to death in 1982.

In careers, the Japanese concentrated first on small farming and independent businesses (gardening, dentistry). They supported one another. Southern California, for example, saw the Japanese dominating the produce market. They established connections from farms to wholesale markets to retail stores. While this type of mutual support isolated the group, it also strengthened their bond as a people.

Business prejudices decreased after World War II. Members of the larger population began hiring Japanese American employees. Other Japanese Americans left farming to start their own small businesses. Then came the movement into the professions. A 1960s study involving 339 Sansei men showed the majority preferred professional careers over farming and small businesses. Some of their popular choices in the professions were to become engineers, teachers, or physicians (Bonacich and Modell 1980, p. 239).

Politics. The first Japanese political successes occurred in Hawaii, where the attainment of statehood in 1959 was directly achieved by young Nisei veterans. Daniel Inouye, a World War II hero who lost an arm fighting with 442nd Regiment, became Hawaii's first Representative and won election to the Senate in 1962. In 1966, three-fourth's of Hawaii's delegation to Congress were of Japanese ancestry: Senator Inouye and Representatives Patsy Takamoto Mink and Spark M. Matsunaga. In the 1970s, three Japanese Americans represented California: Senator S. I. Hayakawa and Representatives Norman Y. Mineta and Robert T. Matsui. The success of these elected officials has done much to bolster the self-confidence of present-day Japanese Americans. Though the group forms less than one percent of the general population, from the late 1970s through the early 1980s Japanese Americans supplied three percent of the U.S. Senate.

Sports and recreation. Baseball is a favored sport among Japanese Americans. Issei fans not only followed the exploits of baseball heroes such as Babe Ruth and Lou Gehrig, they also organized their own leagues in the 1920s. Two teams from Seattle, the Asahi and Mikado, split the Japanese community there into factions, each with its own heroes, pennants and lapel pins. Many Nisei all-Japanese Little League games are popular family events. Also, the Japanese Americans formed their own basketball leagues. Traditional sports of the 20th century include sumo wrestling. Japanese immigrants held annual sumo tournaments in Little Tokyo. Today, the practice of traditional martial arts such as kendo and judo attracts not only Japanese Americans but also Americans of other ethnic backgrounds.

Family life. Japanese culture has always emphasized the strength of family ties, particularly the obligations of child to parent. Even the family's status in the community rested in part on obedience to parents. Although this emphasis has weakened somewhat, the cohesion of the family is given much credit for the success of Japanese Americans in school and business. The father was the central authority figure; the mother's authority stemmed from her role as his representative.

Japanese American families encountered various obstacles over the years. Poverty and an unfamiliar spouse in a strange land made life difficult for many of the picture brides. One Issei woman tells of hardship in the early days (Kitano 1976, p.41).

> Life was intolerable. Everything was different. My husband was not much help. Cooking, shopping, cleaning, washing dishes and washing clothes, taking care of the babies—many Issei women remember getting up after childbirth to go work in the fields—these are some of the things I remember.

Despite their hardships, divorce was rare. Japanese values demanded *gaman*, sticking things out. Recent divorce rates remain low—1.6 percent for Issei, Nisei, and Sansei marriages. The incidence of interracial marriage has risen, though. In the 1970s and 1980s, it jumped to 50 percent in the large cities of California and Hawaii.

A standard event in an Issei household was the family dinner. The Issei mother would serve her husband first, then her children (starting with the oldest and serving boys before girls), and finally herself. While children could talk quietly, parents remained silent for the most part. Praise came to the child who ate most, so boys especially competed with each other. In the Nisei and then Sansei household of the postwar period such scenes became rarer.

Traditional values. Japanese Americans inherited some behaviors that remain even today. An important one is *enryo*, originally the self-effacement "inferiors" were supposed to display to "superiors." In America, others perceived enryo as shyness or passivity: it might keep a Nisei student from speaking up in class, or accepting a second helping at a friend's house. It is described as having contributed to a perception of Japanese Americans as unaggressive and modest. Actually, enryo may have handicapped achievement for some individuals. The value can work only in a culture that understands and makes allowances for it; many Americans appear to be unaware that it exists.

Ties to Japan. Before World War II, some children were sent to Japan for an upbringing or extensive schooling. Though this practice mostly ended with the war, it has been replaced by some schooling and extended visits. Many Japanese Americans have traveled to Japan. With the growth of Japan's economy, Japanese corporations have undertaken operations in the United States. An increasing number of Japanese Americans work for such corporations, although the businesses tend to transfer natives from Japan for high-level positions or hire whites. Japanese Americans look with pride on Japan's prosperity, but it affects them directly no more than it does others. So far their ties to Japan have been cultural rather than economic.

For More Information

See these reading materials:

Daniels, Roger. *Asian American: Chinese and Japanese in the United States since 1850*. Seattle: University of Washington Press, 1988.

Kitano, Harry. *Japanese Americans*. Englewood Cliffs, New Jersey: Prentice-Hall, 1976.

Zich, Arthur. "Japanese Americans: Home At Last." *National Geographic*. April 1986: pp. 512-539.

Contact these organizations:

Japanese American Citizens League, 1765 Sutter Street, San Francisco, California 94115.

Japanese American Curriculum Project, P.O. Box 367, 414 E. Third Avenue, San Mateo, California 94401.

JEWISH AMERICANS
(joo´ish eh mer´uh kins)

Americans whose ethnic and religious ancestry is Jewish.

Population: 5,935,000 (1988).
Location: United States, over 50 percent in the Northeast.
Languages: English, Hebrew, Yiddish, various European languages (German, Hungarian, Czech, Russian).

Geographical Setting

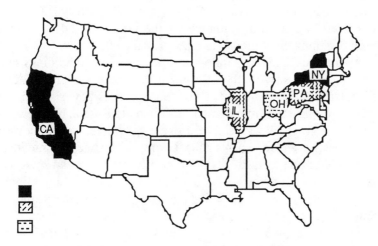

States with greatest Jewish populations.

Located in every state of the nation, American Jews reside mainly in the large metropolitan areas. The Northeast has long been the favored region of settlement, although its share of the population has been decreasing in recent years.

Percent of Jewish American population by region.

Region	Years		
	1981	1987	1988
Northeast	56.9	52.2	51.0
North Central	11.6	11.2	11.0
South	16.3	18.8	19.5
West	15.1	17.9	18.5

Abstracted from: *American Jewish Year Book 1982*,
p. 169; *1988*, p. 227; *1989*, p. 237.

Over two million Jews live in the New York Metropolitan Area, which extends to the city's suburbs and parts of New Jersey. Other large Jewish populations appear in Los Angeles (501,000), Philadelphia (250,000), and Chicago (248,000).

Historical Background

Religious roots. Judaism, the Jewish religion, traces its ancestry approximately 4,000 years back to Abraham, who introduced the then-revolutionary idea of monotheism, or belief in one god. Roughly a thousand years would pass until the era of Moses in the 13th century B.C., when the religion itself began. Shortly thereafter the group settled in Israel (then *Canaan*), beginning their growth as a people called the Hebrews.

Many trouble-filled years followed. Theirs was the tumultuous saga of a culture that would survive the *Diaspora*, the scattering of a people who spread outside their homeland. Over the centuries Jewish communities appeared across Europe from Spain to Germany to Russia. Not permitted to own land in Europe, Jews became artisans, peddlers, and moneylenders, servicing peasants and merchants alike. Living in separate communities, they maintained their own beliefs. Many of the Eastern European Jews lived in *shtetls* (small Jewish towns), whose members were bound by religion, the Yiddish language, certain values, and the scorn of the outside world.

Among the most cherished of the people's values was study. Hebrew Scriptures consist of the Torah, the books of Prophets, and the sacred Writings (Psalms, Proverbs). These comprise the Bible of Judaism. The Torah chronicles history from creation to when the Jews are about to enter Israel after 40 years in the desert. It is read throughout the year to completion, at which point the reading begins anew. The Talmud is a later religious writing, which took centuries to develop. Written by ancient rabbis, it details *halakhah*, or Jewish law, and provides commentary on that law.

Studying the Talmud was a religious duty. Boys and men would devote time each day—often before dawn's early light—to sacred learning.

All this activity occurred in mostly Christian or Moslem lands, where Jewish customs made the group different from everyone else. Jews observed special dietary laws and their Sabbath (day of rest) fell on Saturday, not Sunday. Such oddities, along with their ability to survive economically, brought hostility from outsiders. In troubled times, when crops failed or a czar was assassinated as in 1881, Jews quickly became the scapegoat, blamed for society's ills. *Pogroms*, or massacres of the Jews, erupted. The victims suffered gruesome cruelty—babies were murdered, women violated, and people's eyes put out. One son was killed under the gaze of his father, who was forced to lick his dead boy's blood. Such persecution, along with other hardships, drove hundreds of thousands of Jews to the New World.

Immigration—an overview. Jews migrated to North America in waves of various sizes from different places of origin.

1. The 1630s to 1730s—a few thousand immigrants from Spain and Portugal began American Jewry.
2. The 1830s to the 1880s—250,000 to 300,000 newcomers arrived from German-speaking countries.
3. The 1880s to the 1920s—a massive 2.5 million or more Jews emigrated from Russia and Eastern Europe.
4. From 1937 to 1948—200,000 to 250,000 refugees escaped the horrors of World War II.

Immigration now involves groups of Jews from Russia, Israel, Iran, and South Africa. Their experiences continue to unfold. Among the earlier waves, not only size and place of origin differed but also each wave's experience in the New World.

Spanish-Portuguese immigrants. By the time Christopher Columbus set sail, Jews had lost social standing in Spain. This did not stop them from contributing to the success of Columbus's journey. Abraham ben Samuel Zacuto, a Jewish mathematician and an astronomer, provided almanacs and tables that were instrumental to the voyage. Zacuto and other Jews helped fund the explorer's momentous venture, too. Then, in August 1492, Spain expelled the Jews. Columbus noted in his journal that he was delayed three full days because the harbor was so crowded with fleeing Jews.

The Spanish and Portuguese Jews settled first in Latin America. From Brazil about 24 impoverished Jews migrated to New Amsterdam (New York) in 1654. The birth of American Jewry harks back to this small group. Peter Stuyvesant, governor of New Amsterdam, was hostile to the two dozen Jews. He wanted to deport them, but they refused to be deported. Sending a stream of petitions to Holland, they demanded their rights. Back in Holland, respected Jews pressured the Dutch authorities to control Stuyvesant. They reasoned with him: Jews are self-sufficient and successful in trade. They promise to be an asset to the colony. In the end, Stuyvesant was ordered to let them stay. They could traffic in the fur trade, he agreed, but could not own retail shops. So the Jews went about their business, entering heavily into the fur trade, enjoying mostly friendly relations with the Indians and petitioning for more rights. The English won control of New Amsterdam in 1664. It was renamed New York for the king's brother, James of York, who promoted religious freedom there. By 1683, the Jews had founded their first synagogue, or house of worship, *Shearith Israel* (Remnant of Israel).

Again the Jews went about their businesses, contributing greatly to the growth of America's fledgling economy. Peddling, banking, mining, cotton exporting, and financing the railroad were businesses that involved Jews. The activity depended on the location. Besides New York, communities of Spanish-Portuguese Jews appeared in Rhode Island, Pennsylvania, South Carolina, and Georgia. Jewish businesses in Newport, Rhode Island, for example, included candlemaking factories, sugar refineries, rope-walk plants, and more by the 1760s. In South Carolina, Jewish men worked as merchants, planters, cotton jobbers, and exporters.

Revolutionary War. At the time of the War of Independence, there were some 2,000 Jews living in the colonies. They mostly favored the Revolution, lending both monetary and military support. Jewish merchants stopped purchasing products from England and donated supplies to the army. Haym Salomon raised large sums of money for the cause. Over the years, his role has been somewhat exaggerated. He did not lend his own money to America directly but did sell some 200,000 dollars in government securities, for which he earned a broker's fee. Salomon also lent his own money, interest free, to rebels like James Madison. Turning to the military effort, a fighting unit, the Jews Company, was raised in South Carolina. Over 40 individuals achieved distinction in military service. Two Jewish officers, Colonel Isaac Franks and Benjamin Nones, joined George Washington's staff. Under General Pulaski at the siege of Savannah (see

POLISH AMERICANS), Nones came to the rescue, breaking through British lines with troops.

Victory for the rebels brought independence and complete equality of rights to Jews in America. It was an equality they treasured and did not enjoy elsewhere in the world. Afterwards, Jews tried to resume old activities. Problems resulting from the war took their toll, however, and Jewish life experienced a decline. The community in Rhode Island virtually disappeared, since many Jews had left it during the war. Elsewhere, intermarriage decreased their population. The number of new immigrants fell sharply for a time, then rose with an influx of Jews from Central Europe.

German immigrants. Called German Jews, immigrants from Central Europe outnumbered those from Spain and Portugal by 1830. They would remain the dominant group until the 1880s. After Napoleon's downfall, Europe saw a rise in anti-Semitism, or hostility toward the Jews. Pogroms broke out in places like Frankfurt, Hamburg, and Danzig, and Jews lost rights. Attracting them to America were freedom and economic opportunity. At the time, the American government needed people to settle Louisiana Territory and encouraged immigration. Jewish immigrants settled throughout the new territory, favoring Cleveland, Cincinnati, St. Louis, and New Orleans. Almost always preferring urban centers, Jews moved also to Chicago, Detroit, and San Francisco. The earlier, Spanish-Portuguese Jews sent money to aid these new German Jews, who soon outnumbered the older group. Self-help became a link that connected the different waves of immigrant Jews.

The Germans came from a worldly background. In Europe, many of them had enjoyed economic and social success. They took pride in their German heritage, identifying with the non-Jewish immigrants who came to America from Germany. Many German Jews achieved modest success in short order. They began as peddlers, earning money immediately and adopting Americanisms quite rapidly. (A half century later peddling would likewise affect another group [see ARAB AMERICANS].) If he prospered, the German Jewish peddler went on to become a merchant and then a department store owner. Few peddlers reached this last stage, yet as a group they did well, often rising to the middle class in under ten years. The most prosperous progressed into banking. An example is Joseph Seligman, who manufactured uniforms that he sold to the United States and then had to sell government bonds if he wanted payment. Seligman's team marketed over 250 million dollars in bonds between 1862 and 1864. Turning to banking, he found it far more profitable than the clothing business in the pre-Civil War days. Another success story, Julius Rosenwald, purchased a small watch company. Called Sears, Roebuck, it grew into a huge mail-order business under his guidance. A Jewish elite of wealthy businessmen developed in mid-19th century America, but they were a small minority. Many more Jews remained peddlers or took jobs as tailors or cigar makers. New York City had 1,103 millionaires in the 1860s. While 60 of these millionaires were Jewish, most Jews rose only to the middle class, and some became mired in the lower class.

Slavery and the Civil War. A review of the urban centers in which Jews settled (for example, New York and Charleston) shows they had roots in both the North and the South by the Civil War. In the South, only a few Jewish households owned hundreds of slaves but many possessed one or two slaves. Some *rabbis*, the Jewish spiritual leaders, favored slavery; others opposed it, both sides supporting their position with the Bible. A few anti-slavery Jews marched with John Brown's rebels in Kansas (see AFRICAN AMERICANS), but most Jews championed neither side. They remained neutral, focusing instead on achieving success in business. Their views on slavery, like those of other ethnic groups in the country at the time, were shaped largely by their region and the region's economy. Once war erupted, Jews fought for their respective sides, as soldiers for the Union or for the Confederacy. About 10,000 Jewish men joined both armies in the war, while women formed Jewish volunteer societies for sick and wounded soldiers. These societies were among the first of what would become a huge web of Jewish organizations in the United States. In the heat of war, anti-Semitism surfaced. A town in Georgia banished all Jewish residents when goods grew scarce, and General Grant issued Order Number 11, exiling all Jews from the Tennessee Department. Several communities complied with the Order before President Lincoln made Grant revoke it.

Eastern European immigrants. Conditions for Russian Jews worsened dramatically during the 1880s. The assassination of the czar in 1881 sparked anti-Jewish riots and pogroms. Outside Russia, in London, New York, and Philadelphia, public meetings raised money for the victims. This helped ignite the Third Wave, a massive influx of Jews from Russia, Poland, and other Eastern European regions, who were simply referred to as Russian Jews. Not only anti-Semitism but also economic hardship in Russia drove Jews to America. It became increasingly hard to earn a living in Russia, which gave rise to a new type of Jew in Russia, a *luftmensh*, someone who seemed to live off air without any apparent livelihood. Also, Russia could impose many years of military service on its citizens, and the threat of this prompted Jews to leave. Numbers alone showed the newcomers would dominate American Jewry thereafter. Between 1881 and 1923, over 2.5 million Eastern European Jews immigrated to the United States. This was ten times the number in the earlier German migration.

American Jewish ghetto. The newcomers flocked to New York City's Lower East Side. It became an American Jewish ghetto of sorts, a type of halfway house whose residents brought over vestiges of life from Europe. For example, they spoke Yiddish, a Germanic language with many Hebrew and Slavic elements that would flourish in America for 40 years. Jewish "ghettos" also grew in other Eastern, Midwestern, and Western cities (Boston, Philadelphia, Baltimore, Chicago, Cleveland, and Los Angeles).

The Jewish section of Los Angeles in the early 1900s.

New York City's Lower East Side developed into a bustling neighborhood. Typical housing was the four- or five-story tenement. A narrow brick building, the tenement had two *railroad flats* and one bathroom to a floor. A flat contained four to six rooms spread along the length of the building. The bath was located in the kitchen, so residents would frequent a local bathhouse to wash themselves. From a window of the flat, they looked down on pushcarts and peddlers and often heard the busy whir of hundreds of sewing machines.

Ghetto laborers favored the garment industry or worked in small businesses (markets, butcher shops, delicatessens). Over 60 percent labored in the business of ready-made clothing. Since so many had been tailors in Europe, it was a natural tendency. The garment business developed a pulse of its own in America, though. A manufacturer would cut the cloth into pieces and farm them out to a contractor, who hired immigrants to sew the garments at home. "Piece work," they called it, asking an immigrant to assemble perhaps 20 coats every 14 hours, day after day for six days a week. Later, contractors installed rows of sewing machines in dingy warehouses, *sweatshops*, where workers labored long hours for low wages under poor conditions. Morris Rosenfeld, called the ghetto's finest Yiddish writer, captured the experience in words (Rosenfeld 1898, p 3):

> In the Sweatshop
> The machines in the shop roar so wildly that often
> I forget in the roar that I am...I am a machine. I
> work, and work, and work without end...There are no
> feelings, no thoughts, no reason; the bitter, bloody
> work kills the noblest....

Reading and theater provided relief from the daily grind. Writers vigorously pursued their craft in the ghetto. At least 20 Yiddish newspapers appeared. First issued in 1897, the *Forvits*, or *Jewish Daily Forward*, still circulates today. Even poor workers were avid theatergoers. On the curtain were advertisements and portraits of the play's stars—actors such as Paul Muni, who later won national acclaim. Once the curtain rose, a mixed (children and adults) audience watched silently to the end. Then came a flurry of socializing.

Organizations. The American Jews spun a more elaborate web of organizations than any other ethnic group. They began with institutions like the B'nai B'rith, a charity foundation, and Mount Sinai Hospital in New York. Called *settlement houses*, welfare centers opened in the late 19th century to meet the needs of the Eastern European immigrants (job training, medical exams).

German Jews founded a house called Educational Alliance, acting in the spirit of self-help and on their own behalf. Here again was one wave of Jews helping the next, but for its own benefit too. Anti-Semitism was on the rise in America. Resorts and private schools excluded Jews. A sign at the Grand Union Hotel in Saratoga, New York, said "No Jews or Dogs Admitted Here." Some German Jews linked the rising hostility to the Eastern

Europeans and their foreign ways. If they were Americanized, the Germans reasoned, anti-Semitism would decrease. Tensions developed. Thinking the Germans acted superior, resentful Easterners organized societies of their own. A tendency to divide and form new groups manifested itself, a thorn in American Jewry's side that later would prevent it from speaking with one voice.

Most important among the self-help organizations were the *landsmannschaften* (town societies), consisting of members who immigrated from the same Eastern European town. They were mutual aid societies that met insurance, burial, health, and even employment needs. An employer would look to his landsmannschaft to find a landsmann when there was an opening in his shop.

Religion. An institution of the ghetto and other Jewish neighborhoods was the synagogue, or house of worship. Since Spanish Jews came to America first, their style of worship prevailed for close to 200 years. Followers of this style, called the *Sephardim*, were later outnumbered by Jews who worshipped in the German style, the *Ashkenazim*. Both terms refer to type rather than degree of worship. By the late 19th century, most American Jews were Ashkenazim. They worshipped in the same style but

An early 1900s synagogue on the West Coast.

differed over how strictly to observe that style. The issue resulted in the division of American Judaism into three major branches.

Begun in Europe, *Reform Judaism* came to America with the German Jews. It favored adapting the religion to life in America by abandoning customs viewed as out-of-touch with larger society (for example, the prohibition against musical instruments in a synagogue). Many of the Eastern Europeans were strictly observant Jews, who rejected the Reform movement as too radical a departure from tradition. Far more acceptable was *Conservative Judaism*, a middle-of-the-road approach that embraced aspects of both the Reform and Orthodox movements. The Conservatives adopted a few new behaviors (for example, mixed seating of men and women in synagogues). Most traditional was *Orthodox Judaism*, whose followers opened many small congregations at this time. The three branches organized into formal units over a span of years (Reform began in 1873, Conservative in 1886, Orthodox in 1898). Over time the Conservatives gained the strongest following, winning over many Eastern Europeans from Orthodoxy. Key figures in the movements' growth were Rabbi Isaac Wise for the Reform, Solomon Schechter for the Conservative, and Rabbi Isaac Elchanan for the Orthodox.

Few rabbis came to America before the late 1880s. More immigrated with the Eastern Europeans, and the three branches opened seminaries to train new rabbis in their form of Judaism. Graduates carried the alternative Judaisms into American society and gave new vitality to ancient beliefs.

Politics and labor. Jewish Americans did not focus only on religion and ghetto needs as the 1900s approached. Beyond these immediate concerns, they had national and international concerns. *Zionism*, the movement to recreate a Jewish homeland in Israel, won Jewish American champions like Emma Lazarus (American poet) and Louis Brandeis (Supreme Court Justice). Around this time, a rash of pogroms victimized Jews in Eastern Europe; perhaps the worst occurred in Kishniev in 1903. Americans sent medical supplies, dry goods, and money to the victims. Early-20th-century America was a secure land, full of opportunity for its Jews. During this period, they benefitted from the actions of President Theodore Roosevelt. He encouraged Jewish immigration, admitting thousands of oppressed Romanian Jews, and appointed the first Jewish Cabinet member, Oscar Straus (Secretary of Commerce and Labor). Jews played a key role in national events, greatly aiding the growth the labor movement in America. In 1909, some 20,000 shirtwaist industry garment workers went on strike. The strikers, mostly women, included many Italians (see ITALIAN AMERICANS) and even more Jews. They won the strike, gaining a 52-hour work week, paid holidays, and acceptance of their union. Again involving Jewish garment workers, a 1910 New York cloakmakers' strike won additional benefits. A 1911 fire at the Triangle Waist Company killed 146 women, many of them Jewish, the tragedy leading to stricter government safety controls for workers.

World Wars. Jews fully participated in American life by World War I (1914–1918). Joining the war effort, Jewish soldiers died on the battlefield. The War Department adopted the six-pointed star of David to mark their graves.

Then came the 1920s, a turbulent decade. Anti-Semitism was on the rise, and the Prohibition Amendment against alcohol took effect. Crime grew. American Jews already had some gangsters, men with names like Max Zweibach (Kid Twist). Now organized crime mushroomed in the group. Gangs such as Brownsville's Murder Incorporated appeared, dealing not only in alcohol but infecting the garment and meat businesses too. Like other groups in America at the time, the Jews had individuals who resorted to crime. Anti-Semitism increased as the decade progressed. Leo Frank, the Jewish manager of an Atlanta pencil factory, was lynched. A 1914 mob decided to punish Frank for a murder he supposedly committed despite a lack of evidence that he was guilty of the crime. In the 1920s, colleges tried to reduce the Jewish enrollment, and automobile leader Henry Ford ran a piece in his Michigan newspaper accusing Jews of a conspiracy to rule the world. Anti-Semitism worsened in the 1930s, when hostile radio broadcasts were made by Father Charles Coughlin and pilot Charles Lindbergh spoke against the Jews. World War II struck, but America remained uninvolved for a time. Its Jews did build the boycott against buying German goods that began in 1933. The United States had a quota system that limited the number of Jews who could immigrate, yet it admitted 150,000 refugees from the Nazis. Among them were scientists who helped invent the atomic bomb that would end the war.

Over 550,000 Jewish men served in the Second World War, and they won over 61,000 decorations. Their victories paled, though, next to the six million who died in the *Holocaust*, the attempt by Nazi-controlled Germany to mostly gas Europe's Jews out of existence. Parents, sisters, uncles of the American Jews were trapped in the Nazi death camps. The Americans did not know of the camps before November 1942. Then there was debate about what to do. After 14 months, President Roosevelt established a government body, the War Refugee Board, to mount a rescue effort. Most of its funding came from Jewish organizations. It conducted minor rescue efforts and psychological warfare, trying to convince other Europeans to resist the

Nazis. Later, people wondered why America waited so long to act and why it didn't take more drastic action. Many of the country's Jews felt they should have united to push for a drastic effort (Feingold 1974, p. 277).

> American Jews have been tormented by their failure ever since and much of their subsequent behavior toward Israel, where many of the survivors of the holocaust have settled, can be explained by their feeling of culpability regarding their wartime role.

Postwar issues. About 51 percent of world Jewry lived in America at the end of the war. Some 100,000 Jewish survivors immigrated to America, completing the fourth wave. Now Jews turned to rebuilding a homeland in Israel. The war had convinced them how necessary it was to their survival. In 1948, Israel became a Jewish state. The next two decades saw the opening of synagogues across America and a great integration of Jews into the larger culture. In the 1960s, Jews joined blacks in the Civil Rights movement; two of them, Michael Schwerner and Andrew Goodman, died for the cause. Later, blacks shunned Jewish support and the alliance broke down. Attention shifted to Jewish issues: the fates of Israel, the Soviet Jews, and Jewish America. In 1967, Israel won the Six Day War but its enemies lurked in the foreground. American Jews concentrated on fund raising to help Israel survive and began programs for themselves on college campuses in Jewish studies. In American synagogues, there was new enthusiasm for both tradition and revolutionary change. Reform Jews ordained their first woman rabbi, Sally Preisand, in 1972. The Conservatives followed suit, ordaining Amy Eilberg in 1985. In the background, a movement for women's rights had swept the nation. It is this mix of tradition and response to the times that has produced the American Jew.

Culture Today

Food, clothing, and shelter. The blend of American and Jewish ways is evident in food. *Kashrut*, Jewish dietary laws, limit the foods that may be eaten by traditionalist Jews. Acceptable are mammals who chew their cud and have split hooves (cows), poultry, and fish with fins and scales (salmon). Shellfish are forbidden, as are birds of prey. Traditional Jews keep *kosher*, or obey these dietary laws, which is easier than it once was. Today there are restaurants that offer kosher pizza, kosher Chinese food, and kosher Mexican meals. Jews, in turn, have influenced eating habits in America. Popular across the United States is Jewish delicatessen food. Its specialities include lox, bagels, pastrami, rye bread, and chicken soup, a cure-all that is good humoredly called "Jewish penicillin." Other customary foods are *koogl* (a noodle or potato pudding), *blintzes* (cheese-filled crepes), and *cholent* (a bean stew). Recent Israeli immigrants have added dishes to the Jewish American diet. Most popular is *falafel* (a spiced vegetable and bean patty), now available at fast-food stands.

In the thick of the garment industry, Jews had every opportunity to adopt American clothing styles and they did. Today most Jewish Americans dress like others in the country. An exception is the *Hasidim*, a sect of ultra-Orthodox Jews. Hasidim reject modern ways, much as the Amish do (see AMISH). The men wear long black coats, black hats, and beards in the tradition of their Eastern European ancestors. Their wives shave their hair, then wear scarves or wigs to reduce their appeal to other men. However, these styles are not the norm in Jewish America. Still common among many Jews for synagogue worship are religious garments: the *yarmulke*, a skull cap, and the *tallis*, a prayer shawl. Jews have also influenced American clothing styles. Notably, the merchant Levi Strauss introduced the Levi jean in the 1850s.

Many Jews moved to middle-class neighborhoods during the 1920s and 1930s. In New York, they flocked to Brooklyn and the Bronx and formed gilded ghettos in which they still kept company mainly with other Jews. Jews moved to other regions of the country from 1940 to 1965. Also, there was a movement from cities to suburbs where non-Jews lived. The blend of old and new ways increased. Again the exception was the Hasidic Jews. They remained separate. One group even isolated itself, moving 40 miles from New York City to form its own village. Founded in 1957, the village is called New Square and resembles an old European *shtetl*. Its houses are unremarkable for the region but do not have television sets. Television is forbidden to Hasidic Jews, who are devoted to the religion and regard modern inventions as distractions.

Family life. In the Jewish faith, many religious rituals are performed in the home. Children may see their mothers light candles to welcome the Sabbath or their fathers lead Passover suppers that recall the Jews escape from slavery in Egypt. In short, their first exposure to religion is in the family.

Jewish family patterns came to America from Europe. Great stress was placed on achievement. Sons should accomplish worldly success, become a doctor or make money. Daughters should marry men who had status. Parents worked hard *tzu makhen fun kinder mentshen* (to make their children into fine, upstanding people). In return, parents expected to receive *nachas fun kinder* (pride in the children's accomplishments). Vestiges of this pattern remain today. Now daughters and sons pursue a wider range of occupations, but many still feel driven to achieve worldly success.

In the past, matchmakers arranged marriages. This still occurs in some very Orthodox families, but for a Jewish marriage to be valid both partners must agree to the match. Judaism discourages but accepts divorce. The average birthrate is low, about two children per family. Still practiced is the *bris*, circumcision for a son. In raising children, Jewish mothers tend to openly express their emotions. The stereotype of the demanding, protective, overworried Jewish mother is refuted by social scientists. According to their studies, the image is far too exaggerated. The studies did indicate tendencies. Many Jewish mothers do apparently interfere with their children's problems. Also, they seem to insist on close supervision of a child longer than other American mothers. It is likely that these are legacies from Europe's ghettos, where close supervision was necessary to a family's survival.

Intermarriage, marriage between a Jew and someone not born Jewish, has skyrocketed in American society. As many as two out of five Jews intermarry. Only about a fourth of the spouses convert to Judaism, and in most cases the children are lost to the Jewish faith. The rise in mixed marriages threatens the survival of American Jewry. By traditional Jewish law, children are Jews only if their mother is a Jew. Reform Judaism has recently ruled that it will recognize children raised as Jews if their fathers are Jewish. This is described as a response to the shrinking of American Jewry.

Business. While some old trends in business continue, new ones have also developed. History shows that the majority of the group rose to the middle class. While most Jews still belong to the middle class, a sizeable number are poor. Around 600,000 Jewish Americans live at or below the U.S. poverty level. Many of these Jews are aged.

Job preferences have changed over the years. Few Jews remain blue collar workers, laborers who work with their hands. Once the goal was to become a manager or a small business owner. Since the 1960s, more Jews have bypassed such goals in favor of the professions. Medicine and law are the main choices. While Jews are only 2.5 percent of the American population, they form 20 percent of the country's attorneys.

American Jews concentrated in certain businesses. A quick road to success continues to be finance and banking. Land investment was the final step up the ladder for 19th-century Jews. In this tradition, real estate and construction remain popular fields. The 20th century has seen William Levitt, for example, create tract homes, called Levittowns. In the garment business, Jews still run small factories, but these now compete with large corporations and clothing made overseas. Diamonds are part of another continuing trade. Hasidic Jews as well as others still cut, grind, polish, and sell jewels. In the film industry, men such as Harry Warner of Warner Brothers pioneered the building of studios and enjoyed great control for a time. Today Jews work in film and in other media, but they do not control any of these fields. It is in the toy industry, by founding companies such as Mattel, that Jewish business leaders have been most powerful.

Religion and holidays. A fraction of Jews work as religious leaders: rabbis, cantors, educators. The cantor is the singer who chants the service. Haunting, lyrical melodies have been passed down through the ages by cantors. The majority of today's American Jews affiliate with one branch of the religion. Overall, the breakdown is about 10 percent Orthodox, 40 percent Conservative, and 35 percent Reform. The remainder have no preference. Tradition has found new favor in all three branches. More Hebrew, for example, appears in Reform services today than in the past.

Mordecai Kaplan founded Reconstructionism, a fourth branch of Judaism, in which religion, history, and culture are regarded as equally important. It is a tiny branch, but its members have introduced major changes in the religion. Jewish boys become adults in the *Bar Mitzvah*, a ceremony in which they formally bind themselves to the faith. In 1922, Judith Kaplan, Mordecai's daughter, was the first to have a *Bat Mitzvah*, a ceremony that marks a female's coming of age.

While Judaism has been a flexible religion, certain features are unchanging: the commitment to one god, an ethical life (the Ten Commandments), and the Sabbath. The Sabbath, which falls on Saturday, commemorates the covenant, or special relation, of the Jews to God. It is the holiest holiday. Next is Yom Kippur, the Day of Atonement, a time when sins are forgiven, and the individual is renewed. There is a mixture of religion and history in most Jewish holidays. An eight-day winter festival, Hanukkah recalls the victory of the Jews in 162 B.C., when they rebelled against Syria's demand for an altar to the Greek god Zeus in their Temple. The spring festival Passover, also an eight-day affair, commemorates their flight from slavery in Egypt. Remembrance Day, a sober memorial in May, recalls World War II and the six million who died in the Holocaust. Across America, Jews celebrate such holidays to a greater or lesser degree.

Education and organizations. American Jews have formed scores of organizations over the years. Their purposes range from civil rights (Anti-Defamation League of B'nai B'rith) to culture (Brandeis-Bardin Institute) to charity (American Jewish Joint Distribution Committee) to politics (American

Jewish Congress) to social service (Jewish Family Service) to aid for Israel (United Jewish Appeal) to education (Yeshiva University). Federation councils developed to coordinate the groups. Most recently, a new type of society, the *havurah* (fellowship group) has appeared. This is a small group movement, whose members usually belong to the same synagogue. Made up of 10 to 20 people, a havurah meets monthly in a private home for collective study, prayer, and friendship. It is described as a response to impersonal society.

In education, American Jews favor public schools. Religious education is offered through Jewish day, afternoon, and Sunday schools. Rebecca Gratz helped found the first Sunday school in 1831, serving as its president until 1864. Other pioneers in education were Samson Benderly and Bernard Revel. Benderly headed the Bureau of Jewish Education, promoting high standards for afternoon and weekend schools. Revel added secular studies to Jewish studies at Yeshiva University, opening a liberal arts college there in 1928. There were day schools that offered Jewish and secular education to younger students, but they remained small for much of the 20th century. In 1944, the day schools organized into a national society, *Torah Umesorah*. Non-Orthodox Jews joined the movement in the 1970s, opening their own day schools. The movement mushroomed. America now has hundreds of these schools, and they produce students who are often more traditional than their parents. Still, the majority of American Jews continue to prefer public schools.

Literature and language. After World War II, Jewish writers flourished in America. They have produced acclaimed work in every genre from poetry (Allen Ginsberg) to drama (Arthur Miller) to short stories (Isaac Bashevis Singer) to the novel (Saul Bellow) to children's picture books (Maurice Sendak). Their subjects are the general American experience, the Jewish American experience, and the Jewish experience abroad. More works center on life in the United States than overseas. Among these are Arthur Miller's drama *Death of a Salesman* and Neil Simon's comedy *California Suite*. The list of novels is long. It includes Chaim Potok's *The Chosen*, Philip Roth's *Goodbye Columbus*, E.L. Doctorow's *Ragtime*, and Abraham Cahan's *The Rise of David Levinsky*. Much of the fiction examines how meaningful American life is. Treating Jewish experience abroad, Herman Wouk's *Winds of War* and *War and Remembrance* spin a fictional story about the Holocaust. Elie Wiesel is a nonfiction writer, whose past works include *Night*, a memoir about concentration camp life at Auschwitz. Among the women writers are Gertrude Stein, Grace Paley, Cynthia Ozick, and the poet Emma Lazarus. Her poem "The New Colossus" appears on the Statue of Liberty, and its ending is in a wall of New York International Airport (Vogel 1980, p. 158).

..."Give me your tired, your poor,
Your huddled masses yearning to be free,
The wretched refuse of your teeming shore.
Send these, the homeless, tempest-tost to me,
I lift my lamp beside the golden door!"

Jewish writers have won high acclaim in America. Isaac Bashevis Singer and Saul Bellow each received the Nobel Prize for literature, Singer in 1978 and Bellow in 1976. Bellow has been hailed as the writer who introduced a freer, more conversational style to the American novel. Both authors speak Yiddish, and Singer does all his writing in the language. "Only in America could a Jewish writer win the Nobel Prize in literature for work written entirely in Yiddish." This statement (Bluestein 1989, p. 13) expresses an appreciation often expressed by Jews for life in America.

Yiddish remained the primary language of Jews from the 1880s through the 1920s. Its use has diminished since then, but it is still an everyday language for Hasidic Jews. As with black English, certain Yiddish words have crept into general American vocabulary. Examples are *ganif* (thief), *shlep* (drag), and *kosher* (proper). Yiddish has also been affected by English. For instance, "lawyer" is *advokat* in old Yiddish but has become *loyer* in American Yiddish. More American Jews speak Hebrew than in the past. This increase has been linked to the new Israeli immigrants, the growth of Jewish day schools, and the close, ongoing ties to Israel.

Achievements. Individuals have made large contributions in several fields. Of the scientists, Albert Einstein, is probably most renown. Einstein had some involvement in the invention of nuclear weapons, which he explained after World War II (Clark 1971, p.585).

While I am a convinced pacifist there are circumstances
in which I believe the use of force is appropriate—namely,
in the face of an enemy unconditionally bent on destroying
me and my people.

Other eminent scientists include Admiral Hyman Rickover, who designed the atomic submarine. In medicine, Jonas Salk developed the polio vaccine, and Albert Sabin produced it in oral form. Joseph Goldberger found the cure for pellagra.

In politics, most Jews are Democrats. Those in government have filled staff jobs, and a rising number hold elected offices. Nearly 10 percent of the U.S Senate was Jewish or of Jewish ancestry in the late 1980s. Also, the Supreme Court has seen several Jews serve as Justices, including Felix Frankfurter, Abe Fortas, and Arthur Goldberg.

A host of Jewish American athletes have become sports stars. Abe Attell was a world boxing champion from 1901 to 1912. American speed skater Irving Jaffee won two gold medals in the 1932 Olympics. Hank Greenberg became most valuable player in baseball's American League for 1935. Tennis star Richard Savitt won the Wimbledon matches in 1951. In 1972, swimmer Mark Spitz took seven Olympic gold medals, and football's Hall of Fame welcomed Ronald Mix in 1979. In chess, Bobby Fischer was rated first in the world at age 12.

Jews have excelled in American film and comedy. Among the outstanding filmmakers, Woody Allen (writer, director, producer, and actor) won four Academy Awards for *Annie Hall* in 1977. Steven Spielberg has directed commercial successes such as *Jaws* and *E.T.* Of Barbara Streisand's movies, *Yentl* most closely evokes her Jewish heritage. It is based on a story by Isaac Bashevis Singer, inspired, says Fraydele Oysher, by her own performance as a woman cantor in disguise on the Yiddish stage. The comedians include Lenny Bruce, Red Buttons, the Marx Brothers, Jack Benny, Fanny Brice, and Goldie Hawn. In comic strips, Jules Feiffer contributed greatly to the creation of the adult cartoon in America.

Music is perhaps the field of greatest achievement. The first Jewish music publishers in America formed a group of companies called "Tin Pan Alley." A member of the group was Irving Berlin, the composer of "God Bless America." Berlin also wrote shows to raise money for the army in World War I (*Yip Yip Yaphank*) and World War II (*This Is the Army*). Other giants in the field include the Gershwins and Rodgers and Hammerstein. Combining classic and popular music, George and Ira Gershwin created the show *Porgy and Bess*. Rodgers and Hammerstein developed the Broadway musical, beginning with *Oklahoma* in 1942. Leonard Bernstein composed symphonies. Stephen Sondheim, a lyrics and music writer, won a 1985 Pulitzer Prize for the show *Sunday in the Park*. In singing, opera star Beverly Sills and popular music's Barbara Streisand have won high acclaim. Streisand is regarded as the most successful female vocalist in American history.

"Never again." Jews have opened museums that commemorate the Holocaust in several American cities. These document the killing of six million Jews during World War II. Recording their experiences for posterity, survivors have provided proof that the Holocaust did indeed happen. Elie Wiesel, who won the 1986 Nobel Peace Prize, has spread awareness of the Holocaust through his writings and lectures. Other Jewish Americans and their children work with him to keep the memory of the Holocaust alive so that it will never happen again.

For More Information

See these reading materials:

Eichhorn, David Max, ed. *Joys of Jewish Folklore: A Journey from New Amsterdam to Beverly Hills and Beyond.* Middle Village, New York: Jonathan David, 1981.

Silberman, Charles E. *A Certain People: American Jews and Their Lives Today.* New York: Summit Books, 1985.

Contact these organizations:

American Jewish Historical Society, 2 Thornton Road, Waltham, Massachusetts 02154.

Council of Jewish Federations, 730 Broadway, New York, New York 10003.

Simon Wiesenthal Center (Holocaust), 9760 West Pico Boulevard, Los Angeles, California 90035.

MEXICAN AMERICANS

(mek' si-kin eh mer´ uh kins)

Americans whose ancestors lived in Mexico.

Population: 8,679,000 (1980).
Location: United States (mainly the Southwest).
Language: English, Spanish.

Geographical Setting

Mexican Americans live almost everywhere in the
United States, but partucularly in the Southwest.

The north of Mexico is arid and sparsely populated except for a few large
towns and cities. In these ways, it is not unlike the southwestern United
States, where most Mexican Americans live. Over 90 percent of the region's
population resies in California and Texas. Smaller areas of settlement are in
New Mexico, Colorado, and Arizona. From 1940 to 1970, Mexican
Americans changed from a predominantly rural population to an

overwhelmingly urban one, which they remain today. Outside the Southwest, the group is mostly concentrated in Midwestern cities, such as Chicago, Illinois. resent day. Outnumbering the immigrants are individuals who live in the rapidly expanding border communities of Mexico and commute into the United States. Since Mexico's economy is poor, some of its people move north, hoping to cross the border into the United States. Often they find themselves waiting for that opportunity in a border city such as Tijuana, and sometimes these would-be immigrants obtain permits to work on the United States side of the border and return home at night.

Note on terms. Americans with Mexican ancestors have used several terms to describe themselves. Though widespread, *Mexican American* was rejected by political activists in the 1960s. They preferred *Chicano* (derived from the Spanish *Mexicano*) or simply *Mexican*. All three terms remain common today. The Mexicans who first settled the Southwest were known as *tejanos* in Texas, *nuevo mexicanos* in New Mexico, and *californios* in California. The term for the settlers depended on their geographical location.

Historical Background

Spanish settlement. Beginning with Hernan Cortés in 1519, Spanish explorers roamed Mexico and the American Southwest throughout the 1500s, searching for gold but finding rich silver mines instead. These mines were mostly in the area of what is now Mexico City, so northern Mexico wasn't settled at first. The Englishman Sir Francis Drake's circumnavigation of the world in the 1570s spurred further exploration to the north. The Spanish, it seems, suspected that Drake had discovered the famed Northwest Passage to the Indies somewhere north of Mexico. Juan de Oñate founded San Gabriel de los Españoles in 1598, and a successor established Santa Fe about ten years later. The area was called Nuevo Mexico, and included parts of present-day Texas, Oklahoma, Nebraska, Colorado, and Arizona. Since Drake's Northwest Passage proved as unfounded as hopes of gold had been, the only compelling reason for further settlement was converting the Pueblo Indians who inhabited the area to Christianity. Within about 100 years, some 25 missions were established. Sheepherders and farmers followed. Building fortified villages, these newcomers forced the Indians to work the land.

Settlement continued slowly in the 1600s and was further retarded by the revolt of the Pueblos in 1680. Popé, an Indian leader, succeeded in driving the Spaniards away for over ten years. To the east, the Spanish made the area of Texas a province in 1691, establishing the mission fortress of San

Antonio in 1718. To the west, in California, Father Junipero Serra established his first mission at San Diego in 1769. Serra continued to found missions up and down the California coast. By 1823, the Spanish had 21 such missions in California.

Mexican independence. From the beginning of Spain's contact with the New World, Spaniards had intermarried with the native inhabitants. Most people of Mexican descent are *mestizos*, people of mixed Spanish and Indian ancestry. During the period of Spanish colonialism, tensions erupted not only between the Indians and the Spanish but also between those born in Spain and those born in America. The latter group consisted of two subgroups: the *criollos*, born of pure Spanish parents, and the mestizos. Generally, the criollos felt superior to the mestizos, and the mestizos felt superior to the Indians. In 1810, led by Fathers Miguel Hidalgo and José Maria Morelos, Indians, mestizos, and criollos united against Spain in a war for Mexican independence, which was attained in 1821.

American expansion. Independence weakened Mexico's already fragile grip on her northern possessions. Although the area that would eventually make up the American Southwest comprised nearly 50 percent of Mexican territory, it held less than one percent of its population—about 80,000 people. The isolated colonies in present-day Texas, New Mexico, and California (and a very small one in Tucson, Arizona) had little communication with each other or with the new central government. Most developed and populous was Santa Fe, a colony that sat at the junction of the Chihuahua Trail from central Mexico, the Old Spanish Trail from Los Angeles, and the Santa Fe Trail from Missouri. Blazed by James Becknell in 1822, the Santa Fe Trail would prove crucial in opening up commercial contacts with the eastern United States. Raw goods (hides, tallow, and livestock) were sent east in exchange for finished products.

In the late 1820s, gold was discovered in the Sierra del Oro mountains between Santa Fe and Albuquerque. Attempts by the Mexican government to tighten control of the region led to revolt by New Mexico in the 1830s. Anglos (non-Hispanic whites) had begun to flood into the region to mine and trade. Rebelling against the Mexican government, the nuevo mexicanos, or early Mexican settlers, solidified relations with these Anglo miners and traders. Yankee clipper ships were already sailing around Cape Horn to carry on trade with the Mexican settlers in California. These californios were fiercely self-reliant cattle and sheep ranchers, who also revolted against the Mexican government. The californio leader Juan Alvarado headed an independent government from 1836–1840. It was in Texas, however, that the most violent revolt occurred. Spanish and Mexican immigration had decreased, so the Mexican government encouraged foreign immigration. Led by Stephen Austin, who received a land grant in 1823, livestock traders and cotton farmers poured into Texas. By 1830, 25,000 Anglos had settled in Texas, far outnumbering the area's tejanos, or original Mexicans, who had dwindled to about 4,000. Harsh economic measures, such as heavy customs collection on the U.S.-Texas border, united tejanos and Anglo settlers against the Mexican government. In 1834, Texas declared independence. After initial victories—most notably at the Alamo and at Goliad, where the Texans were defeated—Mexico's forces were routed at San Jacinto in 1836. By 1840, the American, French, and British governments had recognized the new Texas republic.

Annexation, conquest, and purchase. In 1845, under Texan pressure, the United States annexed Texas. Tension mounted between the United States and Mexico, and a border clash provided a pretext for an American declaration of war in 1846. American troops under General Zachary Taylor invaded central Mexico; under Colonel Stephen Kearny they invaded New Mexico. Both Anglos and nuevo mexicanos welcomed Kearny, who, having secured New Mexico, pressed on to California. The American army occupied Mexico City by fall of 1847, and Mexico signed the Treaty of Guadalupe Hidalgo on February 2, 1848. Under this treaty, Mexico ceded her northern territories to the United States in exchange for 15 million dollars. In 1854, for ten million dollars more, the Gadsden Purchase added the Mesilla Valley to southern Arizona and New Mexico.

The sudden Americans. With the exception of the American Indians, never before had the United States attempted to absorb such a large population by conquest. New Mexico had by far the most Mexicans (60,000), then California (8,000), Texas (5,000), and scattered settlements in Arizona and Colorado (2,000–3,000). The Mexican settlers lived in these territories before the Anglos, yet suddenly found themselves subject to Anglo laws.

The Treaty of Guadalupe Hidalgo recognized the Mexicans as American citizens, which should have guarded their political, religious, and property rights. In fact, Mexican Americans were dispossessed of their land and became a scorned working class. They encountered a strange legal and social system in which Anglo customs prevailed over the old Mexican ways. The California Gold Rush of 1849 brought in hundreds of thousands of miners who squatted on Mexican land and forced complicated and expensive legal battles. Often the land had been held for generations without formal documentation. Many *rancheros*, owners of large ranches, lost their lands in court or were bankrupted by court costs. Others perished in or fled from violent attacks. The arrival of the railroad in 1876 finally broke the great Mexican landholding families of southern California. By the late 1880s, Anglos greatly outnumbered the original Mexican settlers. In New Mexico the same process occurred more slowly, with cattlemen, logging companies, and railroads replacing the landholders. By 1910, only 30 percent of the original Mexican owners still held their land. Likewise in Texas, Anglo cotton growers and ranchers displaced smaller tejano landowners, then hired them and newer immigrants to perform cheap labor on the range and in the cotton fields.

An early 1900s immigrant family in the Southwest.

Immigrants. The economic development of the Southwest that followed American acquisition lured Mexican immigrants from the start. Miners from Sonora, Mexico, joined the Gold Rush. Many also found work on the railroads. Most important, however, were technological advances in agriculture. Irrigation had come into wide use, requiring labor-intensive farming. From 1910–1920 cotton spread through Texas, New Mexico,

Arizona, and California due to irrigation. Mexican workers in the Southwest also cultivated fields of melon, grapes, citrus fruits, and sugar beets.

In Mexico, the oppressive regime of President Porfirio Díaz (1876-1911) had concentrated land in the hands of a few wealthy foreign and Mexican investors. Many former landowners descended into poverty. The lower standard of living, along with a population surge, drove as many as 75,000 Mexicans northward by 1890. Many also fled political persecution both during the Díaz years and in the bloody decade that followed the Revolution of 1910, which ultimately overthrew him. Perhaps one million Mexicans died in the fighting between 1910 and 1920; about as many again escaped north. Though some came with enough capital to establish small businesses, the vast majority were forced to work as poorly paid laborers. Since the turn of the century, immigrants have arrived in three main waves: those who fled life under the Díaz regime; those who fled the turmoil of the 1910s and 1920s; and those who came after World War II. This last wave continues today.

Movement north in the 1920s. Beginning in 1921, immigration authorities imposed strict quotas that reduced the number of Asian immigrants. Since these immigrants were a main source of cheap labor for booming West Coast agriculture, growers needed replacements. California began surpassing Texas as the most popular destination for immigrants from Mexico (a trend which continues today). About 500,000 immigrants arrived altogether in this period. Most California arrivals came first to Los Angeles, which by 1925 was second only to Mexico City in its Mexican population. Other immigrant centers arose at Brawley, El Centro, Calipatria, and Calexico. By 1930, about 350,000 Mexican Americans lived in California, supplying migrant labor as far north as Washington. Chicano labor contractors—called *contratistas* or *enganchistas*—provided workers to farmers at a flat rate per head, organizing transportation, food, and minimal lodging for the migrants.

Around 1930, the Mexican American population in Texas was 700,000, twice the number in California. Cities such as San Antonio and El Paso became recruitment centers for employers in the Northeast and Midwest. Mexican Americans worked on the Michigan and Pennsylvania railroads, in Ohio and Pennsylvania steel mills, and in Chicago meat yards. Chicago became the largest center for Mexican Americans outside of the Southwest, attracting former steel and railroad workers, who moved there to take jobs in trucking, construction, and service industries. Aside from the difficulty of adjustment to northern industrial life, European groups in the area considered the Mexicans inferior. Support came from church organizations such as the first Mexican Catholic parish, Nuestra Señora de Guadalupe, in South Chicago's Mexican neighborhoods.

The Great Depression and World War II. The depression (1929–1933), during which many Americans lost their jobs, brought an abrupt end to the second wave of immigration. As jobs grew scarce, "exclusionist" movements led to the Repatriation Program; its goal was the voluntary return of Mexicans who were not legally documented residents. A *Los Angeles Times* estimate put the number of repatriations for 1932 at 200,000. Perhaps 500,000 were deported altogether, many against their will. Threats used to persuade this group ranged from cessation of welfare payments to bodily removal.

With the manpower shortages of the World War II years, however, labor was again in demand. As a result, the Federal government instituted another program to invite Mexicans back into the United States. The Bracero Program operated from 1942–1947, and again from 1951–1964. Braceros (from the Spanish word *brazo*, "arm") were temporary workers recruited under agreements between the Mexican and American governments. From 1942–1947, more than 200,000 braceros worked in 21 states. These early braceros contributed much to the war effort. The second phase of the program was even more significant, with almost 200,000 entering annually in the early 1950s and over twice that in the heaviest year, 1959.

This second bracero program was largely a response to the rapid growth in illegal, or undocumented, immigrations after 1947. Tens of thousands of such illegal immigrants—called "wetbacks" or *mojados* because they often arrived by swimming the Río Grande—entered in the late 1940s. Because of their undocumented status, they were vulnerable to exploitation by employers and by the Immigration Service. A 1948 incident involved 7,000 undocumented workers who were arrested and then paroled to pick cotton in Texas for a wage, said the Mexican government, that was unfairly low.

César Chávez. To remedy such injustice, champions rose in defense of the laborers. César Chávez was a labor organizer in the grape fields of California. From the 1920s, Mexican agricultural laborers had attempted to organize, with little success. Most of the 40 Mexican American unions that formed in the 1930s joined the American Federation of Labor but were ineffectual in the face of violence caused by the growers, smears to discredit existing laborers, and imported Mexican strikebreakers. Chávez's charismatic leadership overcame these obstacles. In 1965, the Filipino-dominated Agricultural Workers Organizing Committee went on strike against San Joaquin Valley growers for better pay and union recognition.

When growers brought in local Mexican Americans as strikebreakers, AWOC's leader approached Chávez's National Farm Workers' Association in an appeal for solidarity. Chávez's union joined the strike; the two groups ultimately merged to form the United Farm Workers' Organizing Committee, which Chávez quickly came to dominate. Chávez, who advocates nonviolence, proved highly effective in enlisting popular support for the strikers' cause. He appeared with political leaders such as California Governor Edmund "Pat" Brown and New York Senator Robert Kennedy, who were instrumental in conveying his case to the broader public. The strike succeeded in 1970 after five difficult years.

In recent years, the economic struggles of Mexican Americans have shifted to the cities. Some of the newcomers gather on street corners to seek jobs as day laborers while others peddle ice cream or vegetables from handcarts in the poorer communities. Meanwhile, Chávez has transcended the platform of a labor organizer to aid in the broader quest for Mexican American rights.

Culture Today

Diversity and unity. Mexican Americans' unique history—first as conquerers and landowners, then as immigrants coming in large numbers from a poorer country—has resulted in a wide variety of cultural experiences. There is not one type of typical Mexican American. Each of the early isolated settlements had its own subculture: tejano in Texas, nuevo mexicano in New Mexico, and californio in California. Nuevo mexicanos, for example, consider themselves more Spanish than Mexican, and to this day their descendants call themselves *hispános*. An early criterion of social class was the degree of *mestizaje*, or ratio of Indian and Spanish blood, in a person. Spanish ancestry was considered desirable, Indian less so. Hence the nuevo mexicanos' insistence on their Hispanic background. Descendants of tejanos who stayed in Texas, by contrast, prefer the term *Latin American*.

Language. Of the many languages absorbed by America's cultural mix none has survived so tenaciously as Spanish. Mexican Americans comprise the largest Spanish-speaking community in the nation. Their "language loyalty" is partly explained by continuing immigration (averaging about 50,000 to 70,000 a year), and partly by the survival of isolated communities. A high proportion of northern New Mexico's hispános speak Spanish today, as do many third- or fourth-generation families in border towns or rural areas throughout the Southwest. Both pride of heritage and self-sufficiency make the language a continuing tradition. Bilingual education in American schools contributes to the language's survival. There have been changes, though. The language of Mexican Americans has been altered by contact with the English speaking majority. English words (*pochismos*) creep into Spanish usage: *el troque* (the truck); *la ganga* (the gang); *huachále* (watch it!). Some colleges offer courses in *calo*, the inventive and colorful slang of the urban *barrio* (neighborhood).

Mexican dress in the days before American rule.

Food, clothing, and shelter. Mexican food, especially in its Americanized form of "Tex-Mex" cuisine, has become an integral part of American eating, particularly in the Southwest. Mexican restaurants appear nationwide, both as family businesses and fast-food chains. Centered around beans, rice, corn, and the many varieties of chili pepper, familiar Mexican dishes include enchiladas, tacos, tamales, burritos, and tostadas. They present variations on a simple theme: spiced beef or chicken wrapped in one of the many cornmeal or flour preparations and served with rice and refried beans.

Once, californio, nuevo mexicano, and tejano rancheros wore practical clothes for work, but adorned themselves in traditional finery for their many fiestas. Men's costumes included deerskin boots with silver or gold studs, satin or velvet breeches (again with silver or gold buttons), a wide-brimmed, flat-topped sombrero, a ruffled shirt with silk vest and wide satin sash, and a leather or embroidered cloth jacket. Women would wear silk or cashmere *rebozos* (colorful scarves to cover the head and neck), a full, dark-colored dress, and satin or velvet shoes. Mexican or Indian workers wore simpler outfits: dungarees, sturdy shoes or perhaps sandals, a rough cotton shirt topped by a *serape* (vest), and a wide-brimmed hat. Today's city dwellers dress like their Anglo neighbors in, for example, blue jeans and shirts .

Housing structures have differed, depending on the area and time of settlement. An early californio's rancho consisted of a number of flat-roofed adobe buildings with packed-earth floors. At first, homes were one-story affairs with two or three rooms. Then settlers expanded and improved their homes, retaining the adobe structure but adding wide shady courtyards and verandas. In New Mexico and Arizona, hostile Indians compelled settlers to concentrate in towns. Homes had walls of adobe two or three feet thick, with barred windows and many storerooms in case of siege.

Barrios. *Barrio* has come to mean "any concentration of Mexican American residents." More specifically, it refers to Mexican American neighborhoods in the large cities. Different types of housing appear in barrio neighborhoods. There are well-kept, small family homes in parts of some barrios. In other areas, barrios have living quarters in decay.

The poverty of barrio areas has been associated with gangs. Sometimes incorporating older members in their activities, the gangs are often linked to violence and narcotics. In the 1970s, concern in the larger Mexican American community gave rise to a number of self-help agencies that offer assistance and counseling to drug addicts. Many communities now have self-help groups that tackle not only drug abuse but also other common problems.

Hard-working families live in the barrios. Typically the men earn 50 to 70 percent of the salaries of others in the same city. They labor long and hard to gain a financial foothold in the nation. Poor laborers and recent immigrants often take work in the construction industry or peddle merchandise. From these jobs, they sometimes move into positions in stores or government offices.

Education. A major difficulty in gaining economic status is that the Mexican American community as a whole tends to have an educational background considerably behind their Anglo counterparts. Many theories have been proposed to explain the apparent lack of interest in the schools. Partly this may stem from a general distrust of organizations which, for some immigrants, were mostly repressive in Mexico. Another explanation relates to history in America. Migrant families who crossed the border to work in agriculture moved from place to place. Also, children worked in the fields along with their parents. These patterns of settlement and work did not encourage educational achievement. At any rate, school attendance does not enjoy the high priority among Mexican Americans that it does among some other ethnic groups in the nation. Dropout rates are high and regular school attendance is frequently poor. This picture changes as families succeed economically and are able to move into less crowded housing in ethnically mixed areas of the cities.

Family life and religion. The traditional center of Mexican culture, family tends to remain most important. Male and female roles are clear-cut in the customary home; the father is dominant, demonstrating *machismo*, or virility, by protecting the family. A wife has responsibility for raising the children, which includes passing on traditional values and setting an example of religious devotion. Daughters are supposed to emulate the purity of their mother and follow her example in caring for the men of the family.

Family ties are strong. Whole families sometimes shop together for the week's groceries or join other families to enjoy the facilities of the local parks. Life rituals such as weddings, baptisms, and funerals once cemented the bond to relatives in the extended family. Today, most families celebrate these rituals differently from in the past. No longer is a baptism followed by an elaborate festival, nor is a wedding an all day affair for relatives more than friends. Funerals still perpetuate ties to aunts, uncles, and cousins; today gatherings after the graveside ceremony allow relatives not only to mourn but also to visit.

The majority of Mexican Americans are Roman Catholics. In most families, women are more observant than men. Rituals such as christenings, baptisms, and confirmations are performed for everyone, but the women attend church on a more regular basis. Perhaps the most important ceremony among Mexican American families is baptism of a young child. It is often associated with the choosing of godparents. In earlier times, a *comádre* (co-mother) and *compádre* (co-father) were chosen to care for the spiritual and bodily health of a child should anything happened to the parents. That is their designated role today, but once close friends served as godparents and now relatives are often selected. Most Mexican Americans expect that the real help in an emergency would come from the immediate or extended family.

Politics. It was only after World War I that Mexican American organizations became politicized. In 1921, the Mexican consul Eduardo Ruiz founded the *Comision Honorifica Mexicana*, which became accepted as a voice of the emerging Mexican American middle class. More recently, the Comision has focused on providing scholarships to Mexican American youths and on supplying a conservative alternative to radical leadership. A more political group, formed in 1921, was the Order of the Sons of America, largely made up of war veterans who sought to encourage awareness of basic political rights in the Mexican American community. A spin-off of the Sons of America formed in Corpus Christi, Texas, in 1929 under the name League of United Latin American Citizens (LULAC). Like the Sons, LULAC sought political awareness, but formulated more specific objectives: economic equality; participation in government, business, and education; higher numbers of Mexican-American professionals, such as doctors, lawyers, and engineers; pride in Mexican heritage; and greater proficiency in English. After World War II, LULAC grew to 15,000 members who were organized into local chapters.

A second wave of Mexican American organizations emerged after World War II. Mexican Americans had fought with exceptional distinction, more volunteering in proportion to their total numbers than any other ethnic group in America. Over 330,000 served, winning 17 Congressional Medals of Honor. Returning veterans felt more confident about their right to a full share in American life. In 1947, Army veteran Edward R. Roybal formed the Community Service Organization in Los Angeles, which encouraged voter registration and helped immigrants acquire U.S. citizenship. The American G.I. Forum fought discrimination against Mexican Americans in veterans' hospitals, then broadened its agenda to include political, civic, and social goals, becoming one of the most important of the politically moderate groups. Like the Forum, the Mexican American Political Association became active in the Democratic Party in the early 1960s, organizing rallies to increase Chicano representation in the party that had traditionally captured most Chicano votes.

Mexican American activists became more radical during the 1960s and 1970s, asserting Mexican ethnicity and downplaying cultural assimilation. Young people organized student groups and formed a revolutionary leadership that was inspired by Latin American revolutionaries such as Ché Guevara. This new leadership spawned several militant groups. Reies Lopez Tijerina led the Alianza Federal de Mercedes (Federal Alliance of Land Grants) in 1963 to military confrontation in an attempt to reclaim the old land grants of the nuevo mexicanos. In 1967, the Alianza wounded two deputies in a shootout; Tijerina was sentenced to two years in prison, and his organization foundered. The Texas leader José Angel Gutiérrez established La Raza Unida in 1970. Literally translated "the race," La Raza suggests an almost mystical union of Spanish and Indian blood. The term is powerfully evocative for Mexican Americans. Gutiérrez invoked it to create a unified party that would supply a complete Mexican American political agenda. His success in local campaigns in Texas inspired Mexican Americans throughout the 1970s.

Since the 1970s, Mexican American men and women have been gaining rights and representation at different levels of government. A Mexican American was elected governor of New Mexico (Jerry Apodaca in 1974), another became mayor of San Antonio, Texas (Henry Cisneros in 1981), and and a third became U.S. Secretary of Education (Lauro F. Cavazos in 1989). Recently, a Chicana movement has encouraged more freedom of self-expression for Mexican American women. By the 1980s, there were over 40 organizations in this movement. The feminists have aligned themselves with progressive Chicano leaders, particularly at university seminars and symposia.

Arts and recreation. The Mexican American movement has found vigorous expression in the arts, combining political and social concerns in many different art forms. Luis Valdez, a playwright, founded the famous El Teatro Campesino (Farm Workers' Theater) in 1965 as part of Chávez's UFWOC. A social protest theater group, the Teatro Campesino presents original productions that blend avant-garde techniques with themes of oppression and Mexican American pride. Social rights champion "Corky" Gonzales authored a highly popular epic poem, "I Am Joaquin," that dramatizes Mexican American self-reliance in a mostly Anglo society. Artists have carried on the Mexican tradition of painting extensive murals that explore social and political issues. This art form, with public walls as its canvas, involves the entire community. An offshoot of mural painting has been taken up by gangs, who paint intricate and highly structured graffiti. In the 1970s and 1980s, the mural painters and gang members collaborated on projects that seamlessly blend both forms. Mexican American writers have also been innovators, publishing novels, plays, poetry, and short stories that use both English and Spanish to examine tensions between Anglo and Mexican culture. In a more traditional vein, salsa and mariachi are popular musical forms. Mexicans encountered German settlers in Texas and developed Tex-Mex *polkeros*, which incorporate such diverse forms as jazz and country music.

Baseball and soccer are major recreational activities in Mexican American communities. Children begin early to play in leagues, and families gather on the weekends to watch the teams compete. Young men, including young fathers, join baseball teams too, competing in community-wide leagues.

Many of today's major league baseball players began as Little League players in the Mexican American barrios; others, such as the Los Angeles Dodger's Fernando Valenzuela, formerly played minor league baseball in Mexico.

Mexican American individuals have achieved acclaim in both sports and the arts. Besides the baseball stars, Jim Plunkett has won several awards in football, and champion golfers include Lee Trevino and Nancy López. Examples of well-known entertainers are singers Vikki Carr, Linda Ronstadt, and Joan Báez, and actors Carmen Zapata and Anthony Quinn.

Holidays. Although Mexican ways have become familiar to America as a whole, they remain most integral to life in the Southwest. Californio-style fiestas are celebrated in many California communities. Citizens throughout the Southwest join Mexican Americans in celebrating *Cinco de Mayo*, the Fifth of May, which commemorates the 1862 defeat of invading French forces by the Mexican Army. In addition to this special holiday, place names from Texas (San Antonio) to Colorado (San Pablo) to California (San Diego) continue to recall the Mexicans who were first to immigrate to the American Southwest.

For More Information

See these reading materials:

Smith, Griffin, Jr. "The Mexican Americans: A People on the Move." *National Geographic*. June 1980, pp. 780-809.

Williams, Norma. *The Mexican American Family: Tradition and Change*. Dix Hills, New York: General Hall, 1990.

Contact these organizations:

Mexican-American Opportunity Foundation, 6252 E. Telegraph Road, Commerce, California 90040.

National Council of La Raza, 810 First Street NE, 3rd Floor, Washington, DC 20002.

MICMAC
(mick´ mack)

Descendants of an American Indian group whose lifestyle centered on the sea and woodlands of eastern Canada.

Population: 12,000 claim Micmac descent, although there may be no pure-blooded Micmac today (1986).
Location: Northeastern Canada.
Language: Micmac (an Algonquian dialect), French, English.

Geographical Setting

The Micmac live in Canada near the St. Lawrence River.

During the 16th century, the Micmac occupied the Canadian region south and west of the Gulf of St. Lawrence. It was a heavily forested area, whose many lakes and rivers ran into fine harbors along the coast. In the early 17th century, French adventurers appeared around the mouth of the St. Lawrence River and the Bay of Fundy (now the provinces of New Brunswick,

Quebec, and Nova Scotia). The region has bitter weather, tormented by the cold arctic winds and the turbulent ocean. Tides are high—often reaching 40 feet in the Bay of Fundy. The first immigrants from Europe found it an inhospitable land in which it was difficult to survive. The abundance of forests, fish, and other wildlife, however, drew French furriers and then settlers from France and Great Britain to the region. Micmac territory changed. Most of today's Micmac live on and off 15 major reserves in Nova Scotia, New Brunswick, and Quebec, and on Prince Edward Island. A few hundred reside in Newfoundland.

Historical Background

A Micmac couple in traditional clothing

Food, clothing, and shelter. The Micmac were a maritime group; they lived always near rivers and streams or the sea. Migrating with the seasons, they moved between the coast and inland camps. This pattern strongly influenced their eating habits. From spring until fall, the Micmac lived on the coast, eating almost solely sea animals: fish, shellfish, birds, and seals. Sometimes the Micmac would catch porpoises or small whales from their canoes.

At summer's end, the Micmac began to pack up for their move inland. They lived inland until spring, locating their camps near a river or stream. During the winter, land animals became much more important in the Micmac diet, though the people continued to fish. They hunted moose with bow and arrow and trapped muskrat and otter. Seals served as food in winter as well as in summer—groups of men would travel to the coast for seal hunts during the seals' birthing season. The Micmac relied also on stored foods, such as smoked fish, dried berries, and nuts to carry them through the winter.

Clothing changed with the seasons, too. Men wore loincloths and deerskin moccasins in the summer. Women dressed in long, one-piece deerskin shirts. When winter arrived, the men added long deerskin shirts; both men and women donned deerskin leggings and heavy fur robes. Porcupine quills, eagle feathers, and shell jewelry decorated the clothing. Garments were further decorated with floral, animal, or geometric designs woven into the material or painted on it. The Micmac used face and body paint and tattoos to ornament themselves. Sometimes a band's symbol, the picture of a salmon, for example, appeared on the skin or clothing, helping to distinguish the members of a band.

The Micmac lived in conical wigwams made of birch or fir bark. Women decorated the wigwams with traditional designs and covered them with extra furs for warmth during the winters. In the summer the Micmac sometimes constructed larger rectangular huts for better air circulation. Wigwams were so comfortable and easy to transport between camp sites that the Micmac continued to live in them into the 1800s.

Social structure. Micmac society included bands, local groups, and households. The people divided their territory into seven districts, a band including local groups that hunted within a given district. The groups in a band came together infrequently, during wartime, for example.

There were three types of governors—a Grand Chief, or *sagamore*, the seven district chiefs, and local chiefs. Grand council meetings were called by the Grand Chief in the process of treatymaking, for example. The district chief called district council meetings. Occurring yearly, a duty of the district chief was redistricting hunting territories based on the sizes of local groups. A local group appears to have included at least 30 members, whose male elders formed a council to assist the local chief.

In social ranking, chiefs belonged to the highest class. Beneath them were commoners and then slaves. There was much equality among the early Micmacs, yet they enslaved captives who had been taken in war.

Under French rule. The Micmac were fiercely independent, warring frequently with the nearby Iroquois. Yet they befriended the French. French furriers married Micmac women, and the two cultures began a long union. The Micmac aided the growing French fur trade. Hunting for furs disrupted their seasonal calendar, however; they were unable to gather as much food during the summer, which made winters very difficult. There were other drawbacks to the presence of the French. The Micmac began to rely on the French for food as well as alcohol. These changes in the Micmac diet, coupled with the diseases brought by the French, caused the population to decline steadily from 1600 to 1850. Still, the friendly relations continued.

When the Micmac learned that their old enemies from Newfoundland, the Beothuk, threatened the French fur trade, the Micmac entered a long war of extermination. Their French allies offered to pay for Beothuk scalps, encouraging the Micmac warriors. The final result was the extinction of the Beothuk by the year 1820. The Micmac also joined the French in war against the Iroquois.

British control. When, in the early 1700s, the British settled in Micmac territory and named part of it Nova Scotia, the Micmac joined the French in resisting the invasion. The British responded by attempting to purge the Micmac population in a series of bloody campaigns. The French and British claims swung back and forth for several years. Then in the 1760s, the British won the rights from France and formally signed a treaty with the Micmac. In exchange for kettles, knives, other European tools, and a parcel of land, the Micmac relinquished their claim to the seashore and neighboring forests. Contact with the French had created a dependency on European living tools.

Canada's influence. By this time, the Micmac had already begun to learn farming techniques from the Jesuit missionaries. Now with their traditional means of survival gone, the Micmac turned to agriculture. British rule limited their travel away from the *reserve* (the area reserved by the British for the use and benefit of an Indian band). So the Micmac resorted to other-than-traditional alternatives. They became sedentary trappers and took jobs in the growing lumber industry or as commercial fishermen. Some Micmac were employed as guides for the early European furriers and settlers. By the mid-19th century, the railroads, lumber mills, and shipping had grown immensely. In addition, potato plantations sprang up around the Micmac reserve and demanded a periodic flow of migrant workers. Demand for Micmac labor was high. However, the new jobs that were filled by the unskilled Indians paid little. Poorly paid and with no means to carry on their old lifestyles, the Micmac became an impoverished people.

Culture Today

Dependency. Aware of the Micmac's economic difficulties, the British governors took action in the early 1900s. Schools were opened and the Micmac were encouraged to attend. A few Micmac began to earn an easier living in professional sports. After World War I, some of the Indians became professional hockey and baseball players. The British also provided new medical services, and Catholic churches and Capuchin monasteries began to minister to the Micmac.

New medical treatments improved health and encouraged a population boom. By the 1930s, the Micmac were threatened with overpopulation. Their economic situation worsened when the Great Depression closed many of the nearby industries. Many Micmac lived on welfare, finding no relief until World War II brought a revival of the industries. After this war, new housing, educational opportunities, and communication through radio and television entered the Micmac world. Many of the Micmac were too poor to take advantage of these new opportunities, however. The presence of new but inaccessible ways boded ill for the group. By 1950, Micmac crime rates had risen above those of the rest of Canada. The response of the Canadian government was to relax controls on the Micmac reserves and to encourage self-determination and independence for the Micmac. As further assistance, Canada began to develop housing for the Indians.

The government attention has done little to overcome the poverty of the Micmac. Canada owns timber mills in Nova Scotia that employ the Indians, but still for low wages and without enough jobs. In the early 1980s, the unemployed Micmac in Nova Scotia outnumbered those who had jobs. Many have moved off the reserve into cities hoping to find greater employment opportunity. The lifestyle of this group is in transition. Yet they have managed to retain a sense of unity. Despite their earlier mixing with the French and British, and their present scattering on and off the reserve , the Micmac have maintained their identity as a distinct people.

Daily life. With the reserve system, the freedom of movement needed for successful hunting decreased. Today Micmac families work for wages and buy their foods at stores. Some have become farmers, but many have become commercial fishermen, tour guides, and lumbermen. Many Micmac men have taken jobs as skilled laborers in the construction industry. To find work, men often leave their homes for the industries of New England.

Micmac women have become nurses, teachers, secretaries, and social workers. Most salespeople in the reserve stores are women. Some of them find employment off the reserve in hotels and restaurants.

Traditional art still appears in designs that are woven into baskets made for sale to shopkeepers and tourists. Basketry is the one skill upon which the Micmac have capitalized, although they produce some leathercraft, beads, and woodwork. The old art of decorating clothing is no longer needed, since members of the group have abandoned their traditional dress. Even those Micmac who live on the reserve now wear Western-style clothing.

Today there are 27 major reserves on which Micmac Indians live. A variety of housing structures appear on the reserves, the results of different government building programs. Still standing are some ancient shacks. Electricity appears everywhere. Otherwise, facilities depend on the particular reserve. It may or may not have a church, school, community center, grocery stores, and a band government office. In business, some reserves specialize in cutting Christmas trees for outsiders or trapping lobster, for example. Many of the reserves cannot capitalize on surrounding wildlife, though, as they sit in areas whose natural resources have been exhausted.

Religion. More than twice as many Micmac have remained on the reserves than have moved to other parts of Nova Scotia. Gathering on the reserve has helped the people retain some old traditions. Although most of the Micmac claim affiliation with the Roman Catholic Church, many cling to old beliefs. Historians are not familiar with the whole belief system of the Micmac religion. A few known beliefs are the faith in *keskamizit*, or "Indian luck," in supernatural helpers, and in the guidance of great hunter ancestors. The religion includes a Great Spirit and many nature spirits. Different forms of life, according to the Micmac religion, may change into one another.

Literature. Micmac legends tell of a mighty warrior named Gluskap. According to early stories, Gluskap was responsible for giving animals their present form. He acted as a teacher of many Micmac skills and a seer capable of foretelling the future. Finally, this mythical figure was characterized as a trickster whose descendants were strong men with supernatural powers.

In Micmac legends, misfortune is attributed to witches and magic potions. Supernatural causes result in forest fires. Among the tricksters are dwarfish beings who dress and act like the early Micmac.

The repetition of the trickster character reveals the value of cleverness among the Micmac. This trait proved useful in dealing with the French and then the British. More recently, it has helped them to support themselves on the reserves in Nova Scotia and to preserve their own integrity and independence. The Micmac preserve this part of their culture by passing on traditional stories and legends. For further continuity, those Micmac who move to urban centers away from the reserve still speak their native language and teach that language to their children.

Family life. In early Micmac culture, marriage was forbidden between members of the same clan. This policy resulted in marriage ties that bound clans and contributed to the Micmac sense of unity. As a rule, marriages involved a period of probation. A prospective husband had to prove his ability to provide for a wife by performing two years of bride service for his future father-in-law. Marriage today is no longer arranged by families the way it once was. As in the rest of North America, divorce has become more common. The number of children born out of wedlock is high. They have long been valued in Micmac society, though.

Children and old people are prized and treated with tenderness in the traditionally strong Micmac family. On the reserve, the family bond is so close that most children stay at home until they near 20 years of age. Then, having reached the age of employment, they begin to leave the reserve. The largest number of off-reserve Micmac is the 30 to 40 age group. Family ties are so strong, however, that later in life (at the age of 50 or 60) many return home to the reserve.

Education. Public education is provided for the Micmac, but this service has seen only limited acceptance. In Nova Scotia, enrollment data shows a high dropout rate after the sixth grade. Of those who remain, less than half graduate from high school. Education, even for those who continue through high school, demands that the Micmac adapt to the larger Canadian culture and seems not to ensure well-paid jobs after graduation. Among Micmac leaders, there has been sharp disagreement about the benefit in types of schooling.

New direction. Since the 1960s, Micmac leaders have actively pursued the advancement of their people by joining pan-Indian movements (for example, the Union of Nova Scotia Indians). These movements, which united different Indian peoples to deal with the outside government regarding their common concerns, have produced some successes for the participants. The Micmac gained control over programs on their reserves. They also addressed land claims, winning money for lands that had been taken from them illegally.

For More Information

See these reading materials:

Callwood, June. *Portrait of Canada.* Garden City, New York: Doubleday, 1981.

Morrison, R. Bruce, and Wilson, C. Roderick, eds. *Native Peoples: The Canadian Experience.* Toronto, Ontario: McClelland and Stewart, 1986.

Woodcock, George. *Canada and the Canadians.* London: Faber and Faber. 1970.

MORMONS
(Mor´mens)

Members of the Church of Jesus Christ of Latter-day Saints,
a religion that originated in 19th-century United States.

Population: 2,958,000 (1989).
Location: United States (1,305,000 in Utah); Canada.
Language: Primarily English (the *Book of Mormon* has been translated
into 80 languages).

Geographical Setting

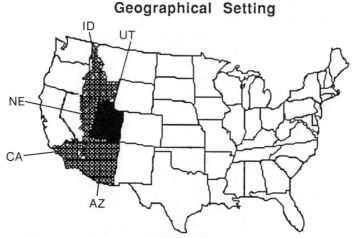

The greatest concentration of Mormons is in Utah,
Arizona, Idaho, Nevada, and Southern California

Mormon religion began in upstate New York (near Palmyra) in 1830.
There on the Hill Cumorah, founder Joseph Smith claimed to have been
given the mandate to lead a new religion as a modern day prophet. Smith led
his followers into Ohio, Missouri, and Nauvoo, Illinois. Chased from
Illinois, the Latter-day Saints (Mormons) continued to the area that is now
Omaha, Nebraka, then on to the Great Basin area of Utah. The terrain was

rugged but fertile. Running North and South, the Wasatch Mountains dissect Utah. Dropping sharply, several thousand feet below the western mountaintops are valleys. The mountains catch the winter snows, then distribute them along a network of small rivers and streams. Pioneering irrigation, the Mormons diverted water to the valleys for farming. They lived within towns but farmed outside them. String towns appeared along the narrow valleys in the second half of the 19th century, and more Mormons scattered on individual farms. Meanwhile, the population grew so rapidly (from 11,000 in 1850 to 87,000 in 1870) it overflowed from Utah into other western states and the province of Alberta in Canada. In the 20th century the tendency to found new towns changed. Mormons instead flocked to urban centers such as Salt Lake City, Provo, and Ogden in Utah. While the Mormon population has increased worldwide, Utah remains the cultural center. Roughly 76 percent of Utah's citizens today are Mormon.

Historical Background

The age of Andrew Jackson. American liberty and prosperity reached new heights during the presidency of Andrew Jackson. However, the decade that followed seemed chaotic to many. Politicians appeared to put personal gain before the national welfare. In religion, sects split from already established groups to form new faiths. Joseph Smith, a poor teenager in upstate New York, searched for the right group to join. He claimed to have a vision in which God and Jesus informed him that none of the divisions was legitimate. In another vision a white-robed angel named Moroni told Smith he had a divine mission. Joseph Smith should bring to the world a book written upon golden plates that had been buried in the Hill Cumorah. Smith dutifully translated the plates from ancient Egyptian into the English *Book of Mormon.* In the book, Mormon is a man, a prophet, and Moroni is his son.

The *Book of Mormon* begins before Christ, with God warning a Hebrew that his people would be conquered by the Babylonians. Heeding the warning, the Hebrew wandered with his followers until they reached the shores of America. An argument between his two sons divided the followers into factions. The Nephites, the religious group, observed the Law of Moses; the irreligious Lamanites preferred the ways of darkness. They fought. In America, Jesus Christ reunited them. Two hundred years of peace followed, then friction erupted again. The Lamanites ultimately conquered the Nephites. Before perishing, the fifth-century prophet Mormon summarized his people's history on gold plates. He entrusted the plates to his son Moroni, who buried them in the Hill Cumorah. This same Moroni was the white-robed angel who appeared to Joseph Smith in his dream. The story continues. Discovered by Christopher Columbus, the American Indians were identified as descendants of the infamous Lamanites. Smith believed God chose Americans to be his people, to redeem humanity. They had done so to the time of the Founding Fathers. By Smith's day, though, Americans had descended from justice into wickedness. Even worse, their churches no longer upheld the ways of Christ. Smith therefore formed a new faith—the Church of Jesus Christ of Latter-day Saints. He referred to his followers not as Mormons but as *Saints*..

On April 6, 1830, in Fayette, New York, Joseph Smith and five other men became the first elders in the Church. Smith took the lead as prophet, the living being who communed with God on matters regarding all humanity. God's divine son Jesus Christ would someday reappear on Earth, Smith believed. Meanwhile, a living prophet like himself would receive revelations from God to direct true believers in the present. Mormonism is unique in its belief in living prophets. Acting on a divine message, Smith created a new faith to restore basic Christian beliefs, prepare for the second coming of Christ, and relay the ancient history.

Mormon beginnings. Smith was from a poor family. Wealthy at first, they had plunged into poverty in upstate New York by 1830. Their hard work brought little reward, and they had been snubbed by prosperous townfolk. So when Smith received a revelation to move his "church" to Ohio he probably had few regrets. His new faith had attracted hostility from outsiders by then. They were upset by the idea of a living prophet receiving messages from God. With departure from New York came over a decade of wandering to their final destination. The *Book of Mormon* speaks of a New Jersulaem to be built upon the American continent. Smith wandered in search of a place to build his new Zion, his city of God. From New York he and 190 followers journeyed to Ohio, then on to Missouri in 1831. They remained in Missouri for nearly a decade, hostility prompting them to move from one county to another.

Anti-Mormons. Confrontations were frequent, and resulted in several dozen Mormon killings. Old residents feared their large numbers, their revelations, their invitations to black people to settle among them, and their claim that God had given them the land. In July, 1833, a "Manifesto of the Mobs" formed to halt the stream of Mormons into Missouri. Still, their numbers increased. Missouri's governor finally banished all Mormons under threat of death. Some 10,000 of them fled to Illinois in 1839. They built the city Nauvoo. Exercising great control, Mormons continued to engage in practices that upset outsiders. Most offensive was the Mormon practice of plural marriage. Smith justified polygamy, or more correctly *polygyny*—marriage of one man to more than one wife—by recalling the Old Testament. Secretly in the 1840s, he urged his worthiest followers to practice plural marriage. They obeyed, the leader Brigham Young quelling his own abhorrence for the custom. Other Mormons objected, defecting from the Church because of the practice.

Despite their strength in Nauvoo, the Mormons suffered beatings, stabbings, kidnappings, and killings in Illinois. Outsiders conducted night rides, burning Mormon farms. In part to win respect for the faith, Joseph Smith ran for United States President in 1844. His opponents were Henry Clay and Martin Van Buren. Followers, a Council of Fifty, aided Smith in his campaign, convinced that his presidency would bring order to America as it had to the Mormon religion. Secretly they prepared for a kingdom of God on Earth, governed by Jesus for a time and then by the Council of Fifty. Their plans came to an abrupt halt due to controversy between Smith and two ex-Mormons. Publishing the *Nauvoo Expositor*, Wilson and William Law argued against plural marriage. Joseph Smith and the Nauvoo City Council attempted to destroy their press, which led to Smith's arrest. Accused of treason, he was jailed without bail. An armed mob of 200 men painted themselves black, then broke into the jail and shot Joseph and his brother Hyrum to death. The date was June 27, 1844. After the two martyrs died, thousands of Mormons had their homes burned and their temple destroyed. Once again the believers were forced to search for new living quarters.

Brigham Young. The death of Joseph Smith brought a split among Church members. Most of them felt the role of prophet should be filled by divine calling, then sustained by a vote of the members. Smith's relatives believed leadership should fall to members of his own family. This smaller group formed the Reorganized Church. The majority of the Mormons voted to accept a new prophet—Brigham Young. Soon, Young led yet another migration, the last and longest. Converts were arriving from Europe at a constant rate to join the spring move west. Those without wagons were furnished handcarts. A ballad of these handcart pioneers reveals their disappointment in the lands they left (Fife 1988, p. 19).

The lands that boast of so much light	The lands that boast of liberty
We know they're all as dark as night	You ne'er again would wish to see
Where poor men toil and want for bread	When you from England make a start
rich men's dogs are better fed.	To cross the plains in your handcart.

A diorama showing the Mormon Batallion on its
march through the Southwest Desert.

Agreeing to a request by the U.S. government, about 500 of the men
separated from their families and marched by a more southerly route to join
in the growing conflict with Mexico. The rest of the migrants trekked
westward along the Oregon Trail, then south to the Great Basin area of Utah,
where they aimed to build Zion—dwelling place of the righteous. It is said
Brigham Young entered Salt Lake Valley on July 24, 1847. Recognizing the
valley from an earlier vision, he quickly announced, "This is the place. Drive
on."

Zion. Mexico, which owned the territory at the time, had left it empty of
settlers. The Treaty of Guadalupe Hidalgo transferred ownership of the
territory to the United States. Numbering 18,000 in 1847, the Mormons
stayed...and grew. Brigham Young sent young male missionaries through
America and Europe to gain converts. In 1849, he founded a Perpetual
Emigration Fund to transport new believers into Utah. His missionaries
chose converts with talents to enhance the self-sufficiency of the society.
Soon 186 communities existed, and farming flourished. The Mormons
initiated a fledgling iron industry and the first irrigation project in America.
Pioneers of the West, Mormon settlers worked hard and prospered.
They farmed to raise their own food and families produced most everything
else they used. Husbands served as providers, usually working at more than
one occupation. Aside from farming, they would engage in mining or
freighting to earn income. Wives mainly kept house and raised children, but
they too worked for money—teaching, selling farm goods, washing clothes,
taking in boarders, or serving as midwives. Though they taught their
daughters to sweep and their sons to cultivate crops, children were active in
the outside world, too. Susa Young Gates, daughter to Brigham Young,

joined the national fight to give women the vote. Also fighting for this cause was the notable Morman leader Emmeline B. Wells.

Brigham Young protected Mormon territory and the group's isolation. When outsiders settled nearby, he planted new colonies nearby as if to declare the land his. Young began with plans for a state named Deseret, not Utah. For a time (1848-1852) the Mormon Church minted its own coins for use in the territory and Young advocated a new alphabet. It seemed the Mormons had finally realized their hopes for a separate, holy society on Earth in the promised land—America.

Brigham Young

Heber Wells

Brigham Young (top left) led the Mormons to Utah. Heber Wells was Utah's first chief of state.

Events in the late 19th century upset the harmony. Fearing the Mormons planned a separate country, the U.S. government cancelled a contract given to the Brigham Young Company for carrying mail. The Church taught Saints to obey ruling governments, yet President Buchanan accused Young of failing to recognize the superiority of federal law. In fact, Buchanan ordered U.S. troops to Salt Lake City. The Mormons threatened to burn their homes and abandon the area. They did, in fact, evacuate 30 miles southward. When troops arrived, the abandoned homes looked so desolately lonely soldiers removed their hats in a gesture of pity. National sympathy shifted in favor of the Mormons, President Buchanan pardoned them, and the Saints returned to their homes.

Another incident did not end so happily. As pioneers headed for California, wagon trains and then the railroad passed the Mormon part of the Rocky Mountains. In 1857, the Mormons heard that army troops were on the way to quash them. They readied themselves for violent action. Several wagon trains were in the region at the time. Trains had already passed through the area peacefully, but now tension mounted. Without approval, some Mormon men paid a visit to the Francher wagon train at Mountain Meadows. They tricked its men, women, and children into separating into groups, then with the help of Indians massacred all but the 18 children. Demanding the responsible Mormons be punished, the cry for justice was interrupted by the Civil War. A Mormon jury convicted John D. Lee in 1876. He was executed at the scene of the crime for engineering the Mountain Meadows Massacre.

Time and again, fear of the increasing power of the Mormon Church caused conflict. Its support of polygamy continued to upset outsiders, but often their main aim was to suppress the economic and political strength of the Church. Objecting to plural marriage, Congress passed measures against its practice—the Morrill Anti-Bigamy Act (1862), the Edmunds Law (1882), and lastly the Edmunds-Tucker Act (1887). Mormons themselves resisted the practice. Estimates have suggested only 10 percent of Mormon men had plural marriages. In 1890, weary of the attacks and well established in Utah, the Church denounced plural marriages. Its president declared his position in an official Manifesto (Alexander 1980, p. 57).

Inasmuch as laws have been enacted by Congress forbidding plural marriages...I hereby declare my intention to submit to those laws, and to use my influence with the members of the Church over which I preside to have them do likewise.

Despite the 1890 declaration, plural marriages continued. Therefore, a second Manifesto in 1904 added punishment for those who disobeyed the ban. The Mormon Church would disown, or excommunicate, them.

A new direction. About the turn of the 20th century, there was a reversal in strategy. Instead of drawing converts to Utah, leaders encouraged them to remain in their countries and build churches there. Missionaries were sent to areas such as South America and Polynesia, continuing also to work among North American Indians. In 1943, the Navajo-Zuni Mission was established.

It became the first mission exclusively designed for the use of Indians. Membership in the church climbed steadily due to all these efforts.

Believing in obeying governments, Mormon soldiers performed their duty on the battlefields of 20th century wars. The Saints sent aid to Mormon and non-Mormon victims after World War II. In 1947 they held a Fast Day for the relief of those in need. About 210,000 dollars was collected and distributed to Europeans of all faiths. For several years they sent supplies to Latter-day Saints in the war-torn countries. Young men resumed their missionary activity after the war. Among the American Indians, more programs were launched. In 1954, Mormons began an Indian Placement Program, taking young Indian students into their homes during the school year. Relations with the American Indians had long been harmonious. As described earlier, they were descendents of the Lamanites–an ancient tribe of Israel–according to the Mormon beliefs. In 1976 a,n Indian rose to the rank of a general authority for the entire worldwide Church.

Probably most signifcant in the 20th century has been the change in the Mormon position on blacks. Few attempts were made to convert black people to the faith at first. Those who entered the Church could become members only, not priests. In the 1960s, with the eruption of the Civil Rights Movement in the United States, pressure began to increase. Why should blacks be denied the priesthood? became the familiar question. In 1978, the living prophet Spencer W. Kimball announced a revelation from God. Worthy men of all races should be able to receive the priesthood.

Missionary activity had succeeded in countries such as Japan by 1970. Now it quickened in nations such as South Africa, where the first Mormon temple on the continent appeared in 1985. There was material aid, too. In the same year, the Mormons of North America held two fasts to benefit the hungry. They raised 11 million dollars for famine victims in Africa and elsewhere. From Washington, DC, Mormons organized the shipment of 180,000 fiction and nonfiction books to African nations. The efforts proved fruitful in terms of world membership, which climbed to seven million by 1990. Mormonism had become the only worldwide religion to have begun in the United States.

Culture Today

Religious beliefs. Mormons believe Christ was not the last prophet but was a supreme prophet. He will, they say, appear on Earth again, so Mormons should prepare the world for his coming. Assuming this responsibility, they consider themselves God's chosen people.

Earthly life is viewed as a small step in an everlasting existence. Mormons believe they lived with God before mortal life, and it is possible for them to live with God again in a future life. Whether or not they will achieve this aim depends on family ties and their observance of Church rules. Mormons think they sin, but hard work and honest repentance absolves them of their sins. Followers abide by 13 Articles of Faith; one article says they are not held accountable for Adam's sin in the Garden of Eden. Thus, Mormons do not believe they must atone for the sins of others. Family is the central religious unit, so ancestors who died without knowing the Mormon faith may be baptized in proxy. In other words, a living family member stands in for the dead. Mormon doctrine holds that being with God in a future life depends on preserving the family through all its lineage. The keen interest in kinship produces Mormon documents tracing ancestry. Vast archives are preserved and updated in Salt Lake City's Family History Library. They have become a center for almost all Americans interested in tracing their ancestry. The Family History Library has millions of microfilmed historical documents that are freely available to people, regardless of their faith.

Family life. The family is the center of the Mormon religion, and prayers are said daily at home. Family members pray individually and as a group. Individuals say grace at each meal and give thanks for the day's blessings at night. As a group, family members kneel on the floor and bow their heads to pray.

Children receive weekly religious lessons from age four. At age eight, they are baptized. Mormons believe people should become their own ministers, that anyone with a Bible and the ability to read can learn Christian truths. A boy becomes a deacon at age 12, a teacher at 14, and a priest at 16. Then many young men go on a mission to spread the gospel.

Members busily engage in Church activities on weekdays, but one night a week—Monday—is reserved for their own family. Called Home Evening, it is time set aside for siblings and parents to share experiences with one another. Involved in social life, the Church encourages young Mormons to meet and marry. Meeting houses have gymnasiums, stages for plays, dance floors, kitchens, and so on. The yearly Gold and Green ball is one of many opportunities for young Mormons to meet and date. At the end of a courtship, a couple requests a *recommend*—a document that permits them to enter the inner sanctury of a Mormon temple. Temple marriage includes a rite that "seals" a husband and wife together for eternity. In contrast to ceremonies that bind couples "until death do you part," a *sealing* joins them beyond mortal life. The religion thereby extends the concept of family for all time. While Mormons may marry outside the temple, their marriages cannot be sealed. Divorce is possible but discouraged. Presently several thousand people in or near the state of Utah practice plural marriage, but they are excommunicated by the Church.

Mormons tend to live longer than many other Americans. This lengthy life span has been attributed to their dietary habits and their avoidance of tobacco and certain beverages.

Food, clothing, and shelter. Mormon girls train to be mothers and wives. While they pursue Church activities and interests outside the home, family always comes first. Some of the rules they follow concern food at family meals. Joseph Smith received a revelation in the religion's early years. Mormons should not consume tea, coffee, tobacco, or alcohol. Called the *Word of Wisdom*, these dietary laws are strictly observed by Mormon temple goers. Otherwise members of the group favor grains and fruits and vegetables in season. Meat is eaten sparingly, saved for times of cold or famine.

With few exceptions, Mormons dress like other Americans. A bride wears a special white robe if she marries in the temple. Green aprons and sacred undergarments are worn by both women and men in the temple. In daily life, clothing is modest. Women avoid low-necked garments; men keep on their shirts. Housing styles vary, stone being an early building material. Both one- and two-story stone houses are among the Mormon structures that have appeared in Northern Utah.

Church structure. Outside the home, Mormons pray in temples and meeting houses. Meeting houses are modest structures, housing chapel and activity spaces. In contrast, the temples are elaborate edifices—not all Mormons are eligible to enter. Sacred rites are performed in the temple, and members must be deemed worthy to join in such ceremonies. If they keep the commandments and are observant Mormons, they receive the recommend—a type of pass into a temple's inner sanctuary.

Churchwide officers are called general authorities and preside over everyone in the faith. Among these officers are the *Presidency, twelve apostles*, and a *quorum of seventy*. Considered the voice of God on Earth, the president is the living prophet. Twelve apostles each exercise domain over a certain part of the world. They are aided by the quorum of seventy, men who are responsible for missionary activity.

Mormons have local as well as Churchwide organizations. Serving several hundred members, a local congregation forms a *ward*. Five to ten wards compose a *stake*. At the head of a ward is the *bishop*. Other local leaders are *elders*, who are also holders of the Melchizedek Priesthood. There are two types and several levels of priesthood in the Mormon faith. (Aaronic priesthood is the lower type; Melchizedek is the higher type.) With work and study, any male member may progress through the various levels to become a *high priest*.

Education and economics. The Church of Jesus Christ of Latter-day Saints has a two-fold commitment to education: (1) to teach Mormon beliefs and (2) to encourage members in their pursuit of worldly schooling so they can earn a living. Aside from public school, Mormons attend religious classes. Sisters (the name for all Mormon women) run a Primary Association for children. Along with the gospel, it teaches appreciation of, for example, novels. Education, in general, is greatly valued by the group. Utah has a well-reputed public school system, and the highest percentage of college-degree residents in the country. Founded by Mormon immigrants in 1850, the University of Deseret is now known as the University of Utah. Brigham Young University is still Church-owned but educates the wider public, too. In fact, BYU is the largest Church-owned school in the nation (over 20,000 students). Notable is its record of far fewer American Indian dropouts than other universities in the UnitedStates.

Mormon graduates tend to earn their income from jobs in practical fields, such as business, medicine, or applied science. Members of the faith are expected to pay *tithes*, or contribute ten percent of their earnings, to the Church. In effect since 1841, tithing pays for Church buildings and provides for the poor. The Church owns farms, canneries, and textile mills, then warehouses and distributes the products. Since the Great Depression in America, it has operated its own Welfare Program. The Church also encourages Mormon families to keep an emergency supply of food and other necessities on hand, enough to sustain the family for a year.

Women and government. Although the priesthood is reserved for men, Mormon women have been active in American life. Eliza Snow, wife an early apostle, demonstrated her business acumen as president of the Relief Society for 30 years. The Society is an educational, charitable organization that has always been run by Mormon women. Aside from her work as a suffragette, Brigham Young's daughter, Susa Young Gates, was a musician, writer, and teacher. Dr. Martha Hughes Cannon, a physician, became the first woman member of the U.S. Senate, and Utah was an early state to allow women the vote (1870).

In the 20th century, Mormon women have reversed their traditional support of the feminist movement, due mainly to potential changes they consider harmful to family life. Their first responsibility is still family and child-rearing.

Mormons of both genders believe in honoring civil authority and actively support the United States government. In politics, the party of choice depends on the individual. Mormons have served in both houses of the U.S. Congress.

Literature. Most popular among Latter-day Saints are religious writings: the Old and New Testaments, the *Book of Mormon* (religious events from 600 B.C. to A.D. 400), *Doctrines and Covenants* (revelations of Joseph Smith and later prophets), and the *Pearl of Great Price* (writings about creation). The popular form of communication among members today is through Mormon newspapers and magazines. There are also personal life histories, providing extensive records of persecution, migration, and spiritual encounters.

Folklorist Austin Fife relates songs and tales passed down through Mormon history. Among these is the "Legend of the Three Nephites," described as ancient American apostles who remain on Earth as Christ's special witnesses until his return. They are characterized as old, bearded men with white hair, who appear and disappear, bringing messages of Christ's gospel, exchanging blessings for hospitality, and performing miracle cures. All three were spotted, one story says, by a sailor in Christopher Columbus's crew.

There is a growing chasm over protective custody of many documents relating to the early Church. Church leaders keep a tight hold on these records, declaring them to be secret. Young scholars, particularly historians, protest this secrecy. They argue the Church is strong and active, able to stand on its own merits, without fear of any controversy that might arise from examination of the Church's early days.

Entertainment and recreation. Mormons participate in acting, dancing, and sports. Opportunities for such activity are organized by the Church. In 1861, Brigham Young helped found the Salt Lake Theater so that "men would have joy." It supported local talent at first. Then with the coming of the transcontinental railroad the theater turned into a major center for dramas and performances by acclaimed artists. Today it is home to six professional theater companies and five dance companies that have won national reputations.

In architecture, the Mormon Tabernacle in Salt Lake City is most renown. Principle architect, Henry Garow, planned a temple constructed internally from huge timbers held together with wooden pegs. Without nails

ts, the building provided meeting space for a congregation
:oustics were so fine the drop of a pin on stage could be
f seat in the house. A grand pipe organ, built by Joseph
Ridges, was installed. In this setting, the Mormon Tabernacle Choir rose to national prominence. It has performed for the public over the radio since 1929 and sings at ceremonies to inaugurate American Presidents.

Mormons are quick to master advances in technology. Already in 1931 they had completed a film of Church history. The Brigham Young Motion Picture Studio, following in this tradition, now produces films on Mormon and other subjects. Its production *A More Perfect Union: America Becomes a Nation* has won awards at an International Film Festival in New York.

Another area of high achievement for Mormons is sports. In 1984, Brigham Young University's football team ranked number one in the nation, and Jason Buck, a member of the team, won the Outland Trophy for most outstanding lineman in 1986.

Holidays. Unique to Mormons is Pioneer Day, July 24. Not a religious but a historical holiday, it celebrates the entrance of Brigham Young and the early pioneers into the Salt Lake Valley. Parades, picnics, and overnight campouts are all part of the festivities. Otherwise, the Mormons celebrate standard national and Christian holidays. They do not recognize Christmas as the birthday of Christ, but as a time to join with other Christians in celebrating the prophet. They believe Christ was born on April 6, a date disclosed to Joseph Smith in a revelation. On the weekend nearest April 6, the Mormons hold a worldwide conference.

For More Information

See these reading materials:

Fife, Austin E. *Exploring Western Americana.* Ann Arbor: UMI Research Press, 1988.

McCarry, Charles. "Utah's Shining Oasis." *National Geographic*, April 1975, pp. 440–473.

Contact this organization:

Mormon History Association, P.O. Box 7010 University Station, Provo, Utah 84602.

NAVAJO
(nav' eh ho')

Latecomers to the Southwest who abandoned their hunting and gathering lifestyle to become sheep herders and farmers and who call themselves Diné.

Population: 158,000 (1990).
Location: Northeastern Arizona, northwestern New Mexico, southern Utah.
Language: Navajo, an Athapascan language, and English.

Geographical Setting

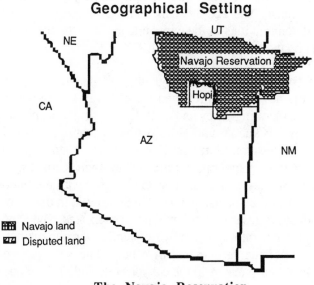

The Navajo Reservation.

The 18,000,000 acre Navajo Reservation lies on high plateaus cut by years of erosion from the Colorado, Little Colorado, and San Juan rivers. Four high peaks mark the limits of the Navajo land, but most of it lies between 3,000 and 8,000 feet above sea level. At the lower levels, the land is desert; plant life is widespread and sage is common. Higher levels are covered with piñon pine and juniper. Still higher, other evergreen trees such as yellow pine and Douglas fir produce some timber for the Navajo. The land is dry, averaging in most regions less than 10 inches of rainfall a year. Among the mountains held sacred by the Navajo are Navajo Mountain (10,388 feet) in the north, and the San Francisco Peaks, of which Mt. Humphries (12,633 feet) is the highest, in the west. Navajo land is rich in uranium ore and in coal, but mining of these ores has not greatly aided the economy.

Historical Background

Origin. Navajo is one of the Athapascan languages. This language links the Navajo to some native groups in Alaska and suggests that the ancestors of the present people were hunters and gatherers who migrated from Asia to the American continent more than three thousand years ago. Similarities with the people of the American plains is further evidence of a people who wandered for more than a thousand years before finally settling among the Pueblo people of the Southwest. As with other Athapascan people, the Navajo name for themselves means The People, Diné. The Diné are believed to have settled in small communities in the canyon lands near the tributaries of the San Juan River by the fourteenth century A.D.

Life among the pueblos. Although they settled in semi-permanent communities, the newcomers preferred the old way of life—raiding and hunting rather than farming. They and their Apache neighbors became feared and distrusted by the Pueblo and Hopi peoples because of their frequent raids on these settled communities. However, the Navajo proved very capable of adapting to new opportunities. They soon learned agricultural methods from those they raided and became familiar with the Pueblo chief product, corn. When the Spanish entered the Southwest in the 16th century, the Navajo tradition of resistance and raiding was repeated. The Diné fiercely resisted Spanish entry into their lands, frequently warring against Spanish settlement and later the settlements of other white settlers. And when pursued, they lost their pursuers in the canyons or sought refuge among their Hopi neighbors. The association with European immigrants was antagonistic, but once more it brought new ways to the Diné. The Spanish brought sheep and horses to the land, and the Navajo became herders.

White settlers. White Americans crossed the Southwest in the 1849 gold rush to California, coming into conflict with the Navajo and other Indians.

Forts and garrisons were established to control the Navajo uprisings. Finally General James Carleton formulated a plan to suppress the Indians permanently. Under the leadership of Colonel Christopher (Kit) Carson, brigades of soldiers would round up the Navajo and Apache Indians and resettle them on a reservation at Fort Sumner, New Mexico. Here the Indians would all become farmers. Those who resisted would be shot and, to discourage hiding out in the canyons, their livestock and farm supplies would be destroyed. The soldiers assigned to this task did not restrict their activities to fighting Navajo warriors; whole villages were sometimes destroyed in their search. Beginning in November, 1863, the Indians were relentlessly pursued and forced on the Long Walk to Bosque Redondo in New Mexico.

The Long Walk. Eight thousand Navajo people were marched to Bosque Redondo and held prisoner there. Finally in 1867 other government units took control and ordered the release of the people. The Navajo returned to part of their original land and to their old ways. But progress was slow since the army had destroyed their flocks and the federal government was slow to replace the losses. An 1868 treaty established a three and a half million acre reservation that reached from northeastern Arizona and northwestern New Mexico to southwest Utah. The treaty land has been expanded over the years so that now the Navajo land includes nearly fifteen million acres.

Recent history. In the 1900s discoveries of oil, uranium, and coal on the Navajo reservation have changed the lives of the people. Pickup trucks rather than horses began to be the favored mode of travel to the trading posts. Often the pickup trucks were rigged to carry large water tanks, so water has become a little more available on the reservation. The new wealth, however, has resulted in a split allegiance among the people. On the one hand, local leaders focus on the ancient traditions and hold all parts of nature holy and inviolable. On the other hand, a strong central government, the Navajo Tribal Council based at Window Rock, has encouraged the people to join a work-for-wages economy to exploit the Navajo land mineral rights. The council reasons that this enables the people to modernize educational and health services. The Tribal Council's position is strengthened by nearly twenty thousand Navajo men who have served in the United States Armed Forces and have learned white ways and the value of money. In past years, Peter MacDonald, president of the Tribal Council tried to lead the Navajo people farther and farther from the traditional lifestyles—even attempting to abolish the Navajo Crafts Guild because pottery-making, weaving, and silver working are not as profitable as uranium mining. In 1989, MacDonald was defeated in his bid for re-election as president. Despite the work of the Council and the new mining interests, most frequently operated by outside financiers, the Navajo people were listed in the 1990 census as the poorest of the Indian groups.

Culture Today

The traditional Navajo home is the hogan.

Shelter. Around the highways and trading posts, Navajos have built frame homes in which to live. In days past, they lived in dugout spaces covered over with logs and mud and called hogans. Since the family is central to Navajo religion and custom, hogans were related to many of the sacred ceremonies. Therefore, even though a Navajo family might live in a frame wooden building, the traditional hogan can often be seen nearby.

A typical community consists of a few homes of relatives. Here the Navajo eat, sleep, raise sheep and practice the arts of blanket weaving and silver jewelry.

A Navajo woman in old-style dress.

Clothing. The Navajo adopted weaving from the Pueblo and Hopi people. Today the women who weave produce rugs, belts, and blankets, dyeing the threads with store purchased dyes and with dyes obtained from the plants around them. The blankets have become popular items among white collectors and tourists. Even so, weaving accounts for only a small part of the Navajo economy. Few of these woven products are now used daily by the Navajo even though the blankets are sometimes used in ceremonial rites. Today's reservation Navajo makes blankets for sale and purchases her own blankets from such sources as Pendleton Woolen Mills. Only a few years ago, the blanket was the most worn by everyone, but now the men dress in levis and western style shirts along with felt cowboy hats. Although they purchase the materials now from stores, women's dress has remained more traditional. Bright velveteen blouses and long skirts are the most common dress. Today, Navajo women are likely to buy "squaw dresses" made in the traditional colorful blouse and long, full skirt style by professional designers. Shoes of white buckskin, tanned leather, or tennis shoes are common for both men and women. One painting of a Navajo shows an old man wearing levis, silver-buckled belt, cowboy hat and tennis shoes, "the white man's moccasins." Deerskin or cowhide moccasins remain popular.

Food. Much of the wealth of the Navajo family is its flock of sheep. Sheep provide wool for weaving, and mutton, the major food of the Navajo. Some vegetables, particularly corn, are grown in family farm plots, but today's Navajo woman is likely to find the vegetables to supplement the mutton meal in cans on the shelves of the market.

Religion. Although clothing habits have changed, the traditional religion is still practiced. The Navajo faith does not center on rainmaking and seasonal rituals as does that of their Hopi neighbors. Rather Navajo ceremonies stress protecting people from diseases, injuries, and evil, or curing ills under the guidance of medicine men. Ceremonies are sung frequently to protect the home of the family. And since this home was traditionally the hogan, that hogan remains important in religious ritual even though the family may elect to live in a white-style frame house. One ritual, The Blessing Way (one of many song-prayers of the Navajo), is sung often by family members for good hope. Another popular rite is the coming of age ceremony called Yubichai.

Navajo myth tells of the time when the Holy Ones (benevolent spirits and the Hero Twins, who were children of Father Sky and Mother Earth) conquered the forces of darkness, evil and disharmony. These Holy Ones are thought to bring disease or injury upon humans to punish them for sins they have committed. Various spirits rule over wind, thunder, water, and other natural materials important to the Navajo. But the chief god is Changing Woman who is believed to have created people and useful crops such as corn. She is imagined as young and lovely and is said to have been the mother of the original eight Navajo clans. In Navajo tradition there is also a mischievous god, Coyote, whose tricks on humans are the plots of many Navajo stories.

Song, painting, and the use of sacred corn pollen are all parts of Navajo religious ceremonies. There are many songs for different events, such as the chants of the Blessing Way for good fortune, the Game Way for successful hunting, the Life Way for curing illness, and the Enemy Way for treating illness or injury brought by outsiders. The dance and song that is the Enemy Way has been renamed by white observers as the Squaw Dance.

Much of Navajo religion has to do with healing. Sickness is treated as both a physical and a spiritual malady, to be cured by ceremonies of chant and sand painting supervised by medicine men. Sand painting is a type of prayer through picture. Its object is often to restore health and harmony to the afflicted by generating a positive charge from the Holy Ones. On a background of clean sand, dry paintings are made with different colors from powders of crushed rock, natural pigments and charcoal. The painting is made inside the patient's hogan. After treatment, the patient leaves the hogan and the sand painting is destroyed in the same order that it was made. In the same spirit of accommodation, Navajo artists now use the crushed rock and pigments to create works of art for sale to the outside world. These are often called sand paintings although they do not have the authenticity of the sacred paintings used in ceremonies.

Traditional religion among the Navajo has been influenced by contact with other Indians and white people. Peyote is a hallucinogenic cactus used by Navajo who have joined the other Indian groups in the Native American Church. This is a blend of traditional beliefs, Christianity, and an even older belief in peyote-inspired contact with the gods. Some Navajo adherents to the Native American Church compare the use of peyote in this religion to the use of wine and bread in communions of Christian churches.

Arts. Navajo craftsmen developed skills in silver working. Today, Navajo silver work takes many forms and continuously incorporates new designs. However, the Navajo silversmiths first gained fame for their production of heavy silver jewelry using a sand casting method. Navajo artists are well known for their abilities as weavers. Several communities weave blankets for sale and have developed their own unique styles. A very popular blanket style is known as Two Gray Hills after the community in northeastern Arizona. Once Navajo women made great use of their ability to weave baskets, but over the years this activity has been restricted to weaving of wedding baskets. Another popular expression of Navajo art originated as religious ceremony. Today, Navajo artists "paint" pictures for sale using various colors of sand and the same designs drawn from their religious beliefs and from nature as are used in blanket weaving.

Painting with other mediums is also popular among some of the Navajo artists. One Navajo painter, R. C. Gorman, is internationally know for water color and oil paintings. His works can be seen at the New York Metropolitan Museum.

Influences of outsiders. Outside people have affected Navajo government and family life in many ways. The Indians had no central political unity until the Navajo Tribal Council was formed by the U.S. Government in 1938. Before that, white settlers and government workers tried to make pacts with the Navajo through the local leaders, only to find that the pact was not binding among Navajo elsewhere. The Tribal Council, now a strong uniting force for the Navajo was created to make negotiations with the Diné easier. Today the Tribal Council consists of a chairman, a vice-chairman, and seventy-four delegates elected by the people of different regions of the reservation to serve for four years. The council meets in an eight-sided building resembling a hogan in Window Rock.

Another exposure to outsiders came during World War II, with many Navajo young men joining the armed forces. Perhaps the most well known of the Navajo contributions to the war effort was made by the "Code Talkers." In seeking a way to communicate that would not be intercepted by the enemy, U.S. Army intelligence sources turned to the Navajo language. Messages sent in this language proved impossible for the enemy to decode. The military men returned to the reservation with new concepts about the outside world. Some remained off the reservation to work in white industries and later retired to the reservation with sources of income that were not common.

Education. Because the people are spread over large expanses of land, much of it requiring more than an acre to support a single sheep, the federal government has established boarding schools in several places throughout the reservation. While these schools help to prepare young Navajo for today's world, they have often been mistrusted because they tend to remove the youth from their heritages. In recent years, Navajo teachers and aides have been more frequently employed in the boarding schools in an attempt to preserve the Navajo way of life. Until 1989, Navajo and other Indians who wanted secondary educations were forced to move away from their families to an Indian School in Phoenix or one in Riverside, California. Today, there is a community college on the reservation at Tsaile.

Recent gains. Navajo families still live in small villages of two or three houses. These houses may now resemble the white farm or ranch house but almost always with the addition of a hogan. Now many Navajo work for wages in the mining industries or for the government. Still sixty percent of the men are unemployed. Although the people have profited as a whole from mining and related activities, poverty is still common. As recently as 1969, the average earnings were less than a thousand dollars a year per family. This figure is a little misleading since the Navajo economy has a strong element of gift and barter that does not involve money. First reports of the

1990 census listed the Navajo as the poorest of the nation's Indian peoples. Meanwhile, the Tribal Council has amassed some financial base which it uses to improve education, develop industry, and promote health programs. This has helped the average Navajo but has not added to the potential sources of individual income. So while the old trading posts turn into supermarkets, Navajo crafts workers turn to roadside stands to market their goods. In this century the Navajo have revived past designs in weaving and have begun to establish regional distinctions that enhance the weaving industry. Navajo jewelers became experts in work with silver and turquoise during their captivity at Fort Sumner. Turquoise became the most popular gemstone, and Navajo men have continued to create silver and turquoise jewelry to the present.

Old vs. new. Still, conflict between the old and the new is evident everywhere in Navajo land. Modern homes of brick and wood appear near hogans. Horses stand beside pickup trucks. Children may now attend boarding schools that provide public education through the community college level on the reservation . In these schools, there is an attempt to blend English and other non-Navajo subjects with the local wisdom.

The Navajos are the second largest group of native Americans, second only to the Cherokee. Many have decided to join the mainstream of American life. They abandon their traditional clothing for colorful western shirts and jeans and become wage earners, sometimes leaving the reservation to do so. Yet the men still wear traditional turquoise and silver work in their belts. They may transform their sand paintings into marketable products, but the details are changed to protect the sacred purpose of the art. And frequently, after a lifetime of wage earning, the Navajo family returns to the old ways on the reservation. Above all, land is still sacred to the Navajo, and they have become even more protective of it because of their conflicts with the Hopi whom they surround.

Today. The economic status of a Navajo family is sometimes unclear because of their policies of gift giving and active reliance on barter, exchanges of goods that do not involve money. Still, the 1990 census lists the Navajo as the poorest of the nation's Indian peoples. Meanwhile, the Tribal Council has amassed some financial base which it uses to improve education, develop industry, and promote health programs. This has helped the education and health of the average Navajo by developing Navajo teachers and nurses but has done little to change the low income state in which most Navajos on the reservation live.

For More Information

See these reading materials:

The Navajo Yearbook. An annual production of the Navajo Agency. Windowrock, New Mexico: U.S. Dept. of Interior, Navajo Agency.

Woodward, Arthur, *Navajo Silver.* Flagstaff, Arizona: Northland Press, 1971.

Navajo artists excel in weaving and carving.

NETSILIK
(net´sel ick)

An Inuit (Eskimo) group of the Canadian Arctic.

Population: 800 (1979).
Location: Canada, the eastern Arctic.
Language: Inuit-Inupiaq Eskimo, English.

Geographical Setting

Canada

United States

The land of the Netsilik is in the far north of Canada.

One third of Canada is the eastern Arctic, an area known to the Inuit as "Our Land." An ice-locked region, the homeland of the Netsilik Inuit lies in the Arctic tundra north of the Hudson Bay. Large land masses spread across the area, islands and peninsulas pointing towards the North Pole. Among them are the flat King William Island and the rocky-hilled Boothia Peninsula. Inland from the sea, many rivers and lakes dot the region. Plant life is limited to lichens, mosses, and grasslike shrubbery. Several animals—seal, caribou (deer), foxes, and fish (lake trout, Arctic char)—withstand the cold. In the freezing winters, temperatures drop to minus 30 degrees Fahrenheit and the sun disappears below the horizon. There are days of 24-hour darkness with a few hours of twilight from the end of November to mid-January. In summer the thermometer climbs to 50 degrees, and the air is misty and cool but bright. From the end of May into August, there is 24-hour daylight.

Historical Background

Explorers. Crossing the Arctic in the 19th century were explorers in search of a Northwest Passage to the Pacific Ocean. Their voyages brought them into contact with various Inuit (Eskimo) groups: the Copper, the Caribou, and the Netsilik. Three explorers, John Ross (1829-30), George Bach (1833-35), and Thomas Simpson (1838-39), had brief contact with the Netsilik. In the next century, the explorer R.E.G. Amundsen discovered the Northwest Passage, then had long-term contact with the people. Amundsen lived with the Netsilik for two winters (1903-05), documenting their ways. Some 20 years later, Knud Rasmussen from Denmark observed the Netsilik for nearly a year, fleshing out Amundsen's description of them. They were a mid-sized people with straight black hair, gray-yellow skin, and large, flat faces. Almost continually on the move, they followed the game on which they survived.

Early hunting. The name *Netsilik* means "people of the seal," the animal hunted by the group in winter. Unlike other activities in Netsilik life, seal hunting was a collective effort. Men would spread over the snow like a fan to locate a seal's breathing hole, each holding a dog by the leash. Later in the year (May) when there was no snow cover, hunters would lie on wet ice, imitating a seal's sounds so they could crawl close enough to harpoon their prey. In July when the snow disappeared, the people moved inland to fish and hunt caribou. Hidden behind stones near a lake, a hunter used bow and arrow to fell caribou on their way to the water. Otherwise, he speared them as they crossed rivers, attacking from his kayak (a one-person canoe that enclosed his waist). For fishing, men used decoys to attract lake trout and Arctic char, then speared them.

Food, clothing, and shelter. A system of partnerships developed to share seal meat, the seal being cut into 14 sections. Each hunter had a sharing partner named after a section of the seal. When a hunter harpooned a seal, his wife doled out sections to the proper sharing partners. The sharing system was a type of insurance against starvation, a constant threat to Netsilik life. According to Rasmussen, seven starved to death in 1919 and 16 more the following year. He also heard that the man Tuneq ate his wife one winter to save himself, then was forever haunted by her ghost.

The large camps broke up when the snow melted in July, ushering in the long, cool foggy days of summer. Then the Netsilik lived in small extended family groups that were constantly on the move, hunting and sharing caribou meat. In times of hunger, children started on the eyes of the animals while parents consumed raw meat. Women cooked the remainder in soapstone pots. Though children enjoyed great freedom, they were forbidden from helping themselves to food. Fathers, in fact, sometimes killed newborn girls because the family lacked food. Since newborn boys would grow into. hunters, they were spared.

Caribou skin provided material for clothing. An inner layer was worn with the hair facing inward next to the body. Over it was an outer layer, its hair turned outward. Men wore two hooded coats, two pairs of trousers, and boots over shoes. Women wore two coats but only one pair of trousers. For decoration, the women trimmed their outer coats with white fur and tattooed their faces and limbs. Sealskin served as waterproof material for summertime clothing.

The Netsilik made use of not only the animals but also the climate for housing. During the winter sealing season, they gathered into four or five large camps. Each camp housed from 60 to 100 people in *igloos*, the Netsilik name for a permanent house of any material. They built snowhouses in their winter camps, each one sheltering two related families. Two fathers could construct a snowhouse in an hour, shaping the snow blocks into a dome and adding a small window of ice. The inside had a small bench with a soapstone lamp and a sleeping platform of snow blocks topped with skins and furs. To avoid melting, the houses had to be kept at freezing point. Caribou-skin clothing kept the Netsilik family warm.

As seasons changed, so did the building materials. In the fall, men built rectangular icehouses with animal skin roofs. In the summer they used sealskin to fashion cone-shaped tents. Except for the large winter camps, the Netsilik mostly lived in small groups (15 to 20 people). Each was an extended family—parents with the father's married sons and the sons' children. The group occupied a cluster of icehouses or tents, the men hunting caribou and fishing together. A headman, the eldest hunter, was leader, deciding where to camp next. The eldest woman controlled the food, men and women eating in two separate circles. In wintertime, several extended families banded together to form the larger camps.

Modeling the clothing material of the North.

Family life. A girl's training began at age seven or eight, when she helped her mother butcher the seals, clean the fish, and melt the ice for drinking water. Boys began helping their fathers hunt at age 10 or 11.

As for marriage, parents arranged unions between their children. There was no ceremony. Upon reaching marriageable age, a girl (age 14) simply moved in with a boy (age 20). Marriage between cousins was preferred, and a man could have several wives. Since girls were sometimes killed at birth, there was a shortage of women. This shortage helps explain Netsilik wife stealing and the practice of wife exchange. Husbands could exchange wives for a time, a practice that was especially likely between men who were "song cousins." These were two song partners who joined together to perform a drum dance at the *gaggi*, the ceremonial igloo.

Drum dances. Netsilik life was lonely, full of long hours of silent traveling and hunting, especially during the winter months of continual darkness. Drum dances relieved the loneliness, an important function since the rate of suicide was high. They also cemented ties between friends and became a vehicle for teaching children or for venting anger. The lack of any organized government meant people who were angry with each other had to resolve their own conflicts. While enemies often resorted to public fist fights, an alternative was to engage in a song duel. An enemy would mock his foe in lyrics, giving him the traits of animals and thereby ending his friendship with the man. Finally, drum dances served a religious purpose. Shamans, the religious leaders, would perform drum dances to stir themselves into a trance.

Religion. Shamans were religious leaders who communicated with the Netsilik spirits to cure the sick, control the weather, and find game for the hunt. Most Netsilik spirits had evil sides that were greatly feared by the people. Nuliayuk, great goddess of sea and land animals, lived in the ocean depths. When angered, the goddess was thought to withhold game from hunters. The people believed in three afterworlds for the dead. Hardworking hunters went to one of two villages of plenty, either high in the sky or deep under the tundra. Lazy hunters went to an afterworld just below the earth's crust. There they had only the butterfly for food.

Change. As early as the 1920s, such beliefs clashed with those of outsiders who came to the area. First, the Hudson's Bay Company established trading posts. Christian missions (Catholic and Protestant) appeared in the 1930s to convert the Netsilik. Slowly native ways changed. From 1945 to 1959, the Netsilik were among the Inuit groups who gave up a life of continual movement for settlement in permanent communities.

The 1960s ushered in a period of more rapid change as Canada's government set up schools and nursing stations for the Inuit. Often children would move to a school while their parents stayed behind in the old camp. Over time the parents followed. By about 1970, the last remaining Inuit camps had been abandoned. A new style of life emerged that had little to do with the ways of the past.

Culture Today

From their camps, the Netsilik moved to three permanent settlements—Spence Bay, Gjoa Haven, and Pelly Bay. The wider area in which these communities lie, the eastern Arctic, attracted outsiders. First came the traders, then the government. The Hudson's Bay Company wanted fur pelts that it could sell elsewhere for high prices. Its traders enticed the Inuit into providing these pelts by paying them in goods (rifles, foreign clothing, new foods) from its trading posts. By meeting their basic needs, the traders left the Inuit free to trap foxes. The trappers got credit at the company store, obtaining goods on credit, then paying with fur pelts later. As more Inuit poured into permanent settlements, however, the Company's ability to meet their needs weakened. Canada's government became involved.

Food, clothing, and shelter. With the rush of Inuit to permanent settlements came makeshift housing. Generally, there were overcrowded communities, unsanitary conditions, and flimsy shelters. R. Quinn Duffy describes the shelters in *The Road to Nunavut* (McGill-Queen's University Press, 1988). Outnumbering the available houses, the Inuit built living quarters from scraps—old box boards and burlap or canvas. The government designed a styrofoam igloo in 1956, but it proved unsuccessful. A wood-frame house covered with canvas and insulated with rock wool followed. Then came the government's temporary "matchbox houses" in 1960 to meet the onrush of settlers. Without bathrooms, stoves, or porches, each matchbox was a single 16-foot square room. Some of these houses were replaced in 1966, but many survived and weathered. In 1978, an Inuit council reported two-thirds of the houses as condemned or in disrepair. Overcrowding and the harsh Arctic climate had done great damage. Later, the government designed a two-bedroom duplex equipped with a storage room for hunters. Yet in 1988, the day still seemed distant when every Inuit family would occupy its own clean living quarters with bathroom, running water, and sewers.

Clothing and food habits changed, too. As with other Inuit groups, the Netsilik began wearing rubber boots, cotton dresses, and loose-knit sweaters in spring through fall. Unlike the warm caribou-skin garments, such store-bought items provided little protection from the severe winter cold, though. (A woman of Pelly Bay claimed that wearing white people's clothing in an igloo would bring sure death.) Therefore, the old-style jackets and sealskin boots remained popular in winter. The Hudson's Bay Company store stocked flour, tea, sugar, and biscuits, new foods to the Netsilik. Over the years they and other Inuit switched from a high protein meat diet to a high carbohydrate diet. Their staple became *bannock*, a homemade bread shaped like a thick, round pancake. The people still eat seal meat, caribou, and fish. They may also purchase canned tuna, canned vegetables, and canned fruits, but more often consume soft drinks, candy, and flour. While the Inuit no longer starve, their overall health has worsened. A 1974 report by Health and Welfare Canada found they had too little Vitamin C and D and calcium, nutrients provided by their earlier diet.

Hunting today. A barge can carry goods into Pelly Bay but not back before the bay freezes. Therefore, everything has to be flown to the settlement. Sites such as airstrips at the Bay have provided new job opportunities for the Netsilik, who now view earning money as necessary for raising a family. Today they survive on a mix of jobs, government aid, and hunting.

Netsilik hunting practices have changed. The men now use rifles, steel traps, fishing nets, and snowmobiles. Hunting seals in large groups and splitting one seal among 14 partners are customs of the past. Today the men hunt seal alone or in small groups. Armed with his rifle, a hunter shoots seal from the ice edge instead of crawling over ice to reach their breathing holes. Also seal hunting takes place year round rather than just during winter. The pursuit of caribou is different, too. Using snowmobiles and rifles allows hunters to shoot the deer anywhere, not just at a lake or river crossing place.

The purpose of hunting has also changed. Now the people track down game not only to meet their own needs but also to sell the animal skins. Fox fur earns higher prices than sealskin, so the hunters have become trappers. In 1974, buyers paid as much as 50 dollars for a quality fox fur.

Co-operative stores. A new source of income is the town co-operative, which fills the high demand for Inuit arts and crafts. Owned, operated, and supplied by the Inuit themselves, co-operatives sell traditional carvings—soapstone lamps, snow goggles, and good luck pieces made of ivory, bone, or stone. A top-quality carving earned 1,000 dollars in the 1980s; souvenirs sold for 100 dollars each. By 1982, the co-operatives employed more Inuit than any other business in the Arctic. They expanded to sell flour, canned goods, and tea in the manner of a general store. The Pelly Bay co-operative became especially well-known for its woven wall hangings and miniature ivory carvings of Arctic life.

Government. The co-operative has given the Netsilik a sense of their own self-worth, not only because of the demand for their arts but also because they operate it themselves. Electing officers of the co-operative gave many Inuit their first experience with voting. Today there are local councils, regional councils, and a Northwest Territories Council (14 of its 22 members were Inuit in 1979). The local councils address matters of immediate concern to the people: dog control, sewage, work policies. Like other Inuit, the

Netsilik gained the right to vote in local elections in 1966. They and other Inuit have united to form a national group, the Inuit Tapirisat of Canada. Its purpose is to influence, for example, the way children in the Arctic are educated.

Education. In 1947, Canada's government began providing schools for the Inuit. Its first goal was to teach them reading and writing in English, health, and simple arithmetic and geography. It used books with zoos and traffic lights and other unfamiliar details to the Netsilik. Since the 1970s, the government has followed a new policy: teaching primary students in their own language and adding instruction in how to survive in the Arctic. Still, many students drop out before Grade 9, the highest grade offered. Attendance is especially poor in summer, when there is 24-hour daylight. Families hunt then, some setting up camp away from town.

Customs. Parents buy their boys rifles and snowmobiles so they can hunt. The boys also play hockey, spending money on skates and a stick. At the same time, it is difficult for the boys to find jobs. In contrast, girls can earn money by working in the arts and crafts shops or sewing for them. So newborn females are no longer considered a greater drain on the family. The killing of baby girls, first discouraged by the missionaries, has stopped. So have wife exchanges. However, many of the Netsilik and other Inuit still commit suicide. In 1981, 41 percent of Inuit deaths were traced to unnatural causes. Suicide was the leader of these causes.

Arts. Aside from the artwork sold at co-operative stores, music remains central to Netsilik life. The young today listen to rock music as well as drum dance songs. In 1978, the most widely-owned instrument at Pelly Bay was a tape recorder. Country-and-western tunes, gospel music, and drum dance songs appeared on the same tape. Lyrics from a typical drum dance song recall days past, expressing a hunter's feelings (Cavanagh 1982, p. 210).

Let me keep remembering.
I was anxious with anticipation
at Natsilik Lake
where you can hope to find [game].
Let me keep remembering.

A man would write his own lyrics. Then his wife sang them while he danced and beat the drum before his song fellow. In print today are over a hundred Netsilik drum dance songs.

Though most Netsilik are now Christians, they still have a storehouse of old myths that recall the original religion. One myth explains how Nuliayuk, mother of all animals, came to be. Once she was an orphan girl who boarded a raft of kayaks bound for new hunting grounds. The raft was crowded, so the other children threw her overboard. When she tried to grasp the raft, they cut off her fingers joint by joint. The joints turned into seals, and she sank to the ocean depths, becoming mother of all beasts. The tale illustrates the struggle for simple survival. Today the Netsilik and other Inuit struggle to survive in a white person's world.

For More Information

See these reading materials:

Condon, Richard G. *Inuit Youth: Growth and Change in the Canadian Arctic.* New Brunswick: Rutgers University Press, 1987.

Steltzer, Ulli. *Inuit: The North in Transition.* Seattle: University of Washington Press, 1982.

Contact these organizations:

Canadian Alliance in Solidarity with the Native People. 16 Spadina Road, Suite 302. Toronto, Ontario, Canada M5R 2S7.

Inuit Tapirisat of Canada, 176 Gloucester Street, 3rd Floor, Ottawa, Ontario, Canada K2P OA6.

316

NEZ PERCE
(nehz´ pehrse´)

Indians of the Northwestern United States, noted
for their helpfulness to early white settlers.

Population: Fewer than 5,000, few pure blooded Nez Percé (1989 est).
Location: The inland valleys and mountains of Idaho and Washington.
Language: English, Nez Percé (related to Yakima and Cayus languages).

Geographical Setting

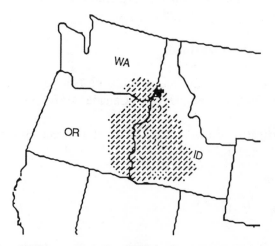

In the 1700s and early 1800s, the Nez Percé roamed the
Great Basin area of Washington, Idaho, and Oregon
Now the Nez Percé reservation is near Lewiston, Idaho.

Between the Cascade Mountains of Washington and Oregon and the
Rocky Mountains in southeastern Washington, Idaho, Montana, and
northeastern Oregon, the land is cut by large rivers that feed the Columbia
River system, rivers such as the Snake, Bitterroot and Salmon. These rivers
flow through canyons cutting a high plateau. In places, this plateau rises into

rugged mountain peaks. The climate here varies with the altitude and with the shelter provided by the valleys and canyons. Pine forests still cover much of the land. Toward the west, the land becomes desertlike. To the east, the mountains give way to the great plains of central United States. Wildlife was once plentiful in this region and encouraged first settlement by Indian hunters and fishers, then by fur traders from Canada and the United States.

The clefts of valleys and canyons isolated early inhabitants of the area, contributing to settlement by a number of different Indian groups. Here the Nez Percé Indians shared living space with the Colvilles, Flatheads, Umatillas, Yakimas, and other smaller groups bearing names often descriptive of the view of the first white explorers.

Historical Setting

A framework and a completed summer dwelling, illustrating the Nez Percé of the 1700s.

Before white men came to their land, the Nez Percé lived in settlements in the river valleys of the inland Northwest as hunters, fishers, and traders. For the most part, they lived peacefully with their neighbors, trading and seeking marriage companions in other tribes as well as in their own. Their two greatest rivals with whom they fought frequent battles were the Shoshone in the south and the Spokans in the Northwest. But even these skirmishes were discontinued under a summer truce kept for trading. At this time, many of the Indian groups of the northwest traditionally gathered at the mouths of the Weiser, Payello or Boise Rivers or along the Columbia River at the Dalles to trade goods and stories. Among these people, the Nez Percé stood out to the first French fur traders because of their habit of painting designs on their faces and sometimes wearing bone or shell ornaments in their noses. These early French traders named the group for the French words for pierced nose.

Nez Percé couple in traditional dress.

When, in 1805, the Lewis and Clark expedition reached the land of the Nez Percé, they found people described in Clark's journal as "stout likely men, hansom women, and very dressy in their way." The men wore white buffalo robes or robes of elk skin decorated with shells or mother of pearl. The women were dressed in long dresses of ibex or goat skin. Both men and women wore beads fashioned from bone. In addition, men painted their faces in multicolor designs and adorned their costumes with feathers. When not wearing the heavy robes, men were dressed only in a leather shirt, long leather leggings, and moccasins.

Early experiences with whites. It was Nez Percé custom to allow anyone freedom of their settlement and to share whatever they had with anyone in need. So, the Clark group was welcomed into the settlement and given food. The Nez Percé befriended the white explorers and volunteered to guide and protect them in their journeys toward the Columbia River. They were to repeat these acts of kindness many times as white settlers made their way through Nez Percé land toward the Columbia Basin. In the early 1800s these were fur traders such as John Coulter and Charles Courtin. One trader, Archibald Pelton, lost in fierce winter storms, wandered into a Nez Percé village crazed by his struggle with the weather. He was taken in and cared for for nearly a year. Another lost group led by a Donald McKenzie reached a Nez Percé settlement in 1811 nearly starved after a long trek over the mountains. The Indians gave them food and shelter, then guided them to the Clearwater River for a safe journey to the Columbia River. The next year McKenzie returned to establish a trading post in Nez Percé territory. As contact increased between white traders and the Indians, the Nez Percé began to see the whites as stingy and demanding.

U.S.–British claims. At this time, both the United States and Great Britain were contending for the Northwest Territory. McKenzie, fearful of being caught in the battles, hid his trade goods and left the area. Upon his return, he found that his caches had been plundered by the Indians who were residents in the area. Since the nearest Indian settlement was a Nez Percé village, McKenzie ransacked home after home until the materials were returned. Another trader, John Clarke, had his cache similarly plundered. He demanded that the goods be returned and set a stakeout to identify the robber. Catching a man in the act of robbery, Clarke erected a gallows and forced an entire village to watch the hanging of the thief. McKenzie remained in the area for several years, once persuading the Nez Percé to cease in a war with the neighboring Snake Indians. Both the Nez Percé and the white traders continued this uneasy pattern of trade and distrust for many years. During the 1820s and 1830s, both British and Americans grumbled about trade with the Indians and wondered what to do about them.

Still, the Nez Percé were influenced by the whites. In 1833 the Indians sent four of their number to St. Louis to inquire about the white man's religion. This trip and the missionary work that had brought Christianity to the Northwest Indians eventually led to the breakup of the Nez Percé people.

Much of the early experiences of whites with the Nez Percé were mixed with experiences with other Indian groups. Two missionary families illustrate this. The Whitman family lived and taught among the Cayuses, while a missionary named Spaulding lived among the Nez Percé. Both worked well with their Indian neighbors, but at one time distrust infected relations with the Cayuse. Disputes among the missionaries about how best to treat the Indians and dwindling supplies to support the missionary work exhausted the missionaries' patience and irritated the Indians. On November 29, 1847, a Cayuse chief asked Mr. Whitman for medical aid. While he was being attended to, another Cayuse struck from Whitman's back and killed him. Whitman's wife was shot in the arm, then carried outside and shot repeatedly. By the time the raid ended 13 white settlers had been murdered. This resulted in a vote by white settlers to raise an army to fight the Indians. Another Indian group, the Umatilla, threatened a Catholic mission and imprisoned a woman there. In another incident 51 captives of the Cayuses were freed only on the intercession of the Hudson's Bay trader, Ogden. Because of their policy of hospitality, the Nez Percé were suspected of participating in all these events. Meanwhile, at least some of the Nez Percé had adopted a pacifist role as taught to them by Christian missionaries. Nevertheless, all these incidents were lumped together to cause white citizens to pressure the government to put all the Indians on reservations.

War with the United States. The army was called out to carry out this plan. In their actions, the government had help from some of the Indians. By 1863, some Nez Percé were firmly Christian while others were not. One chief, Hallalhotsoot (The Lawyer) led a Christian group. Chief Joseph and some other chiefs opposed Christianity. The Lawyer courted the white soldiers by selling Nez Percé land to which he had rights. A treaty giving whites the rights to the Wallowa Valley was signed by some Indian leaders and not by others. Among those who rejected this treaty of 1863 was Chief Joseph of the Nez Percé.

Chief Joseph. He and his followers fought courageously and continuously to preserve their homes. Finally, in the late 1870s Chief Joseph saw that his forces were being destroyed and that there was little possibility of preserving the homeland of his people. With about 500 followers he began a retreat for freedom, planning to cross the valleys and mountains of Oregon and Idaho and move into Canada through Montana. For 1000 miles his band fought and evaded the army forces. Less than 50 miles from his objective, Chief Joseph and his remaining band were trapped and captured. Four hundred thirty-one Indians were put on trains and moved to Leavenworth in Kansas. Here they were kept in conditions that even some of their captors complained of. Not until 1883 were any of the group allowed back to their homeland. Thirty-three women and children returned that year, and 118 more Indians were allowed to go home the next year. Chief Joseph and 150 of the most ardent of his followers, however, were not allowed to return home. They were sent to a reservation near Colville, Washington. In 1903, the chief traveled to Washington to plead the Indian cause before President Roosevelt. He died on the Colville Reservation in 1905. True to Chief Joseph's statement, the Nez Percé have held to his declaration to "fight no more, forever." Since his death, many Nez Percé have lived quietly on or near the reservations at Lewiston, Idaho, along the Clearwater River, at the base of the Bitteroot Mountains, or near Colville.

Culture Today

Food and shelter. Until they were forced to leave their land, the Nez Percé lived a semi-nomadic life in the mountain valleys of Idaho and Oregon. During winter, extended family units built long houses for protection against the weather. One such long house at the time of the Lewis and Clark expedition measured 150 feet in length and had a row of 24 fireplaces down its center, indicating that 24 different family units lived under the one roof. Houses were made of long branches placed in the ground and bent to make an arch over which smaller branches and leaves were placed to make roof and walls. In addition to the living quarters, a Nez Percé community had out buildings such as a woman's building, a separate residence for boys under 14, and sweat houses. Each community was headed by its own chief, so that the Nez Percé "tribe" was really a loosely united collection of small independent extended family units. In the summer, the extended families took down their long houses. Each family gathered its share of the lodge poles and all moved onto the plateau and plains to live in tipis. Part of the problem in negotiations with white settlers was that the white immigrants often did not realize the limited authority of each separate chief.

Men hunted with spears and bows and arrows. The Nez Percé were well known among other Indian groups for the quality of their bows, made from the curled horns of mountain sheep. For hunting, and particularly when the men were forming a war party, short arrows were coated with the venom of rattlesnakes. In addition to hunting, the men fished with spears, nets, weirs. The fish were either eaten immediately or dried on wooden racks for later use. For use in river travel, the men built dugout canoes from the large tree trunks in the area.

Women of the village gathered roots and berries for the family meals. They searched for wild blackberries, huckleberries, and an onion-like tuber of the wild lily. They used fibers from cedar trees to weave water tight baskets. Water was boiled in these baskets and meat and other foods were placed in the water to cook. Women also wove mats for their homes and used wooden bowls and spoons made of animal bone.

Religion. The Nez Percé did not often hold religious ceremonies. Spirits of the dead were thoughat to be threatening to the living. These spirits included spirits of all living things. Shamans had the power to ward off the evil spirits and to heal the sick. But nearly every Nez Percé possesses one or more personal guardians (a Wyakin). Between the ages of nine and fourteen, each child was taken alone to a secluded spot and left without food or water. Their families believed that fear, thirst, or hunger would eventually result in dreams in which the child's guardian would be revealed. Often the guardian appeared in the form of an animal. Having received a revelation about a guardian, the young person was then eligible to learn about shamanism.

Stories of the Nez Percé told of a monster who originated the group, and of encounters with the spirits of the past. As with other Indian groups, Nez Percé stories often centered around a fun-loving spirit coyote. In addition to their stories, the Nez Percé enjoyed singing and dancing. At Guardian Spirit Dances, held randomly during the year, young Nez Percé enjoyed singing songs they felt they had learned from their experience of acquiring a guardian.

Family life. Boys and girls married at a young age—often before they were 14. They were married simply by the boy's moving in with his inlaws. After a short stay there, the new husband and wife built their own shelter and furnished it with a bed of leaves over which a fur cover was placed.

A vanishing culture. Today, so few Nez Percé live on the reservation near Lewistown, Idaho, that there has been talk of disbanding the reservation and its dependence on the federal government. Men, women, and children have abandoned their fur clothing in favor of cloth skirts, shirts, and trousers. Families live in separate frame houses, cook foods similar to those of their white neighbors, use gas and electric stoves, store food in refrigerators, and are entertained in the evenings by television programs. They become housewives, secretaries, teachers, loggers, and businesspeople just as their white neighbors.

Today there are few pure-blooded Nez Percé, and those remaining have abandoned their old life styles to adopt those of the white people who claimed their land.

For More Information

See these reading materials:

Gay, E. Jane *With the Nez Perces, Alice Fletcher in the Field, 1889-92.* Lincoln, Nebraska: University of Nebraska Press, 1976.

Hines, Donald M. *Tales of the Nez Perce.* Fairfield, Washington: Ye Galleon Press, 1981.

Josephy, Alvin M., Jr. *The Nez Percé Indians and the Opening of the Northwest.* New Haven, CT: Yale University Press, 1965.

Nez Percé men today.

324

POLISH AMERICANS
(po´lish eh mer´ uh kins)

Americans whose ancestors lived in Poland or in
Polish territory when Poland lost its independence.

Population: 6,228,000 (1980).
Location: United States, mainly the Northeast and Midwest.
Language: English, Polish.

Geographical Setting

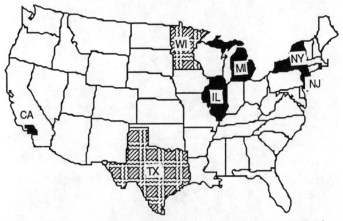

States with the greatest Polish American populations.

Three-fourths of North America's Polish population today resides in the
United States. Originally the Poles migrated to the country in groups, the
majority arriving between 1870 and 1914. Over two million Poles voyaged
to America during this period, the time of mass migration. Favoring Eastern
and Midwestern states, the migrants settled in Connecticut, Illinois,
Michigan, New Jersey, and New York. Earlier in the century some of them
had established farming colonies in Texas and Wisconsin, but over the

decades more than 86 percent took up residence in the cities. Most Poles intended a temporary sojourn in America to earn money, followed by a return to the Polish homeland. Partly for this reason, they remained isolated from other immigrants, forming separate communities in poor areas near large industrial work centers.

Historical Background

Jamestown Polish. From about 1608 to 1800, the Poles trickled onto the American mainland for personal reasons. They distinguished themselves as workers and fighters, contributing to shaping the new world in several ways.

A year after the 1607 founding of Jamestown, a handful of Polish laborers appeared in the colony. Immediately they distinguished themselves as hard workers. Hired to make glass, pitch, and tar, the small band of Poles helped launch American industry. From the start, they won high praise for their steadfast effort in manufacturing its first products. The Dutch and the Poles, said Captain John Smith, were two groups on whom he could depend for an honest day's work. These same Poles are remembered for staging America's first labor strike. In 1619 the Virginia Company allowed Jamestown colonists to form their own lawmaking assembly. Certain groups, the Poles among them, were deprived of the vote. In protest, the Polish colonists refused to continue working. The Virginia Company promptly granted them the right to vote. Recognizing how indispensable they were, it then persuaded the Poles to teach younger colonists how to make pitch, tar, and soap. Polish colonists also taught their neighbors to play *palant*, a game described as a forerunner of baseball.

As the 16th century progressed, Poles appeared in other North American locations. Their presence in New Amsterdam (New York) can be traced to 1643. By 1650, a number of Poles had settled in Pennsylvania. The colonists went about quietly making lives for themselves until the Revolutionary War.

Early Patriots. Two statues of Polish Americans stand in Washington, DC, one of Thaddeus Kosciuszko and the other of Casimir Pulaski. Credit goes to Benjamin Franklin for recruiting both Poles to fight in America's Revolutionary War.

A military engineer, Kosciuszko had been applauded in Europe for his skill in fortifying battlefields. This skill proved instrumental to victory in America, where Kosciuszko made strategic choices. Selecting Bemis' Heights near Saratoga for battle, Kosciuszko then had his men build trenches to fortify their position. It was here that the British General Burgoyne surrendered on October 17, 1777, Kosciuszko clearly affecting the outcome of the war. General Horatio Gates appreciated the fortifications at Saratoga, and had Kosciuszko build a new fort on the Hudson River—West Point. Kosciuszko, like Polish immigrants after him, harbored a love for greenery made obvious in gardens. Himself hauling baskets full of earth to West Point, the general planted an area still known as Kosciuszko Garden.

The general's credits continue. Called Father of American Artillery, Kosciuszko also wrote a first set of regulations, *Manoeuvres of the Horse Artillery*. Well remembered are his attempts to combat human suffering. It is said that at West Point the general divided his rations with hungry British prisoners of war. Returning to Europe to fight for Poland, he left his will with Thomas Jefferson. A few lines reveal Kosciuszko's position on slavery (Renkiewicz 1973, p.46).

> I beg Mr. Jefferson that in case I should die without will or testament he should bye out of my money so many Negroes and free them, that the restant Sum should be Sufficient to give them education and provide for their maintenance.

Benjamin Franklin informed General George Washington that Count Casimir Pulaski was famous throughout Europe for his courage in battle for Poland. Pulaski was to uphold, perhaps even exceed, this reputation with new exploits of bravery for America's colonists. Organizing the Pulaski Legion, he hired soldiers who were former Frenchmen, Germans, and Poles. Pulaski commanded not only infantry but also began the first cavalry, arming his men with Polish lances and a formal set of regulations. In battle at Charleston, when his infantry upset an ambush by showing themselves too soon, his cavalry still forced the British to retreat. Wounded in the thigh by grape shot, Pulaski died at the siege of Savannah. He survives in history as Father of the American Cavalry.

After the Patriots' victory, Poles contributed to the growth and preservation of the new nation. First there was Pieter Stadnitski, a broker whose business dealings brought badly-needed dollars into the United States. From Holland, Stadnitski introduced American bonds to Europeans, persuading them to invest their money in a nation that had not yet proved its worth. Surely he wanted high profits for himself. Meanwhile, though, he helped the fledgling country find cash that enabled it to stand steadily on its independent feet.

Stadnitski died in 1795, the year Poland was divided among Russia, Germany, and Austria. With its largest area under Russian rule, Poland would disappear as a country until 1918. Its society at the time was divided into gentry and peasantry. Some of the gentry, the aristocrats, rebelled. After the Russians put down a revolt in 1831, a number fled to the New World. There they showed a particularly Polish talent for organization that would repeat itself time and again in coming decades. Forming the first Polish American society, an 1834 boat load of 234 exiles elected the Polish Committee to represent them to authorities in New York. Once there, the aristocrats became low-paid wage earners—shoemakers, express riders, road builders, and the like.

Lincoln and Krzyzanowski. New Polish fighters appeared. Fending off the enemy for five days, Colonel Gustavus Schultz was a commander in the Upper Canadian Rebellion of 1838. He was captured, then hung for his part in a revolt that resulted in liberal reforms. Back in the United States, the Civil War was brewing. Some 4,000 Polish soldiers would join the Northern ranks; about 1,000 fought in the Southern army. Outstanding among the Northerners, General Wladimir Krzyzanowski led soldiers in the second battle of Bull Run. Nicknamed "Kris," he staunchly withstood a series of fierce assaults, his horse being shot from under him while he faced the enemy. President Lincoln nominated "Kris" brigadier-general. At the time, the Senate did not award the title, it is said, because no one could pronounce Krzyzanowski's name. Unruffled, Kris went on to save Union soldiers from capture at Gettysburg, then was named brigadier-general in 1865.

Heroines. Krzyzanowski was not the only Polish American honored for steadfast behavior. The nun Sister Mary Veronica (Veronica Klimkiewicz) nursed wounded soldiers. At Gettysburg after washing yet another blood-stained face, she happened upon her brother. She nursed him back to health and went on to complete 75 years of service. When she died in 1930, the country buried the Sister with military honors. Another Pole, Marie E. Zakrzewska (1829-1902), became a doctor, a pioneer for women in medicine. She founded, then ran, the New England Hospital for Women and Children, also establishing playgrounds in cities. While Kosciusko and Pulaski had become fathers of American Artillery and Cavalry, Zakrzewska was known as Mother of the Playgrounds Movement.

Great migration. The number of Polish-born immigrants skyrocketed in the late 1800s. From an estimated 48,557 in 1880, it jumped to 147,440 in 1890 and then 383,407 in 1900. No longer were the incoming Poles largely gentry. Now they were peasantry, but not the poorest peasants. They could afford a crowded two-week steam voyage to *Ameryka* (America). Back in their Austrian-, German-, or Russian-controlled area of Poland, land was often divided into smaller and smaller pieces. It became increasingly difficult to survive, so like other Slavic peoples of eastern Europe, Poles put on their sheepskin coats, or kerchiefs and fringed shawls, and left.

There was much immigrant networking. A worker would hear of a need for laborers at his factory or at a mine, then write family and friends in eastern Europe about the need. Poles were one of a group of Slavic peoples living in Eastern Europe. One peasant, a Slav who lived near the Polish border, had too little land to survive. His friend, a Polish tailor, left for America, then wrote the Slav to come find his fortune there too. So the peasant went. Hungry and jobless in New York, he received relief from another Pole, a man who hired him until he found steady work in a telegraph office. He labored and saved, then sent travel fare to his family who joined him. Such informal networking was common in other cities as well. A grocer, Anton Schermann, is said to have brought more than 100,000 Poles to Chicago.

Polish American workers. Most of the peasants intended not to stay, but to earn money for land back in Poland. Later, they changed their minds, preferring small homes and steady jobs in America. Men usually immigrated first, often to Pennsylvania's coal fields, where they arrived in bunches, each with his own bundle of belongings. The Polish miners worked hard, earning a high reputation for laboring long hours at dangerous tasks. Quite different from farming back home, mining was another form of manual labor. Earlier a few Polish immigrants had begun farming colonies. In fact, the first Polish American settlement to appear in America was a farming community located at Panna Maria, Texas, in 1854. Building pole cabins and sod houses, the farmers braved dry weather, a grasshopper blight, and crime. Their horses were stolen from them one night by outsiders who intended to ridicule and swindle these Poles. Still their settlement survived, the farmers raising cattle and growing corn.

In the 1870s, a few more Poles pursued farming, lured to the Connecticut Valley by agents who met them in New York. They became hired hands, growing tobacco and onions in exchange for food, lodging, and small wages. By about 1900, a farmhand could earn 25 dollars a month. He was thrifty despite the smallness of the sum. He managed to save. Marrying perhaps a Polish servant-girl, who earned nearly four dollars a month, increased his income. Years passed. Finally, the couple saved enough to buy a small farm of their own. In the country, and more often in the city, "slow but sure" was the Polish path to modest success.

Four-fifths of the Poles had become unskilled city workers by 1907. Flocking to Detroit, Pittsburgh, Milwaukee, and Cleveland, they clustered in the nation's major cities. Chicago attracted the greatest number, some 350,000 Poles by 1908, followed by New York (250,000), then Buffalo (80,000). Typically they found jobs in tailor shops, cigar factories, steel mills, and later automobile assembly lines. Employers preferred to hire Poles, since they accepted low wages and were willing to work ten-hour days. Around 1910, the average unskilled Polish laborer earned only 325 dollars a year.

Children made money too, boys breaking up coal and girls working in silk mills, for example. Even children in elementary school were expected to add to the family income. With five to ten offspring per family, the income grew. Soon families could afford to buy small houses, to build a lavish neighborhood church, to send money back to Poland. Over 40 million dollars had reached Poland from America by around 1910.

World Wars I and II. Much of the money sent from America to Poland enabled more immigrants to come. Since Poland was still broken into German-, Austrian- and Russian-controlled areas, the people related not to a country but to different home areas. This changed after World War I. About 215,000 Polish Americans fought in the war. Meanwhile, individuals such as Chicago banker John Smulski argued vigorously to reunite Poland. Divided into three separate areas in 1795, it had remained so for over a hundred years. In 1919, the Treaty of Versailles declared Poland an independent republic again. Polish Americans rejoiced. By 1921, they had contributed over 200 million dollars to this cause. Strong ties developed between Poland and *Polonia*, the community of Poles in America. Polonia was even called the "fourth province of Poland" (the first three being those under German, Austrian, and Russian control). For a time after the war this continued. Polish Americans then returned to building a future for themselves in the United States.

Germany and Russia invaded Poland in 1939, precipitating World War II. Over 4,000 Polish officers were massacred in one camp, then buried in Katyn Forest when it was under Russia's control. (The number of Polish officers massacred at other camps increased the total to about 15,000.) Again Polish Americans acted. After learning of the Katyn Massacre, they founded the Polish American Congress, an organization to help free Poland from outside rule. About 900,000 Polish Americans fought for the Allies in the War.

Considered racially inferior by Germany's government, 2.5 million European Poles, mainly Catholics, perished in the Holocaust. Others were herded into labor or concentration camps and prisons. Afterwards, there was a new rush of immigrants from Poland. They were survivors of the war, intellectuals and professionals rather than peasants, like the mass of earlier immigrants had been. Instead of joining them in the Polish town of an inner city, they tended to settle in suburbs. There was resentment. Polish American workers slighted the professionals, calling them Displaced

Another result of World War II was a weakening of the close-knit inner city community. Polish American workers had fought in the war, their families had achieved some success, and now they began to move. Slowly but steadily, Polish Americans began to leave their separate neighborhoods and join the larger population. Beginning in the 1940s, the movement would continue for the next 40 years. Yet the group has held on to its ethnic identity to the present day.

Bryczinski

Moon Rover: Mieceyslaw Bekkor

Polish Americans—successful farmers and manufacturers, leaders in government and space exploration.

Culture Today

Physically Polish immigrants tend to be short and stocky with broad faces, wide-set grey-to-blue eyes, broad noses, definite cheekbones, and dark brown hair. They have impressed others as a strong, reliable people, whose highest priorities have been religion and family. Beneath the surface are ways of life that help define their character.

The Polish parish. Poles formed their own separate community within a city—Polish Hill in Pittsburgh, for example. They divided their communities into parishes, or church districts. The first parish having appeared at Panna Maria in 1854, the number rose to 800 parishes in America by 1935, then fell slightly to 760 parishes by 1960. Residents of different parishes shared living, business, and religious habits, though these differed somewhat depending on the area. Poles in Los Angeles, California, have been wealthier and less traditional than those in Buffalo, New York, for example. In many communities, though, a familiar lifestyle appeared.

Food, clothing, and shelter. There were similarities in dress. Before leaving Europe, Poles shed their embroidered garments. In America, men would purchase tailor-made suits once they earned enough money. Women bought bright factory-made dresses and hats. Worn as a symbol, the hat meant they had graduated out of the serving class. Priests dressed in decorative garments, handmade by Polish women. Their girls learned to crochet lace draperies and curtains in school.

The curtains cloaked windows in simply built homes. Always some money was spent on a religious piece, a carving of a saint, for example. The common structure in Milwaukee was a modest one-story house. Called "the Polish flat," it would be remodeled up from the ground to add rooms for relatives and borders. Here and in Polish sections of other American cities a community living arrangement appeared—the boarding house.

Called *trzymanie bortników* by the Polish, the system of taking in boarders spread through Polish neighborhoods. A married couple would occupy a sizable house, then rent space to other Poles, usually males. For a monthly three dollars, a late 19th-century boarder might receive sleeping space and cooking services, but he bought his own food. In this way a boarding boss could double his family income. Boarder-keeping flourished into the 1900s, but it was a temporary arrangement for most immigrants. Their goal was a home of their own.

To this end, Poles formed *building-and-loan societies*. Members contributed small sums on a regular basis, building a fund on which they could draw to purchase a home. By 1901 about a third of all Polish Americans owned real estate, often a home purchased in cooperation with an association. Outside the home was a vegetable garden; livestock—cows, goats, and chicken—were common in some areas as well. Inside the typical home had no indoor plumbing, carpets, or fancy furniture until the 1920s. Polish home owners would adopt such conveniences as their fortunes improved.

Food habits went through a similar change. At first the Polish ate simply, preferring cheap pork and beef, smoked fish, dark bread, and home-grown vegetables. They favored beans, barley, oatmeal, potatoes and cabbage, as they had in Poland. Sauerkraut and dumplings with plums (*pierogi*) were early dishes. Beginning in the 1920s, the people ate more meat, particularly smoked pork sausage. Through the years, Polish sausage became standard in the larger American diet.

Family life. The Polish family has traditionally been a patriarchal (father-centered) unit with disciplined children. Among 19th-century immigrant families, men worked hard, women began as homemakers, and children contributed to the income. The household was a working unit. As important as the feeling of affection were the family members' contributions to the unit. Clearly, the husband was head of a household. His income mainly supported the family. While he worked a 10 to 12 hour factory day, his wife stayed home, beginning her workday before dawn. She cooked, cared for the children and possibly the boarders, hauled water to the house, scrubbed wash, and tended the vegetable garden.

Polish women began as a sheltered group. While wives stayed home, single women worked in canneries or silk mills close to their neighborhoods. Some became domestic servants in houses or hotels, the Poles approving of such work as training for future wives. The pattern followed by women changed after jobs grew scarce in the Depression and men went off to fight in World War II. Wives took jobs and kept them. By 1979, 49 percent of all Polish-American women 16 years and older had joined the American work force.

The Polish family was large (five to six children in 1910). Since the struggle for income was of utmost importance, its children began working at an early age. Girls might labor in a textile mill, boys with machines that broke up coal. By 1920, the number of working children had dwindled. Less than 10 percent of the children added to a family income by then. Also the size of the typical Polish family shrank. By 1960, there were 2,076 children to 1,000 women of Polish stock. There was pressure on children to obey their parents but also to rely on themselves.

Religion. Poles are mostly ardent Roman Catholics. Many Jews emigrated from Poland, but they joined the Jewish American rather than the Polish American community.

Upon settling in America, the Poles found the Irish largely in control of the Catholic Church. Services were in Latin and priests managed church funds and property. Back in Europe, church members had managed the money and property. Now there were bitter disputes against priests who tried to exercise complete control. A deeply religious group, Poles refused to accept these conditions. From 1897 to 1904, some of them formed a separate Polish National Catholic Church. It allowed priests to marry, made Polish the Church language, and gave Church members a measure of control. Six priests and six laymen formed a *synod*, a ruling council. Meanwhile, others have remained in the Roman Catholic Church, arguing for it to include more Polish American leaders. Religion for Poles in America has seen new conflicts: church leaders against churchgoers and Polish against other Roman Catholics. Still, the group has kept many of the old rituals alive.

Education. The value Polish Americans attached to schooling changed over the years. A few of the early immigrants were educated individuals. In 1848, Feliks P. Wierzbicki wrote the first English book in the Far West, *California As It Is*, whose subject was California during the Gold Rush days. Most of the early immigrants, however, spent little time on books. Only elementary education was common at first. Around 1911, the familiar pattern was church school from age eight to twelve, public school to age 14, and then work. The church schools taught both American and Polish subjects until about 1918, when they began to drop subjects such as Polish history. As the years passed, public and secondary schools attracted a rising number of Polish Americans. Their numbers were further increased by the Polish immigrants, who arrived after World War II. By 1969, 31 percent of the Polish Americans had obtained education beyond the high school level.

Holidays. Polish Americans celebrate Catholic holidays in customary ways. A ritual still practiced today is the Christmas Eve Supper. Called the *wilia*, the evening meal draws the whole family together. An extra place setting for a stranger and hay on the table are traditions at the meal. There are at least 12 types of food, one for each apostle, ranging from beet soup (*barszcz*) to cookies with raisins, figs, or dates (*mazurek*). Today the supper is still served, but the extra place setting and hay are sometimes abandoned.

Polish Americans carry food in baskets to be blessed in church on Holy Saturday during Easter. Included are eggs to symbolize life and horseradish for Christ's bitter hardships. Later in the year, Assumption Day (August 15) commemorates the ascent of the Virgin Mary into heaven. Back in Poland, it was *Dozynki* day and also celebrated the wheat harvest. Polish Americans of New York made a change. Instead of wheat, they celebrated the harvest of onions. The Polish New Yorkers have staged spectacular parades in the 20th century, including floats with an American flag made of onions and a ship with a swivel gun that shot onions along the route. Of special interest to young people has been St. Andrew's Eve (November 30). It is a custom on this holiday for a young girl to foretell whom she will marry by, for example, peeling an apple nonstop and throwing the peel over her left shoulder to discover the boy's first initial.

Associations. Along with religion, voluntary associations have been a hallmark of Polish America. Its people formed associations for every imaginable purpose—to build a church, to buy houses, to aid Poles in Europe, for protection against misfortune, to further music and art. Almost everyone joined. In the 1910s, about 75 percent of the immigrants belonged to at least one association. Over the years the percentage has dropped. In 1982, only seven percent of Polish Americans belonged to an association. The drop has been slow, though, and the Polish population has grown so membership losses are small. Several associations remain quite strong. Largest is the Polish National Alliance, which dropped from 338,000 members in 1959 to 317,352 in 1975. The PNA began as an organization that offered its members aid in time of need for a small but steady fee. Based in Chicago, it has opened hundreds of branches in other cities. The Polish Roman Catholic Union preserves religious customs in America and the Polish Women's Alliance sends aid to the needy in Poland. Aid from America has been large, on the average about 15 million dollars a year in the 1970s. Not an association but a community center, the *Dom Polski* (Polish Home) appears in some settlements. It services the settlement with a museum, a library, and perhaps a gymnasium.

Change. A network developed in America. Called *Polonia*, it was the Polish American community made strong by connections. Poles spread throughout the United States, each community living in its own separate territory. Communities connected through the parish system, the associations, and personal contacts. Another binding force was the Polish American press, which informed immigrants about American ways and events in Poland. At first these journals were written in Polish, but by 1974, 27 of 107 were written in English and 32 in both languages.

Change among Polish American workers has been slow. Well over half still hold unskilled, blue-collar jobs, though a growing number enter skilled positions or the professions. (Polish American attorneys formed the Polish Lawyers' Association, for example.) There have been individual success stories in both the 19th and 20th centuries. John Lemke opened a tailor shop in Detroit during the 1850s, later purchasing a grocery store, a saloon, and real estate. In the 1960s, Edward J. Piszek served as president of a major food company, then embarked on a campaign to improve the Polish American image.

Polish jokes. The image of Poles as rough, unintelligent people spread through jokes that ridiculed them. Some German Catholic churches in America had Poles sit in separate pews. Movies portrayed Poles as crude characters—for example, Stanley Kowalski in *A Streetcar Named Desire* (1951). While such Poles existed, Kowalski was only one of many different types. Outsiders, though, viewed all Poles in the same negative way, continuing to make derisive jokes. The image especially hurt children, making them feel inferior. In the 1970s, Polish Americans launched a campaign to upset the stereotype. Edward Piszek, for example, took out newspaper ads that reminded readers of Poland's great scientist Copernicus.

Heroes. Polish America's own scientists and heroes upset the image too. In the 1870s, Casimir Stanislaus Gzowski built a bridge over the Niagara Falls between Canada and the United States, an engineering miracle of his time. Frank Piasecki designed and built helicopters in the 1940s. In the same decade, Stanley Musial became three-time winner of baseball's Most Valuable Player Award. A host of other heroes appeared—symphony conductor Stanislaw Skrowaczewski; actress Helena Modjeska in Shakespeare plays; novelist Jerzy Kosinski, who won the 1968 National Book Award for *Steps*; film director Roman Polanski, who received a 1974 award for the movie *Chinatown*; sculptor Korczak Ziolkowski, who on request began carving a statue of Chief Crazy Horse in South Dakota's Black Hills.

Events in Poland also upset the stereotype. Selecting a Pole as Pope, Roman Catholics named Karol Cardinal Wojtyla as Pope John Paul II in 1978. The appointment inspired Polish America with pride. In the 1980s, Poland's workers under Lech Walesa bravely defied Communist leaders. Their courage increased the feeling of pride in America, and jokes took on a new twist, casting Polish workers as freedom fighters.

At first Polish Americans showed little interest in government. Their own associations provided them with a forum for politics. Association leaders gained power among the people and had long terms in office. The first president of the Polish American Congress held his position for 24 years. Later, some heroes appeared in U.S. government. Lawyer Leon Jaworski prosecuted criminals in the Watergate incident, bringing President Richard Nixon's administration to justice. Foremost in politics, Edmund Muskie of Maine became governor, senator, and then candidate for United States President. As voters, Polish Americans elected Democrats fairly steadily until 1984, when 51 percent voted for the Republican candidate Ronald Reagan. It is uncertain which Party most of these voters will favor in the future.

Polka. Polish Americans fought for their contributions to be recognized, and they have succeeded. As early as 1904, they won approval from Congress for a monument to the early hero Kosciuszko   Their polka, a dance brought to the United States by Polish immigrants of the late 19th century, has become a standard form of American music. Several styles of polka music developed over the years—a loose rural style, an orchestrated urban style, a Chicago honky style, and a "country-flavored" style. This last one mixes Polish polka with country music's blue grass fiddling. A music created for dance, polkas had no lyrics until the 1940s. Some of the first lyrics express sadness (Nieminski as cited in Kleeman 1982, p. 158).

> My wife is in the old country,
> And I am in America.
> I work hard, I work hard,
> I work hard in a steel plant.
>
> So I start to work better in this plant,
> So I start to work better in this plant,
> My wife will, my wife will,
> My wife will come in velvet.

More recent songs express lighter moods. Recorded by Dick Pillar and his orchestra in 1979, "Baseball, hot dogs, apple pie and polkas" captures the mix of Polish and American ways. His song "Polish Power Polka" expresses pride in a Polish heritage, declaring that the feeling is here to stay.

For More Information

See these reading materials:

Bukowczyk, John J. *And My Children Did Not Know Me: A History of the Polish Americans*. Bloomington: Indiana University Press, 1987.

Kuniczak, W.S. *My Name Is Million: An Illustrated History of the Poles in America.* New York: Doubleday, 1978.

Contact these organizations:

American Council of Polish Cultural Clubs c/o Joseph Conlin, 1440 79th Street Causeway, Miami, Florida 33141.

Polish American Congress, 1200 North Ashland Avenue, Chicago, Illinois 60622.

PUERTO RICANS
(pwer´ toe ree´ kins)

Mainland Americans whose ancestors lived on the island of Puerto Rico

Population: 2,004,961 (1980).
Location: United States, mainly the Northeast and Midwest.
Language: English, Spanish.

Geographical Setting

Puerto Rico is an island south and east of Florida.
More than half the Puerto Ricans on the mainland
live in New York and Chicago.

Puerto Ricans who live on the United States mainland began arriving
shortly after the end of the Spanish-American War in 1898, when the
Caribbean island passed into American control. From the early migrations to
the present, they have settled primarily in the New York metropolitan area.
Many others live in nearby Newark or in other urban areas of New Jersey,
and in Philadelphia, Pennsylvania. Roughly two-thirds of Puerto Ricans on

the mainland live in these three Middle Atlantic states. Other states with sizable Puerto Rican communities are Connecticut, Illinois, Massachusetts, Ohio, Florida, and California. Over half the mainland's population lives in New York City, which now has a larger Puerto Rican population than San Juan, Puerto Rico's largest urban center. Next to New York City, Chicago has the highest concentration of Puerto Ricans.

Historical Background

Puerto Rico—an overview. Puerto Rico was a Spanish colony from its discovery by Columbus in 1493 until the American takeover of it in 1898. Like other former Spanish colonies, Puerto Rico has retained many Hispanic cultural traits such as the Roman Catholic religion and the Spanish language. In 1917, the United States government granted citizenship to Puerto Ricans, which meant that movement between the island and the mainland has been unrestrained by immigration laws. Strictly speaking, Puerto Ricans who come to the United States *migrate* rather than *immigrate* because they are already citizens. Subject to the draft, they serve in the United States armed forces, but while living in Puerto Rico, they cannot vote in U.S. elections, pay no federal taxes, and have almost no representation in Congress (only a nonvoting commissioner). The island's elected governor heads a government that is responsible for its own domestic policy, but whose foreign relations are subsumed under those of the United States. Puerto Rico's official status is that of a commonwealth.

Racial composition. The island's original inhabitants, the Taino Indians, have disappeared as a distinct people. Most died in the early years of Spanish rule, either through exposure to European diseases or under the slave-labor system the Spanish used to grow cotton, tobacco, and sugar. Many, however, intermarried with the mostly male settlers. As the Indians became scarcer, the Spaniards began importing slaves from Africa, who also intermarried with the remaining Indians and with the settlers. As a result, in the words of Puerto Rican historian Arturo Morales Carrion, Puerto Ricans "are a people of all colors and hues...." (Meltzer 1982, p. 12). Ranging from those whose appearance is "white" to those who look "black," Puerto Ricans tend to think of themselves as just that—Puerto Ricans. They have brought this racially colorblind outlook with them in their migrations to the mainland.

Economic changes in Puerto Rico. Under Spain, Puerto Ricans lived mostly as subsistence farmers—that is, small farmers who grew only enough to feed themselves and their families, bartering surplus items for what they lacked. Some farmed their own small patches of land. For most, however, it was a semifeudal society of landowners and peasants. The average peasant possessed a few pigs, chickens, goats, and perhaps a horse or cow. On a plot of the landowner's acreage, he grew food crops for his table: beans, sweet-potatoes, rice. In exchange for use of the land he worked the master's fields as well as his own, cutting sugar cane, picking coffee and cotton, sorting tobacco leaves. Life offered stability and security, if little hope of advancement.

The United States' presence in Puerto Rico brought rapid and profound changes to the island's way of life. Heavy property taxes prompted both small and large landowners to sell their holdings, usually to American sugar corporations, but also to the very wealthiest Puerto Ricans. Agricultural acreage thus became concentrated in the hands of a few families and absentee corporate owners. Under these owners, sugar emerged as the single crop on which the rest of the economy depended. Men no longer worked for use of the soil but for a wage. There was a brief demand for hired labor in the cane fields only twice a year: at planting time and at harvest. Without income for most of the year, Puerto Ricans moved to the cities in large numbers. Slums appeared around San Juan and other cities. At the same time, improved health conditions lowered the death rate, so the population increased, doubling (to nearly two million) by 1940. This increased population resulted in increased unemployment in both countryside and shantytowns.

In response to these new problems, Puerto Ricans formed the Popular Democratic Party. Led by Luis Muñoz Marin, the P.P.D. (its initials in Spanish) won control of the Puerto Rican legislature in 1940. Muñoz Marin, Puerto Rico's first elected governor after World War II, launched an economic program called "Operation Bootstrap." Designed to attract industry to the island, "Operation Bootstrap" offered American investors tax benefits, labor training, and the chance to pay lower wages than on the mainland. In some ways, Muñoz Marin's plan succeeded: by 1975, it had generated some 150,000 jobs in perhaps 17,000 new factories. Puerto Ricans were manufacturing chemicals, textiles, and electrical instruments. Construction and tourism boomed as Americans discovered the island's tropical beauty. Yet unemployment remained high, despite steady migration to the mainland, dropping only from 13.7 percent in 1950 to 12.3 percent in 1972, still over twice the United States average of 6.1 percent. In the 1970s, moreover, many factories closed as manufacturers discovered that they could pay even lower wages elsewhere. Tourism also slowed, and construction ground to a halt. Unemployment reached at least 18 percent in 1980, while some estimates placed it as high as 40 percent.

Free movement between Puerto Rico and the United States can only have lessened these problems. Without the "safety valve" of migration, many observers agree, poverty and unemployment might have led to serious unrest in Puerto Rico. In essence, a third of the island's population moved to the mainland.

Migration. Thousands of Puerto Ricans migrated to the mainland for employment. Often young males, the migrants sought work as unskilled laborers. They made the journey by ship, the fare costing some of them as much as a year's worth of earnings back home. Some stowed away for the two-to-three-day journey, working off their passage if discovered, enduring pangs of hunger if undetected. The expense and difficulty of the voyage limited the numbers of migrants, as did the scarcity of jobs during the Depression of 1929. Since Puerto Rico's economy is tied to that of the United States, the Depression affected the islanders as well. Their economy had already suffered due to a hurricane in 1928, and it would suffer yet again from a 1932 hurricane, both storms ravaging cotton and coffee plantations.

Employment on the mainland remained an alternative, building its Puerto Rican population. By 1940, over 60,000 had made the trip, almost 90 percent of them settling in or around New York City. Migration slowed during the years of World War II. The dangers of waters infested by German submarines prevented many who might otherwise have found employment in the labor-hungry American market from risking the journey. After the war, however, advancements in air travel allowed larger numbers to migrate quickly at low cost. The 1,600 mile trip to New York decreased from a year's wage to slightly more than a week's, something under 50 dollars. The journey of three days shrunk to six hours. By 1950, the mainland population had grown to over 300,000. Economic prosperity in the United States made jobs plentiful in agriculture, manufacturing, and the service industries.

As the influx continued into the 1970s and 80s, several trends emerged. Not surprisingly, Puerto Ricans born in the United States became proportionately more significant as married couples settled and had children. In 1970, 646,000 were born on the mainland, as compared with 783,000 in Puerto Rico. By 1980, the number born on the mainland had increased to more than half—over one million Puerto Ricans were born in the United States. Puerto Ricans also began to disperse to new areas. Between 1960 and 1970 the number of cities whose Puerto Rican populations exceeded 5,000 grew from 10 to 29. Though they remain a largely urban group, there has been some movement away from inner cities and into suburbs. In Newark in 1970, for example, over 10,000 or roughly one-third of the city's Puerto Rican population lived in suburban areas around its core.

Citizen and stranger. Despite their status as United States citizens, migrants to the mainland have encountered the same difficulties as other ethnic groups coming to America. They experienced language and educational disadvantages, crowded slums or *barrios* ("neighborhoods"), and low-paying jobs. Moreover, the surge in migration after the war provoked hostile reactions, especially in the New York City area.

Puerto Ricans in the United States became more conscious of color as they realized its importance in American society. Writer Piri Thomas, whose popular autobiographical books tell the story of an American-born Puerto Rican growing up in New York during the 1950s and 1960s, recounts his mounting awareness that his dark skin meant lost opportunities.

Workers in agriculture and industry. The first Puerto Ricans to arrive in New York in the early 1900s found employment in the city's cigar factories. One such *tabaquero* (cigar maker), Bernard Vega, remembers how workers donated 25 cents each to pay a reader, who recited aloud in Spanish works of fiction, history, or politics. If dates or facts provoked debate, there was usually someone who insisted on settling the matter by going to the reference books. They called the references *mataburros* (donkey-slayers) and often kept them right there on the work bench. Such spirited discussions certainly enlivened the work place.

After World War II, agricultural workers migrated to the mainland. Beginning in 1947, the Puerto Rican Department of Labor negotiated contracts with some mainland growers, stipulating terms of travel, work, and pay. Contracts brought over about 20,000 migrants each year in the late 1940s, and perhaps 80,000 made the journey without a contract. Together they harvested tobacco, beets, potatoes, apples, and pears, working on farms and orchards in many states. Many returned home at the end of a season, but some remained.

Puerto Rican communities grew as friends and family joined the workers who stayed. Jobs became available in factories, and more communities appeared. In Lorain, Ohio, for example, steel mills and an auto plant attracted Puerto Ricans. They founded a prosperous, middle-class neighborhood here; over half its residents owned their homes in the 1970s. In New York City the garment industry attracted thousands from Puerto Rico in the 1960s and 1970s. Many Puerto Ricans in New York have also worked for the state and federal governments. The 1980s saw them winning higher paying, more responsible positions than had been open to them in the past.

Women in the labor force. In the Hispanic communities of pre-World War II New York, Puerto Rican women made significant economic contributions. Although most thought of themselves as housewives (*mujeres de la casa*), their domestic duties often included activities to supplement the family income. The most popular type of home enterprise was piecework, that is, producing items for sale. They crocheted, sewed and embroidered hats, lampshades, clothing, and artificial flowers. Female relatives of all generations worked together, upholding the strong Puerto Rican tradition of needlecraft. Some women took factory jobs as well, leaving children in the care of friends or relatives. Such informal childcare itself became a source of domestic income, as a caretaker might charge a dollar or two a day for looking after someone else's children. Other women took in lodgers, often relatives who had recently migrated. Aside from supplementing a husband's salary these enterprises fostered a sense of spirit in the Puerto Rican mainland community.

Culture Today

The barrios. As the first groups of contract workers and other laborers arrived in New York after World War II, they carved out neighborhoods in areas that had formerly been occupied by the Italians, Irish, Jews, and others who had moved out to the suburbs. On Manhattan Island they settled what became known as Spanish Harlem, and they also established communities in the Bronx and in Brooklyn. Puerto Ricans soon became a vital part of New York City culture and the city's dominant Hispanic voice.

Poverty has restricted many Puerto Ricans to the barrios, where they live in old housing whose facilities are minimal or nonexistent. Abandoned tenements and empty, rubble-filled parking lots are interspersed with small shops: mostly *bodegas* (food stores) but also other establishments (laundries, pharmacies, record stores, beauty parlors). During winter, children sometimes warm themselves by lighting bonfires in empty lots. The barrios of New York have suffered economic decline as jobs were lost in the 1970s and federal housing subsidies were severely reduced in the 1980s. Crime and drug addiction have also taken their toll, affecting many of the young, who frequently feel embittered and alienated. Introduced above, books by writer Piri Thomas reveal his personal struggles with drug addiction and a term in prison. His work (most notably *Down These Mean Streets* and *Savior, Savior, Hold My Hand*) vividly and movingly depicts the joys and sorrows of life in the barrio.

Frustration has led others to more violent outlets—the urban gangs. Growing out of both a strong Puerto Rican tradition of radicalism and the militant movements of the 1960s, a revolutionary group called The Young Lords, for example, advocated war against businessmen, politicians, and police officials (Garver and McGuire 1981, p. 130). The Young Lords conducted peaceful activities too, providing breakfasts to hungry children and cleaning up barrio neighborhoods. While most Puerto Ricans reject the notion of war against officials, low income and limited opportunities have inspired resentment. Other factors may also contribute to wrongdoing. One study in the 1970s indicated that high-rise housing in poor neighborhoods increases the crime rate. While three-floor, walk-up residences experienced 30 serious crimes per 1,000 families, high rises (13-30 floors) experienced 68. The crime rate, it seemed, rose with the height of the building.

Ties to Puerto Rico. The ease of travel between the island and the mainland has encouraged close communications between Puerto Ricans living in the United States and those living at home. Seasonal workers can come and go cheaply; relatives or friends can be sent for quickly as job opportunities appear. This constant ebb and flow of travelers has slowed assimilation, but at the same time reinforced Puerto Rican cultural values and self-esteem. Up to the 1960s, the returnees were seasonal workers and disillusioned recent arrivals. They have since been joined by other Puerto Ricans from the mainland. As conditions in the barrios worsened in the 1970s and 1980s, thousands of established migrants returned to the island. The trend peaked in 1978, with 27,000 more Puerto Ricans moving back than entering into the United States.

Most of the returnees are first-generation migrants, who are convinced that life in the barrios is not worth the chance of a better-paying job. Sometimes they idealize the sunny island that they left so many years ago. The popular song "En Mi Viejo San Juan" (In My Old San Juan) embodies this nostalgia. Many, however, are of the second or third generation, young people and students who return to discover their Puerto Rican roots. Although they may still have family on the island, they are sometimes disdainfully regarded as *New Yoricans* (those who visit from New York) or *Neo-Ricans* (those who move back to the island for good). Puerto Rican solidarity usually prevails over such antagonisms, however.

Puerto Ricans on the mainland form a Hispanic subculture with its own set of customs brought from the home island. In contrast to Mexican Americans, the Puerto Rican migrants come from the Caribbean, a region with a strong African influence. Their habits—in food and speech, for example—are distinct. Puerto Ricans speak their own variety of Spanish, and they continue to do so after moving to the mainland (Elias-Olivares 1983, p. 226). Their staple foods are rice and beans instead of the Mexican American tortillas and beans.

Education. In America, Puerto Ricans generally have less education than whites, blacks, or other Hispanic groups. Blacks don't have the language problems that continue to hinder Puerto Ricans, especially the recent migrants. Many other Hispanic groups are often wealthier or smaller (and thus more easily absorbed by aid programs).

A complex of factors limits Puerto Rican achievement. Begun in the 1970s, bilingual programs have expanded somewhat but still fail to reach most students who need them. Other factors are even less obvious than language. A 1970s survey found that 30 percent of Puerto Rican children in East Harlem schools were nearsighted, and that fewer than one-quarter of these wore adequate glasses due to the expenses.

Drop-out rates remain high, yet the American-born students compare favorably in most categories with Puerto Ricans born on the island. Median schooling in 1970, for example, was 11.5 years for mainland-born Puerto Ricans (close to the national figure, 12.1); in contrast, Puerto Rican-born children had a median schooling of only 8.4 years. .

Family life. Problems at school are often exacerbated by difficulties at home, especially in urban areas. In the years before and immediately after World War II, family life in mainland Puerto Rican communities was essentially stable. However, continuing poverty and the resulting stress have disrupted this basic social unit. In 1970, 28 percent of Puerto Rican families in the New York area were headed by women alone, as compared with 14 percent for the population in general. Many of these families survive on welfare payments. Without childcare, these women cannot work. Puerto Rican women have left the labor force in large numbers since the 1960s. Among women in the major U.S. racial and ethnic groups, only they have experienced such a decline.

As the two-parent household and informal familial support systems like piecework and childcare have disappeared, so has a social institution that extended family relationships to a social context. The traditional Hispanic relationship of *compádrazgo*, or godparenthood, no longer appears in most New York Puerto Rican communities. A *compadre* was chosen by the child's parents to raise the child as a Catholic in the event that the parents would die; this relationship acted as a strong bond between adults, cementing and formalizing ties of friendship between men. *Compádrazgo* is a central feature of the Hispanic concepts of family and society, and its disappearance has alarmed community leaders.

The traditional family is further disrupted by the high rate of intermarriage, especially in the second and third generations. In 1970, fully one-third of Puerto Rican wives were married to non-Hispanic men; an even higher proportion of Puerto Rican husbands married non-Hispanic women.

Orlando Cepeda

Chi Chi Rodriguez

Rita Moreno

Puerto Ricans have found success in sports and the arts.

The arts. Several cultural organizations and many individuals represent Puerto Ricans in the arts. The *Instituto de Puerto Rico*, led by Luis Quero Chiesa, promotes artistic and cultural events in New York City and holds annual awards for outstanding contributions. The Friends of Puerto Rico shows the work of young Puerto Rican artists in its gallery, as does the establishment *El Museo del Bárrio*. The *Teatro Intar* produces the works of young Puerto Rican playwrights. People's theaters have developed among the Puerto Ricans in America, as they have among other Hispanic groups. Relying on improvisation, these theaters mostly avoid formal scripts. An example of a revealing work by them is *El Alcálde*, or *The Mayor*, a play about discord between Hispanic groups in the Midwest (Huerta 1982, pp. 134-140).

Many individual Puerto Ricans have contributed to and excelled in American entertainment. Jose Ferrer won an Oscar in 1951 for his portrayal of Cyrano de Bergerac. Rita Moreno, Chita Rivera, Raul Julia, and Hector Elizondo have also had highly successful careers on stage, in film, and on television. Jose Feliciano gained national stature in the 1960s and 1970s as a gifted classical and folk guitarist.

Recreation. In sports, Puerto Ricans point proudly to Roberto Clemente, a hero not only for his baseball prowess, but also for his devotion to community service. Clemente shot to national prominence in the 1971 World Series, when his safe hitting led the underdog Pittsburgh Pirates to victory. He spoke out on behalf of both the black and Puerto Rican peoples, fighting for equality through professional sports. In 1972, Clemente led a committee to bring relief to the victims of a violent earthquake in Managua, Nicaragua, and died along with four others when their cargo plane crashed after takeoff from San Juan, Puerto Rico.

Politics. Though Puerto Ricans are becoming more active politically, they have yet to hold elective offices in proportion to their numbers. Herman Badillo, who came to the United States as an orphan in 1941, became the first Puerto Rican Congressman in 1970. His successor, Robert Garcia, is also Puerto Rican. They remain the only two Puerto Ricans sent to Washington, although some have been elected to city councils and state legislatures. In 1977, the group formed the National Puerto Rican Coalition to coordinate national and local Puerto Rican groups. Other organizations include Puerto Rico Mainland U.S. Statehood Students Association, which supports U.S. statehood for Puerto Rico. Much of the political activity is directed at the status of the home island, with people advocating a change to independence or statehood. As a revealing side note, candidates for offices in Puerto Rico often campaign in New York communities to enlist the support of the thousands who regularly return.

Puerto Rican Day Parade. One popular event for such appearances is New York's famous Puerto Rican Day Parade up Fifth Avenue. Started in 1959, the *Desfile Puertorriqueño* includes well-known Puerto Rican and Anglo politcal personalities as well as the poor and homeless of the barrios, who march proudly up the Avenue. Although controversial for its boisterousness, the parade has become a symbol of Puerto Rican unity. Vibrant and colorful, it is one of the best attended of New York's many ethnic parades.

For More Information

See these reading materials:

Meltzer, Milton. *The Hispanic Americans.* New York: Thomas Y. Crowell, 1982.

Wagenheim, Kal. *A Survey of Puerto Ricans on the U.S. Mainland in the 1970s.* New York: Praeger, 1975.

Contact these organizations:

National Conference of Puerto Rican Women, Five Thomas Circle, Washington, DC 20006.

National Puerto Rican Coalition, 1700 K Street N.W., Suite 500, Washington DC 20006.

QUAKERS (FRIENDS)
(kway´ kers)

Members of the Society of Friends, a Christian sect from
17th-century England that sought religious freedom in America.
Known for their belief in nonviolence.

Population: 120,000 (1988).
Location: United States; Canada (mostly west of the
Appalachian Mountains)
Language: English (noted for use of *thee* and *thou*).

Geographical Setting

Originally, Quakers settled in Massachusetts,
Rhode Island, and the Carolinas. Now most
Quakers live in the Midwest and Far West

Though the group has spread to all six continents, today nearly half the
world's Quakers live in the United States. First they settled in the Eastern
region in colonies such as New Jersey and Rhode Island. Venturing into

Massachusetts, the nonviolent Quakers suffered bloodshed in the 1600s, but kept returning to the colony until they were accepted. Quakers moved South into the Carolinas in the 1700s, then to the Midwest, the Far West, and Canada in the 1800s. In the late 1900s, two thirds of North America's Quakers live west of the Appalachian Mountains. Yet many still regard east Pennsylvania as the heart of Quaker life on the continent.

Historical Background

Beginnings. Officially called the Religious Society of Friends, the Quakers began in England in the middle 1600s. They formed as a rebel sect of the Protestant movement underway at the time. Intent on returning to the spiritual, simple ways of early Christians, Quakers adopted habits that brought them jail sentences and persecution. They refused to doff their hats in respect to English lords and ladies or to use titles such as *Your Excellency* when speaking to them. No such titles were used in the Bible, they said. One person was no more deserving than another, and "Your Excellency" might, in fact, be a person of no excellence at all. It was the custom for common folk to use *you* when talking to their social superiors. Instead the Quakers used *thee* and *thou* no matter whom they addressed, considering all members of society equal. They refused to take any oaths, even those required by the king. Taking oaths was needless, they said, because people should tell the truth always. Their belief that war was unlawful resulted in their refusing to bear weapons in combat. The Quakers, like early Christians, thought enemies should settle their differences peacefully. Obeying their consciences, the Quakers lived by these beliefs, even when it meant disobeying men and suffering miserably in jail.

The Quakers adopted radical religious habits, too. They abandoned formal church services and ministers, encouraging each member to find his or her own "Inner Light." This light would speak directly to a person's soul, giving it a *leading*, or message. Thought of as the spirit of God, the Light could reach everyone, Christians and non-Christians alike. Finding the light was most important, not reading holy Scripture, which they regarded as a tool to better understand God. Holding a startling viewpoint for their era, these Quakers were convinced that God was internal rather than external.

A religious-minded shoemaker, George Fox, founded the English Quakers in 1652. It was Fox who introduced the idea that truth rested with the individual. His followers were called Friends of Truth. Curiously, they seemed to tremble, or shake, when preaching. According to one story, Fox was brought before a judge for his religious actions. He admonished the judge to tremble at God's power. The judge replied, "You are the Quaker, not I," and the name stuck. However, Fox's followers called themselves Friends.

Exodus to America. Fox visited America around 1670, then dreamed of forming a colony of Friends there. Already, Quakers had experienced hardship in the New World. In 1656, Mary Fisher and Ann Austin appeared in Boston in the Massachusetts Bay Colony. Officials threw them in jail without trial, burning their Quaker literature. The next year the same Colony passed an anti-Quaker law—a 100-pound fine on anyone bringing a Quaker into the colony and 40 shillings an hour for hiding a Quaker. Quakers were banished, and those who returned would have an ear cropped off. In the next year, three Quakers lost an ear. Others would lose their lives. A statue of Mary Dyer stands in Boston today. Hung in 1660, she was one of four Quakers executed there. Mary was about 43 years old at the time, a mother of a large family. Earlier she had faced hanging, her eyes blindfolded, a rope around her neck, her life spared moments before the act. Drawn to defy a law she found unjust, Mary kept returning to Boston. So she was hung. Then England outlawed killing Quakers, and the Colony passed the Cart and Whip Act. Now returning Quakers were tied to a cart, dragged through several towns, and whipped.

William Penn. Elsewhere, in Rhode Island, in New Jersey, and finally in Pennsylvania, Quakers prospered. In 1679 William Penn and 12 Friends purchased a tract of fertile land. Known then as East New Jersey, it spanned 300 miles by 160 miles. King Charles of England repaid a debt to Penn's fatherwith the sale of this land. It was the King who named the colony *Pennsylvania*. Disliking the name because it seemed vain, Penn planned the colony as a Holy Experiment. It was to be a pure democracy without an army, a navy, or any prejudice against race or class. As for oaths, settlers would not be required to take any. They were to treat prisoners well, to forgo duels or work on Sundays, and to abide by rules about slaves. Relations with nearby Indians got off to a friendly start in 1682.

Arriving unarmed on the ship *Welcome* with 100 Quaker Friends, Penn was greeted by a horde of armed Indians. Their anger dissolved, though, at Penn's earnest desire to pay them for their land. There followed at least 50 years of good relations. Then, the Quaker Thomas Penn (William's son) tricked some Delaware Indians in a land deal known as the Walking Purchase. They had earlier agreed to sell as much land as a man could cover on foot in a day, perhaps 30 miles. Hired by Thomas, two athletes racewalked all day, riding boats over streams. They covered 60 miles. Upholding the bargain, the Delawares lost their land and had to move west.

Other Quakers would come to the support of Indian groups in the future, but the Walking Purchase became a source of ill will.

Quakers built Burlington, New Jersey, on one side of the Delaware River and Philadelphia, Pennsylvania, on the other. As a settlement, Philadelphia was successful from the outset. The colony welcomed people of all faiths, though Quakers were most numerous at first. Living in frame houses neatly lining the town streets, the Quakers worked hard and spent little. Families grew wealthy. Known as fashionable Quakers, they built some grand city houses, often owning country homes, too.

A factor in separating the Quakers from other early Americans was the conservative Quaker dress.

Separation. Outside influences worried Quaker parents, so they isolated themselves in the 1750s largely to keep their children's faith pure. They lost control of government in Pennsylvania in 1765, when they refused to vote a tax for a war against Shawnee and Delaware Indians. Then came the Revolutionary War. In keeping with their antiwar beliefs, most Quakers refused to fight. Six fought for the British and some 450 joined the Patriots. As a result, they were disowned by the Quaker faith. The majority remained neutral and suffered for it, their homes stoned, for example. George Washington, for one, recognized their right not to fight (Bacon 1985, p.75):

> I assure you very especially that in my opinion the
> conscientious scruples of all men should be treated
> with great delicacy and tenderness...

After the war the Quakers isolated themselves more completely, using simple speech, and eliminating art, music, drama, and holidays from their lives. There was no Christmas, because the people believed in treating all days the same. In daily life, they wore plain dark garments and flat, broad-brimmed hats in protest against class distinctions. They kept shops or farms and went to *meeting*, their religious assembly. Meetings were silent. For most of the 1700s, the Quakers observed a type of worship called *Quietism*. The belief was that complete quiet was the only way to receive guidance from the Holy Spirit. So in meeting after meeting no one spoke. Yet life for these Quakers was not totally severe. It is said that warmth and gaiety resided inside their homes. By the 1800s, some groups had broken the silence at meeting, too. They spoke about the Bible or about social issues of the day.

Change. As contact with the outsiders increased, Quakers relaxed in their observance of habits peculiar to them. Their customary styles of dress and speech began to change. In 1827, a split occurred between Orthodox Quakers and the followers of Elias Hicks. Thereafter more splits occurred.

Hicks spoke out against slavery and the use of its products. Among Quakers who agreed with him were James and Lucretia Mott. James Mott would not sell cotton from slave states, and Lucretia refused to use anything made with slave labor. She organized the Philadelphia Female Anti-Slavery Society. Protesting the treatment of women in America, she helped organize the Women's Rights Convention in 1848. Though Quakers opposed war, she explained, there were other nonviolent ways to fight injustice, and fight she would (Greene 1980, p. 262).

> Our principles lead us to reject and to intreat the
> oppressed to reject all carnal weapons....I have no
> idea, because I am a Non-Resistant, of submitting tamely
> to injustice inflicted either on me or on the slave.

Abolitionists. Many Quakers freed their own slaves and helped others escape. On the eve of the Civil War, Quakers were entrenched in the work of the Underground Railroad (see AFRICAN AMERICANS). Levi Coffin, called President of the Underground Railroad, helped scores of slaves escape. Others, such as John Woolman (whose *Journal* became a classic) and poet John Greenleaf Whitter, spoke out against slavery. Then the Civil war erupted and Friends faced a dilemma: the Quakers were opposed to slavery on the one hand and to war on the other. Like George Washington, President Abraham Lincoln recognized their right not to fight if their consciences prohibited them from doing so. Some 250 Quakers fought for the North; the 15th Pennsylvania Regiment was nicknamed Quaker Regiment. Hundreds of Quakers nursed the wounded and raised money for freed slaves. There was some brutality in the North and more in the South against Quakers who refused to fight. Such a Quaker might be strung up by his thumbs or bucked down, head tied to his heels. Some died in prisons.

20th century. Again in World War I Quakers who were drafted refused to fight. Several hundred spent time in prison or in the army stockades because of their refusal. In 1917, the Quakers formed the American Friends Service Committee to provide relief for victims of the War. The War ended, but the Committee continued, aiding coal miners' families in Pennsylvania in 1922 and 1923. World War II broke out. At last, Quakers could abstain from fighting as conscientious objectors of a major church without being thrown in jail. They participated in other ways, helping the Japanese find new homes when Pearl Harbor was bombed. In 1938 under the belief that everyone is capable of goodness, a group of Quakers visited the Nazi Gestapo to plead for the Jews. As part of the American Friends Service Committee, other Quakers traveled overseas to aid victims on both sides of the War. The AFSC, along with its British counterpart, won the Nobel Peace Prize in 1947 for this work. Almost 300 years earlier (1660), the Quakers had created their famous Peace Testimony; it was recited when they received the Prize (Bacon 1985, p. 190).

> We utterly deny all outward wars and strife and fighting
> with outward weapons to any end and under any pretense whatever.
> This is our testimony to the World.

In the Vietnam War, too, Quakers abstained from fighting. AFSC volunteers, protected by their symbol, a red and black star, again aided victims on both sides. Back home, nonviolent Quaker action included a silent outdoor meeting in Washington D.C. to protest America's fighting in the war. They read names of the dead and sent medical supplies to North Vietnam. Since then, nuclear weapons have been probably their greatest concern. Quakers have urged countries to disarm themselves. To persuade leaders, they testify at congressional hearings and hold formal and informal discussions. Some 700,000 people, many of them Quakers, marched through New York in 1983 to support a United Nations session on disarmament.

Culture Today

Over the years Quaker religion has experienced many divisions. After Elias Hicks split from the Orthodox Quakers, other schisms followed. Followers of Joseph John Gurney, or the Gurneyites, split within the Orthodox group. They held that reading the Bible was the path to the Inner Light, not direct revelations. Orthodox and Hicksite groups reunited in the mid-1900s, and other Quaker groups also set aside their differences. Inspired by the educator Rufus Jones, they adopted a common goal. The Quakers aimed to create an outside world that lives by the teachings of Jesus

Social causes. Quakers have a tradition of action on behalf of certain social issues—improved prison conditions, care for the mentally ill, civil rights, Indian rights, and women's rights. Formed in 1943, the Friends Committee on National Legislation was organized to influence U.S. lawmakers. Quaker sympathy for prisoners is an old concern. Thrown into jail for refusing to bear arms, they experienced miserable prison conditions firsthand. Already in 1787, Quakers, along with Benjamin Franklin, helped form the Philadelphia Society for Alleviating the Miseries of the Public Prisons. More recently, a main concern has been capital punishment. The group continues to champion American Indians and their rights. Bringing relief to the Navajo, the Quakers helped the Indians stave off starvation due to a drought in 1947. Another concern is the mentally ill. The early Quakers supported Pennsylvania Hospital, a pioneer facility for treating the mentally ill. Turning to women's rights, Susan B. Anthony, Anna Sharpless, and Lucretia Mott were Quakers. Mott was a minister (the term was used by Quakers for any outstanding speaker). Unusual for the time, women could become ministers in Quaker communities. This, perhaps, inspired their taking leadership roles in outside arenas.

The Meeting. Quaker worship has changed over the years. At first, a group met in a field or a home. Then members of a group would build a separate *meetinghouse*. The "service" was simple. Members sat quietly for perhaps an hour during which a few might receive an inner message to pass on to the group. They spoke. Their message might be a conclusion reached after a daily experience, or a quote from the Bible. Later, some groups held more formal meetings, singing hymns, reading the Scripture, and preaching. Today the structure of the meeting depends on the particular Quaker group.

Some hold silent meetings without paid ministers. Other groups voice the teachings of Jesus Christ. Still others have formed Friends Churches, hiring professional ministers.

By tradition, a group gathers in the meetinghouse—once a week to worship and once a month to conduct business. Several local groups gather four times a year for a large quarterly meeting. Several quarterly groups gather annually for a yearly meeting. In 1985, there were 25 yearly meetings held by Quakers in various areas of the United States. Some of the yearly meetings gathered every five years to discuss work done overseas. When this became too infrequent, the five year meeting changed to a meeting every three years.

At first, Quaker meetings had no set format. In fact, this was an issue members spoke against. The meeting gradually developed into a forum for fellowship, discussion of problems, and business affairs. Decisions are reached in remarkable fashion. No vote is taken on issues. Rather, a clerk records the *sense of the meeting*. If even one member disagrees with the group, no decision is reached. *Elders* exercise control at Quaker meetings. They are spiritual lifeguards, making sure messages relayed in a meeting match with Quaker beliefs and are Biblically correct. If a speaker talks too long or disrupts the peace of the meeting, an elder may stop the speaker with *Friend, I believe we have received the weight of thy message.*

The harshest way to punish a Quaker is to disown him or her from the religion. In the past the penalty for large offenses—bearing arms, for example—was *disownment.* Today's Quakers are no longer disowned for bearing arms. It is now a matter of individual conscience. So some Quakers fought in World War II, though as Friends they were entitled not to fight and declare themselves conscientious objectors.

Although Quakers have no single creed, they have written books of discipline. The book *Faith and Practice* contains examples of conduct in all areas of life, from family and personal matters to education, political duties, and drugs. At meetings, Quakers discuss their behavior in these areas. Also in writing are Queries, or questions, that Quakers ask of themselves at the meetings, such as, Do you manifest a forgiving spirit? They too inspire discussion.

Beliefs. Quakers have no set creed; members have some leeway in which Christian beliefs they adopt. As long as they abide by respect for human rights, each Quaker may develop his or her own ideas of right and wrong. (This helps explain why not all antebellum Quakers opposed slavery, though a great many did.) There are several beliefs most Quakers agree upon. Refusal to bear firearms is one. A second is the refusal to take oaths, and a third is the right of the individual to obey his or her own conscience over the laws of the state.

Family. Refusing to take oaths meant Quakers had to develop their own marriage practices. Formed in the 17th century, these began with parents permitting a man to court their daughter. Other men were to leave her alone until she accepted or refused him. If she accepted, they married at a regular worship meeting. The couple declared their wedding vows without a minister, but before the congregation. Also they signed a certificate, a summary of their vows. Marrying at the Meeting with Friends as witnesses continues today.

When the Quakers isolated themselves in the 18th century, it was largely to create a separate society for their children. The young learned to live righteously, to dress and speak plainly, to control their temper, and to moderate their desires. They studied mainly science and math, since these subjects were favored over the arts. For years, the people saw no need for higher education. Finally, Haverford, a Quaker college, opened in 1833. By 1984, Quakers had opened at least 69 schools in the United States and British Columbia. Today Quakers support many schools in Pennsylvania and a sprinkling of schools throughout the continent, such as Whittier College in California and George Fox in Oregon. Once forbidding arts, colleges now have thriving art departments. At lower levels many non-Quakers enroll in Quaker schools. They learn Quaker history as part of American history and attend Quaker meetings, too. For recreation, children go to Quaker summer camps. Bible study and hymn singing are other camp activities, the purpose being to raise true Christians. Called Young Friends Conference of North America, the first world meeting of Quaker youth occurred in 1985 at Guilford College, North Carolina. It appears that the faith is being passed on.

Arts. As evident in Quaker schools, the group's regard for the arts has changed. Reading was once restricted to the Bible and Quaker history. Fiction writing was frowned upon as frivolous. Quakers such as John Woolman kept journals about their daily life to better understand its meaning. Regarded as the best 19th-century Quaker writer, John Greenleaf Whittier is today considered a minor American poet. Walt Whitman, whose mother was a Quaker, became a major poet. These lines from his masterpiece *Leaves of Grass* (Whitman 1855, p. 35) recall the Quaker focus on making contact with the Inner Light.

> You shall no longer take things at second or third hand, nor look
> through the eyes of the dead, nor feed on the spectres in books,
> You shall not look through my eyes either, nor take things from me,
> You shall listen to all sides and filter them from your self.

By the 20th century, Quaker historians and Bible scholars shared the literature limelight with poets and novelists. Elizabeth Gray Vining, a Quaker schoolteacher, won the 1943 Newbery Medal for her children's novel *Adam of the Road*. Like Vining, Jessamyn West wrote historical fiction. His novel *The Friendly Persuasion* became a popular movie about the crisis Quakers faced during the Civil War. Edward Hicks, a Quaker painter, chided himself for his attraction to art. He turned to farming instead, then gave it up, supporting his family by creating signs and paintings. He is now considered one of America's finest primitive painters; his noted "Peaceable Kingdom" pictures a lion lying down by the lamb. Among the more recent Quaker artists is famed woodcut maker Fritz Eichenberg.

Values. The Quakers' effort to keep their material possessions simple led to their own separate styles in design and in clothing. Simple lines and careful construction produced uncluttered meeting houses of rich wood and grave furniture and glasswork. The variety of styles has since increased. In similar fashion, clothing has changed. Some early American Quakers wore scarlet-colored cloaks, white satin petticoats, and bright blue gowns. Then dress grew plainer, and the group adopted Quaker gray. Styles changed somewhat in time, but Quaker clothing became famous for its somber color, the man's broad-brimmed hat and the woman's Quaker bonnet. Today the group no longer wears special clothing. In conversation the word *thee* is used only to members of the immediate family, if at all. Other habits remain constant. Like Quakers since the 1600s, the people today work hard and save their earnings. Now most of them belong to the middle class, but they continue to limit their desire for material goods.

For More Information

See these reading materials:

Bacon, Margaret Hope. *The Quiet Rebels: The Story of the Quakers in America*. Philadelphia: New Society Publishers, 1985.

Barbour, Hugh and Frost, J. William. *The Quakers*. New York: Greenwood Press, 1988.

Contact these organizations:

Friends Committee on National Legislation, 245 Second Street, N.E. Washington, DC 20002.

Wider Quaker Fellowship, 1506 Race Street, Philadelphia, Pennsylvania 19102.

RUSSIAN AMERICANS
(rush´en eh mer´ uh kins)

Americans whose ancestors were Russian or lived within
the Russian Empire or Union of Soviet Socialist Republics.

Population: 1,380,000 (1980).
Location: United States (mainly New York, New York, and Los Angeles,
California).
Languages: English, Russian.

Geographical Setting

Early Russian migrants hunted fur animals as far south
on the Pacific Coast as Northern California. Later migrants
chose city life mostly in Los Angeles and New York.

The Bering Strait between the Chukchi Peninsula in the United Soviet Socialist Republics (USSR) and Seward Peninsula in Alaska is a narrow strip of water that is often frozen over in winter. To the south this strait opens to become the Bering Sea circled again on the south by an arc of islands, the Aleutian Islands. Exploring this sea, Russian sailors established their first settlements on the islands.

In search of furs, Russian traders then moved to the mainland. They established a capital of Russian America at Sitka near the coast of Alaska. Next the fur traders migrated southward along the coast as far south as Fort Ross, about 100 miles north of San Francisco. Unable to make the fur trade profitable here, these early Russians retreated to Sitka, where they formed a community of 700 to 800. Alaska's harsh winters were not unlike those in their homeland.

Larger groups of Russians began immigrating to other areas of North America over 100 years later. Some of these immigrants came from the poorest European farmlands to find better soil in Oregon and California, on which they established farm communities. Still later, after the Russian Revolution, immigrants left the large towns and cities of the USSR, fleeing political or religious persecution or pursuing idealistic goals. These more recent newcomers established communities in large cities, such as New York, New York, and Los Angeles, California. Outside these communities, Philadelphia, Pennsylvania, and Chicago, Illinois, have large Russian-American populations. There are also communities in areas of North Dakota and in Fort Lauderdale, Florida.

Historical Background

Overview of "Russian" immigration. United States immigration records classify people according to how they identify themselves. In regard to "Russian," the term is often used loosely. It describes not only immigrants of Russian ancestry. Members of ethnic groups who inhabited areas that were under Russian control have also considered themselves Russian. The following description accepts this broad definition, but it focuses mainly on non-Jewish Russians. For an account of the Jewish immigrants, see JEWISH AMERICANS.

Generally, Russians immigrated to North America in four time periods. Arriving in the 1700s was a small collection of fur traders and missionaries. Almost 200 years later, Russians began coming expressly to settle in America. These later settlers arrived in three main waves: 1) aound the 1917 communist revolution in Russia; 2) after World War II; and 3) from 1970 to the present.

Fur traders and missionaries. In 1727, Vitus Bering, a Danish sea captain serving the Russian czar, discovered the Bering Sea and the Bering Strait, which separated Asia and America by fewer than 100 miles. In the 1740s, he landed in the Aleutian Islands and was followed by Russian fur traders and then Russian Orthodox Church missionaries. These pioneers founded settlements on the islands by the 1760s and on the mainland by the 1780s. They established a capital of the new territory at Sitka in Alaska where the early immigrants built foundry and shipbuilding enterprises.

Their explorations took them down the Alaskan Coast as far south as Fort Ross in California. The traders established fur trading posts, factories, and churches, which have had a lasting effect on the native people of the Aleutian Islands (see ALEUTS). However, in the 1790s, Czar Paul I gave North American development rights to a private company, the Russian American Company. While individual leaders of the company had illustrious careers—for example, Alexander Baranov led expeditions as far south as Baja California—amid the competition from France, England, and Spain, Russian enterprises in the new world did not yield the financial return the czar had anticipated. In 1841, Fort Ross in California was sold to John Sutter, and most of the Russian activity moved north to Alaska. By 1867, Czar Alexander II had become so disillusioned that he sold all Russian rights in the Americas to the United States for 7.2 million dollars.

Pre-Revolution immigrants. A scattering of immigrants arrived before the Russian Revolution. In the early 1800s, some immigrants moved to America in search of religious freedom. These people found life under the czars intolerable. Peasants owned little or no land. Their agricultural efforts provided for minimal existence. Often a day's food consisted of two potatoes and some bread. Wages were seven or eight cents for a 12 to 14 hour day in the fields. Boys as young as 12 were drafted into the army for five years, existing on rations that were sometimes less than their meager peacetime meals. Because they had broken off from the Russian Orthodox Church, religious minorities experienced additional hardship. One such group of peasants, the Molokans, were exiled to southern Russia in the 1840s. They and others were threatened with involuntary military service in the atmosphere of growing dissent that led to the Russian Revolution. Escaping these hardships, Russians began to flee to the United States and Canada in the late 1800s and the early 1900s. They established communal settlements apart from the rest of the American citizens or formed settlements attached to major cities.

Several minority groups sought freedom from religious persecution in America during this period. A group known as the Molokans came. Today, about 17,000 Molokans live in Southern California, 3,000 in San Francisco, and another 3,000 in Oregon. After incurring the wrath of the Orthodox Church, about 2,000 "Old Believers" fled to the Pennsylvania mining areas near Pittsburgh and Erie. Nearly 8,000 Dukhobors (literally meaning "spirit wrestlers") moved to Canada, most of them to rural British Columbia, where their numbers have swollen to 30,000. These religious groups had dissented from the Russian Orthodox church. In the future, they would be outnumbered by members of the Russian Orthodox church. A few of these believers also began to immigrate during this period before the Revolution.

Some of the scattered freedom seekers were influenced by the new ideas of socialism and communism. They formed a few nonreligious communities in America that drew on these new ideas. There were Russian immigrants who settled in New Jersey in the early 1890s. Here they established agricultural communities, such as the 14,000-acre Rova Farm, which still prospers. Generally, these collective communities failed or adopted incentives for individual achievement in order to survive.

Pre-Revolution achievements. For the most part, the early immigrants were uneducated peasant farmers, with few skills to help them gain a foothold in the new society. Their chief asset was their willingness to work hard without complaint. A few educated Russians came individually and won distinction in America. Prince Demetrius Gallitzin, 22 years old, arrived in Pennsylvania in 1792. There he converted to Roman Catholicism and became a frontier priest.

Several Russian immigrants distinguished themselves in the Civil War. Vladimir Magazinove deserted his Russian Navy ship in New York Harbor to enlist in that state's artillery. Otto Mears, who had immigrated from Courland, Russia, to San Francisco, enlisted in the First California Volunteers. More famous was Lincoln's only Russian general, John Basil Turchin. Born Ivan Vasilevich Turchininoff, he was trained as an engineer and rose to the rank of colonel in the Russian Army before immigrating to the United States. In 1861, he was called to head the Nineteenth Illinois Volunteers. He led the volunteers in several encounters with the enemy. According to one observer at the battle of Chicamauga, "his impetuosity carried him far into the rebel lines, and he was almost instantly surrounded by the rebel hordes, but the stout old Russian had no thought of surrendering" (Wertsman 1977, p. 92). At Mission Ridge the general led his men in scaling a height. They captured nine guns in a victory so swift that it was over before troop reinforcements could arrive. This battle opened the way for General Sherman's march on Atlanta.

After the war, Peter Demianov made a fortune building railroads, then used it to help found St. Petersburg, Florida (1888), naming the new town for his birthplace in Russia. Also, Vladimir Stolshnikov helped design Carnegie Hall (completed in 1891).

Post-Revolution immigration. Three waves of immigration from the USSR have occurred in the 20th century. One was stimulated by the Russian Revolution and another by World War II. This second wave subsided as a result of emigration restrictions in the Soviet Union until the 1970s. The third wave has continued since then. While Russian Orthodox believers arrived with the first two waves, the third one has overwhelmingly consisted of Soviet Jews.

In 1917, the Russian government of Czar Nicholas II collapsed. It was replaced by a provisional government, which was itself overthrown by the communists led by Vladimir Lenin. Lenin's policies were radical and inspired support of the tsar from many sectors. The result was a civil war that lasted until early 1921. The uncertainty in their home country during and following the civil war caused a number of citizens to leave the USSR. For the most part, these emigrants were better educated than the earlier settlers. In 1920–1922, two million citizens of the new communist nation fled the USSR to Europe. About 30,000 of these found their way to America. More came during World War II, displaced Russians who had been driven from their homeland by war and others who took advantage of the war's turmoil to escape the rule of Joseph Stalin. From the end of World War II until the 1970s, the flow of immigrants was slowed by Soviet regulations. Applicants to leave the USSR often lost their jobs and had to live off their savings for as long as a year, waiting for the necessary emigration papers to arrive.

Altogether about 110,000 immigrants have come to America since 1970. Immigration procedures since the Second World War have changed. At that time, newcomers had to have a sponsor who guaranteed that they would not be a financial burden to the nation. Now the government provides some support while people learn the English language and grow adjusted to their new lives in America. These late comers have a different immigration experience than the earlier immigrants. However, they share a common ambivalence. Many newcomers from the USSR appreciate freedom and opportunity in America but miss some aspects of their lives in the Soviet Union. Consequently, they tend to form groups, whose members are bound together by language, religion, and distrust for government.

Culture Today

Economic development. Russians have typically established separate communities in the central cities of America or in industrial suburbs. Here they open their own stores and service organizations and continue to speak Russian as their basic language. Often the community centers around a church, a Russian Orthodox Church. As the children of the immigrants attend schools, and learn more of the English language, they often move away, leaving an aging population in the old community. This integration into larger society is hastened by the building of supermarkets and larger stores near the community. Eventually the Russian owned small shops disappear, but the bond of family and the respect for property remain.

Food, clothing, and shelter. In many cases, the latest newcomers dress and otherwise act like other Americans almost before they leave their homeland. Old traditions are not as visible among them. Customarily, the family unit serves as the means to pass along traditional values. The father is head of the household, even though both parents frequently work outside the home. At an early age, boys are taught to take on some of the father's responsibilities. Wives take care of the house, cooking and often sewing, and girls at an early age help in these duties. Many of the families live modestly regardless of the wealth of the parents. A goal of the family unit is to save enough to buy homes and to provide the children with a good education, which is viewed as the door to economic progress. In the 1970s and before, the typical family worked hard to buy land and build a small home. Even if the home was only 600 square feet, it was greatly valued. Experiences in the Soviet Union had instilled a deep desire for the independence that comes from home ownership. Some of the Russian American homes were wooden structures with two or three rooms. They had a small kitchen, a small living room, often with a Russian Orthodox Cross, and a bedroom. The rooms were comfortably but not lavishly furnished. The people living in them tended not to openly demonstrate their wealth by buying material goods. Mannerisms and conversation told the other members of the community how much wealth a family had accumulated. In any case, thrift was important to acquire farmlands or shops of their own.

Many Russians quickly become adjusted to the American diet. At first, though, thrift is evident even in the food they eat. Simple foods such as bread and potatoes make up much of the basic diet. Many Russian Americans grew up in an atmosphere in the old country in which having enough bread to eat was a symbol of well being. Bread has therefore been important. Often several kinds of bread would accompany a single meal. The meal might feature bread and potatoes with cabbage and onions. Meat appeared rarely, usually as smoked sausage and always accompanied by hot mustard. Some other traditional dishes are pastry pies, filled with meat and cabbage. Kasha, buckwheat groats, is a typical food. Soups such as borscht—a mixture of beets, cabbage and onions—are eaten with a dollop of sour cream. Newer immigrants have retained many of these eating habits, even though they adopt other American ways almost immediately.

Earlier groups brought their old peasant garb with them: heavy boots, thick felt or hide coats, and drab cotton or woolen pants for men. They exchanged the coats for cotton shirts in warmer weather. Women wore cotton dresses, embroidered hide or felt coats, and brightly colored scarves and shawls. As soon as they could afford new clothes, the early immigrants would adopt American dress. Later immigrants often purchased blue jeans and T-shirts even before leaving the USSR.

Religion. The Russians were converted to Christianity originally by the Greeks. The Russian Orthodox Church, therefore, takes many of its features from Greek Orthodoxy. To read the liturgy, Greeks developed an alphabet for the Russians called the Cyrillic alphabet, after St. Cyril who developed it. Services were once conducted in a slavonic language using this alphabet. Today they are mostly in English.

Russian American families pray and worship together; the Russian Orthodox Church in America has been the single most important marker of their origins. From the earliest days in Sitka, the Church has exerted a strong influence on Russians in America. This was particularly true after the Russian Revolution and subsequent attempts to arrest priests, confiscate church property, and destroy the religion.

Adherents of the church in America have resisted domination by the church leaders in the Soviet Union. The Russian Orthodox Church in America remains independent. The church building, the center of the community, is often distinguished by its golden, onion-shaped domes. While families have religious icons in the home and frequently pray and study scriptures together, the church building is the symbol of their religious bond. Inside, a tall screen separates the altar from the congregation. Several icons are hung on this screen, the iconostasis, Orthodox portraits of religious figures in richly colored woods.

In addition to their Orthodox religion, some Russian Americans have brought with them a belief in faith healing. A healer, the *zamovlat*, acts as an intermediary between an afflicted person and God. It is believed that the zamovlat possesses healing power because of the pureness of his or her soul. Other popular methods of healing and forecasting include palm reading and some forms of black magic.

The Arts. Russia has one of the finest artistic traditions in the world, and Russian immigrants to America have made correspondingly outstanding contributions to the arts. Russian immigrants include three of this century's greatest literary figures: Vladimir Nabokov (1899–1977), Alexander Solzhenitsyn (1918–), and Joseph Brodsky, who is of Jewish descent (1940–).

Born into Russian aristocracy, Vladimir Nabokov lived in Berlin, Paris, and Cambridge before moving to the United States. Best known for his controversial novel *Lolita*, Nabokov wrote much fiction and lectured widely in American Universities. He has been recognized as one of the foremost English language writers of this century.

Alexander Solzhenitsyn began his career as an author while in a Siberian prison camp, where he had been sent for writing criticism of Joseph Stalin. His novel of prison camp life, *One Day in the Life of Ivan Denisovich*, brought him instant fame in 1962. Solzhenitsyn won the Nobel Prize for Literature in 1970, but his writing angered the government of the Soviet Union. He was deported in 1974 and now lives in Vermont.

The poet Joseph Brodsky came to the United States in 1972. His poetry tells about the psychological effects of life in a totalitarian state, and so disturbed the Soviet government that he was sentenced to five years in prison even though he no longer lived in the country. Brodsky won the Nobel Prize for Literature in 1987.

Musical achievements of Russians in America have been equally impressive. Often credited with inventing modern music, Igor Stravinsky (1882–1971) is best known for his early work, especially the ballets *The Firebird, Petrouchka*, and *The Rite of Spring*. Vladimir Horowitz (1904–1989) was one of the century's greatest piano virtuosos. Living in the United States since 1928, Horowitz returned to perform for audiences in Leningrad and Moscow in 1986. He, like Joseph Brodsky, was of Jewish descent. Both of these artists felt a love for the homeland that is shared by many immigrants. Horowitz explained it this way: "I have never forgotten my Russia. I remember the smells when the snow melts and the spring arrives. I had to go back to Russia before I died" (Magosci 1989, p. 97). Mstislav Rostropovich (1927–) has conducted the National Symphony Orchestra in Washington, DC since 1974.

George Balanchine, founder and director of the New York Ballet, is described as the greatest choreographer of our time. A prolific artist, Balanchine has choreographed nearly 200 ballets, 19 Broadway musicals, and four motion pictures. Acclaimed ballet star Mikhail Baryshnikov defected to the United States in 1974. He and Balanchine have been leaders in the development of American ballet.

Well known Russian Americans include (clockwise) Svetlana Alliluyev (daughter of Joseph Stalin), Vladimir Nabokov, and George Balanchine.

The sciences. Russians have also made important contributions to American science. In television, Vladimir Zworykin invented a television camera that proved critical in the development of modern broadcasting. He also developed an electron microscope that, in 1940, allowed magnifications of up to 100,000 times. Igor Sikorsky (1889–1972) was one of aviation's pioneers, building many successful airplanes before developing the helicopter in 1939. In physics, George Gamow helped develop the "big bang" theory explaining the formulation of the universe. He wrote books to popularize the theory.

Government. Russians who came to America were disillusioned with government, first because it prevented them from economic growth, and later because of restrictions on individual freedoms. As a result, Russian Americans tend to remain detached from public institutions. Workers and shopowners reject even the local trade associations because they are reminded of Soviet bureaucracy. One Russian American expresses a general attitude: "Politicians are no good. They only want easy money that they get for doing favors for people" (Gerber 1985, p. 73). This wariness of government has prevented Russians from full participation in activities like the census. It in some ways slows their assimilation into American society. In view of new freedoms now being gained in the Soviet Union and given time in America, this feeling perhaps will change.

For More Information

See these reading materials:

Magosci, Paul R. *The Russian Americans.* New York: Chelsea House, 1989.

Ripp, Victor. *From Moscow to Main Street: Among the Russian Emigrés.* Boston: Little, Brown & Co., 1984.

Contact this organization:

Congress of Russian Americans, P.O. Box 818, Nyack, New York 10960.

SEMINOLES
(sem´eh-nols´)

An American Indian people, who originated in Florida in the 1700s from several tribes who migrated there.

Population: 5,700 (1989).
Location: Florida, Oklahoma.
Language: Mikasuki, Muskogee, English.

Geographical Setting

OK

FL

The Seminole Indians live in Oklahoma and on reservations in southern Florida.

About one-third of the Seminole population lives on reservations and surrounding lands in Florida. Over two thirds (4,100) reside in Oklahoma. Called the Seminole Nation, this arm is headquartered in southeast Oklahoma at Wewoka. The Oklahomans have little collective land, less than 400 acres. Near the turn of the 20th century, their holding was divided and allotted to individuals in the tribe. Oil deposits sat under some of the individual plots.

The Florida Seminoles, after being pushed from the northern borders, clustered in the swampy, isolated Everglades of southern Florida. Today the Florida Seminole land includes swamps, prairies, pines, palmetto, and hardwood hummocks, or low knolls that stand higher than marshland. Flooding is common in the region. Though not all Seminoles live on reservations, there are three in Florida—Big Cypress, Brighton, and Hollywood. Many off-reservation Indians live along the Tamiami Trail west of Miami.

Historical Background

Diverse origins. The Seminoles are a mix of several Indian tribes that fled from Georgia and South Carolina to Spanish-controlled Florida in the early 1700s. The Oconee, Yamassee, Cree, Muskogee, Albama, and Yuchi comprise the core tribes from which the Seminoles were founded. British expansion pushed these tribes southward. Meanwhile, many black slaves fled from the colonies into Florida, where most of them were absorbed by the Indians. The term *Seminole*, first used by Europeans around 1755, probably stems from the Creek word for this mixed group, *simanoli*, meaning "runaway" or "wild." This Creek word is itself perhaps a corruption of the Spanish *cimarron*, used for a tamed animal that reverts to the wild.

Prosperity in northern Florida. When the Seminoles moved into Florida, they replaced the original Timacua and Calusa Indians, who had been wiped out by European diseases and by warfare with other tribes. The new arrivals were welcomed by the Spanish, who thought the Indians might serve as a buffer against the English. Despite the diversity of their origins, the Seminoles rapidly developed a cohesive tribal identity in Florida. An English observer of the 1760s, the naturalist John Bartram, saw clean and prosperous villages, around which the Seminoles raised crops. Customary Indian crops, such as corn, squash, beans, and tobacco, were accompanied by new foods the Spanish had introduced, such as melons and oranges. The Seminoles also acquired domesticated animals (especially horses, cows, and pigs) from the Spaniards and raised herds of cattle. At the same time, they continued to hunt and fish in customary Indian fashion, relying especially on deer, the hides of which they made into clothing. Other favored animals were squirrels, rabbits, racoons, and wild turkeys.

Early society. The Southeastern tribes from which the Seminoles descended shared similar social structures. Language, however, separated them. Most tribes spoke related tongues, but their languages were not mutually understandable. Within a tribe, society consisted of clans of related families. Descent was traced through the mother's line, so children joined her clan. In raising children, responsibility fell to the clan. Bringing up a son was largely the task of the mother's brother. While the father supported his sons, their uncles trained them to be hunters and warriors. Villages contained ten to 50 families. These villages often congregated for religious ceremonies, but they did not share a common leader. It follows that the southeastern Indian's first loyalties were to clan and village, not to tribe. The absence of strong tribal loyalties made it easier for the different tribes to merge in Florida. In the process, the clans of various tribes formed alliances through intermarriage. Two languages, Muskogee and Mikasuki, became most common, though they are not mutually understandable. Along with English, these languages are still spoken today.

Sanctuary for slaves. In the late 1600s, slaves from plantations in the English colonies began escaping to the west and south. Many of them joined Indian tribes in the territory between Florida and the Carolinas, which in 1732, became the English colony Georgia. No longer secure there, fugitive slaves sought refuge in Spanish Florida. There many of them joined Seminole villages, receiving support and protection. While Seminole Indians kept slaves, their form of slavery seemed to exist more in name than in fact. Seminole masters fed and supported their slaves, making few demands on them for labor, enjoying instead the social prestige of being a slave owner. Sometimes the blacks formed their own towns within the Seminole community, engaging in farming and cattle raising. Marriages between the two groups produced a generation of black Indians, creating a taller and darker Seminole.

The black population played an important role in the coming conflicts between the Seminoles and the U.S. government. At first, the blacks served as interpreters and go-betweens in negotiations. Later, as the government attempted to remove the Indians to the West, blacks helped persuade the Seminoles to resist removal, then joined them in the fighting that followed.

First Seminole War. Raids into Florida by plantation owners who wished to reclaim the slaves ended in the First Seminole War in 1817–1818. Andrew Jackson led United States forces and hostile Creek Indians into the Seminole region to destroy villages. Jackson's soldiers, who greatly outnumbered their poorly armed opponents, killed many Seminoles in the fierce fighting that followed. The surviving Indians and blacks retreated into the marshes of central Florida, where they easily evaded capture. As a result of the war, Spain ceded Florida to the United States in 1821. The Seminoles, nevertheless, continued to accept and protect runaway slaves, to the increasing anger of plantation owners. They also kept raiding American Army bases and attacked homesteaders living on their former land in northern Florida. In 1823, under the Treaty of Moultrie Creek, the Seminoles agreed to move onto a reservation in central Florida in exchange for farming equipment, livestock, and 100,000 dollars to be paid over 20 years. In northern Florida, their land had encompassed 30 million fertile, game-filled acres. Their new reservation amounted to only five million acres, and it was marshy land, unfit for farming and with little wildlife.

Second Seminole War. The growing influx of American settlers created pressure to have all Indians removed to the West. In 1830, the Indian Removal Act empowered President Andrew Jackson to relocate the southeastern Indian population to a specified territory in Oklahoma. (Jackson's victory over the Seminoles had helped him win the election for President.) In 1832, seven Seminole leaders, sent to inspect the proposed territory in the West, signed a removal treaty. They had not been authorized to do so by the tribe. Though some Seminole leaders denounced the treaty as illegal, the Army ordered the Indians to relocate. Legend has it that the Seminole war chief, Osceola, once jumped up and drove a knife through a treaty the government officials put before him, declaring that it was the only signature he would give them. Articulate and forceful, Osceola persuaded the Seminoles to defend their land by going to war once more.

For two years, Osceola's warriors inflicted heavy casualties in ambushes and raids, evading capture by quickly melting into the familiar, swampy terrain. In 1837, Osceola and several other chiefs fell into enemy hands. They were underhandedly captured while negotiating with the Army during a truce. Later that year, 11 other chiefs were caught in the same way. The government imprisoned these leaders, first at St. Augustine, Florida, then in Charleston, South Carolina, where Osceola died in 1838. Coacoochee (Wild Cat), who was imprisoned at St. Augustine, escaped with several others and became the outstanding figure in the second half of the war. In the end, he realized the hopelessness of continued Indian resistance. He surrendered in 1841, by which time most of the Seminoles had already been captured and relocated. Overall, about 4,500 members of the tribe made the long, grueling march west in groups of ten to 100 or more. Many died on the way. Some Seminoles, about 500, refused to leave. Instead they fled into the Everglades of southern Florida.

The Second Seminole War was the most expensive Indian conflict ever fought by the United States Army. Aside from the loss of 1,500 soldiers, this conflict cost the government about 20 million dollars. There was a series of skirmishes from 1855–1858, a final attempt to remove the Indians from Florida. Approximately one-fourth of the remaining population did leave; the rest retreated deeper into the Everglades. By 1858, only 150 Seminoles were left in Florida. The wars had caused them to live a nomadic life, camping in small groups. Eventually, they divided into two bands, the Muskogee and the Mikasuki.

Billy Bowlegs, Seminole leader of the 1850s.

Acculturation in Oklahoma. Upon arriving in Oklahoma, the Seminoles were told to share land with their old enemies, the Creeks. The Seminoles set up a government of 25 towns, each with an elected *tustenugee*, or subchief. The subchiefs formed a council that was led by a principal chief. In 1856, after the Seminoles protested, the United States ceded them a portion of the Creek territory. The tribe set about further establishing its own government. By 1860, it had built a council house. The Civil War interrupted the process of recovery, however, dividing the Seminoles. Three fourths of the tribe wanted to remain neutral in this war. However, sentiment in the Oklahoma Territory favored the South. Many Seminoles tried to escape to the Union states, but they were pursued and captured. Ultimately members of the tribe served on both sides. In the Union Army, the Seminoles joined the Indian Home Guard Brigade; the Confederate Army had a Seminole Battalion commanded by Chief John Jumper. After the Civil War, the federal government penalized the Seminoles because some had fought for the South: a treaty in 1866 ceded two million acres of Seminole territory to the government in exchange for a 200,000-acre tract.

After 1868, the Seminoles in Oklahoma consolidated into an area that came to be recognized as the Seminole Nation. The Seminole Nation would remain in existence to the present day, but its collective landholding dwindled down to a few hundred acres. The collective holding of one large tract dissolved in the 1890s. Already other tribes in Oklahoma had been forced to accept allotment, the division of their collective land into individual plots. In 1898, the Seminole Agreement forced allotment on the Seminole. The Agreement promised them a large measure of self-government, but for the next 70 years, federal officials would have the most control.

Meanwhile, contact with outsiders had increased. The first railroad lessened the Seminoles' isolation in 1895. In 1923, the opening of the Greater Seminole Oil Field began the growth of an oil site that drew more outsiders, who stayed. Oil brought great wealth to some of the Indian landowners, even though they now lived on small allotments. Other Seminoles made money in businesses supported by the oil boom. Closer interaction with outsiders encouraged the Seminoles to adopt non-Indian ways. Still, they continued to struggle for self-government. The U.S. government gave the president authority to select the Seminoles' chief. In order to secure signatures on deeds, the government would sometimes appoint a chief who was likely to act as it willed. This tactic backfired when Alice B. Davis (appointed in 1923) and George Jones (appointed in 1925) refused to sign deeds that would sell off Indian lands. Eventually, in 1969, the Constitution of the Seminole Nation of Oklahoma recognized the Seminole Council but made it subject to the rule of the state. In 1970, an act of Congress acknowledged the Indians' right to elect their own chiefs. Other legislation in the 1970s provided funds for school and housing programs to aid the Oklahoma Seminoles.

Struggle for survival in Florida. There was less outside influence in Florida than in Oklahoma. The few Seminoles who had remained in the Everglades were better able to maintain their old customs of hunting, fishing, and farming. By the 1880s, they had established trade relations with the white settlers. The Indians exchanged vegetables, hides, and crafts for cloth, guns, metal tools, tobacco, and coffee. Numbering around 500, they lived in scattered small camps of several households each. In the early 1900s, the Florida state government took steps to encourage development of the Everglades, and Seminole ways were once again threatened. Barges appeared to drain large areas of the swamp land; ranchers and farmers cleared and fenced off land for pastures and citrus groves. The 1920s saw a real estate boom in Florida, as newly-built railroads and highways brought a steady flow of outsiders to growing communities and resorts.

In 1911, the federal government established two reservations: Big Cypress and Dania, later called Hollywood. Big Cypress, the larger of the two, was located in south central Florida, south of Lake Okeechobee. Hollywood sat near what would later become the highly developed East Coast. The government created a third reservation, Brighton, in 1935, situating it on the northern shore of Lake Okeechobee. Meanwhile, many Seminoles continued to live off the reservation, taught by experience to be wary of federal attempts at removal. Since they were slow to move onto reservation land, tribal organization also came slowly. Only when some respected leaders moved to the reservations in the 1950s, did many Seminoles follow. A tribal government begin to emerge.

Government. Drawn up in 1957, the constitution of the Seminole Tribe of Florida organized the tribe's government into a council and a board of directors. The council negotiates with federal, state, and local authorities. It also establishes and enforces laws. The board of directors conducts tribal business affairs and manages tribal lands.

The *Seminole Nation of Oklahoma* now refers to tribal membership, not to land, since the Oklahomans hold almost no acreage in common today. With Wewoka as its capital, the Seminole Nation operates according to its 1969 constitution. Tribal government in Oklahoma consists of a principal chief and a second chief (who are elected every four years) and a 28-member council, two members for each of 14 Seminole clans.

The present tribal governments negotiate with outside authorities for laws, grants, and contracts. Then they implement programs to meet the educational, health, and other needs of their people. Together, the Oklahoma and Florida Seminoles experienced a recent victory. In April 1990, President

George Bush signed the final land settlement between the United States and Seminole Indians. They are to receive 46 million dollars, 75 percent going to the Oklahoma Seminoles and 25 percent to the Florida Seminoles.

Culture Today

The Seminoles remain an Indian people today. Their close alliance with blacks broke down in the pre-Civil War days. Attitudes of nearby whites and conflicts between Indian tribes undermined the friendly relations between the two groups. Remaining separate, Florida Seminoles developed a different way of life than those in Oklahoma. Florida's Indians have been more isolated from outsiders and therefore more able to retain customary ways.

Food, clothing, and shelter. Life in Florida's swampy Everglades dictated an increased reliance on fishing, on hunting otter, skunk, and alligator, and on gathering wild fruits. Log fires provided heat for cooking. Turtle was a favored meat. Three dishes would remain popular over time: *sofki*, a soup made from ground cornmeal boiled with wood ash; frybread, a large, fried wheat-flour biscuit; and swamp cabbage, the tender heart of the sabal palmetto bud. Tasting a bit like celery, swamp cabbage is eaten raw, boiled, or sautéed.

Because of the marshy terrain of the Florida land, the Seminoles built *chickees*, houses on stilts. Constructed of cypress poles and thatched with palmetto fronds, the chickee was open on all sides to admit the cooling breezes, and its floor was raised to avoid floodwaters. Many Seminoles still live in houses based on the chickee design, although large windows have replaced the open walls. The homes now have stoves and refrigerators to cook and preserve food. The 1950s saw the building of cement-block structures, required by the state to provide refuge from the frequent hurricanes that strike southern Florida. While they had many conveniences, the cement structures were uncomfortable in the humid Florida summers. The windowed chickee design followed. Much like an old chickee camp, there are several structures for each family. A unit consists of three separate buildings: a sleeping structure; a kitchen; and a bathroom.

Seminole clothing is highly distinctive. Since the late 1800s, when sewing machines became available, Seminole women have created colorful patchwork garments, sewing long strips of brightly colored cloth into intricate patterns. The women work in groups, sharing designs. Over time, each reservation has come to favor certain patterns. Traditional costumes for women included long skirts from the waist to the ground, a short bolero as a blouse or jacket, and sometimes a light cape draped over the shoulders. Men dressed in patchwork tunics, often secured by a belt or sash. First they wore deerskin leggings, next calico skirts or kilts, and finally khakis or blue jeans. In the 1800s, cotton turbans covered their heads, though today most of the men favor cowboy hats. Contemporary clothing ranges from traditional to modern wear. Young people, especially on the Hollywood Reservation near the crowded east coast of Florida, tend to abandon old styles, but others still wear them. One tradition is disappearing as the young forgo traditional clothing styles. At puberty, Seminole girls would receive a strand of beads. Additional strings were added as gifts and as rewards for acts of virtue. When a woman passed middle age, she would remove the necklaces one at a time until only the first strand remained. This one would be worn to the grave.

In Oklahoma, most of the old Seminole habits are no longer practiced. Families have instead adopted a range of new ways. The Seminole shelter, for example, may be a fine town house, a small farm, or a slight, old structure in the distant country with no running water and only an outhouse.

Family life. Clans still dominate the family organization of the Seminoles, and children still join their mother's line. The Deer Clan, Wind Clan, Beaver Clan, and Bear Clan are groups that continue to exist, but many clans have died out. As a result, the Seminoles relaxed the once strict rule against marriage between members of the same clan. In the family, many households are smaller than they once were. The small, nuclear family is now common, although the three-generation household continues to exist. A household might include parents, single children, perhaps a married daughter and her husband, and an aunt or grandmother on the mother's side.

The family encourages independence and individuality. In the past, punishment was rare. It was acceptable for family members to give advice, but not to give orders. Everyone took responsibility for his or her own behavior. In the present, these customs are evident in the leeway many Seminole teenagers have to make their own choices. This sometimes produces confusion, as teenagers chose between new influences encountered at school and old influences experienced at home.

Education. There is an elementary school covering the first few grades on the Big Cypress reservation. To complete their education, students attend public schools off the reservation. Elsewhere in Florida and in Oklahoma, children attend public schools from the beginning. Not an old value, education has been considered unimportant by some Seminole parents. Many of these parents do not give their children much encouragement to do schoolwork. If a child drops out, they may accept this decision without argument. Or a child who remains in school may grow distant from his or her parents. Students whose families live close to outsiders experience less confusion, since their parents are influenced by surrounding society.

Occupations. The Seminoles often earn a living in a combination of ways, as seasonal jobs provide them with an unsteady income. In Florida, on the Hollywood Reservation, many Seminoles work for the tribal headquarters, selling artwork, running stores, or taking administrative jobs. Others earn money making baskets, carvings, and dolls (whose clothing reflects the Seminole fascination with patchwork). Becoming souvenirs, these items supply shops all over Florida and a tribal store on the Hollywood Reservation. Native villages, both on and off the reservation, recreate Seminole life, featuring attractions such as the powwow ceremony and alligator wrestling. Not traditional, alligator wrestling is a response to tourism, an industry that occupies many Seminoles.

Besides the tourist industry, fruit and vegetable growers in Florida provide some Seminoles with jobs. Others find year-round employment in roadwork. Or they engage in the old activity of cattle raising, which no longer provides enough money to serve as their chief source of income. Unemployment is high, especially on the isolated interior reservations. In fact, the Hollywood Reservation attracts newcomers, because nearby jobs and education have raised prosperity for its Seminoles. Elsewhere in Florida, some of the old occupations continue. Indians trade furs for food and guns or work as hunting guides. Those who remain at Big Cypress and Brighton, or live off the reservations entirely, value their isolation; it allows them to maintain the old ways.

Religion and holidays. In their traditional religion, Seminoles believed in a Great Spirit, symbolizing goodness and purity and a darker force, Yo-he-wa, connected with demons and curses. To placate this dark god, they made offerings twice a year during the Green Corn Dance ceremony. Lasting up to five nights in late June or July, this festival signifies renewal or purification. Its purpose is to bring health and prosperity to the tribe. Accompanied by water drums, gourds, tortoiseshell rattles and flutes, songs for the Green Corn Dance have survived for generations. The festival itself continues today, although most Seminoles have converted to Christianity, joining, for example, Baptist, Methodist, or Presbyterian churches. Conversion began in the 1800s, when many Christian traditions, such as the stories of Adam and Eve, were incorporated into the Seminole mythology.

Conversion did not erase old traditions. Strongest today is the stomp dance religious ceremony. Like other tribes in Oklahoma, the Seminoles have stomp grounds. These are areas where elders traditionally teach the young behaviors, ranging from respect for the earth to foods they must not eat until they reach a certain age. In Seminole society, children belong to their mother's stomp ground. New efforts aim to preserve old ways in Oklahoma, too. A special youth program was designed to train teenagers in Seminole history and tradition so that they can preserve old ways.

For More Information

See these reading materials:

Garbarino, Merwyn S. *The Seminole.* New York: Chelsea House, 1989.

Meltzer, Milton. *Hunted Like a Wolf: The Story of the Seminole War.* New York: Farrar, Straus and Giroux, 1972.

Weisman, Brent Richards. *Like Beads on a String.* Tuscaloosa: University of Alabama Press, 1989.

Contact these organizations:

Seminole Nation of Oklahoma, P.O. Box 1498, Wewoka, Oklahoma 74884.

Seminole Tribal Council, 6073 Stirling Road, Hollywood, Florida 33024.

SENECA
(sen' ih ka)

An Iroquois tribe of North American Indians; one of
the six nations in the Iroquois Confederation.

Population: 5,744 (1989).
Location: United States (New York and Oklahoma); Canada (Ontario).
Language: Seneca (an Iroquian language), English.

Geographical Setting
Canada

Tonawanda
Cattaraugus
Allegany

Once the Seneca hunted and fished on both sides of
Niagara Falls. Now they live on three reservations
in New York State and in Canada.

According to archaeologists, the Seneca have been living in the forested
mountains near Niagara Falls on both sides of the United States–Canadian
border since at least the 11th century. While their villages were concentrated
here, they hunted north to Lake Ontario, south to the Finger Lakes, and as

far east as Lake Cayuga. After the Europeans arrived, the Seneca extended their hunting territory into Ohio and to the shores of Lake Michigan, to the Hudson River to the east, and to Pennsylvania in the south. They ultimately signed a treaty that confined them to four reservations in what is now western New York State: Buffalo Creek, Tonawanda, Cattaraugus, and Allegany. Over the next 150 years, they were continually forced to give up reservation land to whites. While a related group, the Seneca–Cayuga tribe, lives on a reservation in Oklahoma, no records indicate that these Indians were ever part of the Seneca Tribe of New York State.

Today, several thousand Seneca occupy three reservations: Tonawanda, Cattaraugus, and Allegany, and a small parcel called Oil Springs Reservation, all in western New York state. Some Seneca elected to move to Canada, where their descendants still live on the Grand River Reserve.

Historical Background

The Seneca belong to the Iroquois Indian group. While there are many Iroquois tribes, five have been historically connected through the Iroquois League, a federation of tribes that entered a formal pact of alliance. The Cayuga, Onondaga, Oneida, Mohawk, and Tuscarora were the tribes that joined forces with the Seneca. Most of the tribes were located along the southern border of Lake Ontario. Altogether they spread across a stretch of territory in which the Mohawk occupied the easternmost position, and were thus known as "Keepers of the Eastern Door." The Seneca were the "Keepers of the Western Door" because of their position on the western flank. Actually, *Seneca* stems from the Iroquois word for "great hill people."

Longhouses. The Seneca were once divided into a western group and an eastern group, each living in towns. Seneca settlements, or towns, were built on hilltops above streams. They contained longhouses. A log structure, the longhouse came to identify Iroquois peoples. They were called *Haudenosaunee*, "People of the Longhouse." The longhouse was a large structure occupied by six to ten families. Typically, it measured about 25 feet wide and perhaps 100 feet long. There might be 30 people in a house and 30 longhouses in a town, for example. A house group consisted of families related to the senior woman. A core of mothers, sisters, daughters, and the men who married them occupied the shelter. Its simplest unit was the fireside family, a small unit of wife, husband, and children. Usually, a fireside served two families living in facing compartments. Inside a compartment was a low, wide platform, used by the family for sleeping or sitting. Walled by a section of outer house and partitions on either side, a compartment opened onto the family fire located in the central aisle. Streets separated longhouses, and the entire town was confined by a barrier. Along the outer walls of this palisade were raised platforms for lookouts and archers. At the bottom of the hill were the fields, which the Seneca women owned and cultivated. The Seneca practiced slash-and-burn agriculture, with men clearing the land so women could plant. They moved their settlement every eight or ten years to let the earth replenish itself.

Daily life. Women planted corn, beans, squash, melons, tobacco, and sunflowers. Houses and fields belonged to the women, though the men did the building and the governing. For daily activity, the men hunted in the forest. A tribe captured as many as 2,000 deer in a single season. Aside from deer, the men snared bear, and they fished. Both women and children gathered wild foods—roots, berries, and nuts. After drying the berries in the sun, the women baked them into bread. A favorite dish was corn soup, flavored with the meat brought home by the men. The staples were maize, beans, and squash, crops the Iroquois nicknamed "the three sisters." It is known that the clothing was made from buckskin, the people preferring a black-dyed variety of the material. However, records on exact styles are scant. There is record of an 18th-century woman in a dress and an overdress decorated with beadwork and silver brooches. For footwear, the people wore moccasins, changing to corn-husk slippers during summer. They designed snowshoes for travel in winter. On a typical day, members of a longhouse would retire early. They slept on mats on the platforms in their compartments, placing wood or a stone under their heads and covering themselves with animal pelts. The sleepers rose at dawn, giving thanks for life before beginning their daily business.

Iroquois peoples devoted time to practical arts. They crafted pottery, decorating it with little faces around the rim of the container. They also created baskets out of ash splints, elm bark, and corn husks. Using dyed sweet grass and moose hair, women embroidered clothing. Porcupine quills ornamented moccasins and clothing. The women turned animals' teeth or shells into jewelry. For warfare, men painted their faces, three stripes on each cheek to represent the six Iroquois nations in the confederation. Men tattooed their bodies, using geometric forms and clan symbols: the turtle, bear, wolf, beaver, deer, and heron. (A clan consisted of two or more family lines whose members behaved as if they were all one family.) Music and dancing occurred during celebrations of thanksgiving. To play music, the Seneca made over 16 instruments, including flutes, rattles, and drums. They had separate men's and women's dances and a few mixed dances, such as Joined Hands, which was performed in honor of the bean vines.

Wampum. To keep records, the tribe manufactured wampum beads. These cylindrical shell beads, about a quarter of an inch long and an eighth of an inch in diameter, had a hole in the middle. They varied in color from white, to shades of beige, yellow, and pink. The beads were woven into belts and necklaces to document a historical agreement or event. For treatymaking, the wampum belt was made in duplicate, one for each party to the treaty. Custom taught that the wampum confirmed that an agreement was true. The belt, in effect, sealed the agreement. Therefore, treaties involving the Seneca, or other Iroquois, called for an exchange of wampum.

The League of the Iroquois. With the fur trade came continual warfare. By the 1630s, five Iroquois nations—the Mohawk, Oneida, Onondaga, Cayuga, and Seneca—had formed a League in mutual defense against the warfare. According to legend, the idea for the League came from a Mohawk named Hiawatha (not the one from Longfellow's poem) who had lost his entire family to intertribal conflict. Crazed with grief, he wandered in the forest, where he met Dekanawida, a man of great goodness. Dekanawida told Hiawatha about his plan to free the Iroquois from the evils of war by forming a grand league in a long house, where all the tribes would act as brothers. Since Dekanawida had a speech impediment, Hiawatha agreed to speak to the various tribes on Dekanawida's behalf.

In fact, five Iroquois tribes actually agreed to the League. Fifty chiefs from these tribes decided to meet in a grand council. The council would resolve disputes and coordinate defense. At the same time, the five tribes outlawed blood feuds among themselves. In the event of a killing, the injured family was to receive payment and would not retaliate by murdering a member of the aggressor's clan. The five tribes also decided that when a *sachem* (civil chief) who belonged to the Grand Council died, the 49 remaining chiefs would visit his village. They would hold a Condolence Council there for the grief-stricken, then receive from the village a replacement chief to represent them in the Grand Council. While the League provided mutual protection, it did not produce peace. The Iroquois participated in warfare against Indians and whites over the next two centuries.

The fur trade. By 1630, the Iroquois competed against other Indians for direct trade with Europeans. Within ten years they had obtained guns from the Dutch and were harassing tribes along the St. Lawrence River. They destroyed the Hurons and took the bulk of the fur trade away from the Canadian-based French, delivering it to the Hudson River Dutch. By 1676, the League had consolidated its power and dominated the fur trade, which proved to be a mixed blessing. The work was relatively easy and quite profitable, but it brought alcohol and contagious diseases, too. Smallpox, especially, claimed the lives of the Seneca children and old people. Yet the League grew more powerful, controlling the northeast as far west as the shores of Lake Michigan, and south into Pennsylvania and the Shawnee land in Ohio. Around 1722, the Tuscarora, another Iroquois tribe, joined the confederacy—now the League of Six Nations. Like other tribes, the Tuscarora saw white settlers pushing into their territory and joined the League in hopes of keeping out the invaders.

Ben Franklin, George Washington, and the Iroquois. In 1735, the League of Six Nations signed a treaty of friendship with Pennsylvania. Attending the ceremonies, Benjamin Franklin observed the structure of the Indian confederacy. He found in it a partial model for his own plan for a federal union of the American colonies. He later described this vision in the Albany Plan, 1754. With this plan, he tried persuading the colonies of Union, suggesting that they form a federal legislature, which, like that of the Iroquois, might be called a Grand Council. Then came the American Revolution.

The Iroquois League considered the fight between the colonists and the English none of their business and adopted a neutral stance. At the time, there were some 4,000 Seneca. They attended councils with the British in 1777 and were persuaded to support them, though their support was not unanimous. In 1778, Chief Big Trees tried to convince his people to join the rebels. Rumor had it that the rebels were about to invade the Iroquois, so most of them ignored Chief Big Trees and supported the British. Actually, the League divided its allegiance. The Mohawk, Onandaga, Cayuga, and Seneca nations supported the British; the Oneida and Tuscarora sided with the rebels. Drawn into battle at Fort Stanwix, the Seneca fought at Wyoming and Cherry Valley. The Battle of Wyoming (1778) became especially brutal, the British side outnumbering the 300 rebels by four to one. Not only did the British side win but they did so brutally, killing and scalping the wounded with abandon. General George Washington sent soldiers to retaliate against the Indians in 1779; Sullivan's Campaign set out to break the power of the Iroquois enemy. John Sullivan destroyed 40 Indian towns, burning food supplies and cutting down crops. Iroquois power was broken. Thereafter, the Seneca took refuge in Fort Niagara, a British stronghold. They survived on scanty, fort rations until they retreated to the Cattaraugus, Tonawanda, and Allegany areas of New York.

Reservations. In 1783, the Treaty of Paris ended the war. Defeated with the British, the Seneca were at a disadvantage. Some of them moved to Canada, where their descendants remain today. Those who remained had to negotiate with the newly independent Americans. Between 1784 and 1786, a series of treaties certified that the League had forfeited their land and were to remove themselves to reservations. The sachems fought and some refused to sign, but in the end the Indians were forced onto reservations. Control of the old Iroquois lands shifted to the states.

Two Seneca men became prominent during these years: Cornplanter, who was friendly to whites, and Red Jacket, who believed in separation from them. (A note about names: Iroquois custom is not to bestow names that describe personal traits. Cornplanter and Red Jacket are names that came from the whites.) Well-known for his attempt at protecting his people from fraud, Red Jacket became a professional council-speaker, lending his support to whatever council he happened to be representing. Because he appeared to be changing his views constantly, some of the Seneca grew upset. At one point, Chief Handsome Lake denounced Red Jacket.

On the reservations, the Seneca built crude log cabins roofed with bark and continued their traditional ways. Without the outlet of the old raiding parties, young men were underemployed and aimless. The fur trade continued, but each spring trading season culminated in drunken sprees and destructive behavior. The four pillars of Iroquois society—bodily and social health, peace, personal strength and civil authority, and truth and righteousness—were being destroyed.

Handsome Lake. The Seneca had a hard spring in 1799. There was much drunkenness; a man accused of being a sorcerer was murdered, and several women were suspected of witchcraft. Chief Handsome Lake lapsed into unconsciousness. Two hours later, he awoke and said he had been visited by three spirits who had warned him against drinking and witchcraft. Two months later, he announced he was going on a second, longer journey, and again became unconscious. When he awoke, he spoke of more visions. All of Handsome Lake's visions were gathered together to form the *Gaiwiio*, the Good Message, which grew into the Longhouse Religion. It laid down directions: avoid drink, witchcraft, and abortion, treat the aged kindly, and observe the Four Sacred Rituals. These rituals—Feather Dance, Thanksgiving Dance, Personal Chant, and Bowl Game—were part of traditional religion. He also reaffirmed the importance of corn festivals (Planting, Green Corn, and Harvest); the Midwinter (New Year's) festival; and the Thanks-to-the-Maple and Strawberry festivals (the Seneca believed that strawberries showed the path to heaven).

The Seneca believed also in a unifying force, *Orenda*, that could help or harm them. To win favor from the spirits (which lived in everything) they gave Thanksgiving. The world, it was thought, began with Earth Holder, *Tehaohwenjaiwahkonh*, and Great Mother, *Yagentji*. Legend has it that Great Mother, was thrust down to the world, where she had a daughter who died after bearing twin sons. Their mother was buried, and she gave rise to food; maize came from her chest, squash from her body, and beans and potatoes from her fingers and toes. One of her twins was good, the other bad. The exploits of the good twin became legendary.

The Seneca continued to hold these basic beliefs as the 1800s approached. At the same time, the Quakers befriended them, setting up Christian missions and schools. They educated Handsome Lake, whose visions had much in common with their teachings. In 1802, President Thomas Jefferson wrote a letter urging all Iroquois to follow the advice and precepts of Handsome Lake. This advanced the spread of the Good Message, which was adopted not only by Iroquois but also by other Indians. Seneca society changed. While Handsome Lake did not advocate learning to read and write, he did encourage families to hold land individually and men to engage in planting and harvesting. Handsome Lake died on the Tonawanda Reservation. Thereafter, it became the center of the Longhouse Religion.

Seneca Nation revolution. The first half of the 1800s was a momentous time for the Seneca. In 1838, the Ogden Land Company purchased four reservations from them. Valued at two million dollars, the land was sold for 200,000 dollars in an unfair transaction. Most Seneca opposed the treaty. A compromise was finally reached, but it called for them to forfeit the Tonawanda Reservation. Leaders here, John Blacksmith and Jimmy Johnson (grandson of Handsome Lake) began a 15-year struggle to hold onto the reservation.

Meanwhile, tenants of the Cattaraugus and Allegany reservations began a revolution of sorts. The federal government owed the Seneca money that it paid to chiefs, who, in turn, distributed it to Seneca families. Protesting this arrangement, family heads wanted the government to pay this money directly to them. So Allegany and Cattaraugus abolished government by chiefs. Instead, it elected an 18-member council, forming the Seneca Nation. Tonawanda Band and Seneca Nation became separate bodies, with Tonawanda gaining a reputation as the more traditional group.

The fight to keep the Tonawanda Reservation proved successful to a degree. With the money the government had set aside for their removal, the Seneca here were permitted to buy back 7,549 acres. They kept the old council of hereditary chiefs, refusing to switch to elected ones like the other reservations. Civil chiefs, in Seneca politics, passed on the privilege to their descendants. If a chief died, the women decided which descendant would succeed him. In the decades before the Civil War, the Tonawanda Seneca selected one of their young sachems, Ely S. Parker, to be educated by whites so that he could better represent their interests to the government. Parker, a descendant of Handsome Lake, became a civil engineer and then joined the army. He served on General Ulysses S. Grant's headquarters staff during the Civil War. Involved in ending the war, he drafted the terms of General Robert E. Lee's surrender at Appomattox. President Grant then appointed Parker head of the Bureau of Indian Affairs. He was the first Indian to hold the position.

The economy of the people changed during the 19th century from hunting and crop raising to plow agriculture and wage work. By the early 20th century, Seneca men were working as lumberjacks, on the railroads, and in construction. Women farmed and took jobs in nearby mills and small towns. After World War I, Arthur C. Parker, a descendant of Ely Parker, became New York's archaeologist. Parker worried that as the world encroached on the Seneca, there would be no record of their past. So he wrote *An Analytical History of the Seneca Indians,* one of the most complete accounts of his people. He developed a collection of their folktales.

Recent history. The Seneca, like many American Indians, were well-represented among the armed forces in World Wars I and II. This did not win them greater political power, however. Nor did it improve conditions on the reservations. Seneca behavior changed, both on and off the reservation. Inspired by the Civil Rights movement sweeping through America, Seneca extended the right to vote in elections to women in 1964; in 1966, women won the right to hold office.

Meanwhile, the U.S. government built a dam at Kinzua that spelled disaster for Seneca land. The dam flooded one-third of the Allegany Reservation, about 10,500 acres. A large reservoir formed behind the dam. In 1958, the Seneca Nation made an unsuccessful attempt to block the project in U.S. courts. The project proceeded, so they fought for compensation. Aided by the Quakers, the Seneca Nation won 15-million dollars in damages for lost lands and homes. One hundred families had been uprooted by the dam; part of the money was spent to relocate them. Using more of the funds, the Seneca constructed community buildings, equipped with gyms and stainless-steel kitchens. They built an industrial park at Cattaraugus, and began a fund for post high school education. The cost to them has been high, though. Not only was a third of their reservation transformed, but the flooded plain covers sacred sites, like Chief Complanter's grave.

Culture Today

Seneca Indians continue to live on reservations in western New York. A smaller number reside on reserves in Canada. In New York, the Tonawanda Reservation and the Seneca Nation (Allegany and Cattaraugus reservations) operate independently of each other. Reservation sizes vary from 7,549 acres (Tonawanda), to 21,680 acres (Cattaraugus), to 30,469 acres (Allegany). The three New York reservations remain the Seneca heartland.

The Tonawanda Reservation is considered the most traditional of the three New York sites. Even here, though, the people live mostly in frame houses. A few live in trailer homes or updated log structures. On the Allegany Reservation, the 100 families who were relocated due to the Kinzua Dam moved to new suburban settlements on the reservation: Jimersontown and Steamburg. Recently built houses appear here, complete with stainless steel kitchens. Seneca clothing styles resemble those of other New Yorkers, as does their daily diet. Some old food habits persist. In the new stainless steel kitchens, for example, individuals still prepare dishes such as hulled corn soup and corn bread. The old custom of ladling out food equally to everyone at ceremonies has continued in the late 20th century.

Religion. Traditional Seneca maintain the old ceremonies of the past, still holding Green Corn, Strawberry, Maple Sap, and the Midwinter (New Year's) celebrations. Each ceremony opens and closes with a Thanksgiving Speech, perpetuating the old orientation of gratefulness for the earth's bounty.

It was at strawberry time that the Seneca prophet Handsome Lake relayed his visions that led to the Longhouse Religion. There is a Longhouse on Seneca and other Iroquois reservations for the observance of Handsome Lake's teachings. Each fall the Tonawanda Longhouse invites members of the other Longhouses to Tonawada for a meeting. The gathering devotes a few mornings to reciting the Code of Handsome Lake and holds social dances in the evenings. Preachers of the Code recall Handsome Lake's vision and incidents in his life. His messages are repeated: abstain from alcohol, abortion, and witchcraft, and observe Iroquois religious ceremonies. There is also a description of punishments in the afterlife. The Longhouse Religion has fewer followers than in the past, but remains a vital part of reservation life. A set of white and purple wampum belts, made during Handsome Lake's life, contain signs telling the Good Message. They are kept at Tonawanda and studied by its Longhouse religious preachers.

Government. The Six Nations continue to operate as a confederacy. In the 1800s, they formed two separate councils, one in Canada and the other in the United States. These separate Six Nations councils remain in effect today. Among the Seneca reservations, there are two governments. The Tonawada Council includes chiefs elected by clan mothers, as in the past. Male voters elect Tonawanda's officials (a president, clerk, treasurer, marshal, and three peacemakers). The Seneca Nation Tribal Council governs on the Allegany and Cattaraugus reservations. It consists of 16 members elected by both males and females. Though the 19th Amendment gave American women the right to vote in 1920, Seneca Nation women could not vote for or hold tribal offices until the 1960s. Now men and women are eligible to serve on the 16-member council, which governs on the two reservations, and acts as agent for the Seneca Nation in dealings with the United States.

The Seneca Nation has continued to defend the rights of its people. In 1985, it used both the courts and a physical blockade in an attempt to stop the building of a highway across the Allegany Reservation. In the end, the courts overrode the protestors and allowed the construction. In 1990, the Seneca Nation again defended the rights of its people. This time it was over land leased by Allegany Reservation to the town of Salamanca on a 99-year basis. The Reservation also leases land to the towns Kill Buck, Vandalia, and Carrollton. Scheduled to expire in 1991, these leases were judged to be unfairly low priced. Some of them had been written for only one dollar a year. As time passed, white leaseholders did not acknowledge that the land rose in value and some did not pay their rent at all. Ultimately, the Seneca sued a leaseholder, which led to the writing of new leases with higher rents. The Indians have made it clear for the past 20 years that they intend to receive a fair price on any extensions or new leases to the towns. Now that they have made a peaceful, public presentation of their case, the leaseholders have entered into serious negotiations on renewal.

Economy. Like other Indian reservations, the Seneca suffer higher unemployment than the larger American population. They are described, however, as better off than other Indian groups. In 1969, for example, Seneca reservations reported 35 percent unemployment in contrast to over 50 percent for other tribes. Very few Seneca continued to make their living from farming by the 1970s. Today, the reservations employ some Seneca. Their economic opportunities are limited, however, so many take jobs off the reservations in nearby cities. Seneca businesses in Salamanca include a lumber mill and furniture plants. Like other Iroquois, some Seneca work in high steel construction, though the Mohawk are most noted in this field. A profitable business on reservations has been the bingo hall. The Allegany and Cattaraugus reservations operate one, as do other Iroquois and other Indian nations. The Oneida, for example, are an Iroquois group whose bingo hall opened in 1985 and earned over five million dollars in its first year.

Education and recreation. Children of the Seneca Nation attend schools in nearby towns. In 1980, the average educational level was 11th grade. The average education of adults on the Tonawanda Reservation was eighth grade in 1980. Children here also attend nearby public schools. In the past, education was regarded as a game. Games, in general, were regarded as part of the religion, pleasing to the Great Spirit above. Lacrosse is a game that resembles field hockey and originated with the Iroquois Indians. It is described as the oldest team sport in North America that survives today. Making the lacrosse sticks has developed into a small industry for the Indians in Canada, and Iroquois players have formed a team (the Iroquois Nationals) that competes internationally. To play the game, two teams use long-handled, pouched rackets to advance the ball into the opposing team's net. In 1990, the Iroquois Nation was finally allowed to compete in the World Federation Lacrosse Games, along with Team England, Team Canada, and Team U.S.A. They entered as a separate nation.

Among the Iroquois, the Seneca are especially reputed for their skill as runners. In the past, they covered great distances over forested trails in record time. Deerfoot was an acclaimed Seneca runner at the turn of the 20th century.

Societies. Iroquois medicine societies have survived to the present day. Most popular is the False Face Society, whose members wear wooden masks that represent forest spirits (or spirits envisioned in dreams). The False Face Society visits Iroquois houses to cleanse them of disease. Members dip their hands in hot ashes, then blow through them and rub them on a patient as a cure. Other groups are the Husk Face Society and Little Water Society. Wearing braided corn-husk masks, the Husk Faces represent agricultural, not forest, spirits. The Little Water Society makes medicine from animal parts. Such groups each practice their own set of songs and rituals.

Most masks made by the Iroquois are toothless. They have tin eye plates and horse hair. A classic Seneca mask has a hanging mouth and spinelike lines carved into the forehead. Generally, it is desirable for all members of the tribe to own a mask to ward off evil. There are several types of masks, all of which have characteristic expressions and forms. In earlier times, the False Faces carved their grotesque masks from living tree trunks to lure forest spirits into houses.

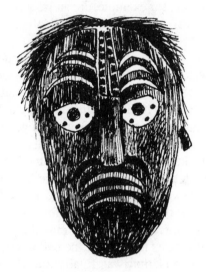

A Seneca mask.

Arts. Today's Seneca still perform traditional dances. The Dark Dance occurs at the Midwinter or New Year's ceremony. This dance takes place in private homes. A series of choral and solo movements on a religious subject, the dance is performed in the dark. The dance begins with an invocation, and the Little People (mythical Pygmies who "live" on the reservation) are supposed to enter in the dark. Later parts of the ritual include a charm-holder's ceremony and a time when everyone tastes strawberry syrup from a saucepan. The Seneca have a collection of other dances for objects and events, from war to snow to strawberries and corn. Among individuals, G. Peter Jemison has won acclaim as a graphic artist. He has illustrated *The Iroquois and the Founding of the American Nation*, a book by Donald Grinde. Jemison has also served in organizations dedicated to perpetuating Indian art, such as the Buffalo North American Indian Culture Center, the Seneca Nation Organization for the Visual Arts, and the Gallery of American Indian Community House.

For More Information

See these reading materials:

Arden, Harvey. "The Fire That Never Dies." *National Geographic*, September 1987, pp. 375–403.

Wallace, Anthony F.C. *The Death and Rebirth of the Seneca.* New York: Alfred A. Knopf, 1970.

Contact this organization:

Seneca Nation Museum, P.O. Box 442, Broad Street Extension, Salamanca, NY 14779.

TLINGIT
(tling´ kit)

An Indian people of the Northwest, known as shrewd traders and skilled artisans; a "totem pole" people.

Population: 8,700 (1985).
Location: United States (southeast Alaska); Canada (British Columbia, Yukon Territory).
Language: English, Tlingit.

Geographical Setting

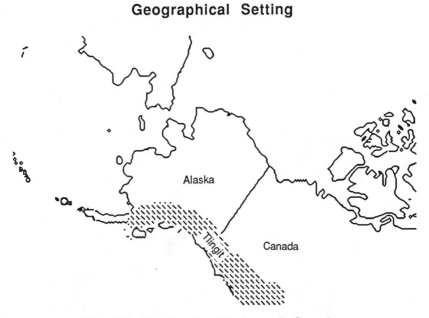

The Tlingits live in Alaska and Canada.

The term *Tlingit* refers to over a dozen Indian groups who speak the same language and share a general location. The ancestors of the Tlingit are thought to have moved from Siberia to Alaska 9,000 or more years ago. Over time, other groups joined them, so by the mid-1700s three native groups lived in the region: Indians, Aleuts, and Inuit (Eskimos). Among Indians of the Northwest coastal region, the Tlingit were the most numerous. It is believed they first lived on islands and the coastal mainland by the Pacific Ocean from Yakutat Bay southward to the present-day city Ketchikan. Later, some Tlingit moved inland. They moved to trap animals for the fur trade in the late 1700s, then to capitalize on gold rushes in the Klondike region during the late 1800s. Both inland and coastal Tlingit exist in the present day.

Much of the Tlingit territory is forested. Spread over 15 million acres, Tongass National Forest now covers three-fourths of southeast Alaska. It is rainforest, rich in animal and plant life, the natural habitat of deer, cedar trees, and spruce trees. Running through the region is a cordillera, a mountain chain, with peaks rising to 8,000 feet. The early Tlingit hunted mountain goats and sheep in the cordillera. Freshwater fish filled their rivers and sea life (seal, sea otter, whale) abounded in the Pacific Ocean, near which most of the bands lived. Nearby lived other Indian peoples, the Haida and Tsimshian. All three groups shaped early lifestyles that depended greatly on the natural abundance of their coastal rainforest.

Historical Background

The largest of the Northwest Coast Indian groups, the Tlingit actually consisted of 13 bands. Each band had its own area and name, and lived independently of the others. Among them were the Chilkat, Sitka, Yakutat, and Tahltan. By the 1720s they had organized into 13 local areas called *kwans* with from one to six villages in each kwan. Tlingit in a given area spoke their own version of the language and practiced their own variation of the customs. Yet the various bands shared some basic survival and social habits.

Food, clothing, and shelter. The Tlingit moved around in pursuit of salmon runs or fur-trade animals, gathering for winter interludes in settlements near supplies of stored fish. Food changed with the area, but there was a rich supply of it. The Tlingit chose salmon as their staple. Men also harpooned sea mammals—seal and sea otter; women gathered clams and berries. For meat, Tlingit hunters snared moose, caribou, snowshoe rabbit, or mountain goats and sheep. Animal skins, wool and furs, provided material for warm clothing.

Interior of an old Tlingit home.

In the north, men and women wore goat's-wool trousers with moccasins attached. Their tops consisted of tailored shirts and deerskin overshirts. In harsh weather separate hoods and fur robes were added. Southern Tlingit wore shredded-bark shirts and robes. When summer arrived, some of the men switched to breechcloths; women wore plant-fiber skirts. At puberty, a girl began wearing a lip ornament. Men pierced their noses and painted their faces. If they were nobles, they wore body tattoos; the designs were their own and could not be used by anyone else.

The coastal Tlingit built great rectangular houses. Made from red cedar wood, each structure measured about 30 by 40 feet. The structure gave off an aura of impressive vastness. It had a gabled roof, no windows, and a low doorway. A dozen or more families lived inside, occupying semiprivate spaces, bounded by mats that hung from rafters. Sleeping platforms ran along the walls, and a sweat bath sat in one corner. The head of a household, who was called the *yitsati*, and high-ranking families lived at the rear. Low-ranking families lived by the door, which faced the sea. A coastal village might have 12 such houses lined up in a row. In front of them sat smokehouses for preserving meats and fish. Farther off were storage caches and birthing structures. Housing differed among the Inland Tlingit. They typically occupied a brush lean-to, which housed two to four families.

Social structure. Tlingit society was organized into two major divisions or moieties: *raven* and *wolf*. Each division contained several clans, and each clan had several house groups. The clan was most significant among all these categories. It had a name, an insignia, and a leader. Children belonged to the clan of their mother, but the family lived in the father's house. At age ten, a son would move into his mother's old house to join the family of his ancestors. Thereafter, the boy was raised by an uncle.

The Tlingit arranged their society into social classes of nobles, commoners, and slaves. Most of the people were commoners. There were also artisans, who would exchange the various items they crafted for food, clothing, and shelter.

Potlatch. Basic to a person's status was ownership. Besides slaves and material goods, the Tlingit owned intangible items—names, stories, crests, and so on. On the surface, the group seemed preoccupied with acquiring riches. They actually amassed wealth to boost their status by giving it away. Gift-giving, like feasting and dancing, occurred at the *potlatch*, a festive celebration that would last for days.

Sometimes a potlatch celebrated a marriage or a young girl's passage into womanhood. Most often it was a memorial for the dead. The Tlingit cremated the dead, then kept the ashes for perhaps a year while the lineage collected enough wealth to host a potlatch. Since they bestowed gifts on all the guests to whom they were indebted, the cost was enormous. Hosts would elevate their status according to the quantity of goods they distributed or destroyed. The more possessions that were shed, the greater the prestige. Later, when the Russians appeared, the nature of the gifts changed. Hosts turned to blankets and money as the main items to give away.

Trade. In contrast to other natives, the Tlingit showed economic foresight. They collected surplus foods, then preserved them for consumption during the four to ten weeks of winter scarcity. Tlingit traders were sharp middlemen, trading all types of goods from boats to baskets to guns. In concluding bargains, the Tlingit proved to be quite shrewd. They would exchange a pile of furs for a gun at the Hudson's Bay Company, then trade that same gun to the Athabaskan Indians for twice as many furs. More numerous on the coast, the Tlingit monopolized trade both there and with the various peoples farther inland. Some of the traders blazed the Chilkat Trail from the coast through the mountains to the interior. It was a treacherous 32-mile route, called the "grease trail" because Tlingit traders dragged eulachon oil over it. Inland, they exchanged the oil to Athabaskan Indians for moose and caribou skins. Later, this well-worn Trail saw the hopeful footsteps of Alaskan gold rushers.

Conflict with Russians. The Tlingit bands fought one another to control sources of fine furs and items for trade. As quarrels escalated, they led to the splitting of family lineages and contradictory claims to insignias, or crests. Feuds over trade, crests, or a woman created war, ended by the payment of a blood price or an elaborate peace ceremony.

The Tlingit feuded with outsiders too. Reputedly, they were a violent people. It is said, however, that they behaved violently not of their own accord but in reaction to others. The actions of the Russians inspired wrath and hostility. Vitus Bering claimed Alaska for Russia in 1741, and the Tlingit killed several of his men. For several decades the Tlingit lived undisturbed. Alexander Baranov brought Russians and Aleuts into the area in the 1790s. The first major conflict occurred at Yschugat Bay, costing the lives of 12 Tlingit, 2 Russians, and 9 Aleuts. The Russians built a fort near Sitka in 1799. In 1802 the Tlingit attacked, killing 20 Russians and 130 Aleuts, and stealing 4,000 sea otter pelts. In 1804, Baranov bombarded Sitka's Tlingit with cannonfire. Led by Chief Ktalean, they fought valiantly but lost.

Farther north, at Yakutat, they experienced more success. Chief Theodore led an attack on the fort here in 1805. So vicious was the fighting that the Russians abandoned this fort and moved farther north. They were accused of robbing Tlingit graves, failing to pay for land, closing streams, abusing women, and taking children away to educate them but actually enslaving them. The Russians dreaded Tlingit raids. They tried winning the Indians over with gifts, and they tried conquering them. Neither tactic worked.

From 1834 to 1854, tensions eased. Ivan Veniaminov, who befriended other natives (see ALEUTS), appeared among the Tlingit to convert them to the Russian Orthodox religion. He learned their language and won their trust. Veniaminov saved many of the Tlingit during a smallpox epidemic. In fact, he considered 1835 a pivotal year in Tlingit history. Having exhausted their own remedies, the *Koloshi* (his name for Tlingit) asked the physician at Sitka to inoculate them against the deadly disease. This was the beginning of their enlightenment, Veniaminov said. The Tlingit impressed him as an enterprising people. Their excellence in trade, he felt, could make them the dominant group in North America, from Bering Strait to the California Sound and beyond. He noted the shrewd methods they employed in their transactions (Veniaminov 1984, p. 429):

When the Koloshi sell their goods, they do not deliver these to
the seller immediately, but wait, learn the situation and
bargain to the limit of possibility and even when they surrender
an item (an important one) for the price agreed upon, they always
ask for an additional cut...

Arguing that the Tlingit had high intellect, Veniaminov pointed to the
splendid array of products they made, from magnificent canoes to helmets
carved in the shape of a fierce human face. Also, he reasoned, they were apt
students. He had witnessed one boy learn Russian in under five months.
After Veniaminov's arrival, relations became more harmonious. The Tlingit
helped the Russians load ice blocks on ships to meet the demand for ice
created by the 1849 California gold rush. Veniaminov left in 1854. That
same year, tensions resumed. Some Tlingit destroyed a Hudson's Bay
Company post, saying it infringed on their territory. In 1855, Russia sent
100 more soldiers to Sitka, which prompted another Tlingit attack.

Americanization. Russia sold Alaska to the United States in 1867,
partly, it is said, because of the unruly Tlingit. From canoes, they watched
the ceremonial transfer of power. Life thereafter changed radically for the
Tlingit. First came the late 19th century gold rushes. Alert to the money to be
made from the miners, the Tlingit hired out their canoes to haul freight. In
1896, the Klondike Gold Rush drew over 40,000 miners to Yukon Territory
near the Inland Tlingit. With the miners came diseases, alcohol, and
opportunities for wage labor. The Tlingit began to rely on cash earnings
rather than hunting, fishing, and trading. Some became prospectors
themselves; other Tlingit took jobs on steamboats or sold their meat and fish
to outsiders.

Just as the Tlingit had fought to protect themselves from Russia, they
defended themselves under U.S. control. In 1912 they founded the Alaska
Native Brotherhood, organizing to protect their rights and better adapt to
American life. There followed a series of successes. The Tlingit won the
right to vote in 1924, along with other American Indians. In 1926, they
elected a Tlingit, William Paull, to Alaska's legislature. They won the right
to file mine claims in 1931.

Their lifestyle changed dramatically after the building of the Alaska
Highway. It was constructed in 1942 as a World War II supply road across
parts of Canada and central Alaska. With the highway came a continuing
stream of new influences into what had been an untouched hunting and
fishing region. Meanwhile the Indians struggled over their rights to land.
They formed the Haida-Tlingit Land Claims Council in 1953. As the years

passed, the controversy continued until it was resolved by the Alaska Native Claims Settlement Act of 1971. The act established 13 regional corporations to administer the settlement. Natives became stockholders. The Tlingit, along with Haida and Tsimshian Indians, received stock in the Sealaska Corporation. In the 1980s, it ran many businesses in southeast Alaska, from fish canneries to construction companies. The net worth of the corporation had reached 500 million dollars by then. Its stock was scheduled to be sold to the public beginning in 1991.

Culture Today

Tlingit villages. The Tlingit have four officially recognized native villages on islands of Southeast Alaska. Only about a sixth of the people live in these villages. The village Hoonah, for example, counted 704 Indian residents in 1969. Government there consists of a mayor and a council. The community has a seafood and a cold storage industry and a few small businesses: a hotel, a theater, and a restaurant. Families there have earned low income and experienced high unemployment. In 1969, over three-fourths did not have jobs.

Employment. The Sealaska Corporation provides about 1,000 jobs, a sizeable number, but hardly enough for everyone in the region. Many Tlingit now rely on cash wages or welfare. At first, gold mines, salmon canneries, and boat loading employed a number of the Tlingit in low-paying positions. Others could find no work. Then government land grants relocated them to forested areas with a logging economy. Their village corporations took out loans to set up logging businesses. Years later, the corporations found themselves heavily in debt. The environment suffered. Forests were devastated to get as much money as possible, and land was resold to the government so that the loans could be repaid.

Some of Canada's Tlingit have worked in railway or highway construction. As in Alaska, they rely partly on the old survival techniques, hunting and fishing. Today's Canadian Tlingit fish and trap to supplement their diet. A few hundred American Tlingit, who live on Admiralty Island, aim to sustain themselves by hunting and fishing as in the past.

Women. Women had considerable status in traditional Tlingit life. Society was *matrilineal*. In other words, children belonged to their mother's, not their father's, clan. Also, women became active in trade. An experienced older woman kept track of prices when selling furs to outsiders such as the Hudson's Bay Company. In Sitka, Tlingit women brought raspberries and halibut fillets to town for sale. They became hired laborers in the vegetable gardens there, too.

Home of a 20th century Tlingit chief.

Family life. The Tlingit's great rectangular houses have been replaced by single family dwellings and apartments. Family customs have changed in the process. Boys, for example, are no longer raised by their maternal uncles. Originally, adolescents received special treatment at puberty. Young males lived together and avoided direct speech or eye contact with sisters. At puberty, a girl retreated to a special hut. She remained secluded for several months, after which a potlatch might be given for the marriageable young woman. Marriage occurred as follows. A boy sent a middleman to a girl's relatives. After they and she consented, the couple engaged in a four-day fast for happiness, broken briefly at midpoint. A month passed before a couple became intimate. Given this traditional waiting period, the Russian custom of immediate intimacy after marriage seemed ridiculous to the Tlingit at first.

A son-in-law would provide for his wife's parents until their death. As the Tlingit aged, they commanded great respect. This attitude was prompted by the belief that older people had a closer connection to the superhuman world.

Religion and education. By 1950, many Tlingit had adopted white ideas of moral behavior and had become Christians. They first adopted the Russian Orthodox faith. With whites during the gold rushes came missionaries from various denominations. Anglican, Roman Catholic, Presbyterian, and Baptist churches began to convert the Tlingit to Christian faiths. In their old community at Sitka, there is a Russian Orthodox Cathedral with a mostly Tlingit congregation today.

Originally, the Tlingit believed in the Supreme Being *Yeíl*, or Raven. Yeíl, it was thought, had created the world. Though fond of human beings, he would punish them from his home deep in the interior of the continent if he was angered. Yeíl had a son who often saved human beings from his father's wrath. The Tlingit also had shamans in their villages, religious leaders who communed with spirits on the villagers' behalf. The Tlingit called on their shamans to heal the sick, control food supplies, or detect hidden enemies in wartime.

Historically, the Tlingit welcomed schools. They were eager to learn the language of white traders, attracted by their goods and their practice of distilling alcohol. At first, the religious groups tackled Tlingit education. The Presbyterians set up schools in 1877. Appearing around 1900, the Roman Catholic or Baptist boarding school appealed to only a minority of the Inland Tlingit. The Bureau of Indian Affairs finally opened a high school for them in the 1960s.

Language and storytelling. By the 1960s, most Tlingit spoke English. They dressed and lived much like their white neighbors. Then came a revival of traditions and a drive for increased civil rights. Once encouraging wholehearted adoption of American ways, the Alaska Native Brotherhood reversed its policy. It became an ardent supporter of customs such as potlatch (see above). Still held in the late 20th century, potlatches have given rise to a resurgence of pride, participants wearing customary garb and painting their faces to indicate clan affiliation.

Despite this revival of tradition, linguists predict the extinction of the Tlingit language within the next 50 years. Parents bemoan the fact that children no longer learn the language. Still, other aspects of their heritage are likely to endure. One of the most cherished is the Tlingit story. Oral storytelling was an art of the early Tlingit. Recounting family histories and legends, an official orator would perform at a potlatch ceremony. The importance of ownership in Tlingit society has already been explained. In fact, certain tales were inherited. Stories were owned, too.

One Tlingit tale features the hero *Kaax´achgóok*, who, like the Greek hero Odysseus, voyaged far from home, coming back to confront changes that occurred during his absence. Another myth ,about Mother Bear, explains a taboo against hunting or eating bears, who were regarded as ancestors. There was a strong belief in transformation, the idea that a whale could be itself, then a bear, then itself again. In keeping with this belief, humans could assume animal form.

Singularly well-known are the tales of *Yeíl*, or Raven, the Supreme Being. A trickster, he supposedly stole the sun and gave it to the Tlingit. Before Yeíl, there was only darkness. A man of this time had a sister with several sons. Suspicious that his own wife was unfaithful and the sons were actually hers, he jealously destroyed them. His sister was grief-stricken. She was losing her sons, one by one. A killer whale counseled her to swallow an ocean pebble, after which she bore Yeíl. His uncle tried to destroy him, but Yeíl always escaped, his adventures becoming Tlingit tales.

Arts—totem poles. Most widely associated with Indians of the Northwest Coast are totem poles. In Tlingit society, the ten-foot poles were mostly memorials in honor of the dead. On a pole was the insignia of the man who paid for the work. He hired members of the opposite moiety to create the totems, or symbolic figures, on the pole. The figures might represent adventures of the man's ancestors with mythological beings. If a pole stood before a house, its bottom figure had an open mouth that served as the doorway. Most Tlingit poles, however, were freestanding structures placed at a clan's grave site. Today they stand mainly in parks and museums.

Aside from totem poles, the Tlingit excelled in the crafting of items such as masks, baskets, and blankets. Carved from wood, masks were used to make spirits visible. The masks had moveable features, such as blinking eyes, opening mouths, and protruding tongues. Women crafted the baskets from spruce root grass. The most popular, the berry basket, flares sightly on top. Outstanding among covers is the Chilkat blanket. While the Tlingit were not the only Indians to weave it, they became its most frequent producer. The blanket was made from cedar bark string and mountain goat hair and had designs in black, yellow, blue-green, and white. These were painstaking copies of painted designs, abstract renderings of crest animals, such as ravens or diving whales. Traded by the Hudson's Bay Company were navy blue blankets, which the Tlingit used to create the button blanket. They added red borders and crest animals to these blankets, then outlined both with iridescent buttons. On one such blanket, three salmon swim across the navy blue, sealike background.

Heroes. Early Tlingit fought valiantly to hold on to their territory and customs. More recently, individual men and women have championed the Tlingit cause under American rule. For example, Susie James (1890-1980) raised her family in Sitka, working in its fish canneries. During the American Depression, her husband fished and she sold handmade dolls and beadwork to help support the family. For over 50 years, Susie served as a midwife, delivering babies in fish canneries and camps. President Harry Truman bestowed an award on this Tlingit for her work. To protect Indian rights, Susie joined the Alaska Native Sisterhood. Frank Johnson (1894-1982) worked in a box factory for five cents an hour as a young boy. In 1927, he completed his university education and became active in the Alaska Native Brotherhood. Frank fished and taught school, educating students about Tlingit traditions. He helped establish labor unions for cannery workers and lobbied for the Alaska Native Claims Settlement Act of 1971.

As a group, the several hundred Tlingit on Admiralty Island in Alaska are heroes, too. Their aim is to maintain a cashless economy, hunting and fishing for survival. To this end, they battle timber companies for the island's resources. They occupy a traditional village there called Angoon. Its residents are nameless champions of the old Tlingit ways.

For More Information

See these reading materials:

Antonson, Joan M. and Hanable, William S. *Alaska's Heritage.* Anchorage: Alaska Historical Commission, 1985.

Holm, Bill. *The Box of Daylight: Northwest Coast Indian Art.* Seattle: Seattle Art Museum, 1984.

Contact these organizations:

Tlingit and Haida Central Council, One Sealaska Plaza 200, Juneau, Alaska 99801.

Sealaska Corporation, One Sealaska Plaza Suite 400, Juneau, Alaska 99801.

Vietnamese Americans
(vee et nah mez eh mer´ uh kins)

Americans whose ancestors were born in Vietnam.

Population: 530,000 (1987).
Location: United States (mainly California and Texas).
Language: English, Vietnamese.

Geographical Setting

Many Vietnamese Americans have become workers
and shop owners in Southern California. A few
have settled in Texas to continue life as fishermen.

Vietnam is a long, slender country in Southeast Asia, lying along the eastern edge of the Indochinese peninsula. Situated between India and China, this peninsula also includes Laos and Cambodia. It was named Indochina because of India's and China's influences on the region's culture.

Today Vietnam is one country, but from 1954 to 1975 it was divided into North Vietnam and South Vietnam. Immigrants came from both South and North Vietnam. About one quarter (130,000) of the Vietnamese in America arrived in 1975, after the fall of Saigon in the Vietnam War. (Previously, only about 20,000 had immigrated to America, mostly wives and children of American servicemen stationed in Vietnam.) While the refugees departed from South Vietnam, some were North Vietnamese who had fled to the South.

The refugees were "processed" by four military installations that served as temporary resettlement camps: Camp Pendleton, California; Fort Chaffee, Arkansas; Fort Indiantown Gap, Pennsylvania; and Eglin Air Force Base, Florida. Initially, areas close to the resettlement camps had large Vietnamese populations, but over time scattered communities of Vietnamese appeared around the country. In Wichita, Kansas, for example, a meatpacking plant sponsored 42 Vietnamese immigrants, starting the community that grew there. A few years after their arrival, many who had settled in rural areas moved again. Favoring warm climates, they swelled Vietnamese communities in California and Texas, where later immigrants tended to join them. California now has the largest Vietnamese population, centered in Los Angeles and Orange counties.

Historical Background

Early Vietnamese history. Northern Vietnam shares a border with China. In its early history the small country was dominated by China, winning independence in 939 A.D. and successfully repelling later invasions by the Chinese. Independence from China did not preclude a strong Chinese cultural influence, however, transmitted mostly by the many Chinese immigrants who dominated Vietnamese commerce. Gradually, highly successful French missionaries gained a foothold in Vietnam that led to French trade with the Vietnamese. French influence solidified after 1777, when a French Bishop, Pigneau de Béhaine, saved the life of a Vietnamese king's nephew during a peasant revolt.

French and American involvement. In 1883, under pressure from the French church, France invaded and conquered Vietnam. A treaty was signed, making the country a French colony.

French rule, which continued until World War II, inspired widespread resentment among the Vietnamese. In 1925, the charismatic leader Ho Chi Minh created the most important of many resistance groups, the Revolutionary Youth Movement, which in 1930 became the Vietnamese Communist Party. The French repressed such groups, whose leaders went underground to direct guerrilla campaigns. The Japanese took control of

Vietnam in 1945, and their defeat soon after left a power vacuum that Ho Chi Minh and his well-organized followers were able to fill. From their base in the north, they fought French efforts to regain control of the lost colony.

The United States had backed France's reinvasion of Vietnam against Ho's Communist Party. At the Geneva Conference of 1954, the United Nations scheduled free elections for 1956, but the United States refused to support them. Instead, America backed the unpopular right-wing nationalist Ngo Dinh Diem, who proposed a separate republic of South Vietnam, of which he would be prime minister. His proposal took effect, and the fighting continued. United States involvement in the conflict between North and South Vietnam escalated from the supplying 800 military advisors and 270 million dollars to South Vietnam in 1956, to the introduction of American troops and heavy bombing in 1965, to the final withdrawal of those troops in 1975. They left behind perhaps six million peasants who were homeless and without a livelihood after all the years of death and destruction.

The first-wave refugees. Without American military support, the government of South Vietnam quickly crumbled. As northern troops advanced toward the southern capital of Saigon in 1975, the United States planned to evacuate and resettle Vietnamese who had supported its policies. In the chaotic spring and summer months, refugees poured into America from Vietnam, and more came from the other Indochinese nations of Cambodia and Laos, which had also suffered intensive American bombing. On April 18, 1975, President Ford established the Interagency Task Force for Indochinese Refugees (I.A.T.F.) to oversee resettlement. Saigon fell on April 30. By that time, the I.A.T.F. had arranged for temporary camps in Guam, the Philippines, Wake Island, Thailand, and Hawaii. From these camps, the I.A.T.F. quickly moved the refugees to the four resettlement centers in the United States (see above, Geographical Setting).

Refugee camps. At the camps, the refugees prepared for American life. They saw American movies and took classes in the English language and in how to find jobs and homes. At Camp Pendleton, in California, the average refugee spent four hours a day studying English. Most of the refugees already had some exposure to American ways, and many of them resisted this forced Americanization. It taught values contrary to their own. For example, classes for children stressed individualism and self-assertiveness as "American" ways of behaving, whereas the Vietnamese stress submission to the wishes of parents. Some parents wanted to exclude their children from such classes. The refugees lived in wood-frame tents or barracks, broken up into cubicles that held about 15 people each. There was little privacy. Outside the cubicle, a refugee stood in line for hours each day, waiting to be interviewed or fed. The Red Cross and other organizations taught classes in child care and helped with college placement. For recreation, the refugees played volleyball or Ping-Pong, watched movies and television, and read newspapers whose articles explained camp operation and different aspects of life in America.

Resettlement. When they closed in December 1975, the camps had processed 130,000 Indochinese refugees. Over 95 percent were Vietnamese. About 8,000 of them had 4,000 dollars per family member, which was considered sufficient for financial security. In order to keep the remainder off welfare, sponsors were found for them by nine private social service agencies (including the Church World Service, the Tolstoy Foundation, and the Hebrew Immigrant Aid Society). Sponsors agreed to provide food, clothing, and shelter until the family could support itself. They were also to provide assistance in finding work, getting children enrolled in school, and further adjustment to American life. Since the financial cost of sponsorship was around 5,000 dollars per Indochinese family, most sponsors were groups rather than individual families. (A valuable record of one American family's sponsorship, however, has been left by Ellen Matthews, in her 1982 book *Culture Clash.*) Government officials tried to disperse the refugees widely so as to minimize economic and social friction in American communities. Accordingly, over half were sent to states in which their total numbers would be under 3,000.

In contrast with those who came later, most of the first wave were members of Vietnam's educated elite. They consisted of professionals and their families. Many had served in the South Vietnamese military or government. Others, having belonged to the wealthier classes in the north, had fled south in the early 1950s and had to flee once again when the Communists came to power there as well. Only about five percent were peasants or fisherman. Over 80 percent were under 35 years old.

Secondary migration. By 1980, perhaps half of the first wave had moved from the towns in which they had first been settled. Most migrated south and west, to warmer areas that more closely approached the tropical climate of Vietnam. Vietnamese communities, which had not existed when the first wave immigrated, drew many to urban areas, especially in California, the most popular secondary destination.

Another motive for secondary migration was to reunite families. As a rule, sponsors tended to limit sponsorship to families of five to seven members. Yet Vietnamese families often spanned three or four generations, containing 15 to 20 or more members. Sponsorship broke many a family into smaller groups, which were resettled in areas distant from one another. Once the refugees had a footing in American society, strong Vietnamese family ties began to reassert themselves.

Second wave: the "Boat People." Emigration from Vietnam slowed in the first few years after the fall of Saigon, with perhaps 20,000 arriving each year. Beginning in 1978, however, fresh political turbulence and natural disasters forced hundreds of thousands to flee their homes in Indochina. Many of them moved first to refugee camps in Thailand, next to U.S. holding centers in the Philippines, Guam, or Thailand, and last to the United States.

Included with the waves of Vietnamese were refugees from Cambodia and Laos. They formed a sizeable portion of the second wave. Altogether about 277,000 refugees from Cambodia and Laos would immigrate to America from 1975 to 1985, as opposed to 482,000 from Vietnam proper. Few Cambodians and Laotians had come in the first wave. It was during this second wave that their numbers escalated. In Cambodia, the overthrow of the brutal Pol Pot regime by a Vietnamese-backed Communist government, along with ongoing famine, caused hundreds of thousands to leave by 1980. Over 150,000 Cambodians were crowded into refugee camps along the Cambodian border with Thailand. In Laos, the policies of the Vietnamese-backed Communist government prompted large groups from the merchant and professional classes to flee. They joined many thousands of Laotian peasants in the Thai camps.

In Vietnam, too, famine and politics drove many to seek refuge elsewhere. The Vietnamese government nationalized private trade in 1978 and took steps to expel its substantial ethnic Chinese minority, which had traditionally made up most of Vietnam's merchant class. Over 160,000 Vietnamese of Chinese descent fled northward into China. In the same year, bad weather led to severe food shortages and general economic hardship. Cambodia and Laos were landlocked, but Vietnam was not. Therefore, many Vietnamese fled from their homeland in small, crowded fishing boats, unseaworthy craft not designed for the open ocean. By November, perhaps 100,000 had survived the perilous trip to Thailand, Malaysia, Hong Kong, or Singapore. According to most estimates, at least as many perished at sea, drowning when their overcrowded boats collapsed or encountering Thai pirates who murdered them. (Many who died met their end after being pushed back to sea because they were unwelcome at their destinations.) The survivors who reached Thailand entered the refugee camps, then moved to the holding centers and finally to the United States. Despite the danger,

Vietnamese left in even larger numbers in 1979. By 1982, around 180,000 of these Vietnamese refugees had been resettled in the United States. Smaller numbers were taken by France, Australia, and Canada.

Culture Today

Ethnic composition. Still in its infancy, Vietnamese American society continues to receive newcomers. The second wave began to slow in 1983. Since then around 25,000 Vietnamese have come each year. Many of the immigrants are young. Some 50 percent of the Vietnamese population in the United States in 1989 was under 19 years of age. Among the earlier immigrants were former officials. Like the first wave, the second contained one-time South Vietnamese military and government officers, most of whom had spent up to two years or more in Communist-run "reeducation centers." These were harsh and squalid camps whose inmates underwent both punishment and indoctrination. In contrast to the first wave, the second also held many peasants and fishermen, whose livelihoods were upset either by the war or by the victorious Communists. In 1977, the Communists began forcing people in Vietnam to relocate to unfamiliar and inhospitable areas. Many fishermen were moved to inland areas where land had been ravaged by wartime defoliation (poisoning of plant life). They would have found farming difficult under the best of conditions and were unable to eke out a living from the barren land. In America, many of the immigrant farmers and fishermen have engaged in their old occupations, each group encountering a different set of challenges. Small-scale farming and fishing have also attracted novices, Vietnamese who are unable to find work in their former occupations.

The fishermen. With its long coastline, Vietnam has always had a large fishing population. Vietnamese immigrants naturally turned to the sea for work in their strange new environment. However, they were unaware of American fishing practices and therefore ignored them, which resulted in much-publicized friction with the established fishing community. Such controversy has been the biggest obstacle for Vietnamese fishermen, who painstakingly struggled through detailed paperwork only to meet these unforseen difficulties. In Seadrift, Texas, for example, Vietnamese joined the important local industry of pot-fishing for crabs without knowledge of informal "territories"—agreed-upon areas in which different local fisherman had special rights recognized by all (except for the Vietnamese). Vietnamese in Monterey, California, had fewer initial problems, mostly because they signed on to crew the boats of established fishermen before running their own, thus gaining exposure to local ways. Established fishermen have also taken exception to what they perceived as careless boat handling and maintenance. In general, Vietnamese fishing style tended, at least initially, to be less technological than that of the Americans. The Vietnamese, for example, employed tools not considered "nautical" by locals, such as rocks instead of specially designed anchors. Intergroup tensions largely receded as language became less of a barrier and as increased prosperity and familiarity allowed Vietnamese to conform more closely to local practices. Now Vietnamese are an integral part of fishing communities in the Northeast, on the Gulf Coast, and in California.

Growers. Small-scale farming and selling of vegetables has been a less troublesome source of income for many Vietnamese. First-wave refugees began growing vegetables to supplement their incomes while in sponsorship situations, and continued to do so after joining urban Vietnamese communities, such as those in California. They have grown cucumbers, squash, carrots, radishes, onions, garlic, and corn for sale in farmers' markets. The whole family participates in such enterprises, which continue to provide a valuable supplement to the minimum wage that many refugees have been forced to accept. Often, the sideline has become a stepping-stone to owning a small market or a food distribution business.

Food, clothing, and shelter. Vietnamese have had difficulty adjusting to the American diet, with its emphasis on red meat and dairy products, which they tend to avoid. Instead, they eat mostly rice, fish, and vegetables, using chopsticks, or *duas*, and a large bowl. They flavor their rice dishes with *nuac cham*, a spicy fish sauce made from anchovies, salt, garlic, chili pepper, lemon juice, water, and sugar. Fish is, of course, popular, and pork and chicken are the preferred meats. For dessert, the Vietnamese favor fruit (bananas, mangoes, papayas, oranges, coconuts, and pineapples) rather than sweets, reserving the latter for special occasions. Before and after a meal they drink tea, often steeped with dried flowers such as jasmine, roses, or chrysanthemums.

In the hot, tropical climate of Vietnam, the people commonly wore light cotton clothes with conical straw hats for protection from the sun. Women dressed in dark pants and short white jackets, taking care to cover their legs, arms, and necks. On formal occasions they donned *ao dai*, delicate silk dresses with intricate print and slits. High-necked and long-sleeved, the *ao dai* are worn with loose silk pants. In America, Vietnamese have abandoned their old dress styles. The changes in clothing have been especially dramatic in the North, where the heat-conditioned Vietnamese have grown accustomed to wearing heavy coats and thick wool caps.

Vietnamese immigrants adopt Western-style dress even before coming to America.

While still being sponsored, many refugees lived in small apartments or houses rented to them by sponsoring organizations. The refugees paid a nominal rent of 50 or 60 dollars a month. After secondary migration, reunited families could pool their resources to obtain a larger home, although it would usually be equally crowded because average family size grew as well. In cities such as Los Angeles, the Vietnamese often live in poor, minority neighborhoods. Few have moved to the suburbs.

Family life. Perhaps the greatest disappointment for the Vietnamese who came to America has been the disruption of traditional family values. In Vietnam, parents exercise strict control over every aspect of their children's lives for as long as the children live in the parents' house, which often means well into adulthood. Close guard is kept over girls, with parents choosing friends and a prospective husband. It is thought that a girl should not escape the control of her parents until she is married. Vietnamese parents also believe that some physical punishment is beneficial for the discipline of a child and it is a loving parent's duty to inflict it. Some parents who discipline their children in such a way have clashed with social agencies or even the police. The resulting embarrassment adds to the confusion they already feel after being resettled.

In the Vietnamese family, the emphasis on discipline is part of the deep connection between parent and child. The parents nourish and care for the children when the children are young. When parents grow old, a child cares for them in turn. The American idea of placing the elderly in nursing homes strikes the Vietnamese as strange and unnatural.

Religion. Although some Roman Catholics from North Vietnam came in the first wave, most Vietnamese are Buddhists. Many Buddhist nuns and monks, driven from Vietnam by Communist policy, have established temples in several American cities. Besides maintaining cultural and religious traditions, these temples supply encouragement and comfort to refugees. Buddhist temples in Vietnam are elaborate structures, but the new temples in America are mostly older buildings transformed cheaply into houses of worship. A simple altar holds a statue of the Buddha, with several candles and incense sticks. On the walls are pictures that depict episodes in the life of the Buddha or illustrate his teachings.

Holidays. The greatest Vietnamese holiday is *Tet*, the celebration of the lunar new year. The three-day celebration usually occurs in February. It is a time for rebirth and bright color. During *Tet*, the Vietnamese forget past mistakes, pay all debts, and forgive others the sins of the past years. The first guest received in the home will influence a family's luck for the rest of the year, so on the first day of *Tet* each family invites special guests. Children open bright red envelopes in which their parents place money for toys and candy. Special, brightly colored foods are served: *banh Tet*, green cakes made from rice, beans, pepper, and pork, and a rainbow of various fruits, especially tangerines, grapefruit, and watermelon.

Also popular is the fall holiday Children's Day, or *Trung Thu*, on which children parade through the streets with paper lanterns shaped like dragons, boats, horses, or toads. In honor of the children, special cakes are served, made from sticky rice filled with peanuts, raisins, and tangerine peel.

"Dust Children." American soldiers in Vietnam had an estimated 50,000 children by Vietnamese mothers during the Vietnamese War. Rejected by Vietnamese society, these *bui doi,* or dust children (so called because they live mostly on the streets), began coming to the United States in the early 1980s. By 1990, some 13,000 had arrived; under the Amerasian Homecoming Act of 1987, over 35,000 are expected to follow over the next three years. The Amerasians have suffered discrimination in Vietnamese society, which resents American actions during the war and values racial purity. Several American veterans' groups have worked to unite the children, now mostly teenagers, with their fathers in America.

Memories of home. The extraordinarily painful circumstances under which the refugees left their homeland and struck out for a new life left many scars. Family members have died; survivors have endured physical and mental brutality, starvation, and extreme deprivation over long periods. Nor did the ordeal end with entry into the United States. Arriving in a time of economic recession, most had to accept low-paying jobs if they were fortunate enough to find employment without waiting for many months. Political violence has also brought tension. The conflict between North and South Vietnam spilled onto American streets in the early 1980s, as anti-Communist gangs gunned down several leftist Vietnamese-Americans in Texas and California. By the mid-1980s, political strife began to diminish. At the same time, studies showed that the early refugees were beginning to catch up with and even surpass the general population's participation in the labor force. Like other Asian Americans, Vietnamese children excel academically, although it is too early for the second generation to have completed their schooling. Despite their progress in America, many Vietnamese hope to return to their homeland one day, given a change in its political and economic outlook. The elderly in particular cherish memories of the peaceful agricultural life that existed before the war. While their children and grandchildren grow up as Americans, they try to reconcile the promise of a new life with their dreams of the old one.

For More Information

See these reading materials:

Fawcett, James T. and Cariño, Benjamin V., eds. *Pacific Bridges; The New Immigration from Asia and the Pacific Islands.* Staten Island, New York: Center for Migration Studies, 1986.

Freeman, James M. *Hearts of Sorrow: Vietnamese-American Lives.* Stanford, California: Stanford University Press, 1989.

Contact this organization:

Vietnam Foundation, 6713 Lumsden Street, McLean, Virginia 22101.

WESTERN APACHE
(west´ urn a patch´ee)

Some of the people that once composed the largest
group of Indians in the Southwest.

Population: 16,000. (1981).
Location: The San Carlos and Fort Apache Indian Reservations in
southeastern Arizona.
Languages: Various languages of the Athapascan language group,
English.

Geographical Setting

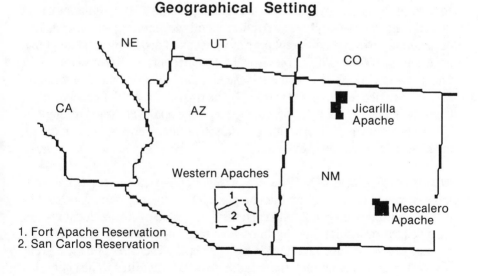

Some of the Apache Indian reservations in the Southwest.

The Apache are not a single people but several different groups that have
grown from small bands of roving hunters and gatherers that traveled

nomadically over a wide range of the great plains, the southwest United States, and Mexico. Each group has its own customs and language variations. The groups have distinctive names: Chiricahua, Lipan, Mescalero, Jicarillo, Kiowa.

The Western Apache are composed of two large groups: the White Mountain Apache living on the Fort Apache Indian Reservation, and the San Carlos Apache living on a more southern San Carlos Indian Reservation. Their cultures are as varied as the land on which they live. The White Mountain Apache live in a mountain area with forests, streams and lakes. The San Carlos Apache live in a more arid desert region south of the White Mountains.

Historical Background

Origin. The ancestors of today's Apache came from northwest Canada through the Great Plains as small groups of hunters. Some, such as the Kiowa, found hunting and gathering lives on the plains. Others, including the Navajo, had found their way to the Southwest by the fifteenth century A.D. Here the Navajo learned from their Pueblo neighbors and soon settled in one place as farmers and herders. Those known as the Apache settled in smaller groups that migrated with the hunting seasons. With limited interest in farming, these people preferred to continue hunting, gathering, and occasionally raiding their neighbors as a means of acquiring food and other necessities. By the 1700s, the Apache had become well-known as both raiders raders to people as distant as the Hopi in the north and the Indians of Sonora, Mexico. Each group was led by its own chief, a chief chosen not by heredity but by his ability to provide for the tribe and to arbitrate differences. Their homes were *wickiups*, branches formed into a cone and covered with the hides of the animals they hunted.

Western Apache. The Western Apache consisted of five tribal units loosely joined by custom and language. Each of these groups consisted of two to four traveling bands, and each band consisted of several local groups, each headed by a chief. Local groups were made up of closely related family clusters of two or three families led by a headman. The chief of a local group was selected from among the headmen of the families. This complex structure made it difficult for Spanish and later white Americans to understand or deal with the Apache. For the most part, these invaders did not realize the limited commitment being made when dealing with a chief, and were then upset to find that a treaty signed with one chief was not binding on all the Apache. Frustrated by this complexity, one Spanish leader, Viceroy

Bernardo de Glavez, hit upon a plan to gather the Apache under a controlling presidio. In 1786, he directed that Apache living near the presidios be supplied not only with food but with plenty of alcohol to serve as a tranquilizer. This worked to some extent. The Apache had never been a united people; rather, small independent groups all depended on raiding others for their livelihood. The Spanish further divided the Apache so that in dealings with the Americans some Apache were friends and aides while others continued their custom of roaming, hunting, and raiding.

White settlers. Unable to contain the Apache, white settlers lived in fear and anger. Throughout the 1800s, they took out their frustrations in mini-wars with small Apache bands and sometimes massacred whole family clusters. By the end of the Civil War, white settlers in Arizona and New Mexico territories were demanding U.S. intervention to confine the Apache. Reservations were established on both sides of the Rio Grande River, and the Indian Service was directed to encourage the Apache to move to them. Some of the Apache agreed, but then became dependent on a government that did not always fulfill its promises. Many Apache chose to live their old lifestyles in the rugged desert and mountain area of the Southwest. They were led by several strong chiefs. Cochise led the Chiricahua Apache, a group from southeastern Arizona and Mexico, for many years and protected them from white intrusion until his death in 1874. In his early leadership, Cochise was cooperative with the white settlers. But in 1861, a United States soldier tried to arrest him for a crime he had not committed. From then on Cochise was an enemy of the white settlers. He died on the Chiricahua Reservation.

Another chief, Mangas Coloradas, led many raids against the military might of the United States. Mangas was a giant of a man in the 1850s, six feet six inches tall and leader of the Mimbres tribe. In his later life, Mangas Coloradas joined Cochise in war against the white army. Defeated in 1862 by a larger army unit equipped with howitzers, Mangas waited a year before he ventured into a mining town to talk peace. But the army's general accused Mangas of plundering wagon trains and refused to talk with him. Instead, he order that the chief be killed. In 1863, Mangas Coloradas was tortured with hot bayonets by soldiers, and then shot.

Victorio, another Mimbres chief, encouraged his people to make peace with the army. In return, the army ordered him and his followers to move from New Mexico to the San Carlos reservation. Victorio rebelled and, in 1877, led his followers into Mexico, where he was eventually tracked down and killed three years later.

In 1883, the last resisting leader, Geronimo, who had been a warrior with Mangas Coloradas, finally surrendered to the army under General Crook with a promise of protection for his people. But once under army control, his people were gathered onto train cars and sent to Florida. There many died, unable to adjust to the different climate and falling victims of new diseases. The remainder were eventually moved to Fort Sill, Oklahoma. By this time, public sentiment was changing, and the Apache had a little more freedom. Geronimo used this new attitude to begin to earn money by selling speaking engagements and "Apache" artifacts made for the purpose. In 1911, while still a prisoner of the army, Geronimo died from an accidental injury after having amassed a fortune for that time of 10,000 dollars.

Return to the Southwest. Later, the United States Government agreed to allow the remaining Apache to return to their homelands. But the people of the Arizona territory objected, so at first the returnees were restricted to the Mescalero Apache Reservation east of the Rio Grande River in New Mexico. Finally, the Western Apache were allowed to return to the Fort Apache area, where they abandoned their old lifestyles and became farmers, ranchers, and herders.

Culture Today

Economy. The White Mountain and San Carlos Apache today have long abandoned their wickiups and live in homes and on farms of wood frame and brick much like their white neighbors. While the land of the White Mountain Apache is mountainous and more suitable for raising cattle, that of the San Carlos Apache is flatter and has been turned to agriculture. The White Mountain Tribal Council controls a tribe-owned herd of Hereford cattle. In addition there are eight independent Apache-owned cattle associations on this reservation. The San Carlos Indians maintain a tribal farm of more than 1,200 acres.

There are other differences in the economies of the two reservations. The White Mountain Indians, living in an area of 26 lakes and many streams and in country where snow covers the land in winter, have capitalized on the recreational potential. The White Mountain Recreation Enterprise controls 300 miles of fishing streams, more than 1,000 campsites, and in Sunrise Park and Ski Lodge and Hondeh, a hotel and motel along with a ski resort with 19 lifts. In addition, the White Mountains contain great stands of pine trees, and the White Mountain Apache operate a sawmill on their land.

The San Carlos Indians live in a more arid area and concentrate on farming, although this group, too, operates a cattle ranch. Here the desert conditions encourage the growth of the jojoba plant. Almost fifty percent of this plant is a fine quality oil, useful for lubrication. The San Carlos people use this oil to make fine candles for market.

The hoop and pole game is popular with Apache men and boys.

Family life. In their earlier days of hunting and raiding for food, horses, and wives, Apache family life centered around those skills and on the ability to move homes from one place to another. A newly born baby was fastened to a cradle board that could be carried on the mother's back. It remained on this board for six or seven months. Children were taught early that making noise of any kind was not desirable, perhaps because of the Apache interest in raiding as a means of livelihood. Sometimes even crying babies were covered with a blanket to teach them to be silent. Girls helped their mothers with such chores as gathering wood for cooking and searching for edible plants. Boys learned through games the art of hunting. One boy's activity called for fashioning small bows and arrows. A boy would shoot his arrow at a target, then others would try to hit that arrow with their own. Hitting the opponent's arrow won that arrow as a prize.

Food. Food today is likely to be from canned or frozen food bought at the market. The old diet of whatever meat was available, corn, beans, and squash has changed. Seldom is there such food as the old ash bread made by mixing ash, water, and meal into a paste, spreading that paste over corn husks laid over a smoldering fire, covering the paste with another layer of corn husks and allowing it to cook through the night.

Clothing. Once the Western Apache dressed in rawhide long leather dresses for the women and shirts and skirts for the men. They decorated this dress with metal bells and beads and wore jewelry made of beads. Today this dress is reserved for ceremonies—the Apache have adopted the dress of their white neighbors except that Apache women still prefer flaired skirts and blouses.

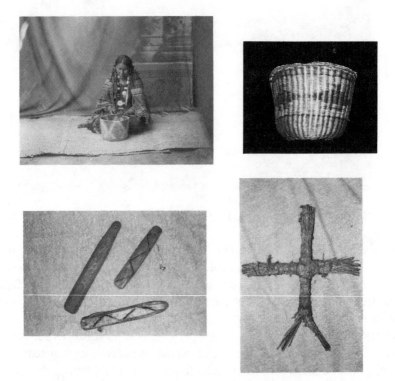

Top: Apache basket maker, basket. Bottom: Bull roarers, straw doll (probably with religious significance).

Education and the arts. In education, too, the Apache are adopting white ways. Children on the reservations attend elementary and high schools, but education is generally not highly prized. Few Apache students go on to colleges or universities.

Industry, clothing, and education have guided a move toward the mainstream of United States society, but the Apache still hold to many of their old beliefs. Having been semi-nomadic, the Apache culture did not encourage possession of material objects. However, the Apache did develop great skills in basketry, choosing to work with a plant called devil's claw to produce a black design. When these baskets were made for family use, they took many forms including a giant basket for storing grain. Today most basketry is done for market, so the large baskets have been abandoned as too time-consuming. In their place Apache produce water baskets (*tuo*), burden baskets, baby carriers, and a number of smaller baskets for sale.

In addition, Apache craftspeople produce dolls carved from cottonwood and dressed in calico, some beaded jewelry, and some silver jewelry. In the late 1970s, the San Carlos Indians decided that they needed to establish an identity in the Indian jewelry market and began to emphasize the semi-precious stone peridot in their work. They developed a tribal enterprise called Tsee yo' Ba Gowa "home of rock jewelry."

One of the most well-known artists who used these colors in his watercolors was Ted De Grazia. De Grazia attended the University of Arizona and earned degrees in both music and art. Following that, De Grazia spent most of his time painting scenes of Apache life, past and present. He also attempted to dispel the reputation for ruthlessness and cold-bloodedness that was put on the Apache during their early struggles with white intruders on their land.

Religion. It is in their religious beliefs that the Apache hold most to the past. Their religion includes the worship of several gods, chief among whom is Life Giver or Earth Maker. There is a female god, White Painted Woman or Changing Woman, and a child god, Child of the Water. In addition, Mountain Spirits are said to live in the mountain caves. In ceremonies, the spirits are impersonated by masked dancers. The most famous of the Apache ceremonial dances is the Snake Dance in which dancers handle live snakes. Dancing is part of most Apache ceremonies. The Apache dance and sing tales of the past accompanied by drums and instruments made by tying a flat stick to a string to be whirled around the head, a *bull roarer*.

Religion is the impetus for many of the Apache folktales. For example, Child of the Water is the hero of many stories in which he is tested by lightning, struggles with a giant, or fights monsters such as the monster eagle or the monster buffalo bull.

Some physical objects have religious importance to the Apache. In addition to the sacred caves, turquoise is considered sacred as is abalone shell. The Apache give religious significance to directions and attach special colors to each: black for east, blue-green for south, yellow for west, and white for north.

Trends today. There is no need for hunting and raiding training. Western Apache boys and girls still have chores within the family to help with cooking or ranching, but their games include basketball and baseball.

For More Information

See these reading materials:

Arizona Highways, July 1977.

Capps, Benjamin. *The Great Chiefs.* Alexandria, Virginia: Time-Life Books, 1975.

Handbook of North American Indians, Vol. 10. Alfonzo Ortiz, ed. Washington, DC: Smithsonian Institution, 1983.

Glossary of Foreign Terms

ao dai Silk dresses worn by Vietnamese women.
baba ghannouj A dip made with eggplant.
banh Tet Green cakes.
barbara A partly underground dwelling.
baidaras Large open boats.
barzcz Beet soup.
bodegas Food stores.
bris Circumcision.
chickee A Seminole house built on stilts.
compadrázgo Godparenthood.
compadres Godparents.
contadini Italian peasants.
Dom Polski Polish community center.
duas Vietnamese chopsticks.
enryo The Japanese value of respect from "inferiors" to their "superiors" in society.
falafel A spicy vegetable and bean patty.
filé Powdered sassafras leaf.
gadugi A work team in Cherokee society.
gaggi A Netsilik structure for ceremonies.
ga-man Withstanding hardship, or sticking things out.
gens de couleur libre Free people of color, a separate social class in early Creole society.
Grossdaadi Haus Home of Amish grandparents.
Halsduch An Amish cape.
halal In Muslim society, meat that is properly slaughtered without being stunned.
halakhah Jewish law.
hanable cey A Sioux's quest for a vision.
hasani Honorable.
havurah Jewish fellowship group.
hummus A Mideastern dip made of ground chickpeas.
hui A Chinese system of borrowing money; a system of credit.
huigan A group, led by merchants, of Chinese Americans from a particular home area.
imam A Muslim prayer leader.
jambalya A Creole dish made with seafood, pork, vegetables, and rice.
kachinas Representations of Hopi spirits.
kachin-tihus Doll-like images of the spirtis.

kamleika A waterproof, hooded parka fashioned from sea mammal intestines.

Kashrut Jewish dietary laws.

ken region of Japan

kenjin people from the same Japanese region.

Kenjin-kai Association of people from the same home region.

koogl A noodle or potato pudding.

kwan A region in Seneca society.

kvass Russian beer.

landsmannschaften Societies of Jews from the same home town.

la terra benedetta Small city gardens on which Italian women grew crops for sale.

latticini food stores. Food stores whose specialty was fresh Italian cheese.

Lepple Flap on back of an Amish dress.

luftmench A person who survives without any apparent livelihood.

mafiosi Gangsters.

mataburros Reference books used by Puerto Ricans to settle intellectual arguments; the literal meaning is "donkey-slayers."

mazurek Cookies with rasin, fig, or date filling.

Meidung Avoiding or shunning a member of the Amish faith who has violated its social rules.

mujeres de la casa Housewives.

nuac cham A tangy Vietnamese fish sauce.

oho nit A Cheyenne game; the literal meaning is "knocking the ball."

Ordnung Social rules of the Amish.

padroni A labor agent or recruited Italians for work in America.

palant A Polish ball game.

passen blanc To pass into white society.

piki A type of thin, Hopi bread.

plaçage A living and financial arrangement between a white man and free woman of color.

rumpspringa Courtship between young men and women in Amish society; the literal meaning is "running around."

seigneurs French feudal lords.

shtetls Small Jewish towns in Eastern Europe.

tabbouleh A Mideastern wheat kernel salad.

tallis A Jewish prayer shawl.

tanomoshi A credit system; a pool of money from which Japanese could borrow.

toion An Aleut chief.

triads Secret Chinese societies that engaged in some illegal activities; tongs.

trzymanie bortników The Polish boarding house system.

tuo Apache water basket.

yarmulke A skull cap worn in Jewish worship.

yisati The head of a Tlingit household, which included a dozen or more related families.

wilia A Polish Christmas Supper.

zamovlat A religious healer in Russian society.

Bibliography

Adler, Bill, ed. *The Kennedy Wit.* New Jersey: Carol Publishing, 1964.

Alexander, Thomas G., ed. *The Mormon People: Their Character and Traditions.* Utah: Brigham Young University Press, 1988.

Allen, James Paul. *We the People: An Atlas of America's Ethnic Diversity.* New York: Macmillan, 1988.

Antonson, Joan M. and Hanable, William S. *Alaska's Heritage.* The Alaska Historical Commission, 1985.

Bacon, Margaret Hope. *The Quiet Rebels: The Story of the Quakers in America.* Philadelphia: New Society Publishers, 1985.

Black, Lydia T. *Atka: An Ethnohistory of the Western Aleutians.* Kingston, Ontario, Canada: The Limestone Press, 1984.

Black, Lydia T., ed. *The Journals of Iakov Netsvetov, The Atkha Years 1828-1844.* Translated by Lydia T. Black. Kingston, Ontario, Canada: The Limestone Press, 1980.

Blassingame, John W. *The Slave Community: Plantation Life in the Antebellum South.* Rev. New York: Oxford University Press, 1979.

Bluestein, Gene. *Ainglish-Yinglish: Yiddish in American Life and Literature.* Athens, Georgia: University of Georgia Press, 1989.

Bonacich, Edna and Modell, John. *The Economic Basis of Ethnic Solidarity: Small Business in the Japanese American Community.* Berkeley: University of California Press, 1980.

Bukowczyk, John J. *And My Children Did Not Know Me: A History of the Polish Americans.* Bloomington: Indiana University Press, 1987.

Cassity, Michael J. *Chains of Fear.* Westport, Conn.: Greenwood, 1984.

Cavanagh, Beverly. *Music of the Netsilik Eskimo: A Study of Stability and Change.* Vol 2. National Museum of Man Mercury Series. Ottawa: National Museum of Canada, 1982.

Ciardi, John. *Selected Poems*. Fayetteville: The University of Arkansas Press, 1984.

Clark, Ronald W. *Einstein: The Life and Times*. New York: World Publishing, 1971.

Collier, Peter. *When Shall They Rest? The Cherokees' Long Struggle with America*. New York: Holt, Rinehart & Winston, 1973.

Crété, Liliane. *Daily Life in Louisiana: 1815-1830*. Translated by Patrick Gregory. Baton Rouge: Louisiana State University Press, 1978.

Daniels, Roger. *Asian America: Chinese and Japanese in America since 1850*. Seattle: University of Washington Press, 1988.

Denton, Frank H. and Villena-Denton, Victoria. *Filipino Views of America: Warm Memories, Cold Realities*. Washington: Asia Fellows, Ltd., 1986.

Douglass, Frederick. *My Bondage and My Freedom*. New York and Auburn: Miller, Orton & Mulligan, 1855.

Duffy, R. Quinn. *The Road to Nunavut: The Progress of the Eastern Arctic Inuit since the Second World War*. Kingston and Montreal: McGill-Queen's University Press, 1988.

Erdoes, Richard and Ortiz, Alfonso, eds. *American Indian Myths and Legends*. New York: Pantheon Books 1984,

Fanning, Charles, ed. *The Exiles of Erin: Nineteenth-Century Irish-American Fiction*. Notre Dame, Indiana: University of Notre Dame Press,

Feingold, Henry L. *Zion in America: The Jewish Experience from Colonial Times to the Present*. New York: Twayne Publishers, 1974.

Fife, Austin E. *Exploring Western Americana*. Edited by Alta Fife. Ann Arbor: UMI Research Press, 1988.

Fischer, David Hackett. *Albion's Seed: Four British Folkways in America*. New York: Oxford University Press, 1989.

Garver, Susan and McGuire, Paula. *Coming to North America: From Mexico, Cuba and Puerto Rico.* New York: Delacorte Press, 1971.

Gerber, Stanford Neil. *Russkoya Celo: The Ethnography of a Russian-American Community.* New York: AMS Press, 1985.

Greene, Dana, ed. *Lucretia Mott: Her Complete Speeches and Sermons.* New York: The Edwin Mellen Press, 1980.

Hazo, Samuel. "Some Words for President Wilson." In *To Paris: Poems by Samuel Hazo.* New York: New Directions, 1981.

Hearn, Lafcadio. *Gombo Zhèbes: Little Dictionary of Creole Proverbs, Selected from Six Creole Dialects.* New York: W.H. Coleman, 1885.

Highwater, Jamake. *The Sweet Grass Lives On: Fifty Contemporary North American Indian Artists.* New York: Lippincott and Crowell, 1980.

Hosokawa, Bill. *Nisei: The Quiet Americans.* New York: William Morrow & Company, 1969.

Huerta, Jorge. *Chicano Theater: Themes and Forms.* Ypsilanti, Michigan: Bilingual Press, 1982.

Indian Reservations: A State and Federal Handbook. Compiled by The Confederaton of American Indians. Jefferson, North Carolina: McFarland & Company, 1986.

Iverson, Peter. *The Plains Indians of the Twentieth Century.* Norman: University of Oklahoma Press, 1985.

Kilpatrick, Jack Frederick and Anna Gritts Kilpatrick. *Walk in Your Soul: Love Incantations of the Oklahoma Cherokees.* Dallas: Southern Methodist University Press, 1965.

Kitano, Harry. *Japanese Americans.* Englewood Cliffs, New Jersey: Prentice-Hall, 1976.

Kleeman, Janice Ellen. *The Origins and Stylistic Development of Polish-American Polka Music*. UC Berkeley: University Microfilms International, 1982.

LoGatto, Reverend Anthony F., ed. *The Italians in America 1492–1972: A Chronology and Fact Book*. Dobbs Ferry, New York: Oceana, 1972.

Lowie, Robert H. *Indians of the Plains*. New York: Doubleday, 1954.

Mallery, Garrick. "Indian Picture Writing." In *The Sioux Indians: A Socio-Ethnological History*. New York: Sol Lewis, 1973.

Meltzer, Milton. *The Hispanic Americans*. New York: Thomas Y. Crowell, 1982.

Murase, Ichiro Mikke. *Little Tokyo: One Hundred Years in Pictures*. Los Angeles: Visual Communications, 1983.

Nelli, Humbert S. *From Immigrants to Ethnics: The Italian Americans*. New York: Oxford University Press, 1983.

O'Conner, Richard. *The German Americans*. Boston: Little, Brown & Co., 1978.

Pido, Antonio J.A. *The Pilipinos in America*. New York: Center for Migration Studies, 1985.

Renkiewicz, Frank, compiler and ed. *The Poles in America 1608–1972: A Chronology and Fact Book*. Dobbs Ferry, New York: Oceana, 1973.

Rosenfeld, Morris. *Songs from the Ghetto with Prose Translation*. Boston: Copeland and Day, 1898.

Singer, David, ed. *American Jewish Year Book*. New York: American Jewish Year Book Committee and Philadelphia: Jewish Publication Society, 1982, 1988, and 1989.

Shannon, William V. *The American Irish*. Toronto, Ontario, Canada: Macmillan, 1966.

Sloan, Irving J. *The Blacks in America 1492–1976*. Dobbs Ferry, New York: Oceana, 1977.

Sturtevant, William C., ed. *Handbook of North American Indians*. 15 vols. Washington, D.C.: Smithsonian, 1978–.

Sung, Betty Lee. *The Adjustment Experience of Chinese Immigrant Children in New York City*. New York: Center for Migration Studies, 1987.

Thornton, Russell. *American Indian Holocaust and Survival: A Population History Since 1492*. Norman: University of Oklahoma Press, 1987.

Veniaminov, Ivan. *Notes on the Islands of the Unalashka District*. Kingston, Ontario, Canada: The Limstone Press, 1984.

Vine Deloria, Jr., ed. *American Indian Policy in the Twentieth Century*. Norman: University of Oklahoma Press, 1985.

Vogel, Dan. *Emma Lazarus*. Boston: Twayne Publishers, 1980.

Wertsman, Vladimir. *The Russians in America 1727–1970*. Dobbs Ferry, New York: Oceana Publications, 1977.

Whitman, Walt. *Leaves of Grass*. Garden City, New York: Doubleday, 1902.

Index

Vieux Carré, 128, 130
Vindication of the rights of
Women, A, 159
Waldschmüller, Martin, 180
Walker, David, 26
Wang, Taylor, 122
Washington, Booker T., 28
Webster, Noah, 162
West, Jessamyn, 358
Western Apaches, 415–423
    geographical setting, 415
    historical background, 416
    culture today: economy, 418;
        family life, 419; food,
        419; clothing, 420;
        education and arts, 420;
        religion, 421; today, 422
White Mountains, 415
White Mountain Recreation
    Enterprise, 418
Whitman family, 320
Whitman, Walt, 357
Whittier, John Greenleaf, 354
winter count, 139
Wisconsin v. Yoder, 61
Wochentliche Philadelphische
Staatsbate, 181
women's rights, 284
Woodenlegs, John, 104
World War I German American
    heroes, 184
Word of Wisdom, 293
Wounded Knee, 145
Yefl, 402, 403
Yo-he-wa, 379
Yom Kippur, 257
Young, Andrew, 30
Young, Brigham, 297–299
Zacuto, Samuel, 245
Zakrzewska, Maria, 327
zamovlat, 366

Zenger, Peter, 181
Ziolkowski, Korczak, 148, 335
Zion, 288